Your Personal
HOROSCOPE
—— 2008 ——

Your Personal
HOROSCOPE
—— 2008 ——

*The only one-volume horoscope
you'll ever need*

Joseph Polansky

The author is grateful to the people
of STAR ★ DATA, who truly fathered
this book and without whom it
could not have been written.

HarperElement
An Imprint of HarperCollins*Publishers*
77–85 Fulham Palace Road,
Hammersmith, London W6 8JB

The website address is www.thorsonselement.com

and *HarperElement* are trademarks of
HarperCollins*Publishers* Ltd

Published by HarperElement 2007

1 3 5 7 9 10 8 6 4 2

A catalogue record for this book is
available from the British Library

ISBN-13 978-0-00-723325-0
ISBN-10 0-00-723325-6

Printed and bound in Great Britain by
Clays Ltd, St Ives plc

This book is proudly printed on paper which contains wood
from well-managed forests, certified in accordance with
the rules of the Forest Stewardship Council.
For more information about FSC,
please visit www.fsc.org

Contents

Your Personal
HOROSCOPE
—— 2008 ——

Introduction

Welcome to the fascinating and intricate world of astrology!

For thousands of years the movements of the planets and other heavenly bodies have intrigued the best minds of every generation. Life holds no greater challenge or joy than this: knowledge of ourselves and the universe we live in. Astrology is one of the keys to this knowledge.

Your Personal Horoscope 2008 gives you the fruits of astrological wisdom. In addition to general guidance on your character and the basic trends of your life, it shows you how to take advantage of planetary influences so you can make the most of the year ahead.

The section on each Sign includes a Personality Profile, a look at general trends for 2008, and in-depth month-by-month forecasts. The Glossary (*page 3*) explains some of the astrological terms you may be unfamiliar with.

One of the many helpful features of this book is the 'Best' and 'Most Stressful' days listed at the beginning of each monthly forecast. Read these sections to learn which days in each month will be good overall, good for money, and good for love. Mark them on your calendar – these will be your best days. Similarly, make a note of the days that will be most stressful for you. It is best to avoid taking important meetings or major decisions on these days, as well as on those days when important planets in your Horoscope are retrograde (moving backwards through the Zodiac).

The Major Trends section for your Sign lists those days when your vitality is strong or weak, or when relationships with your co-workers or loved ones may need a bit more effort on your part. If you are going through a difficult time, take a look at the colour, metal, gem and scent listed in the 'At a Glance' section of your Personality Profile. Wearing a piece of jewellery that contains your metal and/or gem will strengthen your vitality; just as wearing clothes or decorating your room or office in the colour ruled by your Sign, drinking teas made from the herbs ruled by your Sign, or wearing the scents associated with your Sign will sustain you.

Another important virtue of this book is that it will help you to know not only yourself but those around you: your friends, co-workers, partners and/or children. Reading the Personality Profile and forecasts for their Signs will provide you with an insight into their behaviour that you won't get anywhere else. You will know when to be more tolerant of them and when they are liable to be difficult or irritable.

In this edition we have included foot reflexology charts as part of the health section. So many health problems could perhaps be avoided or alleviated if we understood which organs were most vulnerable and what we could do to protect them. Though there are many natural and drug-free ways to strengthen vulnerable organs, these charts show a valid way to proceed. The vulnerable organs for the year ahead are clearly marked in the chart. It's very good to massage the whole foot on a regular basis, as the feet contain reflexes to the entire body. Try to pay special attention to the specific areas marked in the chart. If this is done diligently, health problems can be avoided. And even if they can't be completely avoided, their impact can be softened considerably.

I consider you – the reader – my personal client. By studying your Solar Horoscope I gain an awareness of what is going on in your life – what you are feeling and striving for and the challenges you face. I then do my best to address these concerns. Consider this book the next best thing to having your own personal astrologer!

It is my sincere hope that *Your Personal Horoscope 2008* will enhance the quality of your life, make things easier, illuminate the way forward, banish obscurities and make you more aware of your personal connection to the universe. Understood properly and used wisely, astrology is a great guide to knowing yourself, the people around you and the events in your life – but remember that what you do with these insights – the final result – is up to you.

Glossary of Astrological Terms

Ascendant

We experience day and night because the Earth rotates on its axis once every 24 hours. It is because of this rotation that the Sun, Moon and planets seem to rise and set. The Zodiac is a fixed belt (imaginary, but very real in spiritual terms) around the Earth. As the Earth rotates, the different Signs of the Zodiac seem to the observer to rise on the horizon. During a 24-hour period every Sign of the Zodiac will pass this horizon point at some time or another. The Sign that is at the horizon point at any given time is called the Ascendant, or Rising Sign. The Ascendant is the Sign denoting a person's self-image, body and self-concept – the personal ego, as opposed to the spiritual ego indicated by a person's Sun Sign.

Aspects

Aspects are the angular relationships between planets, the way in which one planet stimulates or influences another. If a planet makes a harmonious aspect (connection) to another, it tends to stimulate that planet in a positive and helpful way. If it makes a stressful aspect to another planet, this disrupts the planet's normal influence.

Astrological Qualities

There are three astrological qualities: *cardinal*, *fixed* and *mutable*. Each of the 12 Signs of the Zodiac falls into one of these three categories.

Cardinal Signs	Aries, Cancer, Libra and Capricorn The cardinal quality is the active, initiating principle. Those born under these four Signs are good at starting new projects.
Fixed Signs	Taurus, Leo, Scorpio and Aquarius Fixed qualities include stability, persistence, endurance and perfectionism. People born under these four Signs are good at seeing things through.
Mutable Signs	Gemini, Virgo, Sagittarius and Pisces Mutable qualities are adaptability, changeability and balance. Those born under these four Signs are creative, if not always practical.

Direct Motion

When the planets move forward through the Zodiac – as they normally do – they are said to be going 'direct'.

Grand Trine

A Grand Trine differs from a normal Trine (where two planets are 120 degrees apart) in that three or more planets are involved. When you look at this pattern in a chart, it takes the form of a complete triangle – a Grand Trine. Usually (but not always) it occurs in one of the four elements: Fire, Earth, Air, or Water. Thus the particular element in which it occurs will be highlighted. A Grand Trine in Water is not the same as a Grand Trine in Air or Fire, etc. This is a very fortunate and happy aspect, and quite rare.

Grand Square

A Grand Square differs from a normal Square (usually two planets separated by 90 degrees) in that four or more planets are involved. When you look at the pattern in a chart you will see a whole and complete square. This, though stressful, usually denotes a new manifestation in the life. There is much work and balancing involved in the manifestation.

Houses

There are 12 Signs of the Zodiac and 12 Houses of experience. The 12 Signs are personality types and ways in which a given planet expresses itself; the 12 Houses show 'where' in your life this expression takes place. Each House has a different area of interest. A House can become potent and important – a House of Power – in different ways: if it contains the Sun, the Moon or the Ruler of your chart, if it contains more than one planet, or if the Ruler of that House is receiving unusual stimulation from other planets.

1st House	Personal Image and Sensual Delights
2nd House	Money/Finance
3rd House	Communication and Intellectual Interests
4th House	Home and Family
5th House	Children, Fun, Games, Creativity, Speculations and Love Affairs
6th House	Health and Work
7th House	Love, Marriage and Social Activities
8th House	Transformation and Regeneration
9th House	Religion, Foreign Travel, Higher Education and Philosophy
10th House	Career
11th House	Friends, Group Activities and Fondest Wishes
12th House	Spirituality

Karma

Karma is the law of cause and effect which governs all phenomena. We are all where we find ourselves because of karma – because of actions we have performed in the past. The universe is such a balanced instrument that any act immediately sets corrective forces into motion – karma.

Long-term Planets

The planets that take a long time to move through a Sign show the long-term trends in a given area of life. They are important for forecasting the prolonged view of things. Because these planets stay in one Sign for so long, there are periods in the year when the faster-moving (short-term) planets will join them, further activating and enhancing the importance of a given House.

Jupiter	stays in a Sign for about 1 year
Saturn	2½ years
Uranus	7 years
Neptune	14 years
Pluto	15 to 30 years

Lunar

Relating to the Moon. See also 'Phases of the Moon', below.

Natal

Literally means 'birth'. In astrology this term is used to distinguish between planetary positions that occurred at the time of a person's birth (natal) and those that are current (transiting). For example, Natal Sun refers to where the Sun was when you were born; transiting Sun refers to where the Sun's position is currently at any given moment – which usually doesn't coincide with your birth, or Natal, Sun.

Out of Bounds

The planets move through the Zodiac at various angles relative to the celestial equator (if you were to draw an imaginary extension of the Earth's equator out into the universe, you would have an illustration of this celestial equator). The Sun – being the most dominant and powerful influence in the Solar system – is the measure astrologers use as a standard. The Sun never goes more than approximately 23 degrees north or south of the celestial equator. At the winter solstice the Sun reaches its maximum southern angle of orbit (declination); at the summer solstice it reaches its maximum northern angle. Any time a planet exceeds this Solar boundary – and occasionally planets do – it is said to be 'out of bounds'. This means that the planet exceeds or trespasses into strange territory – beyond the limits allowed by the Sun, the Ruler of the Solar system. The planet in this condition becomes more emphasized and exceeds its authority, becoming an important influence in the forecast.

Phases of the Moon

After the full Moon, the Moon seems to shrink in size (as perceived from the Earth), gradually growing smaller until it is virtually invisible to the naked eye – at the time of the next new Moon. This is called the waning Moon phase, or the waning Moon.

After the new Moon, the Moon gradually gets bigger in size (as perceived from the Earth) until it reaches its maximum size at the time of the full Moon. This period is called the waxing Moon phase, or waxing Moon.

Retrogrades

The planets move around the Sun at different speeds. Mercury and Venus move much faster than the Earth, while Mars, Jupiter, Saturn, Uranus, Neptune and Pluto move more slowly. Thus there are times when, relative to the Earth, the planets appear to be going backwards. In reality they are always going forward, but relative to our vantage point on Earth they seem to go backwards through the Zodiac for a period of time. This is called 'retrograde' motion and tends to weaken the normal influence of a given planet.

Short-term Planets

The fast-moving planets move so quickly through a Sign that their effects are generally of a short-term nature. They reflect the immediate, day-to-day trends in a Horoscope.

Moon	stays in a Sign for only 2½ days
Mercury	20 to 30 days
Sun	30 days
Venus	approximately 1 month
Mars	approximately 2 months

T-square

A T-square differs from a Grand Square in that it is not a complete square. If you look at the pattern in a chart it appears as 'half a complete square', resembling the T-square tools used by architects and designers. If you cut a complete square in half, diagonally, you have a T-square. Many astrologers consider this more stressful than a Grand Square, as it creates tension that is difficult to resolve. T-squares bring learning experiences.

Transits

This refers to the movements or motions of the planets at any given time. Astrologers use the word 'transit' to make the distinction between a birth or Natal planet (see 'Natal', above) and the planet's current movement in the heavens. For example, if at your birth Saturn was in the Sign of Cancer in your 8th House, but is now moving through your 3rd House, it is said to be 'transiting' your 3rd House. Transits are one of the main tools with which astrologers forecast trends.

Aries

♈

THE RAM
Birthdays from
21st March to
20th April

Personality Profile

ARIES AT A GLANCE

Element – Fire

Ruling Planet – Mars
   Career Planet – Saturn
   Love Planet – Venus
   Money Planet – Venus
   Planet of Fun, Entertainment, Creativity and
      Speculations – Sun
   Planet of Health and Work – Mercury
   Planet of Home and Family Life – Moon
   Planet of Spirituality – Neptune
   Planet of Travel, Education, Religion and
      Philosophy – Jupiter

Colours – carmine, red, scarlet

Colours that promote love, romance and social
   harmony – green, jade green

Colour that promotes earning power – green

Gem – amethyst

Metals – iron, steel

Scent – honeysuckle

Quality – cardinal (= activity)

Quality most needed for balance – caution

Strongest virtues – abundant physical energy, courage, honesty, independence, self-reliance

Deepest need – action

Characteristics to avoid – haste, impetuousness, over-aggression, rashness

Signs of greatest overall compatibility – Leo, Sagittarius

Signs of greatest overall incompatibility – Cancer, Libra, Capricorn

Sign most helpful to career – Capricorn

Sign most helpful for emotional support – Cancer

Sign most helpful financially – Taurus

Sign best for marriage and/or partnerships – Libra

Sign most helpful for creative projects – Leo

Best Sign to have fun with – Leo

Signs most helpful in spiritual matters – Sagittarius, Pisces

Best day of the week – Tuesday

Understanding an Aries

Aries is the activist *par excellence* of the Zodiac. The Aries need for action is almost an addiction, and those who do not really understand the Aries personality would probably use this hard word to describe it. In reality 'action' is the essence of the Aries psychology – the more direct, blunt and to-the-point the action, the better. When you think about it, this is the ideal psychological makeup for the warrior, the pioneer, the athlete or the manager.

Aries likes to get things done, and in their passion and zeal often lose sight of the consequences for themselves and others. Yes, they often try to be diplomatic and tactful, but it is hard for them. When they do so they feel that they are being dishonest and phony. It is hard for them even to understand the mindset of the diplomat, the consensus builder, the front office executive. These people are involved in endless meetings, discussions, talks and negotiations – all of which seem a great waste of time when there is so much work to be done, so many real achievements to be gained. An Aries can understand, once it is explained, that talks and negotiations – the social graces – lead ultimately to better, more effective actions. The interesting thing is that an Aries is rarely malicious or spiteful – even when waging war. Aries people fight without hate for their opponents. To them it is all good-natured fun, a grand adventure, a game.

When confronted with a problem many people will say 'Well, let's think about it, let's analyse the situation.' But not an Aries. An Aries will think 'Something must be done. Let's get on with it.' Of course neither response is the total answer. Sometimes action is called for, sometimes cool thought. But an Aries tends to err on the side of action.

Action and thought are radically different principles. Physical activity is the use of brute force. Thinking and deliberating require one not to use force – to be still. It is not good for the athlete to be deliberating the next move; this will only slow down his or her reaction time. The athlete must act instinctively and instantly. This is how Aries people tend to behave in life. They are quick, instinctive decision-makers and their decisions tend to be translated into action almost immediately. When their intuition is sharp and well tuned, their actions are powerful and successful. When their intuition is off, their actions can be disastrous.

Do not think this will scare an Aries. Just as a good warrior knows that in the course of combat he or she might acquire a few wounds, so too does an Aries realize – somewhere deep down – that in the course of being true to yourself you might get embroiled in a disaster or two. It is all part of the game. An Aries feels strong enough to weather any storm.

There are many Aries people who are intellectual. They make powerful and creative thinkers. But even in this realm they tend to be pioneers – outspoken and blunt. These types of Aries tend to elevate (or sublimate) their desire for physical combat in favour of intellectual, mental combat. And they are indeed powerful.

In general, Aries people have a faith in themselves that others could learn from. This basic, rock-bottom faith carries them through the most tumultuous situations of life. Their courage and self-confidence make them natural leaders. Their leadership is more by way of example than by actually controlling others.

Finance

Aries people often excel as builders or estate agents. Money in and of itself is not as important as are other things – action, adventure, sport, etc. They are motivated by the need to support and be well-thought-of by their partners. Money as a way of attaining pleasure is another important motivation. An Aries functions best in their own businesses or as manager of their own departments within a large business or corporation. The fewer orders they have to take from higher up, the better. They also function better out in the field rather than behind a desk.

Aries people are hard workers with a lot of endurance; they can earn large sums of money due to the strength of their sheer physical energy.

Venus is their money planet, which means that Aries need to develop more of the social graces in order to realize their full earning potential. Just getting the job done – which is what an Aries excels at – is not enough to create financial success. The co-operation of others needs to be attained. Customers, clients and co-workers need to be made to feel comfortable; many people need to be treated properly in order for success to happen. When Aries people develop these abilities – or hire someone to do this for them – their financial potential is unlimited.

Career and Public Image

One would think that a pioneering type would want to break with the social and political conventions of society. But this is not so with the Aries-born. They are pioneers within conventional limits, in the sense that they like to start their own businesses within an established industry.

Capricorn is on the 10th House (Career) cusp of Aries' Solar Horoscope. Saturn is the planet that rules their life's work and professional aspirations. This tells us some interesting things about the Aries character. First off, it shows that, in order for Aries people to reach their full career potential, they need to develop some qualities that are a bit alien to their basic nature: They need to become better administrators and organizers; they need to be able to handle details better and to take a long-range view of their projects and their careers in general. No one can beat an Aries when it comes to achieving short-range objectives, but a career is long term, built over time. You cannot take a 'quickie' approach to it.

Some Aries people find it difficult to stick with a project until the end. Since they get bored quickly and are in constant pursuit of new adventures, they prefer to pass an old project or task on to somebody else in order to start something new. Those Aries who learn how to put off the search for something new until the old is completed will achieve great success in their careers and professional lives.

In general, Aries people like society to judge them on their own merits, on their real and actual achievements. A reputation acquired by 'hype' feels false to them.

Love and Relationships

In marriage and partnerships Aries like those who are more passive, gentle, tactful and diplomatic – people who have the social grace and skills they sometimes lack. Our partners always represent a hidden part of ourselves – a self that we cannot express personally.

An Aries tends to go after what he or she likes aggressively. The tendency is to jump into relationships and marriages. This is especially true if Venus is in Aries as well as the Sun. If an Aries likes you, he or she will have a hard time taking no for an answer; many attempts will be made to sweep you off your feet.

Though Aries can be exasperating in relationships – especially if they are not understood by their partners – they are never consciously or wilfully cruel or malicious. It is just that they are so independent and sure of themselves that they find it almost impossible to see somebody else's viewpoint or position. This is why an Aries needs as a partner someone with lots of social grace.

On the plus side, an Aries is honest, someone you can lean on, someone with whom you will always know where you stand. What he or she lacks in diplomacy is made up for in integrity.

Home and Domestic Life

An Aries is of course the ruler at home – the Boss. The male will tend to delegate domestic matters to the female. The female Aries will want to rule the roost. Both tend to be handy round the house. Both like large families and both believe in the sanctity and importance of the family. An Aries is a good family person, although he or she does not especially like being at home a lot, preferring instead to be roaming about.

Considering that they are by nature so combative and wilful, Aries people can be surprisingly soft, gentle and even vulnerable with their children and partners. The Sign of Cancer, ruled by the Moon, is on the cusp of their Solar 4th House (Home and Family). When the Moon is well aspected – under favourable influences – in the birth chart an Aries will be tender towards the family and want a family life that is nurturing and supportive. Aries likes to come home after a hard day on the battlefield of life to the understanding arms of their partner and the unconditional love and support of their family. An Aries feels that there is enough 'war' out in the world – and he or she enjoys participating in that. But when Aries comes home, comfort and nurturing are what's needed.

Horoscope for 2008

Major Trends

Last year was a good and successful one for most of you. There was a great enlargement of your horizons. Your mind was expanded in many ways. For many of you this came from more foreign travel, where you were exposed to different lands, different cultures and different possibilities. For others it came through higher education. And for still others it came through what we call 'religious revelation' – where the mind is expanded and enlightened through the actions of a Higher Power. When the mind is enlarged, there is optimism. There are infinite possibilities in life. This year, your widened mental capacities are going to gain you practical and concrete results. They will not remain 'up there' in the abstract world – as concepts or religious ideas. They will be put into practice. The first result of this will be seen in your career, a very successful area of life in 2008. This year will see a lifetime career peak for many of you. You will reach the heights – the pinnacles. And as sure as night follows day, you will see new pinnacles to be achieved after that. (More on your career later on.)

Friendships and group activities have been important for many years now, and this trend is still in force this year. The whole area is becoming 'spiritualized' – refined – lifted up.

Spirituality has been important for many years as well. And this trend is also still in effect. Your true friends are your spiritual friends. The group activities that call to you are spiritual group activities.

Last year Saturn made an important move out of Leo into Virgo – from your 5th House to your 6th House. Thus the year ahead is very much a work and career year. A year for succeeding through hard work and sheer productivity. The breaks will come, but you will have earned them.

The other major headline for the year ahead is Pluto's move out of Sagittarius into Capricorn. Again this relates to the career, which we will discuss later on. But it also has health consequences. For Pluto is a very long-term planet. He stays in a Sign anywhere from 15 to 35 years! So his move is a long-term trend. This year Pluto is just flirting with Capricorn – he will move in and move out. But he will announce what is to come: upheavals in your corporate hierarchy, the blasting away of career obstructions, a revamping of your old order of life. Those of you born early in the Sign of Aries (from March 20 to 25) will feel this transit the most; those born later in the Sign will feel it in coming years.

Your most important areas of interest this year will be career (all year), health and work (all year), friendships and group activities (all year), spirituality (all year), religion, philosophy, higher education, foreign travel (January 1 to January 27 and June 14 to November 27).

Your paths of greatest fulfilment this year are friendships, group activities and the career.

Health

(Please note that this is an astrological perspective on health and not a medical one. For the medical perspective, please consult your doctor.)

Health is basically good this year. Perhaps energy is not as strong as it was last year, with two long-term planets now moving into stressful aspect with you. But still, most of the long-term planets are either kind to you or leaving you alone. One or two stressful aspects are not enough to cause any serious illness. We only get concerned when we see a 'gang up' of planetary stresses.

Of course there will be periods in the year where health is more vulnerable and you need to rest and relax more and watch your overall energy. We will deal with these more fully in the monthly reports. But in general these periods are from January 1 to January 20, March 4 to May 9, June 21 to July 22, September 22 to October 23 (and especially until October 4), and December 21 to December 31 (and especially from December 27 onwards).

The good news about health is that your 6th House of Health is very strong this year. You are not letting problems fester or get worse. You are making health a high priority and seem willing to undertake serious, disciplined daily regimes. What I also like here is that you are interested in long-term cures and not short-term fixes.

Saturn in your House of Health shows that you are more conservative, more traditional in your approach to health. You want therapies that have been well tested and that have stood the test of time. You are less apt to experiment these days. Generally, this shows a preference for orthodox medicine. But sometimes it can show a preference for the more traditional forms of alternative therapy (many of which are very ancient and just as traditional as orthodox medicine).

With Mercury as your health planet, it is always important to pay more attention to the lungs, arms, shoulders and small intestine. There are many natural ways to do this – but if you like you can work with the chart supplied. In addition, this year it is important to pay more attention to the spine, knees, teeth, bone structure, gall bladder and overall skeletal alignment. Knees should be given more support when exercising or indulging in sport. Make sure you are getting enough calcium for bone health. Regular visits to a chiropractor will help you keep your spine in alignment. Yoga, tai chi, Pilates and Alexander Technique are also good for the spine.

With Saturn in your 6th House of Health, this is a good year for losing weight and breaking addictions. Saturn helps the willpower (and we all need all the help we can get when it comes to these things).

Saturn is your career planet. His position in your House of Health is giving us many other messages. First off, it underscores the importance of health this year. (From a spiritual perspective, it shows that health and healing – both of the

Reflexology

Try to massage the whole foot on a regular basis, but pay extra attention to the points highlighted on the chart. When you massage, be aware of 'sore spots', as these need special attention. It's also a good idea to massage the ankles and top side (as well as the soles) of the feet.

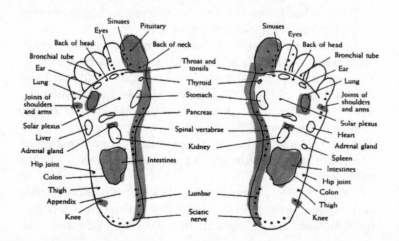

self and others – is the spiritual mission for the year ahead.) It shows that good health for you means more than just the 'absence of symptoms' but also a healthy career. A career that is expanding, growing and evolving. Career problems can actually impact on your physical health if you are not careful. It also shows that you are involved with the health of a parent or parent figure and you are as much concerned with his or her health as your own. (Surgery might be recommended to them this year, but detox will often do as much good.)

Mercury (your health planet) is a fast-moving planet. During the course of a year he will move through all the Signs and Houses of your Horoscope. Thus you are the kind of person who has variable – constantly changing – needs in health and who responds to different kinds of therapies at different times. These short-term issues will be covered in the monthly reports.

Home and Family

Your 4th House of Home and Family is not a House of Power this year. This means it is not much emphasized. Other things in your life are more important. Generally I read this as a good thing. You are pretty much satisfied with the status quo and have no need to make important changes. You are content. The lack of planetary power in this House also shows that the planets aren't pushing you one way or the other. You have more personal freedom in home and domestic affairs this year. You can shape this area according to your specifications. But the problem with that is lack of interest. Generally we don't make changes unless we are forced to. Thus the status quo tends to prevail.

With two Lunar Eclipses this year which impact on the home and family, there will certainly be periods of drama and excitement. But these will be short-term phenomena. The Lunar Eclipse of February 21 and August 16 test family relationships, make family members more temperamental, bring dramas into their lives and bring up hidden flaws in the home. When the dust settles, things will be better than before.

There are also two Solar Eclipses this year – and these will impact on children (if you have them). The Lunar Eclipses impact on the family as a whole, the Solar Eclipses impact on children. Many of these changes are quite normal – the child reaches puberty and has a sexual awakening, or moves out, or goes off to university, or marries. But still these events are 'disruptive' and create major changes for both parents and children.

If you are planning major construction in the home – renovations and the like – March 4 to May 9 and June 21 to July 22 are good periods for this.

If you are planning to beautify the home – paint, decorate, buy art objects, etc. – June 8 to July 12 is a good period.

A parent or parent figure is contemplating surgery. Looks to me like a cosmetic type of surgery. But there are other natural ways to achieve the same result – diet, yoga and meditation. This person is having a bittersweet kind of year. On the one hand there is prosperity and much travel, but there are also many personal crises. Much of it has to do with the self-image and self-concept. If this person hasn't been careful in dietary matters there can be a cleansing of the physical body.

Children might also undergo surgery (though they should always get second opinions) but in general the health looks good. If there have been health problems there should be good news by the time the year is over with.

Finance and Career

Finance *per se* doesn't seem a major interest in the year ahead. Status, prestige, advancement, elevation – in other words, the career – is much more important and this is where the action is in the coming year. A very strong career year.

With Jupiter in your 10th House of Career all year, many of you will be promoted and receive pay rises. And this seems to be what you are shooting for. Not so much to make money, but to achieve the elevation from which money can naturally be made. It's as if you are putting off earnings to achieve greater status. You are setting up the conditions by which earnings will increase down the road.

Of course you will have earnings in the coming year – in spite of the fact that the Money House is basically empty. But this will simply maintain the status quo.

Success will come through much hard work, taking on more responsibility, many dramas and changes. This is a turbulent area in the year ahead – turbulent but good. You are attaining success the hard way – through old fashioned hard work. As you do this, you will create much good luck for yourself – as Jupiter's beneficence steps in. Even if you get promoted without doing too much hard work, the promotion will bring that with it. The good news is that you will see the result of your work – many people are not that lucky.

There is more travel involved with the career as well. Your willingness to travel will play a big role in your success. Many of you have got all the education you needed last year, but any educational opportunity that arises, especially if it is related to the career, is good.

Finally you will need to make dramatic changes in the career. This can be with your attitudes, your career path, or the methods by which you are pursuing it. These changes – and they might go against the grain – will help you achieve the heights.

Destiny will also play its role – as you play yours. As you do the work required and make the changes that it is possible for you to make, other changes – dramatic ones – either in your industry, with your bosses, your corporate hierarchy, with the government or government regulations, are going to happen to clear your path. These shakeups can seem frightening, but hold firm; ultimately they are for your good.

We are seeing these changes in a number of ways. Pluto – a very dynamic power – moves in and out of your 10th House this year. And, Saturn camps out very near an eclipse point from February until August. If obstructions to your success need 'blasting', it will happen. Nothing can stop you this year.

Pluto's move into your 10th House (which only tentatively begins this year) is the beginning of a long-term trend. By the time Pluto finishes his transit (in 20 to 35 years) your career is going to be totally changed. Your industry is going to be changed. Impurities in your industry (perhaps crimes or injustices that were going on behind the scenes) will get revealed and cause havoc. You will die and be reborn, from a career perspective, many times. Out of this will come a fearlessness – an endurance – that will always keep you on top.

Pluto's move into Capricorn also has world level implications. Capricorn rules the traditional structures of the world – the government and corporate structures – and these will be subjected to many a crisis in coming years. We will hear of more revolutions in different parts of the world. Keep in mind that Pluto cannot kill something that is vital and healthy – only the flawed and effete are vulnerable. In this respect, Pluto's violent tendencies, are a cosmic good – they demolish what needs to be demolished. The good will always endure.

Your most prosperous period this year will be from April 17 to May 24. This will be the financial peak.

Love and Social Life

Your 7th House of Love and Marriage is not a House of Power this year, Aries. It doesn't seem to be a major interest as compared to other things. This lack of planetary impetus does give you more freedom in this area – freedom to create your love life as you would like it to be. But few people exercise their freedoms when the interest is not there. Also, the fact that we don't see major power in your 7th House shows a basic contentment with the love life as it is. Thus there is no need to make dramatic changes. Thus I expect a status quo type of year. Marrieds will tend to stay married and singles will tend to stay single.

The real action this year is in the area of friendships. This seems a lot more interesting to you than romance. And this area seems very exciting these days. New and very interesting friends are coming into the picture. These are not 'run-of-the-mill' kinds of people. They are unconventional and glamorous. They lead glamorous lives and you get to share it with them. The people you are meeting now are spiritual and creative types. Hanging around these kinds of people is doing wonders for your own spiritual and creative life, too. The only problem here is instability. These kinds of people tend to be here today and gone tomorrow. But there are spiritual lessons here, too – learning to deal with social instability – learning to embrace abrupt social changes. New friends come, old ones go. The social life is very spontaneous – it is always a NOW kind of proposition – making future plans seems difficult.

Of course singles will be dating and perhaps even falling in love. But marriage (especially if it is the 1st one) doesn't seem in the stars. The social peak this year – the period when romance is most likely to flourish and when the social life will be most active is from August 19 to October 23. In any given month, there will be monthly romantic peaks and we will deal with those short-term issues in the monthly reports.

Since your love planet, Venus, is a very fast-moving planet. In a given year she will move through all the Signs and Houses of your Horoscope, love, social and romantic opportunities tend to come to you in a variety of ways and places – all depending on where Venus is at any given time. Also, you are the kind of person whose needs in love change constantly, and this too depends on Venus. Again, we will cover these things in the monthly reports.

Those who have been working on the second marriage could easily have tied the knot, last year – the opportunities for serious romance and marriage were very strong. This year marriage opportunities come as you pursue your career goals – and with people involved in your career. But truth be told, your aspects for this were much better last year than now.

Those working towards their third marriage are having a great social life – very exciting – but though the opportunities are there marriage doesn't seem recommendable. You will need someone who gives you a lot of space and a lot of personal freedom (but be prepared to return the favour!) Serious romantic opportunities come as you pursue your spiritual life and growth – at meditation seminars or spiritually-oriented retreats, or charity-type functions.

Self-improvement

Your spiritual life has been important for some years now. There has been much inner growth going on. This trend is still important. There are many, many paths to the Divine – as many as there are people. But for you, you need something that is transcendent – that leads to the ultimate heights, but is scientific and rational as well. Paths such as Hermetic Science or Jnana Yoga seem very attractive and you will get good results from them. The spiritual side of Astrology (and there is a strong spiritual dimension to it – it is much more than just reading the future) would also be very good. Many people don't understand that Spirit is ultimately rational and operates by scientific laws. Yes, there are aspects that are 'unknowable' – but, over time, even the 'unknowable' becomes known.

This rational and scientific understanding will help you decode the scriptures of all traditions and reveal why certain religious practices were instituted. It was not random or haphazard.

It is also a period where you need to experiment more in the spiritual life – to learn what works for you by trial and error. Personal experiment will lead you into knowledge not written in any book or taught by any system.

Saturn, as we mentioned earlier, is now firmly in your 6th House of Health and Service. Since, in your chart, Saturn is showing your spiritual mission for the year ahead, we see that it involves health and healing. If any of you are not well, your mission is to get well, and then to help others get well. If you are well, your mission involves healing and service to others.

Month-by-month Forecasts

January

Best Days Overall: 5, 6, 14, 15, 22, 23
Most Stressful Days Overall: 1, 7, 8, 20, 21, 27, 28
Best Days for Love: 1, 5, 6, 14, 15, 23, 24, 27, 28
Best Days for Money: 5, 6, 7, 14, 15, 16, 17, 23, 24, 25

As mentioned in the yearly forecast, you are in a banner career period this year – and this month is a peak within the peak. First off, 70 to 80 per cent of the planets are above the horizon. Your 10th House of career is super strong – 60 per cent of the planets will either be there or move through there this month. Wow! The planets that are moving through are mostly beneficial – helpful. It is understandable (and advisable) that you let go of home and family issues for a while and focus on the career.

Your ruling planet, Mars, is Retrograde most of the month (until the 30th). So you might be feeling doubts or lack of direction. But conquer your doubts and push forward with your career goals. If you feel you deserve that promotion or pay rise make your case fearlessly. (Probably these things have already happened.) You are in demand, both in your company and your industry. You are a 'hot commodity' – recognize your worth. Happy career opportunities are manifesting both within your present situation or with other companies.

On a personal level you seem 'way outside' your normal boundaries and perhaps this is the cause for some of the doubt and uncertainty you feel. You are in strange territory. Students are studying (or reading) subjects outside the normal curriculum. Sales or marketing people are in strange locales.

The focus on the career is in effect all month, but after the 20th there is more interest in friendships and group activities. Intellectual interests, as we mentioned, are also important this month.

Finances start to become important towards the end of the month – on the 24th as your financial planet crosses your Midheaven. Finances will be strong this month – you have big, financial ideas and goals. Money comes from foreign sources or foreign clients or foreign investments until the 24th. After that it comes from pay rises, the support of parent or parent figures, or authority figures. Those involved in your own businesses should investigate government contracts. Until the 24th you are a big and rash spender. Afterwards you seem more conservative and cost conscious – if you are buying big-ticket items, it's probably better to wait until the 24th (the only problem is that Mercury will be Retrograde then).

Love, too, becomes more important after the 24th (your love and financial planet is identical – Venus). For singles, there are romantic opportunities at the office after the 24th. Before that it is in religious or educational type settings. Until the 24th you seem very rash in love, afterwards, you are more cautious.

Health needs watching all month, but especially until the 20th. (Try especially to rest and relax more on the 7th and 8th – but it will be difficult.)

Happy romantic and financial surprises come on the 30th/31st.

February

Best Days Overall: 1, 2, 10, 11, 19, 20, 28, 29
Most Stressful Days Overall: 3, 4, 17, 23, 24
Best Days for Love: 3, 4, 13, 14, 23, 24
Best Days for Money: 3, 4, 12, 13, 14, 21, 22, 23

Happy romantic and financial surprises are coming on the 1st and 2nd. Perhaps there is opportunity for a foreign trip. Students hear good news about university or graduate school. Career is still going great.

Health is much improved over last month. By the 17th energy levels will be super–abundant.

Most of the planets are still above the horizon and your 10th House (career) is still much stronger than your 4th House of Home and Family. You can safely let go of family issues and responsibilities and focus on the career. You benefit your family most by succeeding in the outer world. You are not neglecting your family only serving them in a different and better way.

Friendships, groups, organizations and group activities are the major interests this month (aside from career). Spirituality, too, is very important. Both these interests are very merged. Your friends tend to be spiritual or spiritually involved too. This is a good period (especially after the 19th) to go on spiritually oriented retreats, get involved in charities, and attend spiritual lectures or seminars.

Singles still find love opportunities at the office, with superiors or bosses, as they pursue the career goals, or with people who are involved in their career. You seem conservative in love – you want the person of high status – the good provider – the person who can help your career. Love is more practical than romantic. But after the 17th the attitudes change. You want more – you want friendship with the beloved – a feeling of equality – good communication – mutual freedom. After the 17th love opportunities come at group activities, organizations and spiritual type settings.

Mars is now moving forward. It receives beautiful aspects. Another good health signal. But more importantly your confidence is back. Yes, you are still in strange locales and unfamiliar settings, but you are OK about it. The fear and apprehension is gone.

Finance doesn't seem a big deal this month. Especially after the 17th. You seem content with finances as they are. A status-quo kind of month.

Two eclipses this month shake up the world (and probably bring changes in your corporate hierarchy or industry) but you seem relatively untouched. (Friends and parent figures are having very dramatic experiences though). Still it won't hurt to take a reduced schedule around February 7 (Solar Eclipse) and February 21 (Lunar Eclipse).

March

Best Days Overall: 9, 17, 18, 27, 28
Most Stressful Days Overall: 2, 3, 15, 16, 22, 23, 29, 30
Best Days for Love: 4, 5, 15, 22, 23, 24, 25
Best Days for Money: 2, 3, 4, 5, 11, 15, 19, 20, 24, 25, 29, 30

This is a bit of a tumultuous month on various levels, but it is also a spiritual month – a month for spiritual growth and understanding – and this will be a help and protection against the tumult. Mars will be in stressful aspect with Pluto from the 4th to the 8th – thus you should drive more defensively, watch your temper, and avoid tense or conflicting types of situations. If you are provoked take a few deep breaths before answering – and perhaps it is better not to answer. (This aspect will affect the world at large, so it will be interesting to read the headlines this period.) Saturn, your career planet, will re-stimulate the lunar eclipse of point on February 21 towards the end of the month. This brings shakeups in the corporate hierarchy, dramas with parents or parent figures, and career shifts. (On a world level you will hear about all kinds of crises in government – and perhaps even the fall of some governments.) Your career is still very good, so I see these career shifts as positive – but still they are disruptive.

Your love and financial planet, Venus also re-stimulates eclipse points this month – bringing dramas – and disruptions – in love and finance. Be more patient with your spouse, lover or partner during these periods (the 2nd to the 5th and the 13th to the 16th). Probably you will be shown why present financial thinking has been unrealistic. Avoid speculations those periods too. In the end though, in spite of these financial dramas, prosperity is intact. Your financial intuition is super from the 13th onwards and if you trust it, you'll come out richer than before.

When Mars enters Cancer on the 4th, there will be three long-term planets in stressful aspect to you. Take it easy. Rest and relax more. Enhance health by giving more attention to the ankles (until the 15th) and to the feet afterwards. Foot and ankle massage will do wonders for you. Air therapies (breathing exercises, fresh air, air bathing) are powerful until the 15th. After the 15th water therapies (soaking in a tub or whirlpool, swimming, boating, being around water) are more powerful. Many new revelations on the spiritual dimensions of health are happening this month. (There is in general more spiritual revelation happening.)

The dream life is very active this month. ESP experiences happen more frequently. There is pleasure in seclusion and spiritual studies. There are new insights into the scriptures. A very good month to go on spiritual retreat or be involved in charitable activities.

Love opportunities happen at groups or organizations – or through friends until the 13th. Afterwards the opportunities are at spiritual or charitable kinds of events. For many of you this is your birthday month – the beginning of your personal new year. So it is good to review the past year, make corrections, and set goals for the year ahead.

Love is much more idealistic after the 13th. The highs of love can be very high, but the lover is much more sensitive and easily hurt. Watch your voice tones and body language. Little things can have enormous impact. For those on a spiritual path, this is a period to cultivate unconditional love.

Most of the planets are still above the horizon and your 10th House is still very strong – so keep your focus on the career.

April

Best Days Overall: 5, 6, 13, 14, 23, 24
Best Days for Love: 4, 13, 14, 18, 19, 24
Most Stressful Days Overall: 11, 12, 18, 19, 25, 26, 27
Best Days for Love: 4, 13, 14, 18, 19, 24
Best Days for Money: 4, 7, 8, 13, 14, 16, 17, 24, 26, 27

Though you still have three long-term planets in stressful aspect to you, health seems much better this month (actually it began to improve on the 20th of last month). Three long-term planets stress you, but the short-term planets are helping you out. Enhance health by giving more attention to the feet (until the 2nd), the head and face (from the 2nd to the 18th) and the neck and throat afterwards. Head and face massage will do wonders for you from the 2nd to the 18th. You are not only helping the head, but strengthening the entire body – the head has reflex points to the whole body – likewise the face. Neck massage and cranial sacral therapy will be powerful from the 18th onwards. The neck is a place where tension tends to collect – and energy gets blocked up there. So be aware when this happens and consciously relax it.

On the 6th there is a shift of planetary power from the upper half to the lower half of the Horoscope. Career is still very important and successful, but you are entering a period where you need to pay more attention to the home and family. You also need to get more into emotional harmony and balance. Success is wonderful, but it's time to start 'feeling right' as well. With Mars in the Sign of Cancer (your 4th Solar House) all month most of you are realizing this and doing this.

After all the excitement of last month, this is a calmer month. Financial and love opportunities are running after you. Nothing much you need to do. On the 6th (for some of you it will happen after) a nice financial windfall comes. Personal items come to you, too – clothing, jewellery or accessories. This is a time to invest in your self and your image. Happily you can afford it – for on April 19, you enter a yearly financial peak. Money comes easily, in fun sort of ways – perhaps as you are on the golf course or theatre or at a party. Speculations seem very favourable – and it might be wise to invest modest amounts on lottery tickets after the 19th. (Next month will also be good for this.)

Your 1st House of Self is very powerful this month. Some 70 to 80 per cent of the planets are in the independent East. This is Aries heaven. This is a time to create your life as you want it to be – no need to adapt or people please (though you should never be rude or disrespectful to others). This is a time to please yourself. Make life conform to you rather than the other way around. You are supposed to have life on your terms now. Build your life, but build wisely, for there is an inescapable law that will make you live with your creation – good, bad or indifferent.

This is a month of great personal pleasure and sensual fulfilment. You are in a yearly personal pleasure peak (it began on the 20th of last month).

If you are buying big-ticket items after the 19th seems better. There will be a lot of earth in the Horoscope – and buying decisions will probably be better.

There are still dramas going on in your industry and with authority figures in your life.

May

Best Days Overall: 2, 3, 11, 12, 20, 21, 30, 31
Most Stressful Days Overall: 8, 9, 15, 16, 23, 24
Best Days for Love: 4, 5, 13, 14, 15, 16, 24, 25
Best Days for Money: 4, 5, 13, 14, 23, 24, 25

The planetary power is still very much in the independent East – so keep in mind our discussion of last month. It is a time to make things happen, to have your way, and to create conditions as you desire them to be. Please yourself and others will also be pleased.

You are still very much into your yearly financial peak. Wealth increases easily and substantially. Still a good time to invest modest daily amounts in the lottery – the period of May 10 to May 14 and May 17–21 is best for speculations. Remember the cosmos doesn't have to give you the good through a lottery – it can come to you in many ways – but those periods bring increased riches – beautiful pay days.

You tend to be a rash and impulsive spender and investor, but this month (and the year as a whole) you are more conservative. There is a lot of earth in the Horoscope right now – 50 to 60 per cent until May 20. A huge percentage. So you are more careful, more apt to get value for your dollar and thus a good time to make important investment or buying decisions (especially if large sums are involved).

Finance is still the major interest until May 20. After that the focus is on intellectual interests, communication, teaching, sales and marketing. This is a time to catch up on all those letters and phone calls you owe. A great time for taking courses in subjects that interest you. Keep in mind, though that Mercury will go Retrograde on the 26th – so be more careful with your communication. If you are doing mass mailings or advertising campaigns start them from the 20th to the 25th – before Mercury goes backwards.

Love is very practical these days. Love opportunities come as you pursue your financial goals or with people involved in your finances (until the 24th). After that the opportunities come in the neighborhood, with neighbors or at educational type settings. Until the 24th, you are allured by wealth and pleasure. The sensual aspects of love allure you. The good provider, the giver of material gifts, the one who can take care of you – this is the kind of love you like. After the 24th you crave more mental compatibility. Good communication is important to you. You want to love the person's mind as well as the body. You show love through communication. And this is how you feel loved. If a person is not communicating with you, you feel that he or she doesn't love you (this might not be true, but this is how you feel).

Having fun also seems important this month – especially after the 9th when Mars, your ruling planet, moves into the 5th House. But as we mentioned this is the kind of month where you can have fun and still prosper.

Health improves after the 9th, but you can make it even better by giving more attention to the neck and throat (until the 3rd) and to the arms, shoulders, lungs and small intestine afterwards. Air based therapies are powerful after the 3rd (fresh air, being in windy places, breathing exercises, air bathing). Avoid making dramatic changes to the diet or health regime after the 26th.

June

Best Days Overall: 7, 8, 16, 17, 18, 26, 27
Most Stressful Days Overall: 5, 6, 11, 12, 13, 19, 20
Best Days for Love: 3, 4, 11, 12, 13, 14, 15, 24, 25
Best Days for Money: 1, 2, 3, 4, 9, 10, 14, 15, 19, 20, 24, 25, 28, 29

Most of the planets are below the horizon and your 10th House of Career gets weaker after the 14th. (Pluto moves back into your 9th House.) In the meantime your 4th House of Home and Family is becoming very strong – beginning on the 18th. So, it is time to take a little bit of a breather from the hectic career pace and find simple pleasures in the home and hearth. Now is the time to attend the graduations, the plays, and be there for the family. Parents or parent figures are still experiencing dramatic events and might need you. Focus more on feeling right, feeling in harmony, your inner state. As you do this, when it is time to get back to the career, you will do it with more vim, vigour and enthusiasm. (Also keep in mind that Retrograde activity is greatly increased this month – 40 per cent of the planets are Retrograde – so there is not much happening out there in the world and you might as well focus on family.)

Intellectual interests and communication are still the major focus early in the month – until the 21st. But be more careful with these things as Mercury is Retrograde. Make sure you are clear when you communicate – that the other person heard and understood you and that you understood them. This can save a lot of heartache later on. (This is especially true in love.)

After the 21st the focus is on children and family. (Children seem a focus all month – but more so after the 21st.)

Earnings are enhanced through good communication (perhaps investing in good equipment and upgrades) sales, marketing and advertising. Good use of the media is important. People need to know about your product or service. A financial hit – perhaps an unexpected expense – on the 17th–20th is short term. Prosperity is still intact. (Be more patient with your spouse or lover during this period, too.) After the 19th you are spending more on the family and home, and family members are more financially supportive of you – in various ways. It can be through actual physical cash, or just as likely, by providing financial opportunities or ideas.

Like last month, love is in educational settings – at lectures, school or seminars. There are opportunities with neighbors. Love is close to home these days – no need to travel far and wide. There is still a need for good communication with the beloved – to be on the same intellectual wavelength. But after the 18th your love needs change. You want more sensitivity, nurturing, emotional support. You want to feel emotionally intimate with the lover – to be able to share your feelings – no matter what they are – as well as ideas. Emotional sensitivity, psychological depth will allure you more than a brilliant mind. You also want a person who has strong family values and a strong commitment to family. After the 18th the lover is apt to be more emotionally sensitive – perhaps even temperamental and moody – be patient. Be aware of the mood he or she is in. In a good mood love will be wonderful, in a bad mood, you might as well stay home.

Health is more stressful after the 21st, but not a serious thing. Basically you need to rest and relax more, maximize your energy. Continue to enhance health through arm and shoulder massage and through giving more attention to the lungs and small intestine. Avoid making major changes in the diet or health regime until after the 19th.

July

  Best Days Overall: 4, 5, 14, 15, 23, 24
  Most Stressful Days Overall: 2, 3, 9, 10, 16, 17, 30
  Best Days for Love: 2, 3, 9, 10, 13, 24
  Best Days for Money: 2, 3, 6, 7, 13, 16, 17, 24, 26

Mars – a very important planet in your Horoscope – he is your Ruler – is re–stimulating the Lunar Eclipse point of February 21 – from the 1st to the 8th. This is likely to be a very stressful period, so try to rest and relax more, avoid arguments – even if provoked – drive defensively and avoid high stress activities. (Do what you need to do, but let go of things that can be re-scheduled.) Now when a planet re-stimulates an eclipse point it is almost as powerful as the actual eclipse itself. Thus if you haven't been careful in dietary matters, there could be a detox of the body. It will be a period where you need to re–define your image and personality too.

Home and family continues to be important, but you still seem very ambitious (Mars is travelling with your career planet, Saturn from the 1st to the 13th.) You will have to balance both the career and the home life. You seem to have important involvement with bosses, authority figures, parent or parent figures or the government that period. After the 13th you can refocus on the home and on feeling good. It's a time to charge the emotional batteries.

The major focus this month is on home, family, children and health issues. Work also seems very important – and demanding.

The focus on health is a good thing this month, as you need to give it more focus – especially until the 22nd. You seem into vigourous exercise – which is good – and eating better. You also seem more involved in daily disciplined health regimes. A good month for diet and weight-loss programs – especially until the 13th. The health of a parent or parent figure seems delicate and you are personally involved. Health can also be enhanced through giving more attention to the arms, shoulders, lungs and small intestine (all month but especially until the 10th); the stomach and breasts (from the 10th to the 26th); the heart (from the 26th onwards). Air therapies – fresh air, air purity, wind surfing or wind bathing – are powerful until the 10th; water therapies – soaking in a tub or natural spring, whirlpools and spas, boating and swimming – are powerful from the 10th to the 26th; Fire therapies – sunshine, heat, saunas, hot water bottles – are powerful after the 26th.

Finances are status quo this month. Financial support and opportunity comes from family and family connections until the 12th. After the 12th speculations become more favourable – and they become even more favourable after the 22nd. Financial opportunities can come through children (out of the mouth of babes) and as you're having fun. Serious investors should look at real estate (until the 12th) and gold, gaming companies, electric utilities, and entertainment afterwards.

Venus will re–stimulate the Solar Eclipse point of February 7, from the 26th to the 29th. Avoid financial risk taking or speculations that period. There is some financial disruption – but short lived. Overall prosperity will not be affected by this.

Job-seekers seem aggressive this month – some more elevated position is available, but there are bumps on the road.

Venus' re-stimulation of the eclipse point also affects love
– so be more patient with the beloved that period (the 26th
to the 29th) – the marriage or current relationship gets
tested.

August

Best Days Overall: 1, 2, 10, 11, 20, 28, 29
Most Stressful Days Overall: 5, 6, 12, 13, 14, 26, 27
Best Days for Love: 1, 2, 5, 6, 21, 22, 23
Best Days for Money: 1, 2, 3, 4, 12, 13, 22, 23, 30, 31

Last month two important planets re-stimulated eclipse
points – making these periods like 'mini-eclipses'. This
month we have two actual – real – eclipses.

Though these eclipses are relatively benign for you, it
won't hurt to take a reduced schedule during those periods.

The Solar Eclipse of August 1 occurs in your 5th House of
Children. Thus there are dramatic events with the children if
you have them – or with people who are 'like' children to
you. It will test a love affair too (not a marriage) and if it is
flawed it will probably dissolve. There can be disruptions in
creative type projects as well. Since Mercury is impacted by
this eclipse, there can be job changes and changes in the
health regime. Communication equipment and cars get
tested as well. If there are fundamental flaws in these things,
you will find out about them now.

The Lunar Eclipse of August 16 occurs in your 11th
House of Friends and Organizations. This eclipse will test
friendships and bring important changes in your spiritual
regime and practice. There are dramas in the lives of friends.
There are shakeups in a spiritual organization or ministry
that you are involved in. Every Lunar Eclipse tests the home
and family life. Family members are apt to be more temperamental. If there are hidden flaws in the home, now you find
out about them.

This is a great period for a vacation. Your 5th House of
Fun is very strong and you are in the mood for leisure. Also

40 per cent of the planets are Retrograde and things are slow in the world. You won't be missing much by taking a holiday.

After the 22nd the focus is on health and work. Health is good this period, but you want to make it even better. You are very into 'physical fitness' as much as health and this is where the interest is coming from.

Job-seekers have good fortune this period – all month is good – but especially after the 22nd. Those who employ others will expand their staff.

The planets make a major shift towards the end of the month. By the 30th the dominance will be in the upper half of the Horoscope – the sector of ambition and outer achievement. Seventy to 80 per cent of the planets (a huge percentage) will be in the upper half of the Horoscope. So get ready to start focusing on your career and outer life.

Speculations are still favourable until the 22nd (but most favourable until the 5th). But the bulk of your earnings are coming from work. The work place is not only the place that supplies the paycheck, but also romance and romantic opportunities (after the 5th). You (and you are probably attracting these kinds of people) are looking for perfection these days. And this can lead to too much criticism and analysis. Sure, your motives are good, you want to love to be perfect – but criticism (especially the destructive kind) won't make it perfect – it will just kill whatever you have. Singles will have to work harder to show warmth to others. Venus doesn't like the Sign of Virgo.

September

Best Days Overall: 6, 7, 8, 16, 17, 24, 25
Most Stressful Days Overall: 1, 2, 3, 9, 10, 22, 23, 29, 30
Best Days for Love: 1, 2, 3, 11, 12, 21, 29, 30
Best Days for Money: 1, 2, 9, 10, 11, 12, 18, 19, 21, 27

Retrograde activity is lessening this month. Jupiter and Pluto start moving forward on the 8th and 9th. Until the 24th only

2 planets (20 per cent of the planetary power) will be Retrograde. (Last month 40 per cent were Retrograde). Mercury will Retrograde on the 24th, but this will be a short-term trend. The planetary momentum is forward, the world is moving forward, gridlock is over with, you make rapid progress towards your goals.

Health, health regimes and work are still the major focus until the 22nd. Love and romance is a focus all month – but especially after the 22nd. You are in a yearly social peak now. Singles might not marry now, but they will meet people who are 'marriage material'. Aries are always aggressive in love, but this month (and last month from the 19th onwards) even more so. If you like someone you are not shy, you let them know. You don't wait around for the phone to ring – but take the initiative. You are 'out there' pursuing love and love opportunities. You are in fact, creating your social life.

Not only that, but you have the knack – and it is a knack – of combining social and financial goals. The social life expands the earnings. Earnings expand the social life. A business client could invite you to a party or play cupid. Or, you go to a party and meet someone who can be important financially. One merges in to the other and it is hard to tell which is which.

Health needs more watching all month, but especially from the 22nd onwards. Naturally rest and relax more and listen to your body. Enhance health by giving more attention to the heart (until the 22nd); the spine, knees, teeth, bones and skeletal alignment (all month and all year); the kidneys and hips. Hips can be regularly massaged. The spine can be kept in shape through yoga, Pilates, Alexander Technique or seeing a chiropractor. (Also see the foot reflexology chart on how to strengthen these organs.)

Air-based therapies are powerful this month. If you feel under the weather go out in the fresh air and let the wind blow all over you. You will feel better. Keep harmony with the friends and the lover – as this can be root cause for problems this month.

The power in the upper half of your Horoscope is even stronger than last month. By the 22nd, 80 to 90 per cent of the planets will be above the horizon of your chart. A clear message, serve your family by being successful in the outer world. We see forward motion in the career in other ways too – Jupiter in your 10th House of Career starts moving forward on the 8th after months of Retrograde motion.

October

Best Days Overall: 4, 5, 13, 14, 22, 23, 31
Most Stressful Days Overall: 6, 7, 19, 20, 26, 27
Best Days for Love: 1, 11, 12, 21, 22, 23, 26, 27
Best Days for Money: 1, 6, 7, 11, 12, 15, 16, 21, 22, 24, 25, 31

By the 15th (as Mercury starts to move forward again) 80 per cent of the planets will again be moving forward. The momentum of the heavens is forward – onward and up-ward. Go for your goals. Keep your eyes on the prize.

Most of the planets have been in the Western sector of your chart for some months now – and this is still true. You are in a strong social period where you need to cultivate the good graces of others. Your skills and abilities are important – but not enough. People also have to like you and get on with you.

You are still very much into your yearly social peak until the 23rd. With your interest so strongly focused on others, success is bound to happen. You are willing to overcome the various social challenges that arise.

Career definitely takes priority over the home and family but from the 15th to the 23rd – as the Moon becomes the 'handle' of a 'bucket type chart' – family becomes more important than usual. You will have to juggle between the two – and perhaps even let career matters go for a brief period. But the period is brief, and ambitions return as strong as ever.

Until the 18th focus on the prosperity of other people – especially of your spouse or business partners. Try to see things from their financial interest. See where you can enhance it. As you do this, you will find that your own prosperity comes to you very naturally. For serious investors, bonds and the bond market look interesting. There are financial opportunities in 'creative financing'. Your line of credit will increase. Those of you who are looking for outside investors should take the initiative now – until the 18th.

Until the 18th you are in a good period for reducing debt and for eliminating waste – extra expenses – needless expenses. This will make you financially healthier. After the 18th you can focus on expanding your income (and it will happen). But you need to prepare the ground for the expansion. You are very prosperous after the 18th.

Health still needs watching until the 23rd. Enhance health with more attention to the kidneys and hips and with air based therapies. Love 'disharmonies' need to be eliminated too – especially if there is a health problem.

Love is very passionate – very sexual – until the 18th. The physical, sexual chemistry is the major attraction. But after that (no one can maintain this kind of intensity for very long) the focus is more on philosophical and religious compatibility. You look for lovers who can teach you things – expand your mind. There are often love affairs with teachers or professors under these aspects. You can enhance love by foreign trips or by attending religious services together as a couple.

November

Best Days Overall: 1, 10, 11, 18, 19, 27, 28
Most Stressful Days Overall: 2, 3, 4, 16, 17, 22, 23, 30
Best Days for Love: 1, 11, 12, 20, 21, 22, 23, 30
Best Days for Money: 1, 2, 3, 4, 11, 12, 13, 20, 21, 30

Retrograde activity is even less than last month. The planetary momentum is overwhelmingly forward this month. By the 2nd, 90 per cent of the planets are forward. By the 27th, it will be 100 per cent. So the world is moving ahead and so are you. Stuck and stalled projects are now moving forward again. This is Aries heaven – especially after the 21st. A go-go-go kind of month. Things happen fast. It is exciting.

The major interest this month are sex, other people's money, debt and the repayment of debt, and the deeper things of life – depth psychology, occult studies, past lives, life after death and personal transformation.

Most of you will be dealing with death on some level this period. Sometimes it's hard to avoid it – the newspapers and TV are full of it. In most cases it will be a psychological confrontation – you have dreams about it, or someone you know has a near death experience. The object here is to conquer some of the fear associated with it and to understand the subject on a deeper level. Those on a spiritual path will be dealing with the death of ego on some level. The death of the ego generally doesn't happen all at once, but in stages. And you are in one of those stages. Rejoice when this happens, as resurrection is sure to follow.

This is a great month (until the 21st) to detox the body – herbally or mechanically – and detox the mind and emotional life. Also good to get rid of old possessions you no longer need. This will make room for the new and better that wants to come into your life. Things not needed are not evil *per se* – it is just considered 'effete material' that clogs up the works – clogs the channels.

Your 9th House becomes very strong beginning the 16th and even stronger on the 21st. Thus foreign lands call to you. There will be travel opportunities – both for business and pleasure. There is a greater interest in religion and philosophy that period. (People who are strong in the 9th House by birth, will prefer a philosophical discussion over a night out on the town – it is considered much more pleasurable than that – and this is how you are this period.) This is not a permanent condition, but only a phase. It should be enjoyed.

Happy educational opportunities also come.

Prosperity is unusually strong this month. You are better off doing serious shopping or investing after the 12th when your financial planet moves into Capricorn. Purchases will be sounder and more conservative.

Mars, your ruling planet, re-stimulates the Solar Eclipse point of August 1 from the 6th to the 11th. Take a reduced schedule and avoid risk-taking activities. Spend more quiet time at home. (Also read the newspapers that period – the headlines should be dramatic.)

Mercury your health and communication planet will re-stimulate eclipse points from the 10th to 11th (this is the stronger transit as Mars is also on an eclipse point then) and from the 18th to the 21st. This could test your communication equipment, bring some upheavals at work or with co-workers, and cause a change in your health regime. Overall health seems good this month. You have the energy of 10 people. The main danger is hyper-activity – pushing the body beyond its limits, causing burn-out.

December

    Best Days Overall: 7, 8, 15, 16, 24, 25, 26
    Most Stressful Days Overall: 1, 13, 14, 20, 21, 27, 28
    Best Days for Love: 1, 11, 20, 21, 30, 31
    Best Days for Money: 1, 9, 10, 11, 17, 18, 20, 21, 27, 28,
        30, 31

A very powerful career month – another yearly peak begins on the 21st. Some 80 to 90 per cent of the planets are above the horizon – a huge percentage. But even more dramatic than that is that 60 per cent (and sometimes 70 per cent) of the planets will either be in, or move through, your 10th House of Career. (Your 4th House, by contrast, is empty – only the Moon will move through there on the 13th and 14th.) So let go of the family for a while. Hire someone to do the cleaning and the housework, and focus on the career. This is the best way to serve your family and achieve emotional harmony. Outer success will make you feel right.

Religion, philosophy, metaphysics, foreign travel and higher education are still important until the 21st. Higher education or travel that relates to the career, seems best for you.

But all this career success is taxing on your health and energy. Health definitely needs watching all month – but especially after the 21st. You are going to be very busy, no question about it, but you can work smarter and not harder. Delegate wherever possible. Keep your priorities straight and focus only on those things. Don't make three trips, when one will do. Organize yourself better. Listen to your body, if there are strange pains, stop what you're doing and rest. If they persist check them out.

Enhance health by giving more attention to the liver and thighs until the 12th and to the spine, knees, teeth, bones and skeletal alignment after the 12th (these organs have been important all year and now even more so.)

Very happy love experiences happen on the 1st and 2nd. Financial windfalls happen then too. There is romantic opportunity with someone of high status then (and this relationship will probably get tested from the 14th to the 18th). Pay rises and promotions could happen all month, but the 1st and 2nd are likely times. (Those are good days to play the lottery – but your good can happen in many other ways too.)

Love is practical – down to earth – bottom line-oriented – until the 8th. The person of high status, the person who can help you financially or careerwise – the person of power – this is alluring to you. You feel you can 'learn to love anyone' so long as the basics – the practical issues – are in place. After the 8th you change. You want more equality with the lover. You want friendship and not just 'another job'. Also you want more social freedom. Love opportunities happen at group activities, organizations or through the introduction of friends. (Groups or organizations – friends in the right places – are important on a financial level, too.)

Enhance your finances by being up to date technologically. Be a little more experimental – think out of the box – try new things. You need to learn what works through trial and error. Sure you might make a few mistakes (and you'll find out from the 14th to the 18th) but that's part of the learning process. Correct your mistakes and move on. Prosperity is still very much intact – and even a mistake or two is not going to damage it long term.

Taurus

ຽ

THE BULL
Birthdays from
21st April to
20th May

Personality Profile

TAURUS AT A GLANCE

Element – Earth

Ruling Planet – Venus
   Career Planet – Uranus
   Love Planet – Pluto
   Money Planet – Mercury
   Planet of Health and Work – Venus
   Planet of Home and Family Life – Sun
   Planet of Spirituality – Mars
   Planet of Travel, Education, Religion and
      Philosophy – Saturn

Colours – earth tones, green, orange, yellow

Colours that promote love, romance and social
   harmony – red–violet, violet

Colours that promote earning power – yellow,
   yellow–orange

Gems – coral, emerald

Metal – copper

Scents – bitter almond, rose, vanilla, violet

Quality – fixed (= stability)

Quality most needed for balance – flexibility

Strongest virtues – endurance, loyalty, patience, stability, a harmonious disposition

Deepest needs – comfort, material ease, wealth

Characteristics to avoid – rigidity, stubbornness, tendency to be overly possessive and materialistic

Signs of greatest overall compatibility – Virgo, Capricorn

Signs of greatest overall incompatibility – Leo, Scorpio, Aquarius

Sign most helpful to career – Aquarius

Sign most helpful for emotional support – Leo

Sign most helpful financially – Gemini

Sign best for marriage and/or partnerships – Scorpio

Sign most helpful for creative projects – Virgo

Best Sign to have fun with – Virgo

Signs most helpful in spiritual matters – Aries, Capricorn

Best day of the week – Friday

Understanding a Taurus

Taurus is the most earthy of all the Earth Signs. If you understand that Earth is more than just a physical element, that it is a psychological attitude as well, you will get a better understanding of the Taurus personality.

A Taurus has all the power of action that an Aries has. But Taurus is not satisfied with action for its own sake. Their actions must be productive, practical and wealth-producing. If Taurus cannot see a practical value in an action they will not bother taking it.

Taurus' forte lies in their power to make real their own or other people's ideas. They are generally not very inventive but they can take another's invention and perfect it, making it more practical and useful. The same is true for all projects. Taurus is not especially keen on starting new projects, but once they get involved they bring things to completion. Taurus carries everything through. They are finishers and will go the distance so long as no unavoidable calamity intervenes.

Many people find Taurus too stubborn, conservative, fixed and immovable. This is understandable, because Taurus dislikes change – in the environment or in the routine. They even dislike changing their minds! On the other hand, this is their virtue. It is not good for a wheel's axle to waver. The axle must be fixed, stable and unmovable. Taurus is the axle of society and the heavens. Without their stability and so-called stubbornness, the wheels of the world (and especially the wheels of commerce) would not turn.

Taurus loves routine. A routine, if it is good, has many virtues. It is a fixed – and, ideally, perfect – way of taking care of things. Mistakes can happen when spontaneity comes into the equation, and mistakes cause discomfort and uneasiness – something almost unacceptable to a Taurus. Meddling with Taurus' comfort and security is a sure way to irritate and anger them.

While an Aries loves speed, a Taurus likes things slow. They are slow thinkers – but do not make the mistake of assuming they lack intelligence. On the contrary, Taurus people are very intelligent. It is just that they like to chew on ideas, to deliberate and weigh them up. Only after due deliberation is an idea accepted or a decision taken. Taurus is slow to anger – but once aroused, take care!

Finance

Taurus is very money-conscious. Wealth is more important to them than to many other Signs. Wealth to a Taurus means comfort and security. Wealth means stability. Where some Zodiac Signs feel that they are spiritually rich if they have ideas, talents or skills, Taurus only feels wealth when they can see and touch it. Taurus' way of thinking is 'What good is a talent if it has not been translated into a home, furniture, car and holidays?'

These are all reasons why Taurus excels in estate agency and agricultural industries. Usually a Taurus will end up owning land. They love to feel their connection to the Earth. Material wealth began with agriculture, the tilling of the soil. Owning a piece of land was humanity's earliest form of wealth: Taurus still feels that primeval connection.

It is in the pursuit of wealth that Taurus develops intellectual and communication ability. Also, in this pursuit Taurus is forced to develop some flexibility. It is in the quest for wealth that they learn the practical value of the intellect and come to admire it. If it were not for the search for wealth and material things, Taurus people might not try to reach a higher intellect.

Some Taurus people are 'born lucky' – the type who win any gamble or speculation. This luck is due to other factors in their Horoscope; it is not part of their essential nature. By nature they are not gamblers. They are hard workers and like to earn what they get. Taurus' innate conservatism makes them abhor unnecessary risks in finance and in other areas of their lives.

Career and Public Image

Being essentially down-to-earth people, simple and uncom-
plicated, Taurus tends to look up to those who are original,
unconventional and inventive. Taurus likes their bosses to
be creative and original – since they themselves are content
to perfect their superiors' brain-waves. They admire people
who have a wider social or political consciousness and they
feel that someday (when they have all the comfort and security they need) they too would like to be involved in these
big issues.

In business affairs Taurus can be very shrewd – and that
makes them valuable to their employers. They are never
lazy; they enjoy working and getting good results. Taurus
does not like taking unnecessary risks and do well in
positions of authority, which makes them good managers
and supervisors. Their managerial skills are reinforced by
their natural talents for organization and handling details,
their patience and thoroughness. As mentioned, through their
connection with the earth, Taurus people also do well in
farming and agriculture.

In general a Taurus will choose money and earning power
over public esteem and prestige. A position that pays more –
though it has less prestige – is preferred to a position with a
lot of prestige but fewer earnings. Many other Signs do not
feel this way, but a Taurus does, especially if there is nothing
in his or her personal birth chart that modifies this. Taurus
will pursue glory and prestige only if it can be shown that
these things have a direct and immediate impact on their
wallet.

Love and Relationships

In love, the Taurus-born likes to have and to hold. They are
the marrying kind. They like commitment and they like the
terms of a relationship to be clearly defined. More importantly, Taurus likes to be faithful to one lover, and they
expect that lover to reciprocate this fidelity. When this

doesn't happen, their whole world comes crashing down. When they are in love Taurus people are loyal, but they are also very possessive. They are capable of great fits of jealousy if they are hurt in love.

Taurus is satisfied with the simple things in a relationship. If you are involved romantically with a Taurus there is no need for lavish entertainments and constant courtship. Give them enough love, food and comfortable shelter and they will be quite content to stay home and enjoy your company. They will be loyal to you for life. Make a Taurus feel comfortable and – above all – secure in the relationship, and you will rarely have a problem.

In love, Taurus can sometimes make the mistake of trying to control their partners, which can cause great pain on both sides. The reasoning behind their actions is basically simple: Taurus people feel a sense of ownership over their partners and will want to make changes that will increase their own general comfort and security. This attitude is OK when it comes to inanimate, material things – but is dangerous when applied to people. Taurus needs to be careful and attentive to this possible trait within themselves.

Home and Domestic Life

Home and family are vitally important to Taurus. They like children. They also like a comfortable and perhaps glamorous home – something they can show off. They tend to buy heavy, ponderous furniture – usually of the best quality. This is because Taurus likes a feeling of substance in their environment. Their house is not only their home but their place of creativity and entertainment. The Taurus home tends to be truly their castle. If they could choose, Taurus people would prefer living in the countryside to being city-dwellers. If they cannot do so during their working lives, many Taurus individuals like to holiday in or even retire to the country, away from the city and closer to the land.

At home a Taurus is like a country squire – lord (or lady) of the manor. They love to entertain lavishly, to make others feel secure in their home and to encourage others to derive the same sense of satisfaction as they do from it. If you are invited for dinner at the home of a Taurus you can expect the best food and best entertainment. Be prepared for a tour of the house and expect to see your Taurus friend exhibit a lot of pride and satisfaction in his or her possessions.

Taurus likes children but they are usually strict with them. The reason for this is they tend to treat their children – as they do most things in life – as their possessions. The positive side to this is that their children will be well cared for and well supervised. They will get every material thing they need to grow up properly. On the down side, Taurus can get too repressive with their children. If a child dares to upset the daily routine – which Taurus love to follow – he or she will have a problem with a Taurus parent.

Horoscope for 2008

Major Trends

Last year was a period of intense inner growth – both on a psychological level and on a deeper spiritual level. Home and family conditions were burdensome and challenging. It was not safe to express your true feelings and many of you learned how to direct them without repression. Many of you explored the occult sciences – past lives, karma, life after death – all to help you understand your emotions. Health, too, was not as good as it should have been. But happily all these tests are over with. Health is much improved over last year, and there is prosperity, too.

The major challenge in the year ahead will be in dealing with children, learning how to set a right order and discipline for them, and in your personal creative life. It will take more work to unlock your latent creativity than usual. But if you do the work, it will come out.

As mentioned, this is a year of prosperity. Jupiter in Capricorn all year makes fabulous aspects to you. It is a year for travel, too – foreign travel – and for expanding your mental horizons. The wanderlust is upon you both physically and mentally. More on this later.

Career has been important for many years and this trend continues this year. In fact the same forces that were in effect last year are still in effect in 2008. You face more or less the same kind of challenges. More on this later on.

Last year was, for most of you, a period of expanded sexual activity. This seems to be cooling down a bit, as other things in life become interesting.

Your most important interests this year are children, creativity, fun; religion, higher education, foreign travel, philosophy; sex, past lives, life after death, the prosperity of other people, debt issues, personal transformation (January 1 to January 27 – June 14 to November 27); career; friendships and group activities.

Your paths to greatest fulfilment this year are career, foreign travel, higher education, philosophy, metaphysics and religion.

Health

(Please note that this is an astrological perspective on health and not a medical one. For the medical perspective, please consult your doctor.)

As mentioned, health is much improved over last year and will get even better in coming years. Saturn moved a way from a stressful aspect to a harmonious aspect late last year. Saturn will be in harmonious aspect to you for at least two years. Jupiter is in harmonious aspect to you all year. And, the major headline of the year, Pluto will start coming into harmonious aspect to you this year and for many years to come.

There is only one long-term planet making difficult aspects to you – Neptune. All the rest are in positive aspect. If there have been health problems you will see dramatic improvements in the year ahead (many of you felt them last year, too).

So overall energy is high. With energy, the immune system functions as it should, and prevents many problems. With energy we are in a better mood, and this, too, is an important factor. With energy horizons open up to us that weren't there before – we become more successful. So all of this is good news on many levels.

Sure, there will be periods during the year where energy is not up to its usual standards – these things come from the transits and are temporary – they are not trends for the year. When the difficult transits pass the normal good health returns.

This year your most vulnerable periods are from January 20 to February 19; July 22 to August 22 and October 23 to November 22. Try to rest and relax more those periods.

Your already good health can be enhanced further by paying more attention to the kidneys and hips – always important organs for you. The hips can be regularly massaged. The kidneys can be strengthened in many ways – acupuncture, acupressure, diet, foot reflexology (see chart opposite), hand reflexology, kinesiology and hosts of other natural ways.

Another positive health indicator this year is your empty 6th House. This shows that health is not a major interest. You sort of take it for granted. No need to give it special attention or focus.

Venus, your health planet, is a fast-moving planet. She will move through all the Signs and Houses of your Horoscope in any given year. Thus your health needs – and the things that help you – tend to vary very quickly – it all depends where Venus is at any given time and the kind of aspects she is receiving. We will deal with these short-term issues in the monthly reports.

The health of your spouse or partner can be enhanced through vigorous physical exercise (as much as can be comfortably handled) – muscle tone is very important. If he

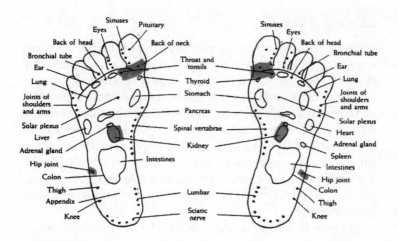

Reflexology

Try to massage the whole foot on a regular basis, but pay extra attention to the points highlighted on the chart. When you massage, be aware of 'sore spots', as these need special attention. It's also a good idea to massage the ankles and top side (as well as the soles) of the feet.

or she feels under the weather, hot and spicy foods seem good – things like garlic, onions or jalapeño peppers.

Children seem a major focus this year. There seems to be many changes going on with them – changes of the image, the self-concept, and perhaps cleansings of the physical body. Though they seem in general more conservative this year, from a health perspective they need to be more experimental – try out new things, new therapies and the like. Foot and ankle massage will be very beneficial. Ankles should be given more support. Shoes should fit right.

The health of parents or parent figures also seems improved over last year. One of them might be contemplating surgery – but in spite of this health will be OK.

Home and Family

Home and family issues were ultra important for the past few years. In fact the whole area of life was very challenging and burdensome. But by now, you have learned the lessons you needed to learn and you can focus on other things.

Your 4th House is not a House of Power this year. You have more freedom – more latitude to shape this area as you like. Your hands are not tied as they were the past two years. But, will you take advantage of your freedom to make dramatic changes? Probably not. You just don't have that much interest here. I presume that the status quo will prevail this year.

There will be some excitement at home and with the family – some dramas – but they seem short lived. The Solar Eclipse of August 1 occurs in your 4th House. This will bring some dramatic events with family members, make them more temperamental, and bring out any hidden flaws in the home.

Many of you have wanted to move for some years now. You felt cramped at home. Not enough space – both physical and emotional. But you were prevented. Now – especially this period – from August 1 onwards – might be the time to do it.

Those of you who have children seem to be having a rough time. They seem depressed and in low spirits. Perhaps they are involved in legal issues that are stressful. A love affair could have been painful. Self-esteem and self-confidence could be a lot better. Parents can be a big help now. But this is a time for the children to learn endurance, discipline and patience. It is a character building kind of year for them. In the end, if they pick up their responsibilities, they will be better people. Also they will unlock a lot of latent creativity that they didn't know they had. Necessity is the mother of invention. It's the kind of period where you have to do your duty no matter how you feel. Duty comes before feeling good. Pleasure should be derived from doing something difficult well – and from doing what is supposed to be done. Learning to discipline them properly – neither overdoing it nor under doing it – is a challenge. They need discipline – but in a very balanced way.

The family life of parents or parent figures are status quo. There are some dramatic events with these figures brought on by the Solar Eclipse of February 7 and the Lunar Eclipse of August 16. These bring image changes, a redefinition of the personality and detoxes (if they haven't been careful in dietary matters) of the body. But it doesn't look like they are moving. (Perhaps next year, but not this year.)

Your spouse or current love wants to invest in entertainment equipment for the home – big-ticket items.

If you are planning construction or major renovation of the home May 9 to July 1 is a good time. If you want to beautify the home – paint, decorate or buy art objects – July 12 to August 6 is a good time. This period is also good for entertaining from home or attending family type gatherings.

Finance and Career

Though money is always important to you – always a major focus – this year it is not as much a focus as usual. Your 2nd House of Finance is not a House of Power. I read this as positive. First off, it shows that things are going well and there's no need for many major changes or initiatives. Secondly, it shows that you have more freedom to shape this area as you like. The planetary powers are not obstructing you. You can create the financial life that you desire.

The career – your outer life – seems more of a focus this year. More important than mere money. With a solid career position, a good professional reputation, you can always make money. But not so easy the other way around.

The challenges that we see in the career are the same we've been seeing for many years now – the same planets are still involved. Your problem is how to succeed in a worldly way while still being idealistic, while doing something that is right for the planet, and without having to sacrifice your spiritual values. A tall order. The world seems to respect the 'bottom line' and not idealism. In the world people succeed in cutthroat kinds of ways. Yet these things don't sit right with you. Somehow – and everybody finds their own personal solution – you have to integrate spiritual values with a worldly work – and work that will bring success. Some people, with these kinds of aspects actually choose a spiritual type of career – professional philanthropy, careers in hospitals, welfare centers, or with altruistic causes, the ministry or arts. Some pursue a worldly career but get heavily involved in charities and causes on the side. Other people manage to merge a mundane work with something spiritual – i.e. building a health spa and community – or building a spiritual community with places of worship and health facilities – this combines the natural talents of Taurus with something idealistic. This should give you a few ideas, but you will each find your own solution. There are many scenarios not mentioned.

Those of you who choose a mundane kind of career will gravitate to film, electronic media, radio, TV, Internet and art. This doesn't mean that you have to be a performer (although many Taurus people are good performers) – it can be on the business or technical side of these industries, too.

One of the things I like about your career these past few years is how you manage to have the right friends in the right places – friends who can and do help you. Your networking abilities have seldom been better. Thus you can advance your career by joining clubs and professional organizations and getting involved. Those of you who market products, should focus more on organizations.

Generally you tend to be conservative and dislike too many changes. But with regard to career it is just the opposite. You like constant change. And, this year you are getting it. There are two eclipses in your 10th House of Career this year – a Solar Eclipse on February 7 and a Lunar Eclipse on August 16. This is going to shake things up both in your industry and in your corporate hierarchy. But these changes will work out well for you.

Your most important career period will be from January 20 to April 6. Your most important financial period will be from April 19 to July 10.

Love and Social Life

Your 7th House of Love and Marriage is not a House of Power this year. This is how life is – a wheel. Some years certain things are important and some years not. This is an area of great free will – as the planets are not pushing you one way or the other.

Generally, when the 7th House is empty, we read it as a status quo kind of year. But this year, we see big and major changes going on. You are only seeing the beginnings of it – but the trend will go on for many years to come. Pluto, your love planet, has been in Sagittarius your 8th Solar House since November 11, 1995. This year it makes a major move into Capricorn, your 9th House. It will flirt in and out of Capricorn this year and by November 27 it will move in for the next 20 or so years.

This is going to have profound implications for both singles and marrieds. For marrieds, this shift shows a shift in your spouse or partner's interests and focus. For many, many years your spouse was focused on finance and material security. Now it will shift more to intellectual type interests. What is the point of being materially secure if we can't expand our minds? Your partner will want and need more intellectual stimulation. Also, good communication with you. In the past, problems in the marriage could be settled through sex or through material means. Now good communication will be necessary. If you want to enhance your marriage start taking courses together or attend lectures as a couple. Develop the mental bonds. And since Pluto is going into the 9th House it might be a good idea to attend religious services together as a couple, or get involved in the activities of your church, synagogue, mosque or ashram – as a couple. Romantic trips to exotic places will also do much to enhance the marriage.

Similar changes are happening for singles. In the past the physical and sexual chemistry was the most important thing. And while it will still be important, there is a need to fall in love with the lover's mind as well as the body. There needs to be a 'philosophical harmony' as well as good physical chemistry. Religious issues will become more important. Incompatible philosophies of life will sink any relationship.

Singles will now find love opportunities in educational milieus – at lectures, seminars, school and university functions. Religious functions are also the scene of romantic opportunities. Foreign countries and foreigners have been alluring for many years and the trend will continue for many more years. A trip to a foreign country can lead to finding Mr or Ms Right. A trip to a foreign country will also enhance an existing relationship. There is more to love than just sex – and this is the lesson of the coming Pluto transit.

While I don't think singles (those working towards their first marriage) will marry this year, there are still many opportunities for romance in the year ahead. A love affair with someone older – perhaps a teacher or mentor type is happening.

Those working on the second marriage have wonderful opportunity this year – marriage is very likely. Again foreign countries, religious or educational type settings are where the meetings are likely to happen. The person will be conservative and traditional.

Your most active social period this year – and the period where you are most likely to have serious romance – will be from September 24 to November 22.

Self-improvement

In Astrology we read the 10th House and its ruler in two ways. When we read from a worldly, mundane perspective, we read it as a person's worldly career. This we have discussed. But the 10th House has a deeper, spiritual meaning. It shows a person's mission and purpose for a life (when we read the Natal Horoscope) or for a given year (such as what we are reading now). Every person has a special God-given mission to achieve. It is always something great and wonderful – but not always what the world would consider great and wonderful. Sometimes this mission calls a person to humility, to do for others, to be there for the family or a specific child. Sometimes the mission involves healing, or inventing something new, or long dispassionate research in some field of knowledge that no one else can do. Always it is a call to contribute something important to the world – though the world may or may not recognize it. True happiness – inner satisfaction – comes when we are fulfilling this purpose. This year, your spiritual mission, involves your friends. You are supposed to be there for them – to assist them. Also it is to enlarge and refine your ideas about what friendship is – to arrive at the true essence of it. It's not about what your friends can do for you, it's about what you can do for them. (When you are doing the right thing, they too will be doing the right thing.) Your mission also involves certain organizations – groups. You are supposed to assist them in some way. As you get more involved with them, the specifics will become apparent.

This is going to be a fun year – fun and prosperous. But Saturn in the 5th House cautions not to overdo it. Sure enjoy life – that is the purpose of life – but keep it in right proportion.

Learning to discipline children – and especially the administration of 'tough love' is another challenge in the year ahead. It is easy to be the 'good guy' and allow everything – but is such an attitude in the child's best interest? Taurus needs to think long and hard about this. We're not talking abuse or cruelty here – just right limits and discipline. If your inaction creates a problem 30 years from now – when it could have been corrected early on – who is to blame? You or the child?

Month-by-month Forecasts

January

Best Days Overall: 7, 8, 16, 17, 25, 26
Most Stressful Days Overall: 2, 3, 9, 10, 22, 23, 29, 30, 31
Best Days for Love: 2, 3, 5, 6, 14, 15, 23, 24, 29, 30, 31
Best Days for Money: 7, 16, 18, 19, 24, 25, 27, 28

Your year begins with most of the planets above the horizon. Your 10th House of Career becomes very powerful beginning the 8th and continues to strengthen as the month progresses. Your 4th House of Home and Family is basically empty – only the Moon moves through there on the 22nd and 23rd. A clear message: Focus on the career and let go of home and family. In fact, your family will even support you in this – for ultimately, this is how you serve them best. On the 20th you enter a yearly career peak – and there is much success, elevation and opportunity happening.

Career is important all month – and all year – but so are higher education, foreign travel, religion and metaphysics. A very happy and active area this month. Happy travel and educational opportunities are coming. Students hear good news on the university or graduate school front. In general students at the university level are having a successful year.

This is the kind of month where you enjoy philosophical and metaphysical discussions as much as a night out at the club or theatre. It's the kind of month where you almost can't escape philosophical revelation. You can be sitting at the restaurant, and there is a lively religious discussion going on at the next table; or your local minister presses you to attend services; or you meet romantic partners who enjoy these kinds of discussions. Whether you like it or not, the cosmos is going to educate and enlighten you this month.

Finances are status quo this month. Try to make important purchases, investments or financial decisions before the 23rd when Mercury starts to Retrograde. After that it is a good time to review your financial life and strategy to see where you can make improvements. (Keep in mind that the other planet involved in your finances – Mars, is also Retrograde until the 30th.) Raises and promotions are likely this month. Earnings opportunities come from your good professional reputation, the favor of elders, parents, parent figures or authority figures in your life.

Those of you who are looking for outside investors or to borrow big amounts of money, have a successful month. The 31st seems a powerful day for this kind of thing.

Love too seems status quo. There is a happy love opportunity from the 23rd to the 25th. There is a happy sexual encounter on the 31st.

The month begins with most of the planets in the Western, social sector of your Horoscope. This shows a need to cultivate the social graces and to do things by consensus – not independently. But this starts to change on the 20th as the planetary power shifts to the East. By next month, there will be more personal independence in your life. You will have more power to create conditions as you want them to be.

February

Best Days Overall: 3, 4, 12, 13, 21, 22
Most Stressful Days Overall: 6, 7, 19, 20, 26, 27
Best Days for Love: 2, 3, 4, 11, 12, 13, 14, 20, 21, 23, 26, 27
Best Days for Money: 3, 4, 6, 7, 12, 13, 14, 15, 21, 22, 23, 24

Your yearly career peak is in full swing. Your 10th House of Career is the most powerful in the Horoscope. Your 4th House of Home and Family is still empty (except when the Moon moves through there on the 19th and 20th). Career success is happening and pay rises and promotions (if they haven't already happened) can still happen. You are personally elevated this month – from the 17th onwards. You are world – in charge – of higher status than

ur family. You are honoured and appreciated

are – not just for your career achievements.

es are stronger this month. Mars is now moving

and Mercury starts to move forward on the 19th –

yo   thinking and strategy start to clarify. Continue to avoid making important investments, purchases or financial decisions until the 19th.

Professional investors should look at blue-chip type stocks – especially in the high-tech industry. Airlines also seem interesting. You will have important financial intuitions and hunches early in the month – but since Mercury is still Retrograde – sit on them and digest them. Get confirmation.

With Mars in your Money House the danger is of rash or risky financial behaviour. But once you've thought things through – after the 19th – bold actions will pay off.

There are two eclipses this month. The first is a Solar Eclipse on the 7th (in the US it is the 6th) that occurs in your 10th House of Career. This eclipse seems strong on you so take a reduced schedule. This eclipse brings important career changes. There are shakeups in the corporate hierarchy where you work. A promotion also changes the whole career situation. There are dramas with parents, parent figures and authority figures in your life. Since this eclipse impacts on Neptune, your planet of friends – there are dramatic events in the lives of your friends. Friendships will get tested.

The other eclipse – a Lunar Eclipse on February 21 (in the US the 20th) – occurs in your 5th House. This brings dramatic changes with children. Often births happen under this aspect. There are dramas with the siblings – and big changes in your neighbourhood. Cars and communication equipment get tested.

After the 19th friendships and group activities become a focus. You meet friends who are like family to you. Also through these activities you can further your career too.

Last month (on the 27th) your love planet changed Signs. It is now in your 9th House. Singles should look for romantic opportunities in educational or religious type settings – at university, or the church, synagogue or mosque. Look for people you can learn from and with whom you have a good philosophical compatibility. A strong sexual chemistry is always important, but if there is nothing more than that – the relationship will not have a long life span.

March

  Best Days Overall: 2, 3, 11, 19, 20, 29, 30
  Most Stressful Days Overall: 4, 5, 17, 18, 24, 25, 31
  Best Days for Love: 1, 4, 5, 10, 15, 18, 19, 24, 25, 28, 29
  Best Days for Money: 2, 3, 4, 5, 11, 13, 14, 15, 19, 20, 24,
    25, 27, 28, 29, 30

The Eastern sector of the Horoscope is now dominant. Some 60 to 70 per cent of the planets are now there. Other people are always important, but they don't determine your destiny. You have more free will to create conditions as you want them to be. If others don't go along with you – you can act independently. So have your way in life, but with wisdom. One of the problems with having your way is that you have to live with the consequences of it – so build wisely and lawfully.

The planetary momentum is forward this month – 90 per cent of the planets are in forward motion. So progress is rapid – both in the world and in your personal life.

The major interests in the month ahead are career (until the 15th); friendships, group activities and organizations (all month); spirituality (beginning the 20th).

Career is still more important than family issues. And still active and successful. You are still being honoured, appreciated and elevated. Pay rises and promotions are still likely.

Mars leaves your Money House on the 4th and thus the financial impetuousness is reduced. You are your normal conservative Taurus self. Until the 15th financial opportunities are still coming from the career, the good professional reputation, parents or parent figures. The powers that be in your life – those who are above you – are helping and supporting your financial goals. You have their grace. After the 15th the financial intuition is very strong – and more reliable than the past few months. Financial opportunities come from friends and from involvement in organizations. Professional investors should continue to look at high technology, airlines and blue-chip companies until the 15th, and oil, natural gas, energy, shipping, water industries afterwards. There are surprise financial windfalls on the 27th–28th. A parent or boss is unusually generous. Financial intuition is exceptional over these two days.

Spirituality is important this month. Especially with family members. A sibling could be meeting a guru or spiritual mentor. A good month for spiritually oriented retreats, seminars or meditations. Also good for charitable and altruistic activities. You are getting close to your birthday – your personal new year – and this will be a good time (especially after the 20th) to spend more time in seclusion, reviewing your past year, correcting mistakes, and setting goals for the year ahead. Such time is well spent as you will enter your new year with clarity and purpose.

Health and overall energy are much better than last month. Enhance health by paying more attention to the ankles (until the 13th) and to the feet afterwards. Spiritually oriented therapies are very powerful after the 13th.

April

Best Days Overall: 7, 8, 16, 17, 25, 26, 27
Most Stressful Days Overall: 1, 2, 13, 14, 20, 21, 22, 28, 29
Best Days for Love: 4, 6, 7, 13, 14, 15, 16, 23, 24, 25, 26
Best Days for Money: 5, 6, 7, 8, 9, 10, 14, 15, 16, 17, 25, 26, 27

Late last month Saturn started to re-stimulate the Lunar Eclipse point of February 21. He more or less camps out on this point all month. For students this shows that they are earning their success now – there are bumps on the road –

perhaps they change their main area of study – perhaps there are shakeups in the university – perhaps the rules have changed. Very tumultuous. A legal issue is getting very bumpy, too – in the end it seems successful but there is a rough patch now. Faith in general is being tested and the personal religion, the personal philosophy of life, is becoming more refined.

Career is still strong but starting to wind down. Late last month there were two career successes. And you seem to have achieved your major aims. Pretty soon now – by next month – the planetary power will shift to the lower half of your Horoscope and it will be time to emotionally recharge and start to take care of family responsibilities.

Religion, philosophy, higher education and foreign travel are important all year and this month as well. Friendships and group activities are still important until the 6th. Spirituality is important all month – and perhaps the strongest interest in the month ahead. Still a very good period for spiritual retreats, meditation, review, introspection and being involved in selfless charitable activities. The world is a nice place, but periodically it's healthy to take a holiday from it.

On the 19th the Sun moves into your own Sign, signalling a yearly personal pleasure peak. Spirituality doesn't mean that you deprive the body of its pleasures – as you will learn this month. The body – which is of the animal kingdom – is treated with kindness and respect. You are in a period of fulfilling your sensual desires.

The Sun is also your family planet and this is showing the growing importance of family and domestic issues in your life. Family seems very supportive. A parent or parent figure is coming to visit or taking a deeper personal interest in you.

Finances are excellent this month. Mercury (your financial planet) crosses your Ascendant beginning the 18th. This brings financial windfalls and personal items to you. You are spending on yourself and you can afford to. Financial opportunities are seeking you out, you don't have to run after them – the financial powers of your world, are going out of their way to please you. Even more important than this, the element of Earth – your native element – is very strong this month. After the 19th there are 50 to 60 per cent of the planets in this element. This tends to practicality and prosperity. Further, people with your particular talents are worth more – appreciated more.

Health is excellent this month. You can enhance it further by paying more attention to the feet (until the 6th) the head, face and adrenal glands (from the 6th onwards). Spiritual therapies are powerful all month. Head and face massage is powerful from the 6th onwards.

Love is good and will get even better from the 17th onwards. You are looking good – radiant and magnetic and the opposite sex takes notice. Your love planet starts to go Retrograde on the 2nd and it will be that way for many more months. So this is a time for singles to let love develop as it will, and not try rush or force things. Important love decisions – such as marriage or divorce – should be delayed. Over the next few months you will have time to review your relationship and see where improvements can be made. In the meantime enjoy the many love opportunities that come.

May

    Best Days Overall: 4, 5, 13, 14, 23, 24
    Most Stressful Days Overall: 11, 12, 18, 19, 25, 26
    Best Days for Love: 3, 4, 5, 12, 13, 14, 18, 19, 22, 24, 25,
        31
    Best Days for Money: 4, 5, 6, 7, 13, 14, 15, 16, 23, 24, 25,
        26

Most of the planets are in the East (like last month) and your 1st House of Self is still very strong. You are at the maximum period of personal independence and now is the time to create or recreate conditions as you want them to be. The world will adapt itself to you. The universe wants you to be happy, and will consent to your constructive desires. This is a time for having things your way.

You can downplay the career this month (even though it still looks very good and successful) and start to focus more on the family. Time to find your 'central core' – the true feeling of harmony and to function from there. You are in the 'night cycle' of your year, and you need to work in the ways of the night – dreaming, visualizing, recharging, drawing within – these are powerful now. Clairvoyants say that the Earth dreams in the winter, and then expresses herself in the spring and summer. Thus it should be with you.

You are still well into a yearly personal pleasure peak – so enjoy. Pamper yourself. Enjoy the delights of the sense. So long as you don't overdo it, health is not affected.

Health is excellent this month. Overall energy is high. You can enhance it further by paying more attention to the neck and throat (until the 24th) and the arms, shoulders, lungs and small intestine afterwards. Don't let financial ups and downs affect your health. Earth-based therapies are very powerful all month (50 to 60 per cent of the planets are in Earth Signs – so there is a strong connection here) but especially until the 24th. If you feel under the weather, spend some time in old forests, or caves, or mountains – places where the earth energy is strong – and you will immediately feel better. Also mud baths, mud packs, soaking in mineral springs or mineral baths are good. After the 24th air-based therapies are good – fresh air, wind, windy places, breathing exercises.

Aside from personal pleasure you are also entering a yearly financial peak this month. It begins on the 3rd and becomes very powerful on the 20th. A very prosperous month. There is only one fly in the ointment – Mercury, your financial planet, starts to Retrograde on the 26th. Try to make your important financial decisions before then.

But even Mercury's Retrograde is not going to stop earnings. It can introduce glitches and delays – but earnings will still come – and come in a big way. You can ease things by taking better care of how you communicate about finance or in your financial affairs. Don't take things for granted. Spell everything out. Make sure the other person understands you and that you have understood them. A little precaution in the beginning can save much heartache later on. If you must purchase big-ticket items, make sure the store or vendor has a good return policy.

Love should still be good – you look great and have great personal magnetism. But marriage? That's another story. Not right now.

June

Best Days Overall: 1, 2, 9, 10, 19, 20, 28, 29
Most Stressful Days Overall: 7, 8, 14, 15, 21, 22, 23
Best Days for Love: 1, 3, 4, 8, 9, 14, 15, 18, 24, 25, 27
Best Days for Money: 1, 2, 3, 4, 9, 10, 11, 12, 19, 20, 21, 22, 28, 29, 30

Career is getting a little challenging this month. Your career planet, Uranus, is going Retrograde on the 27th. (Neptune, the other planet involved with your career went Retrograde on the 26th of last month.) Further, Uranus is receiving some stressful aspects until the 21st. So, you might as well focus on the home, give the children more attention, attend the graduations, soccer games, and plays. Career issues will need time to resolve. There are no really 'quickie' solutions here.

You are still well into your yearly financial peak. Mercury's Retrograde is creating some uncertainties, but the New Moon of the 3rd is going to clarify these things. Nothing much that you need to do – the Moon will bring you the information, normally and naturally as the month progresses. Family is supportive financially – and probably you are spending more on the home, too. Professional investors should look at telecommunication, transport and media stocks. Retailing also seems interesting. Trading needs more care until the 19th – when Mercury is Retrograde trading opinion often reverses – darlings become dogs and vice versa.

Like last month you are spending on yourself. Your personal image and overall demeanor plays a huge role in earnings these days. After the 18th, though, this becomes less important.

Finances are important all month, but after the 18th the focus is more on communication and intellectual interests (and these start to become much happier after the 19th when Mercury moves forward again). A good period for taking courses in subjects that interest you and attending lectures and the like. A time to feed your mind. (Neglect of the mind is often the root cause of many a feeling of 'unease' – something bothers us and we can't figure out what it is – often it is the mind complaining.) The mind is important from a health perspective as well. Good mental health is important all month.

Good marketing and good use of the media is the most important thing for profits now. Whatever your service or business – whatever the size – people need to know what you're offering. Professional investors should focus on the same industries we discussed last month – telecommunications, media and transport. Trading is more profitable after the 19th.

Health is still excellent, but you can enhance it further by paying more attention to the arms, shoulders, lungs, small intestine and overall air purity until the 18th and to the stomach and breasts afterwards. Emotional (as well as mental) health becomes important after the 18th.

Love is a little challenging after the 19th, but it is short term. (Family members and the beloved are not in synch.) Your love planet makes another shift back into your 8th House – and old love attitudes return. Sexual chemistry and magnetism are more important than philosophical compatibility. But this attitude will change in November – and for many years to come.

July

Best Days Overall: 6, 7, 16, 17, 26
Most Stressful Days Overall: 4, 5, 11, 12, 19, 20
Best Days for Love: 2, 3, 5, 11, 12, 13, 15, 24, 25
Best Days for Money: 1, 6, 7, 10, 16, 17, 22, 26, 28

40 per cent of the planets are Retrograde this month – a high percentage. Activity in the world and in your life is slowing down. Couple this with the fact that the two planets involved in your career – Neptune and Uranus – are also Retrograde and that your 4th House of Home and Family is much stronger than your 10th House of Career. Most of the planets, like last month, are below the horizon. No question about it. Let career issues go for a while. You won't be able to ignore them completely, but many issues there will take time to resolve. Give your attention to your family. Be there for them. Cultivate the feeling of 'emotional harmony' – work on the career by inner methods rather than outer ones.

There are major spiritual changes going on this month – especially from the 1st to the 8th. You are changing your regime and practice – many of your attitudes and opinions on this subject are getting tested and the false ones will go by the wayside. There are shakeups in a charity or spiritual organization you are involved with. (Mars is re-stimulating the Lunar Eclipse point of February 21. There will be dramatic events in the world at large during this period, too – read the newspapers.)

Communication and intellectual interests are the main focus until the 22nd. After that the focus is on family and psychological issues.

Family relationships seem harmonious this month. Probably there will be more family gatherings and more entertaining from home. (After July 12 seems best, but all month is basically good.) Family – and especially a parent – seem financial supportive too. It's not just that they supply physical cash – though that could happen, too – but they provide financial opportunity and good contacts. Also money is being invested in the home – perhaps you are buying big-ticket items for the home, or spending more on the family. Serious investors should look at residential real estate, industries that cater to the home, restaurants, and lodging industry for profit opportunities. Trading and the retail industry seem profitable from the 10th to the 26th.

Sales, marketing and good PR still seem essential for earnings until the 26th. This is the time to do those mass mailings, telemarketing, or advertising campaigns (from the 3rd to the 18th is best.)

Your financial planet moves very quickly this month – a good sign. Financial confidence is strong and you make speedy progress towards your goals. You are more moody in finances from the 10th onwards, so make sure you are in a 'right state' – calm, peaceful, relaxed, before making important purchases or financial commitments. Sleep on things until you feel calm.

Health is more delicate after the 22nd – be sure to rest and relax more. Venus (both your personal and health planet) will re-stimulate an eclipse point from the 26th to the 29th and this is a period where you should avoid risky or stressful things. Take a reduced schedule. If you haven't been careful in dietary matters, there can be a physical detox then. Enhance health through better care of the diet, the emotional well being, and the stomach and breasts. After the 12th give more attention to the heart. If you keep your energy high you will go through this with flying colours.

Your love planet is still Retrograde, so there is a lack of direction here. But in spite of this you will see improvement after the 22nd.

August

Best Days Overall: 3, 4, 12, 13, 14, 22, 23, 30, 31
Most Stressful Days Overall: 1, 2, 7, 8, 9, 15, 16, 28, 29
Best Days for Love: 1, 2, 7, 8, 9, 11, 21, 22, 23, 29
Best Days for Money: 1, 2, 3, 4, 12, 13, 22, 23, 24, 25, 30, 31

Many of the trends that we wrote of last month are still in effect. Your 4th House of Home and Family is still stronger than your 10th House of Career. Your career planets are still Retrograde. And 40 per cent of the overall total of planets are Retrograde. Give more attention to the family and to your emotional well being (your health will improve, too). Cultivate emotional harmony. Feeling right is more important for you than doing right.

Your 5th House of Fun becomes very strong this month and when you consider that nothing much is happening in the world – there is a lot of gridlock going on – you might as well schedule a holiday now. (But you can also spend more time on leisure activities.)

Home and family is still the dominant interest this month – and this is as it should be. Now is the time to make up for all the soccer games, plays and other family events you missed. Quality time with the family will do more for you (and for them) than another business deal (which may or may not materialize right now).

Children are also important this month and you have a knack for getting on with them right now – let's just say, a better gift than you've had all year. You are better able to understand them on their level, to relate to them as equals – for your own inner child is strong now. Joy is the way to reach them.

Finances are good all month but the 10th to the 29th seems the strongest financial period. Speculations are very favorable this period – but I like the 14th to the 19th best. (This might be a good time – from the 14th to the 19th – to invest modest amounts in the lottery – or to take a junket to Las Vegas or Atlantic city or some such place near you. Keep in mind that your good – this is a powerful period – can come in many other ways, too.) This is a period where money comes to you in happy ways. While you're enjoying yourself, or involved in leisure activities. Happy money is the best money. You are also spending more on leisure, too. Professional investors seem very fortunate this month. People who earn their money in entertainment or creative kinds of fields are also having a banner month. The family as a whole – a parent or parent figure – is having a banner financial month too.

For singles this is a month for love affairs – uncommitted things. Even if you think you've met Mr or Miss Right, this is not a time to rush to the altar. Your love planet is still Retrograde. Also, after the 22nd, you might be of another opinion. Love becomes more challenging.

Health still needs watching until the 22nd. Give more attention to the heart until the 22nd. After the 5th also pay attention to the small intestine and the diet. This is a great month to lose weight and to make your image and appearance more perfect. Spiritual approaches to healing become powerful after the 19th.

Keep in mind that there are two strong eclipses on you this month – all the more reason to rest and relax more. The Solar Eclipse of the 1st will test the home and the family relationships. The Lunar Eclipse of August 16, will bring career changes. Both of the eclipses bring dramas with parents or parent figures.

Health and overall energy will improve dramatically after the 22nd. It's not only that the planetary aspects are kind to you – it also has to do with the fact that you're having fun – and joy is one of the greatest healing forces.

September

Best Days Overall: 9, 10, 18, 19, 27, 28
Most Stressful Days Overall: 4, 5, 11, 12, 24, 25
Best Days for Love: 1, 2, 4, 5, 8, 11, 12, 17, 21, 25
Best Days for Money: 1, 2, 9, 10, 11, 12, 18, 19, 20, 21, 27, 29, 30

Continue your focus on the home, family and emotional life. Career is going to become important soon enough. Get as much re-charging in as you can. By the 24th, the planetary power will be balanced between the upper and lower halves of the Horoscope. And, by next month, the upper (outer) half of the chart will be dominant.

Also Retrograde activity is much less than the past few months. Only 20 per cent will be Retrograde – the planetary momentum is forward now. Play time is soon over.

Your 5th House of Fun, Creativity and Children is still strong until the 22nd. But so is your 6th House of Work. You are working hard and playing hard. But the serious work ethic will take over after the 22nd.

Job-seekers have good fortune this month. Those who employ others, likewise. Job-seekers can easily find work through friends, social connections and family. Minister types – psychics, spiritual channels – are also helpful in this regard.

Health is still good. Not only that, but you have been focused here since last month. You are taking care of your health – involved in disciplined health regimes – involved in health oriented life styles. Part of the interest is coming from vanity – the healthier you are the better you look – the physical appearance is dramatically affected. But this is not the only reason. Doing health oriented things as a family can enhance the family relationship (going to the gym or health spa together).

Health can be enhanced even further by paying more attention to the kidneys and hips (until the 24th) and to the colon, bladder and sexual organs afterwards. (Safe sex becomes more of an issue after the 24th.) Detox regimes are powerful then too.

Finances are good this month, but they get more complicated after the 24th as your financial planet, Mercury, goes Retrograde. Try to make your major purchases or important decisions before then. Traders should exit their risky positions before then too (if possible). This month money comes the old fashioned way, through work. But Taurus is not afraid of work, and this is a positive financial signal.

Love is much improved now. Venus is in the romantic Sign of Libra until the 24th. After that she enters your 7th House of Love. You are about to enter a yearly social peak. Also, your love planet is starting to move forward (after many months of Retrograde motion) on the 9th. Thus social confidence is back to what it should be. Social judgement is much improved. Serious love can happen now – whether this will lead to marriage is another story. But you are meeting people who are 'marriage material'. Love is still very physical and sexual this month – especially after the 24th. But this attitude is about to change.

October

Best Days Overall: 6, 7, 15, 16, 24, 25
Most Stressful Days Overall: 1, 2, 9, 10, 22, 23, 28, 29, 30
Best Days for Love: 1, 2, 5, 11, 12, 14, 21, 22, 23, 28, 29, 30, 31
Best Days for Money: 6, 7, 9, 10, 15, 16, 17, 18, 24, 25, 28, 29

This month the planetary power shifts from the lower to the upper half of the Horoscope. It begins on the 4th and gets even stronger on the 23rd. Your 10th House of Career – though not unusually powerful – is still stronger than your 4th House of Home and Family. It is time to focus on your outer goals and to serve your family by being successful in the world.

Your social life is also picking up steam. It will be strong all month, but your yearly social peak really begins on the 23rd. Enjoy. You are reaching out to others. You are creating your social life, not just waiting for things to happen. You are out there looking – and the law is, seek and ye shall find. Singles have many, many opportunities and different types to choose from – glamour people, spiritual types, creative types, health professionals, athletes and family types. You have a huge menu to choose from. (Sometimes this is not so good – it can create confusion – but this is a good confusion to have.)

Sexual activity also increases. Whatever your age, the libido will be stronger than usual. And, with the health planet in the Sign of Scorpio until the 18th – the challenge will be to keep things in moderation. Too much can impact on the health. And, health needs more watching from the 23rd onwards.

Enhance health by resting and relaxing more and staying focused on essentials. Safe sex is more important than usual. Give more attention to the colon, bladder and sexual organs – there are many natural, drugless ways to do this. Detox regimes are powerful all month – and there is a problem, try detox first. After the 18th enhance health by paying more attention to the liver and thighs. Water-based therapies (soaking in a tub, whirlpool or Jacuzzi – soaking in a natural spring or lake – swimming and boating) are powerful until the 18th. After that fire therapies are strong. Head for the warmer climates – if you can't, make sure you stay warm. Stay out in the sunshine more.

Finances are still delicate until the 15th as Mercury is still Retrograde until then. This won't stop earnings, but only slow things down. Delay important purchases or financial decisions until after the 15th. Money still comes from work and social connections.

Family unity can be enhanced by working together as a family – like a team – and getting involved in health as a family. After the 23rd family unity is enhanced through social means – attending the same parties, or entertaining from home – or scheduling family-type gatherings.

November

    Best Days Overall: 2, 3, 4, 12, 13, 20, 21, 30
    Most Stressful Days Overall: 5, 6, 18, 19, 25, 26
    Best Days for Love: 1, 11, 12, 19, 20, 21, 25, 26, 29, 30
    Best Days for Money: 2, 3, 4, 7, 12, 13, 14, 15, 16, 17, 20, 21, 27, 28, 30

A lot of important developments are happening both personally and in the world this month. First off, 90 per cent of the planets are moving forward – by the 27th, ALL the planets are moving forward. So the pace of events heats up. Long-stalled projects both on a worldly and personal level start moving forward again. The planets involved with your career are also starting to move forward this month. So the pace of career progress is picking up. (The upper half of the Horoscope is totally dominant now – by the 4th, 80 to 90 per cent of the planets are above the horizon.) You are focused on the outer world and making good progress. The seeds you planted in the 'night time' of your year are now starting to grow.

Your love planet makes an important move on the 27th. This time for good. It moves from your 8th House to your 9th House and there is now a whole shift in your love attitudes. Things that pleased you before – or that you thought you wanted – will probably not satisfy. You want more than just sex. You want intellectual and philosophical communion. Perhaps you are seeing this clearly because of the unusual sexual activity going on this month. The satiation leaves your mind more clear to see priorities. Very often we need to go through an experience to see its limitations. The love life seems very happy though and there is a happy romantic meeting from the 11th to the 13th. For the unattached it is a meeting of someone special. For the attached it is significant social opportunity – very happy.

Finances are basically good but there are some bumps on the road on the 10th–11th and the 18th–21st. These are disruptive kinds of events – perhaps sudden expenses, a disappointment, or a revelation about your financial condition. You need to make some changes and when you do, everything will straighten out. Your overall prosperity is still very much intact – but perhaps you needed a little push to get you going. Until the 4th money comes from work. Social connections are important all month from the financial perspective. You mingle with rich people this month. A joint venture or partnership is likely (or the opportunity for it might come). This is a good month to borrow to pay off debt. Outside money comes easily. Many of you are planning the estate or involved with tax issues. Professional investors should look at bonds and the bond market from the 4th onwards.

You are still in a yearly social peak until the 21st. After that the focus is on the deeper things of life, occult studies, life after death, depth psychology. A period for making deep psychological progress, Personal transformation and re-invention is important too. Good for detox regimes of all sorts – physical, emotional and mental. (Health, which needs more watching until the 21st, is enhanced by all these things.)

Health improves dramatically after the 21st. You can enhance it further by paying more attention to the liver and thighs (until the 12th) and to the spine, knees, teeth, bones and skeletal alignment afterwards.

December

    Best Days Overall: 1, 9, 10, 17, 18, 27, 28
    Most Stressful Days Overall: 2, 3, 15, 16, 22, 23, 30, 31
    Best Days for Love: 1, 9, 11, 17, 20, 21, 22, 23, 27, 30, 31
    Best Days for Money: 1, 7, 8, 9, 10, 11, 12, 17, 18, 27, 28

Health is much improved over last month and by the 21st you will have the energy of 10 people. If there have been health problems there are sudden and miraculous cures. Even long-standing health problems can clear this month.

The focus, early in the month is on personal transformation, personal re-invention, the prosperity of partners and other people, estate and tax issues, debt and the repayment of debt, occult studies, past lives and life after death. But then, on the 21st, the focus shifts to foreign travel, higher education, religion, philosophy and metaphysics. A very happy travel and educational opportunity comes early in the month (the 1st to the 3rd). Students hear good news about university or graduate school. A legal issue has a fortunate outcome. There is much philosophical and religious revelation the whole period (but especially on the 1st–3rd).

The Hindus consider the 9th House the most fortunate of all the Houses. And this is where the power is this month. So you are optimistic about life, prospering and fortunate in most areas of your life.

Most of the planets are still above the horizon and your 10th House becomes powerful on the 8th as Venus crosses the Midheaven of your chart. You can let go of home and family issues and focus on your blossoming career. When Venus crosses the Midheaven you can expect personal elevation – rises and promotions – honours – appreciation. You are, figuratively speaking, at the top – in charge – above everyone in your life. A nice feeling. (This won't last too long, but enjoy it while it lasts.)

You can enhance your already good health through detox (until the 21st), paying more attention to the spine, knees, teeth, bones and skeletal alignment (until the 8th) and to the ankles after the 8th.

Love seems very happy this month – with a few bumps on the road. Your love planet receives stimulation from Mercury from the 12th–14th. This brings happy romantic opportunities for singles, and the opportunity for a joint venture or business partnership. The Sun travels with Pluto on the 21st and 22nd – this brings family gatherings, or meeting someone special through a family connection. (Family is trying to arrange something for singles). When Mars travels with Pluto from the 26th to the 30th love will get tested. The problem is intensity and passion – this can lead to jealousy and possessiveness. True love will survive this. (Watch the headlines in the world that period – they will be dramatic.) Love opportunities are now in educational, religious or foreign settings.

Until the 12th work to pay off debt. If you need to borrow or need outside investors that period is also good. Your spouse or lover is more generous with you. After the 12th there is stronger prosperity. Earnings will increase. Speculations are very favourable from the 29th to the 31st – and you might want to invest modest amounts – harmless amounts – on a lottery ticket. This period will also bring a big financial opportunity to you. Investors should focus on conservative, traditional blue-chip type companies after the 12th.

Gemini

♊

THE TWINS
Birthdays from
21st May to
20th June

Personality Profile

GEMINI AT A GLANCE

Element – Air

Ruling Planet – Mercury
   Career Planet – Neptune
   Love Planet – Jupiter
   Money Planet – Moon
   Planet of Health and Work – Pluto
   Planet of Home and Family Life – Mercury

Colours – blue, yellow, yellow–orange

Colour that promotes love, romance and social
   harmony – sky blue

Colours that promote earning power – grey,
   silver

Gems – agate, aquamarine

Metal – quicksilver

Scents – lavender, lilac, lily of the valley, storax

Quality – mutable (= flexibility)

Quality most needed for balance – thought that is deep rather than superficial

Strongest virtues – great communication skills, quickness and agility of thought, ability to learn quickly

Deepest need – communication

Characteristics to avoid – gossiping, hurting others with harsh speech, superficiality, using words to mislead or misinform

Signs of greatest overall compatibility – Libra, Aquarius

Signs of greatest overall incompatibility – Virgo, Sagittarius, Pisces

Sign most helpful to career – Pisces

Sign most helpful for emotional support – Virgo

Sign most helpful financially – Cancer

Sign best for marriage and/or partnerships – Sagittarius

Sign most helpful for creative projects – Libra

Best Sign to have fun with – Libra

Signs most helpful in spiritual matters – Taurus, Aquarius

Best day of the week – Wednesday

Understanding a Gemini

Gemini is to society what the nervous system is to the body. It does not introduce any new information but is a vital transmitter of impulses from the senses to the brain and vice versa. The nervous system does not judge or weigh these impulses – it only conveys information. And does so perfectly.

This analogy should give you an indication of a Gemini's role in society. Geminis are the communicators and conveyors of information. To Geminis the truth or falsehood of information is irrelevant, they only transmit what they see, hear or read about. Thus they are capable of spreading the most outrageous rumours as well as conveying truth and light. Geminis sometimes tend to be unscrupulous in their communications and can do great good or great evil with their power. This is why the Sign of Gemini is called the Sign of the Twins: Geminis have a dual nature.

Their ability to convey a message – to communicate with such ease – makes Geminis ideal teachers, writers and media and marketing people. This is helped by the fact that Mercury, the ruling planet of Gemini, also rules these activities.

Geminis have the gift of the gab. And what a gift this is! They can make conversation about anything, anywhere, at any time. There is almost nothing that is more fun to Geminis than a good conversation – especially if they can learn something new as well. They love to learn and they love to teach. To deprive a Gemini of conversation, or of books and magazines, is cruel and unusual punishment.

Geminis are almost always excellent students and take well to education. Their minds are generally stocked with all kinds of information, trivia, anecdotes, stories, news items, rarities, facts and statistics. Thus they can support any intellectual position that they care to take. They are awesome debaters and, if involved in politics, make good orators.

Geminis are so verbally smooth that even if they do not know what they are talking about, they can make you think that they do. They will always dazzle you with their brilliance.

Finance

Geminis tend to be more concerned with the wealth of learning and ideas than with actual material wealth. As mentioned they excel in professions that involve writing, teaching, sales and journalism – and not all of these professions pay very well. But to sacrifice intellectual needs merely for money is unthinkable to a Gemini. Geminis strive to combine the two.

Cancer is on Gemini's Solar 2nd House (of Money) cusp, which indicates that Geminis can earn extra income (in a harmonious and natural way) from investments in residential property, restaurants and hotels. Given their verbal skills, Geminis love to bargain and negotiate in any situation, but especially when it has to do with money.

The Moon rules Gemini's 2nd Solar House. The Moon is not only the fastest-moving planet in the Zodiac but actually moves through every Sign and House every 28 days. No other heavenly body matches the Moon for swiftness or the ability to change quickly. An analysis of the Moon – and lunar phenomena in general – describes Gemini's financial attitudes very well. Geminis are financially versatile and flexible. They can earn money in many different ways. Their financial attitudes and needs seem to change daily. Their feelings about money change also: sometimes they are very enthusiastic about it, at other times they could not care less.

For a Gemini, financial goals and money are often seen only as means of supporting a family; these things have little meaning otherwise.

The Moon, as Gemini's Money Planet, has another important message for Gemini financially: in order for Geminis to realize their financial potential they need to develop more of an understanding of the emotional side of life. They need to combine their awesome powers of logic with an understanding of human psychology. Feelings have their own logic; Geminis need to learn this and apply it to financial matters.

Career and Public Image

Geminis know that they have been given the gift of communication for a reason, that it is a power that can achieve great good or cause unthinkable distress. They long to put this power at the service of the highest and most transcendental truths. This is their primary goal, to communicate the eternal verities and prove them logically. They look up to people who can transcend the intellect – to poets, artists, musicians and mystics. They may be awed by stories of religious saints and martyrs. A Gemini's highest achievement is to teach the truth, whether it is scientific, inspirational or historical. Those who can transcend the intellect are Gemini's natural superiors – and a Gemini realizes this.

The Sign of Pisces is in Gemini's Solar 10th House of Career. Neptune, the Planet of Spirituality and Altruism, is Gemini's Career Planet. If Geminis are to realize their highest career potential they need to develop their transcendental – their spiritual and altruistic – side. They need to understand the larger cosmic picture, the vast flow of human evolution – where it came from and where it is heading. Only then can a Gemini's intellectual powers take their true position and he or she can become the 'messenger of the gods'. Geminis need to cultivate a facility for 'inspiration', which is something that does not originate in the intellect but which comes through the intellect. This will further enrich and empower a Gemini's mind.

Love and Relationships

Geminis bring their natural garrulousness and brilliance into their love life and social life as well. A good talk or a verbal joust is an interesting prelude to romance. Their only problem in love is that their intellect is too cool and passionless to incite ardour in others. Emotions sometimes disturb them, and their partners tend to complain about this. If you are in love with a Gemini you must understand why this is so. Geminis avoid deep passions because these would interfere with their ability to think and communicate. If they are cool towards you, understand that this is their nature.

Nevertheless, Geminis must understand that it is one thing to talk about love and another actually to love – to feel it and radiate it. Talking about love glibly will get them nowhere. They need to feel it and act on it. Love is not of the intellect but of the heart. If you want to know how a Gemini feels about love you should not listen to what he or she says but rather observe what he or she does. Geminis can be quite generous to those they love.

Geminis like their partners to be refined, well educated and well travelled. If their partners are more wealthy than they, that is all the better. If you are in love with a Gemini you had better be a good listener as well.

The ideal relationship for the Gemini is a relationship of the mind. They enjoy the physical and emotional aspects, of course, but if the intellectual communion is not there they will suffer.

Home and Domestic Life

At home the Gemini can be uncharacteristically neat and meticulous. They tend to want their children and partner to live up to their idealistic standards. When these standards are not met they moan and criticize. However, Geminis are good family people and like to serve their families in practical and useful ways.

The Gemini home is comfortable and pleasant. They like to invite people over and they make great hosts. Geminis are also good at repairs and improvements around the house – all fuelled by their need to stay active and occupied with something they like to do. Geminis have many hobbies and interests that keep them busy when they are home alone.

Geminis understand and get along well with their children, mainly because they are very youthful people themselves. As great communicators, Geminis know how to explain things to children; in this way they gain their children's love and respect. Geminis also encourage children to be creative and talkative, just like they are.

Horoscope for 2008

Major Trends

For the past few years you have been learning the lessons of discipline of speech and thought. To talk less, but with more depth and understanding. To think less, but with more depth and penetration. It was a period of deepening the mental and communication skills. This lesson is over with and now, there is a need to manage the emotional life. There are more family burdens in the year ahead – more responsibilities – and you can't get out of them. You have to pick them up and use them for character building. (More on this later on.)

Last year was a very powerful social year. Many single Gemini married or got involved in serious relationships. Many entered into business partnerships. All expanded their social life and met new and important friends. Now the focus is on more serious things – depth psychology, past lives and their impact on the present, death, rebirth, life after death and personal transformation.

Career has been important for many years and the trend continues in the year ahead. Change, experimentation, instability seem the order of the day. Learning to deal with career instability is the spiritual lesson this year. How to be secure amidst all the insecurity.

Religion, philosophy, metaphysics, foreign travel have been important for many years now and will continue to be important this year. There are two eclipses in your 9th House of Religion and Philosophy this year and this promises major change in these areas.

Though romance seems settled, the year ahead seems more sexually active.

Your important areas of interest this year are career; religion, philosophy, metaphysics, higher learning and foreign travel; home, family and emotional issues; personal transformation, personal reinvention, life, death, life after death, debt and the prosperity of partners.

Your paths of greatest fulfilment this year are religion, philosophy, higher learning and foreign travel; personal transformation, personal reinvention, life, death, life after death, paying off debt and the prosperity of partners.

Health

(Please note that this is an astrological perspective on health and not a medical one. For the medical perspective, please consult your doctor.)

Last year when Saturn moved into Virgo, health started to become very delicate. Three long-term planets were making stressful aspects to you. This year the burden is lighter as Pluto, starts to move away from a stressful aspect. He moves out of Sagittarius where he has been since 1995 and into Capricorn.

Still, you are not out of the woods. Pluto will still be in stressful aspect from January 1 to January 27 and from June 14 to November 27. The most critical periods to watch are from February 19 to March 20; July 1 to September 22; November 16 to December 21. These are times when the short term planets also start to stress you out. These are times to rest and relax more – take a holiday if you can – and focus more on health. Focus on the essentials in your life and let the inessentials go. Do everything possible to maximize your energy. Delegate tasks where possible. If you give health more attention you should pass through these periods with flying colours.

Pluto, the planet mentioned above, also happens to be your health planet. Its move from Sagittarius to Capricorn has major health implications. It shows a new attitude to health and new ways to enhance your health. Yes, you CAN do much to enhance your health. Yes, you CAN prevent problems from developing – and the Horoscope gives us some important clues.

Pluto rules the colon, bladder and sexual organs. So these organs always need more attention. Safe sex is more of an issue for you than for other Signs. Also there is a need for sexual moderation. Neither too much nor too little. If you listen to your body, it will tell you when enough is enough. With your health planet now moving into your 8th House of Sex, everything we say is reinforced. Also, libido seems much stronger this year, you will tend to be more sexually active than usual and might tend to overdo things.

Your health planet in the Sign of Sagittarius (January 1 to January 27 and June 14 to November 27) shows a continued need to pay more attention to the liver and thighs. Thighs can be regularly massaged and the liver can be strengthened in many natural ways. (See the reflexology chart opposite.)

Your health planet in Capricorn (January 27 to June 14 and November 27 to December 31) shows a need to pay more attention to the spine, knees, teeth, bone structure and overall skeletal alignment. Regular visits to a chiropractor might be a good idea this year (and long term). Make sure you are getting enough calcium for your bones. Give the knees more support when you exercise or indulge in sports. Yoga, Pilates and Alexander Technique are good ways to strengthen the spine, too.

The health planet in the 8th House shows that you will benefit from detox regimes over the long haul. Good health is not about adding things to your body, but about getting rid of what doesn't belong there. There are many detox methods out there – herbal and mechanical. They are all good. Fasting on a regular basis will be good for serious problems. (If you combine it with prayer it is even more powerful.)

With the health planet in 8th House many of you might be contemplating surgery. Perhaps surgery has been recommended as a solution. Always get second opinions, and remember that 'fasting is like a surgeon's knife'.

Your health planet in the Sign of Capricorn also shows a shift in health attitudes – you seem more conservative about health matters and most of you gravitate to orthodox medicine. The new and untried therapies don't suit you. You want things that have been well tested and well documented.

The main health danger this year is neglect. Your 6th House of Health is basically empty. Your tendency would be to ignore things or take health for granted – when you

Reflexology

Try to massage the whole foot on a regular basis, but pay extra attention to the points highlighted on the chart. When you massage, be aware of 'sore spots', as these need special attention. It's also a good idea to massage the ankles and top side (as well as the soles) of the feet.

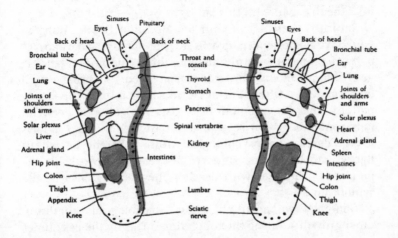

shouldn't. You will have to almost force yourself to pay more attention this year.

Home and Family

Your 4th House of Home and Family is very important this year (and it will be important next year, too.) A difficult and challenging area of life this year.

Saturn moving through the 4th House shows extra family burdens, as mentioned. Often it produces the feeling of 'being cramped' in the home. You feel a lack of space – physical and emotional. You want to move, but are blocked by circumstances and so there is feeling of discomfort. Your real solution is not to move but to make better, more efficient use of the space you have. Your space needs better management not physical enlargement. Saturn is calling you to greater creativity.

When Saturn is in the 4th House the family situation is such that it is not safe to express your true feelings. The tendency is to repress them. When they do get expressed (you can't keep doing this forever) the expression is way, way out of proportion to the cause that triggered it – and then matters get worse. So, there is a need to 'direct' the moods and feelings without repression. This is done by spiritual means. (More on this later.)

Saturn is the ruler of your 8th House of Death. Many of you have experienced deaths in the family – perhaps of parents or parent figures in your life. This is not helping your overall mood. But this transit need not bring actual physical death. Often it brings a transformation of the family pattern. There is an emotional separation going on between family members that so transforms the family, that it feels like a death – a psychological death. (Parent or parent figures can be having surgery this year, or near-death experiences – brushes with death – these events also fit the symbolism.)

Generally we make the most psychological progress – inner growth – during the tough times. During the easy times we have no need to do the work necessary for this growth. So this is the ultimate spiritual purpose of what is going on.

A purification is happening on the emotional level – all effete patterns or responses are going to be done away with. Perhaps they were useful to you in the past, but now they are not.

Normal psychological therapies won't be enough for you this year. From your Horoscope, the issues are coming not from childhood, but from past life experiences – and many of you will be delving into this in the year ahead.

This is a wonderful year to do a physical house-cleaning. Get rid of all the household possessions that you no longer need. Make room for the new. If you are feeling cramped in the home, watch how much more space you will have.

This is a good year for remodeling the home. This might be better than an actual move. The whole year is good for this, but especially from July 1 to August 19. If you are redecorating or beautifying the home – buying art objects and the like – August 6 to August 30 is a good time.

Finance and Career

Your 2nd House of Finance is not a House of Power this year. Not a major interest. I read this as a good thing. Finances are basically good – you are pretty much content – and you have no need to pay special attention here. Generally it shows a status-quo kind of year.

Your spouse or partner, however, is a different story. He or she is VERY focused here and is prospering greatly. You seem better off prospering your spouse or partner than focusing on your own prosperity. As you do this, your own prosperity will come to you quite naturally. Also your spouse or partner seems very generous with you.

This year your 8th House of Other People's Money is the House of Power. This shows that money can come to you through insurance claims, royalties or inheritance. Hopefully no one literally dies, but you may be named in someone's will – or be appointed an executor.

You have great access to outside money this year. Your line of credit will be increased. You can attain financial goals through creative financing and re-financing of existing debt. This is also a good year to get out of debt. Debts are easily made (people are willing to lend to you) but also easily paid.

If you have good ideas, there are outside investors waiting for you. Doesn't seem a problem to raise money for any worthwhile project.

Many of you older Geminis (and perhaps even not so old ones) are planning your estate these days. Estate and tax issues are influencing many a financial decision now.

If you have tax disputes or issues with the government, there is a best-case scenario outcome.

From an investment perspective bonds, the bond market (especially government bonds or the bonds of conservative blue chip companies) are good. There are good profit opportunities with troubled or even bankrupt companies – the bonds of these companies. Many a City fortune has been built in this way.

Your most personally profitable periods this year will be from June 18 to July 22. This is on an overall level. But every month will bring its peaks – much depends on where the Moon is at any given time (and the aspects she receives). We will deal with this in the monthly reports. (The Moon is a fast-moving planet and she moves through all your Houses in any given month.)

Love and Social Life

After last year, love and social issues are fading into the background. Most of you either married or got involved in serious relationships. The social life doesn't need much attention. Your focus is now elsewhere.

Sex seems more important than romance this year. Even for singles. It's the sexual attraction that seems to matter. (Keep in mind our discussion of this in the health section.)

Love is very physical. Singles are allured by the person of high position, the good provider, and the sexual chemistry.

Good communication is always important to a Gemini, but this year not so much. Philosophical and religious harmony are always important, too – but this year less so.

If there are still some singles out there, romantic opportunities come in weird places this year. Places where you would least expect it; at funerals and wakes; as you pay a courtesy call to a bereaved person; at séances or past life regression seminars or sessions; at remembrance services for the dead. Death need not be morbid – it can be the scene of romance.

Romantic opportunities can also come at the accountant's or financial planner's office. Going to get a mortgage can become something much more than that. Paying the tax bill can become a romantic adventure.

Those working towards their second marriage are having a good time. The social life looks happy and active – but marriage? Not clear from this chart. Perhaps you are better off enjoying your freedom. The romantic opportunities come at spiritual retreats, prayer circles, or meditation seminars – also as you pursue your career goals. You are mingling with high and mighty people. Perhaps involved with your bosses.

Those in or working towards their third or fourth marriage are having a status-quo year. Marrieds will tend to stay married and singles will tend to stay single.

A single sibling is having a good time – seems involved with spiritual or glamorous people – but marriage might be better next year.

Your most active social periods this year will be from January 1 to February 17, October 18 to November 12, and November 22 to December 31.

Self-improvement

Your emotional life is really the main headline for the year ahead. Saturn moving into your 4th House wants to establish some order here – a right order – a cosmic order – and Saturn is very good at what he does. He knows how to arrange things so that this will happen. It is best to cooperate with him – things go easier.

So there is a need to examine your moods and emotions – your emotional responses. There is a spiritual way to do this. It is called self-observation. You observe your moods and feelings – your reactions under different stimuli – dispassionately – without judgement. You are only the observer. As you observe, you will see what things are counterproductive and even destructive. You will see what they do to your relationships and the impact it has on your actual physical body. Once you see and understand these things you can take some action. Please note, there is no repression or holding back. You just observe. If you see your emotions are too violent, you can express them harmlessly (instead of pouring out on others) by writing them out on paper (and then throwing the paper away) or talking them out into a tape recorder (and then erasing the tape). Observe yourself all the while. Insights will come into you that will be incredible. Just the act of observation itself often transforms a negative state into something positive. Because you are not attached to the emotion, it only has its own stored up energy to work with – you are not feeding it – not making it worse. And, you find that it has a life span – it changes. Its energy is weakened. So long as you don't feed it, even if it comes back, it will not be as strong – it will be manageable. Little by little over time, the root cause behind the emotion will be exposed and will dissolve. You will be free. But this takes discipline and practice.

As mentioned, some of your emotional patterns – the root cause of the painful ones – will lie in past lives. And this is a good year to explore these issues.

You will find that your family relationships – your relationships with almost everyone close to you – are merely a continuation of things that have been going on for many, many lives. It is shocking and liberating at the same time.

Aside from this, you have a very special spiritual mission this year. It involves religion and philosophy – delving deeper into it – especially your personal religion – being involved in the church, synagogue, mosque – and also with institutions of higher learning.

Month-by-month Forecasts

January

Best Days Overall: 1, 9, 10, 18, 19, 27, 28
Most Stressful Days Overall: 5, 6, 12, 13, 25, 26
Best Days for Love: 5, 6, 7, 14, 15, 16, 23, 24, 25
Best Days for Money: 7, 8, 16, 17, 20, 21, 24, 25, 27, 28

The whole year ahead is about balancing home and career, but this month, with 80 to 90 per cent of the planets above the horizon, you can shift emphasis to the career. We're not talking about ignoring home and family – you won't be able to do that – but just shifting some emphasis. It's a matter of proportion. Good communication is always important to you and important in enhancing the family life, but this month you can enhance things at home through philosophical discussions or attending religious services as a family. There needs to be philosophical unity in the family.

The entire month is good for detox and getting rid of possessions you no longer need. Detox of the mind and emotions also seems important. The home especially needs to be cleaned of things that are just cluttering up the house – especially until the 8th.

With your 8th House powerful all month, this is a time to pay off debt, cut costs and financial waste. It is also good to refinance debt at more favourable terms and to attract outside investors to your projects. Tax and estate issues also seem very important.

The 8th House also rules personal transformation and re-invention and this is a big interest for many of you.

Though overall health needs watching this year, this month seems OK. Your health planet makes an important (but temporary) move into Capricorn on the 27th. Thus you will need to take better care of the spine, knees, teeth, bones and skeletal alignment. Regular back massage and visits to a chiropractor are good after the 27th and until June. Until the 27th pay more attention to the liver and thighs. (Regular thigh massage is good.) If problems arise check out your love and sex life and bring harmony there.

Finances are status quo this month. But in general you will have more energy and enthusiasm for finance from the 8th to the 22nd as the Moon, your financial planet, waxes. You can schedule yourself accordingly. The 8th to the 22nd are good for making investments or for saving – for things that you want to see 'grow'. The 1st to the 8th and the 22nd to the 31st are good for paying off debt – things that you want to see 'shrink'.

Your spouse or partner is generous with you all year, but especially this month. Prosperity comes as you help other people prosper.

Money can come from estates, trust funds, insurance claims and royalties this month. (This is the trend for the year ahead, but especially for this month).

Love seems happy and idealistic this month. Singles are attracting spiritual and glamour types of people. Marriage isn't likely but still there is fun and romance. Something more serious – someone of 'marriageable standards' – comes into your life on the 31st. The sparks really fly and the chemistry is hot.

Some 70 to 80 per cent of the planets are in the West – including your ruler, Mercury. So downplay self-will and cultivate the good graces of others. With dynamic Mars in your Sign this is easier said than done. You want everything in a hurry and want it your way. You can be more combative and self-assertive than usual – so temper this tendency. Your good comes from others, not so much from your independent efforts.

February

Best Days Overall: 6, 7, 14, 15, 23, 24
Most Stressful Days Overall: 1, 2, 8, 9, 21, 22, 28, 29
Best Days for Love: 1, 2, 3, 4, 12, 13, 14, 21, 22, 23, 28, 29
Best Days for Money: 3, 4, 6, 7, 12, 13, 15, 16, 17, 21, 22, 25, 26

Two eclipses this month insure that there will be lots of excitement and shakeups – both in the world and on a personal level.

The Solar Eclipse of February 7 (February 6 in the US) occurs in your 9th House. But it impacts on Mercury, your ruler, and on Neptune, your career planet. A strong eclipse, so take a reduced schedule – a few days before and after. No need to hide under your bed or anything like that – do the things that need to be done, and reschedule inessentials for another time. Especially avoid risky or stressful activities. This eclipse is bringing career changes and dramas with parents, parent figures, bosses and authority figures in your life. For students it shows an educational shakeup – a change of schools, or areas of study – perhaps a shakeup in their school. If you haven't been careful in dietary matters, a detox of the body could happen. And, even if detox doesn't happen (I hope not) there will be re-definition of the image and the personality. In future months you will be dressing differently – presenting a different image to the world.

We see some shakeups in the family by the second eclipse, too – the Lunar Eclipse of February 21 (February 20 in the US). Again, a parent or parent figure is involved. Perhaps there is a surgery (or the recommendation for same), perhaps a near-death experience or encounter with death. (This is usually a psychological encounter and not a literal physical death). Hidden flaws in the home or family relationship get revealed. Once revealed, you can correct them.

Health needs more watching from the 19th onwards. Enhance health with more rest and better care of the spine, knees, teeth, bones and skeletal alignment. Sexuality needs to be kept in moderation.

Mars in your own Sign gives you more energy and personal magnetism, but it can push you to go beyond your physical limits. You might be trying to break athletic records, when you shouldn't – you are exercising more these days, but after the 19th keep the workouts light and relaxed. If you feel pain in any part of your body – stop, or slow down.

Love is still very hot on the 1st and 2nd. If you haven't met a special someone last month, the 1st and 2nd is still a good time. You are still in a very sexually active month. Even older Geminis will have more libido – more urge – than usual.

Your 9th House of Religion, Higher Education, Philosophy and Metaphysics is strong all month – a major focus now. Happy educational opportunities come – and what Gemini is going to pass that up! There will be happy travel opportunities. Most importantly there is philosophical and religious revelation happening for you – if you want it. Probably the Solar Eclipse of the 6th will bring a shakeup in a religious organization you are involved with.

On the 19th the Sun crosses your Midheaven and enters your 10th House of Career. You begin a yearly career peak. There is great career progress happening and you should focus on it. (Yes, you are distracted by family issues then, but as soon as possible get back to the career.) Career is enhanced through willingness to travel, educational preparedness, and good marketing. No one knows how to market like you – so this is another positive.

Finances are status quo, but go better from the 6th to the 20th as the Moon waxes.

March

Best Days Overall: 4, 5, 13, 14, 22, 23, 31
Most Stressful Days Overall: 6, 7, 19, 20, 27, 28
Best Days for Love: 2, 3, 4, 5, 11, 15, 19, 20, 24, 25, 27, 28, 29, 30
Best Days for Money: 2, 3, 6, 7, 11, 15, 16, 19, 20, 27, 29, 30

Career is still the major focus in the month ahead. Some 80 to 90 per cent of the planets are above the horizon and your 10th House of Career is very strong. Even family seems ambitious for you, and you for them. On the 15th Mercury crosses the Midheaven bringing you elevation and status. Pay rises and promotions can happen then. (This is a good career day for family members too.) You are honoured and appreciated. Your worth is recognized. Continue to enhance your career through communication and marketing. After the 13th social means enhance the career – parties – attending them or hosting them. This period is also good for entertaining important clients – wining and dining them – also those who are important to your career.

Health still needs a lot of watching now. The demands of career are great but you have to listen to your body – career success will mean nothing without your health. Pay more attention to the heart, spine, knees, teeth, bones and skeletal alignment. Health and energy improve somewhat after the 20th – but still needs watching. With your 6th House of Health empty, you will have to force yourself to pay attention.

At home, do things to make the home safer. Also perhaps the plumbing needs to be checked.

Finances look very good this month. First off, the career is going well and that generally helps the bottom line. Mars enters your 2nd House of Finance on the 4th. (Mars is 'out of bounds' all month and this suggests that you are taking risks and venturing far from your usual territory for earnings or investments.) You are aggressive in financial matters.

Friends are going way out of their way for you. Networking abilities are good. Be careful of rash or impulsive spending now. On a spiritual level you are entering a period where you need to overcome financial fear. However, a healthy caution is not fear.

Love is status quo this month. In general, love and social matters are happier and go easier before the 20th than afterwards.

Your 11th House of Friends and Organizations becomes strong after the 20th and this seems more important than romance. You enter a period where fondest hopes and wishes come true and where you formulate 'new' fondest hopes and wishes.

A child of appropriate age has an important career opportunity on the 6th–7th. He or she has an encounter with someone prominent. Singles have a romantic opportunity with someone prominent, too.

Friends have dramatic type experiences from the 4th to the 8th. They need to be more careful and avoid risks. A friendship can get tested during this period, too.

A dream or ESP experience on the 9th is guiding your career.

April

Best Days Overall: 9, 10, 18, 19, 28, 29
Most Stressful Days Overall: 3, 4, 16, 17, 23, 24, 30
Best Days for Love: 4, 7, 8, 13, 14, 16, 17, 23, 24, 26, 27
Best Days for Money: 5, 6, 7, 8, 11, 12, 13, 14, 16, 17, 25, 26, 27

Most of the planets are still above the horizon and your 10th House of Career is still strong. You can safely let go (to a degree) of family concerns and focus on your career. But your interest in career matters is gradually weakening. The main focus in the month ahead is friendships, group activities and organizations and spirituality (after the 19th).

Mars is still in the Money House and many of the trends written of last month are still in effect. Be fearless in finance, but not rash. Have faith in your abilities and your power to earn, but this doesn't mean that you behave foolishly. Once a plan is carefully thought out, then act on it boldly and with confidence. Professional investors are taking on more risk and debt. Military contractors, makers of athletic equipment or athletic wear and construction equipment seem like interesting investments. Financial power and enthusiasm is strongest from the 6th to the 20th, as the Moon waxes. Paying off debt is better from the 1st to the 6th and from the 20th to the 30th – as the Moon wanes.

Love is much happier this month. Especially after the 18th. There is a happy romantic experience on the 28th–29th. Romantic (and other) guidance comes to you through psychics, spiritual channels, minister types this month. In fact, now that your 12th House of Spirituality is strong (after the 18th) it is good to get more involved with these kinds of people and to go on spiritually oriented retreats, attend spiritual lectures and seminars and involve yourself in altruistic 'impersonal' kinds of projects. Inner spiritual growth is never divorced from the world (though it seems to be) – always it leads to greater effectiveness in the world. Spiritual values may seem to conflict with your career goals – but if you go deeper into things, you will see that they don't. The conflict is superficial.

Career is enhanced by good communication (until the 2nd), social methods (until the 6th), and a willingness to travel and expand your knowledge.

Spirituality is enhanced by a good rational understanding of the spiritual world. Take your intellect along with you for the ride. The mind is not your enemy (not this month anyway) but your friend and ally.

Family issues can be enhanced by inculcating a 'team' spirit in the home. Family activities should be 'group' activities. There needs to be more of a democratic spirit at home too (especially until the 18th). After that spirituality and spiritual understanding will enhance family life. Meditation and unconditional love will be a big help.

May

Best Days Overall: 6, 7, 15, 16, 25, 26
Most Stressful Days Overall: 1, 13, 14, 20, 21, 28, 29
Best Days for Love: 4, 5, 13, 14, 20, 21, 23, 24, 25
Best Days for Money: 4, 5, 8, 9, 13, 14, 23, 24, 25

We have a lot of Earth in the Horoscope this month (and we had a lot last month). This makes people as a whole more practical and down to earth. You, on the other hand, tend to be an intellectual – an ideas person – and perhaps you are not as appreciated as the more practical types are. However, you can use this knowledge to your advantage – especially if you sell or teach. Emphasize the practical aspects of whatever you are teaching about or selling. You will connect better with your audience.

The planetary power is now mostly in the Eastern sector of your chart. Your 1st House becomes very powerful beginning the 20th, while your 7th House of Social Activities is basically empty. (Only the Moon visits there on the 20th and 21st.) This is a time to please yourself. To have things your way and to have life on your terms. No need to compromise with your happiness now – you have the power to create new conditions or change conditions that displease you. If you are happy, the world (and those who are your true friends) will also be happy. You know best what is right for you – so act on your knowledge (preferably before the 26th.)

Spirituality is still important until the 20th – keep in mind last month's discussion. Since many of you will have birthdays coming up, the spiritual focus should also include a review of your past year, the correction of mistakes (religious people call it 'repentance' – re-thinking), and the setting of goals for the future. Your birthday is considered your personal new year, and it is important to start the year off on the right foot and with the right attitude.

On the 20th you begin a yearly personal pleasure peak. It will be a time for the good things of life – the delights of the senses – the good food, good wine, nice clothing and the like. Enjoy. It is a time to pamper yourself. Your body is your best friend – it serves you valiantly – it is good to treat it right.

Health is much improved this month. Pluto, your health planet, went Retrograde early last month and so it is not a time for making dramatic changes to your diet or health regime. Study things more before you act. This is a time for reviewing your current state of health and seeing where you can make improvements.

Job-seekers need more patience now, too. Pluto's Retrograde doesn't mean that you can't get a job, only that you need to research the job opportunities more carefully – ask questions and read the small print on all contracts. That dream job might not be all that it sounds like.

Your love planet goes Retrograde this month as well (in fact, Retrograde activity is reaching its height for the year – by the end of the month 40 per cent of the planets will be Retrograde). So this is not a time for making important love decisions one way or another. Singles should let love develop as it will, in its own time and way. Those with marital problems should not schedule a divorce either. Review. Get clarity. Investigate options. Perhaps improvements can be made.

Health is good now. You are in one of your best health periods of the year.

June

Best Days Overall: 3, 4, 11, 12, 13, 21, 22, 23, 30
Most Stressful Days Overall: 9, 10, 16, 17, 18, 24, 25
Best Days for Love: 1, 2, 3, 4, 9, 10, 14, 15, 16, 17, 18, 19, 20, 24, 25, 28, 29
Best Days for Money: 1, 2, 3, 4, 5, 6, 9, 10, 11, 12, 19, 20, 24, 28, 29

Your yearly personal pleasure peak is still in full swing. Have things your way. Enjoy your life. Spend on yourself. Pursue your personal interests. Enjoy the delights of the senses. Create conditions as you want them to be. Let the world adjust to you.

Though your love planet is still Retrograde, singles are having many love opportunities. Only these are more 'fun and games' types of relationships – not serious committed things. What is interesting is that these relationships are pursuing you – they come to you. You look great. Personal magnetism is strong. You have charisma this month. And, with Venus in your own Sign, you dress with flair and style. Normally, with Venus in your Sign it's a great time to buy clothing and personal accessories – things that enhance your image. Only now, this year, Mercury is Retrograde, and this complicates the whole situation. If you must buy those personal items, make sure the shop has a good returns policy. Save all your receipts and original boxes.

Late last month the planetary power shifted from the top to the bottom half of your chart – most of the planets are now below the horizon. You are in the 'night period' of your year. Night is a time for dreaming, for gestating and digesting. Not so good for outward action. Career is still important (and will be for many years to come) but now it is good to pursue it in the ways of the night – plant career seeds in the mind, visualize what you want, get into the right psychological state for future career success to happen. Also it is time to focus more on family. (Both of the planets involved in your career are Retrograde this month, too – thus there is not much going on there – so you might as well focus on the home.)

On the 18th you begin a yearly financial peak. Finances are going to become a major focus. And, where there is strong interest, there also is success. This is 90 per cent of success. Much of what we see will not be a surprise, communication, sales, marketing and promotion are the main paths to profit. This is Gemini's forte. Venus in your Money House shows luck in speculations, easy money, money that is earned in happy ways. Artists and creative people will sell more of their creative product now. And since Venus is your spiritual planet, intuition is going to play a huge role. Probably you will increase your charitable giving, and deepen your understanding of the spiritual laws of affluence.

Health is good now. Your health planet is still Retrograde and once again changes Signs. It moves out of Capricorn and into Sagittarius. Enhance health by paying more attention to the liver and thighs.

The home should be made more safe and secure. Plumbing still needs to be checked. A parent or parent figure is still having adventures.

July

Best Days Overall: 1, 9, 10, 19, 20, 28
Most Stressful Days Overall: 6, 7, 14, 15, 21, 22
Best Days for Love: 2, 3, 6, 7, 13, 14, 15, 16, 17, 24, 26
Best Days for Money: 2, 3, 6, 7, 11, 12, 16, 17, 23, 26, 30

Retrograde activity increases this month and the pace of events are slowing down in the world and with people around you – but, for you personally, things are moving forward (with the exception of the career). You seem unaffected by the slow-down.

Like last month, most of the planets are below the horizon and your 4th House of Home and Family gets strong (Mars enters on the 1st). Both of your career planets are Retrograde all month. Your focus on home and family will not harm the career. A lot of issues there will only be resolved with time.

A friend, who is having a lot of dramas in his or her life, is coming to stay for a while. This is a wonderful month to do construction or renovation in the home – if you need it. Tempers with family members are more volatile and passionate these days. Perhaps a DIY construction project in the home might alleviate this and foster family harmony. Joint athletic activities also seem good. It might be good to go to the gym, or jog together as a family – or attend the football or cricket match as a family. Your personal involvement – just paying more attention to family members – will help until the 10th. From the 10th, family harmony is enhanced through financial means – financial support, material gifts and the like. After the 26th good communication is important – and perhaps it would be good to attend lectures or seminars as a family unit. This gives some common intellectual ground, and interesting discussions can happen afterwards.

You are still in a yearly financial peak. A very prosperous month. Speculations are still favourable until the 12th. Like last month, good sales, marketing and promotion are very important.

Job-seekers still need to research offers better as your work planet is still Retrograde. Those who employ others, likewise. Check out CVs more thoroughly. Be careful not to ignore details.

Job-seekers will have better success after the 22nd. (But continue to resolve all doubts.)

You will have more energy and enthusiasm for finances from the 3rd to the 18th, as the Moon waxes (you will have enthusiasm all month, but especially this period). From the 1st to the 3rd and from the 18th onwards use spare cash to pay off debt.

Love is a bit challenging this month. It seems that your financial focus is an issue and perhaps you're ignoring the social life or the current love. Perhaps there is a disagreement about finances. A love affair will get tested on the 26th–29th. With your love planet still Retrograde, this is not a time to make major love decisions one way or another. Continue to review your love life to see where and how improvements can be made.

A health scare from the 10th to the 12th is probably nothing, but merely a wake-up call to take better care of the health. Mars move into Virgo, and Pluto's move back into Sagittarius (last month) have increased the stress on you. So rest and relax more, massage the thighs regularly, and pay more attention to the liver. More sunshine is probably good for you, too.

August

Best Days Overall: 5, 6, 15, 16, 24, 25
Most Stressful Days Overall: 3, 4, 10, 11, 17, 18, 30, 31
Best Days for Love: 1, 2, 3, 4, 10, 11, 12, 13, 21, 22, 23, 30, 31
Best Days for Money: 1, 2, 3, 4, 10, 11, 12, 13, 21, 22, 23, 26, 27, 30, 31

Two eclipses this month insure that the month ahead will be dramatic. Read the newspapers and check the headlines.

The Solar Eclipse of August 1 is strong on you as it impacts on Mercury, your personal and family planet. You need to take a reduced schedule all month, but especially around the eclipse periods. This eclipse brings shake ups at home, with family members or with parents or parent figures. It will test the home and communication equipment and cars. Hidden flaws in these things will come to light so you can correct them. If you haven't been careful in dietary matters there could be a cleansing of the physical body. There will be a re-definition of the image in coming months – for you are changing the way you look at yourself – the way that you define yourself.

The Lunar Eclipse of August 16th occurs in your 9th House and impacts on Neptune, your career planet. Again this brings dramas with parents or parent figures. Also there are shakeups in your corporate hierarchy and possible career changes. There are shakeups in a religious institution you belong to, and many of you will change your religious affiliations. Students have dramas with university. Perhaps the school they wanted, doesn't pan out, and they change to another. Or they change institutions or areas of study on their own. Since the Moon rules your finances, every Lunar Eclipse brings financial change – dramatic – and a re-definition of the financial plan, strategy, or investments.

Often people change their banks, brokerage accounts, accountants or financial planners under this aspect.

Health needs watching this month – there is a lot of planetary stress on you – even without the eclipses. So maximize your energy as much as possible. Listen to your body. Rest when tired. Don't be embarrassed to take a nap when you're tired. Continue to pay more attention to the heart, liver and thighs and to detox regimes.

Finance doesn't seem as important as last month – though the eclipse on the 16th will force you to make some changes. You'll make them and move on. Financial enthusiasm is strongest from the 1st to the 16th and on the 30th and 31st. Pay off debt from the 16th to the 30th.

Early in the month communication and intellectual interests are important (these are always important to Gemini – but now even more so.) This is a time to catch up on your reading and letter-writing.

Home, family and domestic issues are important all month – and the events here seem dramatic, as mentioned. Good communication will enhance family harmony until the 10th, and afterwards it requires your personal, physical involvement.

Love seems happy and romantic after the 5th. Family members are playing Cupid for singles. Love can happen at family gatherings or through family connections.

September

Best Days Overall: 1, 2, 3, 11, 12, 20, 21, 29, 30
Most Stressful Days Overall: 6, 7, 8, 14, 15, 27, 28
Best Days for Love: 1, 2, 6, 7, 8, 9, 10, 11, 12, 18, 19, 21, 27
Best Days for Money: 9, 10, 18, 19, 22, 23, 27, 29

Last month, the planets made an important shift from the Eastern sector to the social, Western sector. Some 80 to 90 per cent of the planets are now in the West – a trend that will continue for many months. Your period of independence is over with. Now you need to cultivate your social skills. Up to now you have been pleasing yourself, now you need to please others and get on with them. Though your talents be astronomical, if people don't like you, it will mean little. The like-ability factor is very important these days. Sometimes the cosmos gives us things because of our own efforts. And, sometimes it likes to give us by grace – this is one of those latter kind of times.

Home, family and children are very important all month. Many of you are connecting with the 'child within' – this not only enables you to connect with children – but to enjoy life as well. It is said that the adult can never know true joy – this comes from the inner child. If you want to be happy – want more fun in your life – study children. They are happy without any reason for it. They emanate joy. Having fun with the family – doing fun type things together – will also enhance the family relationship.

Both of your career planets are still Retrograde so there's not much going on right now – not much you can do anything about. With your 5th House strong, this is a good month for a holiday.

Love is getting happier this period especially until the 22nd. Oh, there are bumps on the road – especially when Mars squares your love planet from the 5th to the 10th. But progress is happening. Your love planet starts to move forward on the 8th, bringing back your normal social confidence and judgement. Also many planets in romantic Libra are also fostering a mood for romance. The problem is that many of you are not sure what you want – commitment or fun and games. The relationships that happen after the 22nd don't seem like marriage material. Married couples can have strong temptations in that department. But the important thing is that you are clear, you know what you want, and can start moving forward towards it.

Finances are status quo this month. You have more energy – greater earning power – from the 1st to the 15th and on the 29th and 30th. From the 15th to the 29th use spare cash to pay off debt.

Health improves dramatically this month. On the 9th your health planet starts to move forward after many months of Retrograde motion. A positive health signal. On the 22nd the Sun moves away from a stressful aspect. The gang-up of planets against you is dissipated.

Mercury, your personal and family planet, goes Retrograde on the 24th so avoid making important purchases for the home or family decisions then. Try to wrap these things up before the 24th.

October

Best Days Overall: 9, 10, 17, 18, 26, 27
Most Stressful Days Overall: 4, 5, 11, 12, 24, 25, 31
Best Days for Love: 1, 4, 5, 6, 7, 11, 12, 15, 16, 21, 22, 23, 24, 25, 31
Best Days for Money: 6, 7, 9, 10, 15, 16, 17, 18, 19, 20, 24, 25, 28, 29

Most of the planets are still below the horizon and the two planets involved with your career are still Retrograde. So, still best focus on home, family and psychological issues. Still best to focus on right feeling and right state. Pretty soon now, the career situation will change and you won't have this luxury – so take advantage while you can.

Your main focus this month is still on children, fun and creativity. A party time of year. You are into another one of your personal pleasure peaks so enjoy. Work is important too and will become more important on the 23rd, but if you pamper yourself now, you will have renewed enthusiasm for work.

If you need to make important decisions with the family or children – or to buy big-ticket items for the home or children, after the 15th is better than before. This is when Mercury starts to move forward again.

With the 6th House powerful (and Mars also in that House) you are working harder than usual. The pace at work is frenetic. Job-seekers have good fortune this month, but mostly because they are seeking work more aggressively. Job opportunities come from friends, neighbours, siblings and as you are having fun.

Health is good this month and you have a strong focus here – especially after the 23rd. Health is enhanced in a variety of ways this month, through taking better care of the heart, the adrenal glands, kidneys, hips, liver and thighs. Vigorous exercise seems good this month, too.

Love is becoming more active and happier, too. Your love planet started to move forward last month. This brought clarity and a return of social confidence. This month, Venus is moving into your 7th House of Love on the 18th. This is a prelude to the yearly social peak that will begin next month. For singles, Venus in the 7th House brings opportunities for love affairs, rather than marriage. For marrieds, it is a good time to bring the romance back by going on a second honeymoon or doing fun things together. Love opportunities happen in the usual places – at parties, the theatre, clubs, sporting events and the like. Since Venus is also your spiritual planet, spiritual-type seminars, meditation groups, yoga retreats are also the scene of romance. The workplace has long been as much a place of romance as a workplace – and this hasn't changed this month. Glamorous people are coming into your life.

Most of the planets in the social Western sector are also helping romance. Other people are more important to you; you are more personally popular. You have a stronger interest in others.

Finance is still status quo – which I consider good. There is basic contentment here. Earnings will be strongest from the 1st to the 14th and from the 28th onwards. Focus on paying off debt and cutting costs from the 14th to the 28th – as the Moon wanes.

November

Best Days Overall: 5, 6, 14, 15, 22, 23
Most Stressful Days Overall: 1, 7, 8, 20, 21, 27, 28
Best Days for Love: 1, 2, 3, 4, 11, 12, 13, 20, 21, 27, 28, 30
Best Days for Money: 2, 3, 4, 7, 8, 12, 13, 16, 17, 20, 21, 27, 28, 30

The planetary power shifts this month – from the lower half to the upper half of the Horoscope. Not only that, but your two career planets (Neptune and Uranus) start moving forward after many months of Retrograde motion. So career is starting to become important and starting to move forward again. The gridlock that we saw for many months is about over. Stuck projects or developments are now getting unstuck.

On the 21st as the Sun moves into your 7th House of Love, you enter a yearly social peak. For singles this brings marriage opportunity or relationships that are like a marriage. These are more serious and committed kinds of relationships. You have a big menu to choose from as there are many types of people who are in your 7th House – athletic types, friendship types, family types (people with strong family values), intellectuals, teachers and writers, spiritual and creative types and glamour kinds of people. Wow!

Venus will start to travel with Jupiter, your love planet, on the 29th and 30th (and on the 1st of next month too) and this brings a very happy romantic meeting or experience.

Married Geminis will just be socializing more and meeting new friends. Probably there will be more weddings they are attending.

There is still a great focus on health and work until the 21st – a good thing, too – because afterwards health becomes much more delicate and needs watching. First off rest and relax more and pace yourself better. Maximize energy as much as possible. Pay special attention to the heart now. Take naps when you're tired. Delegate tasks wherever possible. Exercise is still good (especially until the 18th) but take more relaxed workouts. The social life is great, but avoid people who drain you – look for people who lift you up – who energize you.

Finances are status quo – again. Earnings will tend to be strongest from the 1st to the 13th and from the 27th onwards. From the 13th to the 27th the focus should be on cutting debt, waste and expenses.

Your spouse or partner is prospering this month (it has been a prosperous year in general, but this month even more so). And thus your spouse is more generous with you. If you are looking to borrow money, increase your line of credit or attract outside investors, after the 12th (and especially on the 29th and 30th) is good.

Job-seekers still have good success.

December

Best Days Overall: 2, 3, 11, 12, 20, 21, 30, 31
Most Stressful Days Overall: 5, 6, 17, 18, 24, 25, 26
Best Days for Love: 1, 9, 10, 18, 21, 24, 25, 26, 27, 28, 30, 31
Best Days for Money: 1, 7, 8, 9, 10, 13, 14, 15, 16, 17, 18, 27, 28

Your personal social peak is in full swing and will last longer than usual – right through the new year and beyond. Love is happy and active. There are marriage opportunities for singles. New and important friends are coming into the picture.

Your 8th House was powerful last month and becomes even more powerful this month – 60 to 70 per cent of the planets are either there or moving through there this month. A huge, huge percentage. So it is not only an important love period, but a highly sexual period, too. (Even older Geminis will have a stronger libido than usual.)

This power in the 8th House shows that your spouse or partner is very focused on finances and having a yearly – and perhaps lifetime – financial peak. Naturally this will translate into greater generosity towards you.

But this power in the 8th House also shows other things. If you need to borrow or pay off debt, it is easy this month. Outside investors are there if you have good ideas. Money can come from inheritance, insurance claims or royalties. Professional investors have a sure touch with the bond market (especially government bonds, or the bonds of conservative blue-chip type companies).

Debt needs watching now – it is so easy to borrow that the temptation will be toward frivolity – this can be dangerous. Borrow to invest in things that will go up in value, not in things that will have no value a year from now.

Health still needs watching until the 21st. Keep in mind last month's discussion. Safe sex and sexual moderation are always important to you (Pluto is your health planet), but this month, with the 8th House of Sex so powerful, it is even more important. Detox regimes of all kinds – physical, mental, emotional and financial are all good this month.

There are dramas in the lives of friends from the 28th to the 30th. There can be some disturbance at work, too. Job changes can happen. Keep your cool. Take a few deep breaths before responding to anyone.

Avoid speculations from the 14th to the 18th. There are dramatic events with children that period. A love affair gets tested.

Cancer

$\odot$

Personality Profile

CANCER AT A GLANCE

Element – Water

Ruling Planet – Moon
   Career Planet – Mars
   Love Planet – Saturn
   Money Planet – Sun
   Planet of Fun and Games – Pluto
   Planet of Good Fortune – Neptune
   Planet of Health and Work – Jupiter
   Planet of Home and Family Life – Venus
   Planet of Spirituality – Mercury

Colours – blue, puce, silver

Colours that promote love, romance and social harmony – black, indigo

Colours that promote earning power – gold, orange

Gems – moonstone, pearl

Metal – silver

Scents – jasmine, sandalwood

Quality – cardinal (= activity)

Quality most needed for balance – mood control

Strongest virtues – emotional sensitivity, tenacity, the urge to nurture

Deepest need – a harmonious home and family life

Characteristics to avoid – over-sensitivity, negative moods

Signs of greatest overall compatibility – Scorpio, Pisces

Signs of greatest overall incompatibility – Aries, Libra, Capricorn

Sign most helpful to career – Aries

Sign most helpful for emotional support – Libra

Sign most helpful financially – Leo

Sign best for marriage and/or partnerships – Capricorn

Sign most helpful for creative projects – Scorpio

Best Sign to have fun with – Scorpio

Signs most helpful in spiritual matters – Gemini, Pisces

Best day of the week – Monday

Understanding a Cancer

In the Sign of Cancer the heavens are developing the feeling side of things. This is what a true Cancerian is all about – feelings. Where Aries will tend to err on the side of action, Taurus on the side of inaction and Gemini on the side of thought, Cancer will tend to err on the side of feeling.

Cancerians tend to mistrust logic. Perhaps rightfully so. For them it is not enough for an argument or a project to be logical – it must feel right as well. If it does not feel right a Cancerian will reject it or chafe against it. The phrase 'follow your heart' could have been coined by a Cancerian, because it describes exactly the Cancerian attitude to life.

The power to feel is a more direct – more immediate – method of knowing than thinking is. Thinking is indirect. Thinking about a thing never touches the thing itself. Feeling is a faculty that touches directly the thing or issue in question. We actually experience it. Emotional feeling is almost like another sense which humans possess – a psychic sense. Since the realities that we come in contact with during our lifetime are often painful and even destructive, it is not surprising that the Cancerian chooses to erect barriers – a shell – to protect his or her vulnerable, sensitive nature. To a Cancerian this is only common sense.

If Cancerians are in the presence of people they do not know, or find themselves in a hostile environment, up goes the shell and they feel protected. Other people often complain about this, but one must question these other people's motives. Why does this shell disturb them? Is it perhaps because they would like to sting, and feel frustrated that they cannot? If your intentions are honourable and you are patient, have no fear. The shell will open up and you will be accepted as part of the Cancerian's circle of family and friends.

Thought-processes are generally analytic and dissociating. In order to think clearly we must make distinctions, comparisons and the like. But feeling is unifying and integrative.

To think clearly about something you have to distance yourself from it. To feel something you must get close to it. Once a Cancerian has accepted you as a friend he or she will hang on. You have to be really bad to lose the friendship of a Cancerian. If you are related to Cancerians they will never let you go no matter what you do. They will always try to maintain some kind of connection even in the most extreme circumstances.

Finance

The Cancer-born has a deep sense of what other people feel about things and why they feel as they do. This faculty is a great asset in the workplace and in the business world. Of course it is also indispensable in raising a family and building a home, but it also has its uses in business. Cancerians often attain great wealth in a family type of business. Even if the business is not a family operation, they will treat it as one. If the Cancerian works for somebody else, then the boss is the parental figure and the co-workers are brothers and sisters. If a Cancerian is the boss, then all the workers are his or her children. Cancerians like the feeling of being providers for others. They enjoy knowing that others derive their sustenance because of what they do. It is another form of nurturing.

With Leo on their Solar 2nd House (of Money) cusp, Cancerians are often lucky speculators, especially with residential property or hotels and restaurants. Resort hotels and nightclubs are also profitable for the Cancerian. Waterside properties allure them. Though they are basically conventional people, they sometimes like to earn their livelihood in glamorous ways.

The Sun, Cancer's money planet, represents an important financial message: in financial matters Cancerians need to be less moody, more stable and fixed. They cannot allow their moods – which are here today and gone tomorrow – to get in the way of their business lives. They need to develop their self-esteem and feelings of self-worth if they are to realize their greatest financial potential.

Career and Public Image

Aries rules the 10th Solar House (of Career) cusp of Cancer, which indicates that Cancerians long to start their own business, to be more active publicly and politically and to be more independent. Family responsibilities and a fear of hurting other people's feelings – or getting hurt themselves – often inhibit them from attaining these goals. However, this is what they want and long to do.

Cancerians like their bosses and leaders to act freely and to be a bit self-willed. They can deal with that in a superior. Cancerians expect their leaders to be fierce on their behalf.

When the Cancerian is in the position of boss or superior he or she behaves very much like a 'warlord'. Of course the wars they wage are not egocentric but in defence of those under their care. If they lack some of this fighting instinct – independence and pioneering spirit – Cancerians will have extreme difficulty in attaining their highest career goals. They will be hampered in their attempts to lead others.

Since they are so parental, Cancerians like to work with children and make great educators and teachers.

Love and Relationships

Like Taurus, Cancer likes committed relationships. Cancerians function best when the relationship is clearly defined and everyone knows his or her role. When they marry it is usually for life. They are extremely loyal to their beloved. But there is a deep little secret that most Cancerians will never admit to: commitment or partnership is really a chore and a duty to them. They enter into it because they know of no other way to create the family that they desire. Union is just a way – a means to an end – rather than an end in itself. The family is the ultimate end for them.

If you are in love with a Cancerian you must tread lightly on his or her feelings. It will take you a good deal of time to realize how deep and sensitive Cancerians can be. The smallest negativity upsets them. Your tone of voice, your irritation, a look in your eye or an expression on your face can cause great distress for the Cancerian. Your slightest gesture is registered by them and reacted to. This can be hard to get used to, but stick by your love – Cancerians make great partners once you learn how to deal with them. Your Cancerian lover will react not so much to what you say but to the way you are actually feeling at the moment.

Home and Domestic Life

This is where Cancerians really excel. The home environment and the family are their personal works of art. They strive to make things of beauty that will outlast them. Very often they succeed.

Cancerians feel very close to their family, their relatives and especially their mothers. These bonds last throughout their lives and mature as they grow older. They are very fond of those members of their family who become successful, and they are also quite attached to family heirlooms and mementos. Cancerians also love children and like to provide them with all the things they need and want. With their nurturing, feeling nature, Cancerians make very good parents – especially the Cancerian woman, who is the mother par excellence of the Zodiac.

As a parent the Cancerian's attitude is 'my children right or wrong.' Unconditional devotion is the order of the day. No matter what a family member does, the Cancerian will eventually forgive him or her, because 'you are, after all, family'. The preservation of the institution – the tradition – of the family is one of the Cancerian's main reasons for living. They have many lessons to teach others about this.

Being so family-orientated, the Cancerian's home is always clean, orderly and comfortable. They like old-fashioned furnishings but they also like to have all the modern comforts. Cancerians love to have family and friends over, to organize parties and to entertain at home – they make great hosts.

Horoscope for 2008

Major Trends

Last year (and for the past few years) you were learning financial lessons. Learning to be in control of your finances and not letting them control you; learning to eliminate waste, live within your means, stretch a pound to the fullest, and take a long-term perspective on wealth; to learn to increase wealth in evolutionary rather than revolutionary ways. For most of you there was a huge financial reorganization. By the middle of last year these lessons were learned and the focus shifted to communication and intellectual interests. This trend continues this year, too. It is all about deepening the thought process, studying things in a more thorough way, learning to control your thinking and speech.

Last year there was great emphasis on health and work. Many of you landed dream jobs. Those of you who employ others enlarged the workforce. This year the focus shifts to love, romance and social issues. The year ahead will be a banner love and social year. More on this later on.

For many years there has been great interest in the deeper things of life – the meaning of life in general and the meaning of your own life. There have been explorations into past lives, life after death, rebirth and a focus on personal transformation. Religion and philosophy have been very important. These interests continue – perhaps even stronger in the year ahead.

Pluto has been in your 6th House of Health and work for many, many years – since November of 1995. This year he makes an important move into your 7th House of Love. So, over time, there is going to be a complete transformation of your love attitudes, friendships and marriage. This will not happen all at once, but as a process. This whole area of life is going to get purified.

Your most important interests this year are communication and intellectual interests; health and work (from

January 1 to January 27 and from June 14 to November 27); sex; debt, personal transformation, the prosperity of other people, occult studies, reincarnation, death and life after death; religion, philosophy, foreign travel and higher education.

Your paths of greatest fulfilment in the year ahead are love, romance and social activities; personal transformation, sex, occult studies, reincarnation and past lives.

Health

(Please note that this is an astrological perspective on health and not a medical one. For the medical perspective, please consult your doctor.)

Pluto's move out of Sagittarius and into Capricorn has important health implications for you. It is a stressful transit. Of itself, it is not enough to cause any major problems but it does impact somewhat on your overall energy. This year only two long-term planets are in stressful aspect (and Pluto will only be in stressful aspect part of the year). Health is reasonable, but energy is not as strong as last year. The time to get more defensive is when the short-term planets start to make stressful aspects – this will be from March 21 to April 19; August 19 to October 23 and from December 21 to December 31. These will be periods to rest and relax more and to pay more attention to your health.

The good news here is that there is much you can do to enhance health and prevent problems before they develop. Pay more attention to the liver, thighs (ruled by Jupiter, your health planet) and to the spine, knees, teeth, bone structure, gall bladder and overall skeletal alignment. (Your health planet will be in Capricorn, which rules these things.) Since these are the most vulnerable areas – and problems, should they happen, would most likely begin there – keeping them healthy and fit is good preventive medicine.

This is a good year for regular visits to a chiropractor. Yoga, Pilates and Alexander Technique are also excellent for the posture and spinal alignment. Perhaps you need more calcium in the diet to strengthen the bones. Regular back and thigh massage would also be very helpful. Knees should be given more support when exercising.

Most of our readers already understand that disease winds up in the physical body but never originates there. Always it has its roots in the more subtle dimensions and bodies. Thus if a person wants true and lasting healing he or she must also deal with the spiritual or subtle roots of the problem. The beauty of the Horoscope is that it shows us these things very clearly.

With you, the spiritual causes of possible problems lies in the love life, the marriage and the social relationships. (Your health planet is in the 7th House this year.) Thus if a problem occurs, review this area of life and restore the harmony – forgive whoever needs to be forgiven, and also forgive yourself. Also check – and you must be ruthlessly honest with yourself – if you have been abusing the love force in

Reflexology

Try to massage the whole foot on a regular basis, but pay extra attention to the points highlighted on the chart. When you massage, be aware of 'sore spots', as these need special attention. It's also a good idea to massage the ankles and top side (as well as the soles) of the feet.

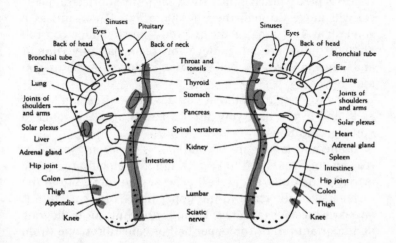

some way – using it manipulatively – using it to harm instead of to bless. And then make the correction. Chances are, if you do this the health problem will just melt away on its own. It will have no energy to support it. Even if you need the services of a health professional, the healing will go much more quickly and easily.

The second possible spiritual cause that needs investigation is your personal religion, your religious and philosophical beliefs, your view of the world and of life in general. (These things are ruled by Jupiter, your health planet). If there are false beliefs there will be much pain and suffering in the life. For a person will interpret events based on these things, will have negative emotional reactions to events that don't warrant it, and eventually this philosophical problem will also manifest in the physical body as some form of ailment. Happily, this area is important in your life these days and you are breaking with many false beliefs. I consider this a positive health signal.

Home and Family

Home and family are always important to you, Cancer, but this year less so. Everything is a matter of degree. Your 4th House is pretty much empty this year (only short-term planets will move through there temporarily). I read this as a good sign. This area of life is pretty much under control. Though things are not perfect you seem basically content and have no need to make drastic changes. A status-quo kind of year.

But also keep in mind that you have more freedom in this area, and if you like, you can shape this area according to your specifications.

Home and family are becoming less important for other reasons too. You seem to be getting more ambitious – more active in the outer world. Last year, Jupiter moved from the lower half of the chart to the upper half. This year Pluto is also crossing over (albeit back and forth). But this is showing an important trend. The upper half of your Horoscope (from a long-term perspective) is much, much stronger than the lower half. Next year Pluto will be in the upper half on a permanent basis. Four out of the five long-term planets will be in the upper hemisphere. Career – and not family – is starting to dominate your interests over the long haul. If you can pursue your career from a point of emotional harmony, you will be ultra-successful – and have happiness, too.

Venus is your family planet and she is fast moving. During the year she will move through all the Signs and Houses of your Horoscope. So the family situation and family needs, will tend to fluctuate depending on where Venus is at any given time – and depending on whether she is stressfully or harmoniously aspected. We will deal with these issues in the monthly reports.

If you are planning heavy construction and major renovations in the home, August 19 to October 23 is a good period. If you are planning the beautification of the home – painting, wall papering, decorating and the like – August 30 to September 24 is a good time.

Finance and Career

Your 2nd House of Finance is not a House of Power this year, so we expect a status-quo kind of year. I read this as a good thing. You've learned the financial lessons of the past two years. You've become financially healthier and more responsible. You are more in control of your finances and there's no need now to make dramatic changes. You seem content.

Many of you entered into business partnerships last year. And, if not, it is still likely to happen in the year ahead. These partnerships (or joint ventures) seem lucrative and successful.

Though money matters don't seem a big deal to you, your spouse or partner is very focused here. It's as if you have delegated this area of life to your spouse. Probably a wise idea. Your spouse is in a strong period of prosperity. Not just this year, but next year, too. This translates as more generosity to you. Your spouse seems 'visionary' in finances this year. The dream – the big idea – captures the imagination. If truth be told, they are merely following intuition. The financial intuition is very powerful this year. And, as our readers know, one moment of a real intuition – the merest instant of it – is worth many years of hard labour. Your spouse or partner is going deeper into the spiritual dimensions of wealth – that is, the focus is on tapping into the 'supernatural' and not the 'natural' source of supply. This is a whole different way of thinking and many of your spouses moves may seem nonsensical to you (and to others), but this is the rationale behind it. If your spouse is having financial problems it probably means that they are not 'prayed up' – not in right alignment with the Spiritual Power. The solution is to get aligned as quickly as possible.

The power that we see in the 8th House of Other People's Money also shows inheritance (no one may literally die, but you may be named in someone's will or be an executor of a will), money from insurance claims, or from royalties or trust funds. Your personal line of credit will increase in coming years – especially next year. Your access to outside money will increase. If you have good ideas you seem well able to attract outside investors to your projects. The whole thrust in the year ahead is the prosperity of others – your partner and spouse especially.

The power in your 8th House shows that many of you are planning your estates these days. Estate and tax issues are weighing heavily on financial decision-making.

There is a Solar Eclipse in your Money House on August 1 this year. This shows that you will make very important and dramatic financial changes. These changes long needed to be made and you probably procrastinated, now the eclipse forces the issue. With this kind of eclipse people change their investments, their accountants, financial planners, banks or brokers. More importantly they change their financial thinking and strategy. The eclipse tends to reveal the flaws in these things.

With the Sun (a fast-moving planet) as your financial planet, money and earnings opportunities tend to come to you in a variety of ways and means. It all depends on where the Sun is at a given time. We will discuss these short-term trends in the monthly reports.

Love and Social Life

This is definitely the major headline of the year ahead. Your 7th House of Love and Marriage is strong this year and for many years to come. It is going to be one of your main interests.

Singles of appropriate age are likely to marry this year. If not actual marriage, there may be a relationship that is 'like' a marriage. Something serious and significant. All of you will be dating more, attending more gatherings and parties and meeting up with new and significant friends.

But there are some challenges here. Two people and two opportunities come to you. One is something with a powerful sexual chemistry, but not serious – it just seems fun and games – just sex – while the other is something more serious. Both will vie for your interest. Both have their charms. In the end, though, it seems likely that you will opt for the more serious one.

You are always pretty traditional when it comes to love and marriage. You like a clearly structured – clearly defined – relationship. Each party has their role and duty. Most of you are not into gender bending. This trend is even stronger in the year ahead. You like your lover older, more established, more stable than you. You are attracted as much by the lover's status in the world and ability to provide as you are by the other charms. You sort of see marriage as another 'career move' – a way to advance yourself. Marriage is not about 'romance' *per se* but about practical issues. Once these practical issues are there, you feel you can learn to love anyone.

With these kinds of aspects the danger is that you will drift into a 'marriage of convenience' instead of one based on true love. You will have to observe yourself closely this year.

There are other challenges to love this year – hopefully you will be able to avoid them with right understanding. Your love planet is in the Sign of Virgo (which rules health) and your health planet is in your 7th House of Love. This gives us many messages. There is a very strong connection between health and love (some of the health issues have already been discussed). It shows that you are allured to doctors, nurses, healers and health professionals. Romance is likely to happen to you as you pursue your normal health goals – at the gym, yoga studio, health food shop or doctor's surgery. But on a deeper level this is showing that you have a passion (much more than usual) for a healthy love life – a healthy social life – a healthy relationship. You have a passion for perfection – the perfect love. Nothing wrong with this *per se*, but you need to be careful of how you go about it. The tendency is to start analysing every little thing – to search for pathologies in love, the way a doctor searches for pathology in the body. Pretty soon, if you're not careful, you will find yourself awash in pathologies and problems – losing sight of the overall picture. The tendency to criticize will be strong (again this comes from the desire for perfection) and if the criticism turns destructive, it will destroy the mood of romance. Most of you know that romance is 90 per cent magic and only 10 per cent logic. And nothing will destroy the magic more quickly than destructive criticism (even from good motives). Also romance is of the heart, but your tendency is to relate from the head – the mind – and this too is not conducive to romance. (Many of you might not be like this personally, but could be attracting lovers who are like this – both scenarios are likely.)

So, save your analysis for another time – not during romantic moments. A few days afterwards, you can review things and see where they can be improved. Keep criticism constructive at all times. If the situation can't be improved refrain from criticism – even in your heart.

It is helpful to keep in mind that perfection is never handed to us on a silver platter. In heaven everything is perfect. Here on Earth, perfection is a goal that we shoot for.

It is a road, a process. Be patient with yourself and your partner. As long as you keep improving your relationship – you are on the road to perfection – though not yet at the goal.

Other venues for romance this year are at educational settings – at lectures, seminars, or school. Love is close to home – in the neighbourhood – and perhaps with neighbours.

Those working towards their second marriage have been having a good time and enjoying their social freedom, but this year they might tie the knot in spite of this.

Those working towards their third marriage have a status-quo year – marrieds will tend to stay married and singles will tend to stay single.

Self-improvement

Keep in mind our previous discussion about love – for this is an important area for self-improvement in the coming year. In love both the head and the heart have their places. The heart of course should be the most important thing.

But the heart without the mind can lead to much pain and many mistakes. So you are right to be more in the head – but the danger is overdoing it.

You are cautious in love this year – and caution is a good thing. But be careful that caution doesn't become fear – or that fear is masking itself under the guise of caution. Caution, letting love develop as it will, is a healthy thing. Fear is pathology.

Those involved romantically with Cancerians will have to deal with this pragmatism. The Cancerian might not even believe in romantic love this year and your job will be to convince him or her that it exists.

The second area of self-improvement is in the mentality and communication skills. This is a period for setting these things in order. You need to learn to organize and structure your thought process – bring it under your control. Thinking is not the enemy but 'chaotic, disjointed thinking' is. Courses and seminars on communication skills seem a good idea this year. Learning to turn your mind off when not in use is also helpful (this is done through meditation and spiritual practice). When you talk make sure you have the facts and that your homework is done – the cosmos won't let you get away with unresearched speech. You will be called on it. When you are studying something take more time with it – go deeper – don't leave a subject until you understand it inwardly (don't just be satisfied with knowing enough to pass a test).

Cancerians who are in school will need to work harder this year – but the hard work will have long-term benefits.

Month-by-month Forecasts

January

Best Days Overall: 2, 3, 12, 13, 20, 21, 29, 30, 31
Most Stressful Days Overall: 1, 7, 8, 14, 15, 27, 28
Best Days for Love: 5, 6, 7, 8, 14, 15, 16, 23, 25
Best Days for Money: 7, 8, 16, 17, 22, 23, 24, 25, 27, 28

This month you are right in the midst of a yearly social peak. Now the whole year ahead is going to be socially strong and happy – but this month even more so. Some 60 per cent of the planets will either be in – or move through – your 7th House of Love and Marriage. Romance is happening and wedding bells are ringing. With the Sun, Venus and Jupiter in your 7th House this month – you couldn't ask for better love aspects.

Reinforcing all this is the fact that 80 per cent – sometimes 90 per cent – of the planets are in your Western, social sector. Other people, relationships, social graces are very important this month. As long as you hang out with the right kind of people this is fine, but for the younger Cancerians, peer pressure will be very strong – the wrong kinds of friends can lead to trouble.

This is a period where you get your way through the good will of other people and not because of your talents or through personal independence. Difficult right now to change conditions. You just need to be more adaptable.

Finances, too, depend on social connections, friendships, your spouse or lover. After the 20th you prosper by putting the prosperity of others ahead of your own. You need to think of the financial interest of others – but especially your partner or current love – ahead of your own. As you help others to prosper your own prosperity happens – very naturally and easily.

A business partnership or joint venture is very likely this month. (The same aspects that rule marriages also rule business partnerships.)

Professional investors should look at the blue-chip, traditional companies until the 20th and then to bonds and the bond market afterwards. After the 20th the high-tech industry also looks interesting (but I like the bonds of these companies better than the stocks).

After the 20th it is good to 'detox' yourself on a financial level. Get rid of possessions that are no longer needed. Eliminate waste and cut needless expenses. This will clear the decks for the new prosperity that wants to come.

Health needs watching this month – especially until the 20th. Pay more attention to the heart, the liver, thighs, spine, knees, bones, and skeletal alignment. Regular back and thigh massage will be powerful. Being in places with a strong Earth energy – mountains, old forests, caves – will also lift you up. Crystal therapy is powerful this month, too.

February

Best Days Overall: 8, 9, 17, 26, 27
Most Stressful Days Overall: 3, 4, 10, 11, 23, 24
Best Days for Love: 3, 4, 12, 13, 14, 21, 23
Best Days for Money: 3, 4, 6, 7, 12, 13, 15, 16, 19, 20, 21, 22, 25, 26

Though the Sun has moved out of your 7th House of Love, your yearly social peak is still intact. Romantic Venus is in your 7th House (joining Jupiter there) and making fabulous aspects to your love planet. Romance only deepens now. Singles who haven't yet met Mr or Ms Right are still likely to meet them this month.

Many singles are reconnecting with old flames – these will either re-kindle or the old issues between you will get resolved.

With your 8th House strong this month, this is a sexually active kind of month – another good signal for love. No matter what your age or stage in life, libido will be stronger this month than usual.

The power in the 8th House shows that detox regimes of all sorts (not just on a financial level) are good. This is a month for personal transformation and reinvention. And, these things don't happen unless we change our mental and emotional patterns. You can change your body and image cosmetically – through cosmetics, different clothing and jewellery – but this is not transformation. This is merely covering the 'old' person with a different coat of paint. Transformation happens when we change on the *inside*.

Last month we saw a shift from the lower half of the Horoscope to the upper half. This happened late in the month. Right now there are 80 per cent – sometimes 90 per cent – of the planets above the horizon. A huge, huge percentage. (Your personal planet, the Moon, will spend half the month above the horizon as well.) So, you can safely let go of family issues and focus on your career. You will never ignore your family, but you serve them best, by succeeding in your career. (They want this for you too.)

This shift took place just as your career planet Mars was starting to move forward (after months of Retrograde motion). Career issues are straightening out. Long-stalled projects are getting unstuck. There is movement and progress happening (a lot of this is behind the scenes and you may not be aware of it).

You can enhance your career by getting involved in charities and altruistic activities. Spiritual channels, ministers and psychics have important career guidance for you. Your dreams are also giving career guidance – but you need to pay attention.

Health is much improved this month. By the 17th it will get even better. By the 19th better still.

Job-seekers had good success last month and the trend continues this month, too.

There are two eclipses this month – but you don't seem too affected by them. The Solar Eclipse of the 7th (the 6th in the US) brings long-needed financial changes both for you and your spouse or partner. The Lunar Eclipse of the 21st (20th in the US) will test communication equipment and cars. Students will have changes in their education (pre-university students). The image and personality get redefined.

March

Best Days Overall: 6, 7, 15, 16, 24, 25
Most Stressful Days Overall: 2, 3, 9, 22, 23, 29, 30
Best Days for Love: 2, 3, 4, 5, 10, 11, 15, 19, 24, 25, 29, 30
Best Days for Money: 2, 3, 6, 7, 11, 15, 16, 17, 18, 19, 20, 27, 29, 30

Many of the career trends discussed last month are still in effect. Your urge for success is incredible – and by itself is enough to make it happen. But this month, your career planet makes an important move into your own Sign. This happens on the 4th. This is showing many things – the most important is that career opportunities are seeking you. You don't need to run after them. You are in demand. Your ambitions are intensified even more than last month. You are dressing for success – dressing in keeping with your status (and in many cases, with the status that you aspire to). You are magnetic and charismatic. You have the image of a leader – a manager. From a health perspective, you are exercising more and more athletic than usual. You excel at these things this month. Athletes are breaking their previous records – performing at a very high level.

Health in general is good – especially until the 20th. You have the energy of 10 people and achieve a lot very quickly (90 per cent of the planets are in forward motion – and this is also helping here). After the 20th you should slow down a bit and rest and relax more. Overall health is good then, too, but energy levels are not as high as before the 20th.

One of the problems with Mars in your own Sign is that it makes people more independent and self-willed – and this is not a time for that. Most of the planets are still in the Western sector and you still need the good graces of others. Too much self-assertion will be counter-productive. Also, Mars in your own Sign (it behaves very much like a drug – an amphetamine) makes people more in rush – things have to be done yesterday. There is a rashness that needs to be curbed. Temper can be a problem, too. Use this energy positively – to get things done, to lead, to excel in sports – but avoid temper and conflict.

Love is still very happy this month – but too much temper, self-will, self-assertion can be a problem here as well. Love gets bumpier after the 20th, but have no fear, your overall love life is still wonderful. A real relationship will not dissolve over this.

Finances are good this month. Your financial planet will be in the prosperous 9th House until the 20th. Financial horizons are huge. Financial goals are larger than life. Your intuition is exceptional as well – and speculations are favourable until the 20th. After the 20th finances are a bit more challenging, but your interest is so strong (the Sun will be the most elevated planet in the chart) that you are willing to overcome all the challenges that arise. Until the 20th earnings come from foreign sources, foreign investments, and through the advice of ministers and religious types. (Probably you are giving more to these people, too.) After the 20th money comes from pay rises, promotions, the support of parents, parent figures, the government and authority figures. They all seem supportive of your financial goals. If you have issues with the government, now (after the 20th) seems a good time to resolve them.

Your good professional reputation has tangible bottom-line results this month. On the 20th you enter a yearly career peak. Enjoy.

April

Best Days Overall: 3, 4, 11, 12, 20, 21, 22, 30
Most Stressful Days Overall: 5, 6, 18, 19, 25, 26, 27
Best Days for Love: 4, 7, 13, 14, 15, 24, 25, 26, 27
Best Days for Money: 5, 6, 7, 8, 13, 14, 16, 17, 25, 26, 27

Love is very bumpy this month (especially until the 20th). Your love planet camps out on an eclipse point all month. This will test your current relationship in many ways. Also it will bring dramatic events in the life of your spouse or partner. Relationships that are mediocre can dissolve now. The good ones will only get better because of the testing. After the 20th things will improve as the love planet starts to receive good aspects. But hold on for the ride.

You are still in the midst of a yearly career peak – until the 19th. And this focus on the career (and the demands of it) is probably contributing to the testing of love. (Emotional and family issues are also testing love. Communication with your beloved could be a lot better.) Even family is getting in on the act – they too seem more ambitious – both personally and for you. They are supporting your career goals and you are supporting theirs.

After the 6th the boundaries between home and office seem blurred. Hard to tell where one begins and the other ends. If you work in an outside office, you are making it more 'homelike'; if you work at home, you're making the home more like an office.

Venus moving across your Midheaven also has other messages. You can enhance your career through social means – attending or hosting the right kinds of parties. Social and family connections are playing an important role. There can be an opening in a family-type business. Good communication and marketing are also important. Mercury crosses your Midheaven and enters the House of Career on the 2nd.

Finances are a bit more challenging this month, but earnings still come. You just have to work harder for them. Until the 19th they come from pay rises, promotions and the support of parents, parent figures or bosses. After the 19th they come from networking, friendships and involvement with organizations. Fondest financial wishes come to pass after the 19th – but will you be satisfied? Not likely.

Health needs more watching until the 19th. The main thing is to rest and relax more and maximize energy. Continue to enhance the health in the ways mentioned in the yearly report – pay more attention to the heart, liver, thighs, spine, knees, teeth, bones and skeletal alignment. With Mars still in your own Sign, you are exercising more – so make sure you give the knees more support.

May

Best Days Overall: 1, 8, 9, 18, 19, 28, 29
Most Stressful Days Overall: 2, 3, 15, 16, 23, 24, 30, 31
Best Days for Love: 4, 5, 13, 14, 22, 23, 24, 25
Best Days for Money: 4, 5, 11, 12, 13, 14, 23, 24, 25

The Sun left dynamic Aries last month. Mars is moving out of your Sign on the 9th. Overall Retrograde activity is increasing and, by the 26th, 40 per cent of the planets will be in Retrograde motion. The dominance of the Fire element (which encourages frenetic activity) is now replaced with cautious Earth. Things are slowing down in the world. You have some breathing space. Progress will be more measured and not frenetic. As a result, health is also much improved.

By now you have achieved many career goals. You have been successful the past few months. And though you are still ambitious, your interests are shifting to other things. Friendships, group activities, organizations are important. After the 20th spirituality will become important. This is good. Life was not designed for only one thing or one area. Life is a wheel, and every segment of the wheel has its charms and lessons.

Finances are becoming more important this month, too. Mars moves into your Money House on the 9th. This shows many of the trends of last month – for Mars is your career planet. So it shows that money comes from the career, your status in a company or industry, your good professional reputation, the intercession or support of elders, bosses, parents or parent figures.

Mars in Leo and in the Money House is a VERY specula-tive position. You are into big and quick money. You are a risk-taker. You throw caution to the winds. You are a rash spender and investor. So this is the danger. With this posi-tion no amount of lecturing will stop you from being specu-lative, but you can limit your risks – hedge yourself, speculate with only a percentage of your assets and not everything. It is great to be able to buy what you want whenever you want – but do more research and check prices and terms.

The good news is that 50 to 60 per cent of the planets are in Earth Signs this month – and this makes people more practical, down to earth and cautious – thus it will temper some of your urges.

Family unity can be enhanced through group activities (and developing the team spirit in the family) until the 24th. Afterwards spiritual understanding – the revelation of a higher power becomes very important. Also it might help to get involved in some cause or charity as a family unit.

Health is good this month.

Love is improving. Your love planet is starting to move forward on the 3rd and this is bringing greater clarity and social confidence. (But Saturn is still on an eclipse point and love is being tested.)

June

Best Days Overall: 5, 6, 14, 15, 24, 25
Most Stressful Days Overall: 11, 12, 13, 19, 20, 26, 27
Best Days for Love: 1, 3, 4, 9, 10, 14, 15, 19, 20, 24, 25, 28
Best Days for Money: 1, 2, 3, 4, 7, 8, 9, 10, 11, 12, 19, 20, 24, 28, 29

Your 10th House of Career is empty this month and the planets are getting ready to shift from the upper to the lower half of the chart. (This will begin on the 18th, but will be more established next month.) Career is winding down. You have achieved important goals. Of course there are more goals waiting to be achieved – but these will need more time and development. You're getting ready to focus on your main love – home, family and the emotional life.

In the meantime focus on the inner life – the spiritual life. Work on your connection to the Spirit within you. All the frantic career activity of recent months probably disconnected you and now you have to re-establish the connection. People often wonder why the Divine allows so many negative things to happen on the planet and to people. But if you analyse (and this is a good month for that) you will see that the problem is not with the Spirit – but with us. Spirit is willing, but people – humans – are just not paying attention. As you start to refocus your attention, watch how problem after problem simply melts away. You have been getting in the way of your own progress.

This is an excellent month for going on spiritually-oriented retreats, seminars or meditation workshops. It is great to review your past year (as you are having a birthday this month or next month), correct past mistakes and set goals for the future. Your birthday is your personal new year and you want to start it on the right foot.

On the 18th, as Venus enters your Sign, you enter a yearly personal pleasure peak. This is a time for the fulfilment of sensual desires and fantasies. For taking care of

Number One. You are not your body – but the body is your friend and servant. Treat it right. Pamper yourself.

Most of the planets are now in the Eastern sector of your chart and your 1st House is very strong. (Your 7th House of Others is also strong – but the 1st House is the strongest it will be this year.) So now is the time to create conditions as you desire them to be. If a condition or situation irks you or displeases you – change it to your liking. You have more independence now. Personal initiative (and not the grace of other people) is important. You don't need to worry about pleasing others – if you please yourself – create conditions of happiness – others will also be happy.

Health is excellent this month – especially after the 21st. You look great. Magnetic. You have style and grace. You like yourself and the opposite sex likes you, too. Love is still getting tested until the 21st – think of your relationship as a diamond – it needs some polishing. When the polishing is over with, it will shine all the brighter.

Mars is still in your Money House – so refer to what was written last month.

July

    Best Days Overall: 2, 3, 11, 12, 21, 22, 30
    Most Stressful Days Overall: 9, 10, 16, 17, 23, 24
    Best Days for Love: 2, 3, 6, 16, 17, 25, 26
    Best Days for Money: 2, 3, 4, 5, 6, 7, 11, 12, 16, 17, 23, 26

Your yearly personal pleasure peak is still in full swing. You are not only enjoying life, receiving many personal kinds of items (clothing and accessories) and communication equipment, but you also look great. You have style, magnetism and charisma. If there are challenges in love it's not because of your appeal – there are other issues involved – perhaps financial disagreements with your beloved or disagreements involving parents or parent figures. But these are short lived. Your love life overall is good.

This is still a time for personal independence – and this could also be putting stress on your love life now. You have the power to create conditions as you like them to be – to have life on your terms – and you should.

Though career is on the back burner now (by the 10th the dominance of power will be in the lower half – the night side – of your Horoscope) there are some career shakeups going on – especially from the 1st to the 8th as your career planet re-stimulates the eclipse point of February 21. This brings shakeups within your corporate hierarchy and in your industry – major change. This could affect your career as a side-effect. There are also dramas in the lives of parents or parent figures.

Your spouse or current love seems very ambitious this month – perhaps he or she is travelling a lot on business.

On the 22nd you enter a yearly financial peak. Prosperity will be very strong. The main reason for it is your interest and focus. Friends, social contacts, siblings and neighbours are also supporting your financial goals. No need to travel far and wide for financial increase or opportunity – it's there in the neighbourhood – especially after the 26th. Networking, being up on the latest technology, good use of the media – both print and electronic – also seem important and bring financial bonuses. When Mercury, your spiritual planet, enters your Money House on the 26th, intuition becomes important. You have to be alert to the spiritual messages that are always being sent. Be alert for unusual phenomena in your life – a strange insect camps out on your window, a bird makes a strange gesture, note the animals that you come in contact with – all of these things have financial import for you, if you can decode the message. Sometimes the messages come in other ways – through dreams, psychics and astrologers. This is the short-cut to your financial goals.

Professional investors should look at gold, electric utilities, entertainment, gaming, copper, the beauty industry, telecommunications, transport and media companies. A nice menu – select what appeals to you.

Health is good this month.

Love gets tested early in the month.

August

Best Days Overall: 7, 8, 9, 17, 18, 26, 27

Most Stressful Days Overall: 5, 6, 12, 13, 14, 20

Best Days for Love: 1, 2, 3, 12, 13, 14, 21, 22, 23, 30

Best Days for Money: 1, 2, 3, 4, 10, 11, 12, 13, 21, 22, 23, 28, 29, 30, 31

Earnings are still strong and your focus and concentration are good. This is 90 per cent of the key to success. Focus on your financial goals – and stay focused. Don't waver for a minute. You become what you focus on. Everything that you have right now came from 'past focus'. Attention is one of the great magical tools with which we shape our lives.

There are two eclipses this month – and one of them, the Solar Eclipse of the 1st – affects the financial life. I read this as a good thing. Your success, your prosperity, is forcing you to change your financial thinking and strategy. Perhaps you formed certain plans from a 'fearful' or 'poverty' consciousness – now you must revise these plans or investments or strategies. This eclipse seems benevolent to you, but it won't hurt to take a reduced schedule anyway. These eclipses roil up the energy of the whole world and it is not advisable to do risky or high-stress things. (You might be OK, but others might not be.)

The Lunar Eclipse of the 16th occurs in your 8th House. This affects the finances of your spouse or partner – he or she also needs to make important changes. If you are involved in estate, tax or insurance issues, this eclipse brings a dramatic turning point. Things go forward one way or another. Every Lunar Eclipse affects your image and personality – your self-concept – and this one is no different. So, once again, the cosmos gives you the opportunity upgrade, refine and improve. As you do, you will certainly change the way you dress, your hairstyle, and the image you project to others. This eclipse impacts on Neptune, the ruler of your 9th House. For students, this brings a change in educational plans – there can be changes of schools, changes of areas of study or shakeups (or dramatic events) in the school they attend. For non-students this shows a crisis of faith – belief systems, personal religion and world view get tested. If found wanting, these things will get revised or thrown out. On a psychological level the eclipse can bring dreams or encounters with death – this is for your benefit so that you can have a healthier concept of it.

Health is basically good this month, but starts to get more delicate towards the end of the month – after the 29th. Try to rest and relax more.

Love is reasonable. There are opportunities for business partnerships or joint ventures after the 22nd. Singles have love opportunities in the neighbourhood or educational settings. Avoid being critical or perfectionist. Force yourself to come from the heart rather than the head – this will go a long way to easing problems. This looks like a socially active kind of month.

September

Best Days Overall: 4, 5, 14, 15, 22, 23
Most Stressful Days Overall: 1, 2, 3, 9, 10, 16, 17, 29, 30
Best Days for Love: 1, 2, 9, 10, 11, 12, 18, 19, 21, 27, 28
Best Days for Money: 9, 10, 18, 19, 24, 25, 27, 29

Job-seekers have good success this month – especially until the 22nd. Jupiter starts to move forward on the 8th after many months of Retrograde motion. The Sun and Saturn are also making wonderful aspects to Jupiter. A prosperous month as well – especially until the 22nd. Lady Luck is with you. Speculations are favourable. But the good luck seems more likely on the career front – a dream job opportunity comes. Serious investors should explore the health industry (until the 22nd) and the beauty industry (fashion, cosmetics, jewellery, art, perfumes), copper and sugar afterwards.

(Telecommunication, transport and media stocks also look interesting before the 22nd – and property is worth a look afterwards.)

This month the major focus is intellectual interests and communication. A great period (until the 22nd) to catch up on your letter writing, emails, phone calls and to take classes in subjects that interest you. A very good period (before the 15th) to launch an advertising campaign or mass mailing.

After the 22nd the focus is on home and family (actually this whole area will be important all month, but more so after the 22nd). Even your career planet is in the 4th House this month. This shows that the powers that be in your career are supportive of your family goals and interests. Many of you will do more work from home. From a spiritual perspective, your mission in life – for this month – is the family – to be there for them. You will solve a lot of problems by making them your priority – let them know that they come first. Doing things as a group – group activities and spiritual understanding – will also improve the family situation.

You are spending more on the family this month and perhaps buying some big-ticket items for the home. This helps family unity. A good month (before the 24th) to do heavy construction, repairs or redecorating.

Love is happy this month. The love planet makes beautiful (and exact) aspects with Jupiter this month. Singles will meet a special someone. A current relationship deepens. Happy social experiences come. Office romances are likely, too.

Health needs more watching all month – but especially after the 22nd. There doesn't seem to be anything very serious, only that energy is not up to its usual standards – and thus you can be more vulnerable. The solution is just to rest more. Focus on what is really important and don't waste precious energy on inessentials. With your health planet moving forward on the 8th, you can implement changes to your health regime and diet.

October

Best Days Overall: 1, 2, 11, 12, 19, 20, 28, 29, 30
Most Stressful Days Overall: 6, 7, 13, 14, 26, 27
Best Days for Love: 1, 6, 7, 11, 12, 15, 16, 21, 22, 23, 24, 25
Best Days for Money: 6, 7, 9, 10, 15, 16, 17, 18, 22, 23, 24, 25, 28, 29

Last month, the planets made a major shift from the Eastern to the Western sector of your chart. By now you have made the changes that you wanted to make. You've explored personal independence. Now you have to live with the changes – now you road-test your creation and see how it works. If you built well and wisely, the fact that it's difficult to make changes won't be an issue. But if you built haphazardly, it can be irksome and very difficult to make changes independently – you'll have to wait until your next cycle of independence comes (next year) to correct things. Now you more or less have to adapt as best you can to conditions. (However, it won't hurt to make note of what needs to be changed – this way when the time comes, you'll be ready.)

Home and family are still the dominant interests this month. Investing in the home and spending on the family seem like good investments. (This will also create more family harmony – finance is one of the important ways to achieve harmony this month.) Good communication and spiritual understanding are also important.

Your mission this month is twofold. First, to be there for your family and children. Second, to enjoy your life, to put joy into your life – to enter the spaces of happiness. (Seems weird that this would be a spiritual mission, yet there are times when this is vital – personal happiness refreshes us to do our other work better. There is a saying in the Talmud that on Judgement Day everyone will have to give an accounting for every joy not taken. It was intended that people be joyful.) Also there is some creative-type project that needs your attention – it could be personal, or a project involving others.

On the 23rd you enter into another of your yearly personal pleasure peaks. A party period. A time to explore the rapture of life. A time to look at some of the serious events in life – in the world, and for you personally – and to laugh. The gates of Hell themselves will not prevail against laughter and true happiness. The minute happiness is introduced, Hell ceases to be hell. It is destroyed. (Something to remember with the many planets in Scorpio this month and when the seamy side of life is prominent in the world.)

Health needs watching until the 23rd. Keep in mind last month's discussion. After the 23rd there is a dramatic improvement. If there have been health problems you will see 'miraculous' or spontaneous-type healings.

Love is still very happy and moving forward nicely. It gets even better after the 23rd. More passionate – more intense – more physical. A sexually active kind of month. Singles have many options – serious love – or many 'fun and games' opportunities.

November

Best Days Overall: 7, 8, 16, 17, 25, 26
Most Stressful Days Overall: 2, 3, 4, 10, 11, 22, 23, 30
Best Days for Love: 1, 2, 3, 4, 11, 12, 13, 20, 21, 30
Best Days for Money: 2, 3, 4, 7, 8, 12, 13, 16, 17, 18, 19, 20, 21, 27, 28, 30

Some 80 to 90 per cent – a huge percentage – of the planets are in the social, Western sector this month. Your 7th House of Others has been strong all year and gets even stronger this month. Your 1st House of Self, by contrast, is empty – only the Moon moves through there on the 16th and 17th. (This will be a monthly personal pleasure peak.) So the message is very clear: Tone down self-will and self-assertion. Get your way through consensus and compromise. Let others have their way – so long as it isn't self-destructive. Your way is probably not the best way this period. With these kinds of aspects, peer pressure is very strong. The desire to be accepted by others is overpowering – and with good reason – this is how your good comes to you. However, very important – especially for the younger Cancerians – to hang around with the right kind of people. The peer pressure of bad company is like a psychic poison.

Love is fabulous this month. On the 12th Venus will re-enter your 7th House of Love for the second time this year. (Generally she only visits a Sign and House once in a year – your Love House gets two visits this year. Combine this with Jupiter being in this House all year and you can see why this is such a great social year.) Pluto also moves back in (for a second visit) to this House on the 27th. This brings more 'fun and games' kinds of opportunities. It's as if you have a choice now – go for the diamond or just have fun. Either choice seems happy. There is a Mr or Ms Right or a Mr or Ms Fun for all of you. Even children of appropriate age are having wonderful romantic opportunities.

Finances also seem happy. The financial planet is in the fun-loving and speculative 5th House until the 21st, then moves into bullish Sagittarius. You spend a lot, but earn a lot. Money comes as you're having fun, or involved in leisure pursuits – until the 21st. This is 'happy money'. After the 21st it comes the hard way, through work. You are spending more on children and leisure pursuits this month, too. Also on health. Speculations are favourable all month.

Professional investors should look at bonds and the bond market, gold, electric utilities, energy, entertainment and gaming companies until the 21st, and at publishing, travel companies, for-profit universities and the health industry afterwards.

Your 6th House of Health and Work is strong all month, but especially after the 21st. You become more serious and work-oriented. Job-seekers have success. Those who employ others will find workers rather easily. You are working very hard after 21st – but you seem very committed to work. Very motivated. Your job (as well as your health – and the healing of others) is your spiritual mission for the month ahead (from the 16th onwards).

Health is good this month. Part of the reason is that you are very focused here – you have a strong drive and interest. Thus you are taking care of problems before they get worse. Also you seem more willing to get involved in preventive measures (healthy lifestyle, right diet, exercise and the like) and this will stand you in good stead next month, when health becomes more delicate. The cosmos tends to give us the cure before the problem happens – but we need to be alert.

December

Best Days Overall: 5, 6, 13, 14, 22, 23
Most Stressful Days Overall: 1, 7, 8, 20, 21, 27, 28
Best Days for Love: 1, 9, 10, 11, 17, 18, 20, 21, 27, 28, 30, 31
Best Days for Money: 1, 7, 8, 9, 10, 15, 16, 17, 18, 27, 28

The major headline this month is love. No question about it. Now, 70 per cent (!) of the planets are either in your 7th House or will move through there this month. You enter another yearly social peak now – and perhaps even a life-time social peak. If you haven't met anyone special yet (though this is hard to believe), this is a good month for it. Most of you are involved in serious kinds of relationships, and this is a month where the relationship deepens and moves forward. You take the next steps – this could be an actual marriage, or you move in with the beloved (or vice versa) or move the relationship forward in other ways.

With so much power here in the House of Love, failure is just inconceivable. You will succeed beyond your dreams.

Until the 27th your spiritual mission is your job. Yes, a mundane job can be a very spiritual thing if done properly and with understanding. There are certain things at the job that only you – no one else – can do. And you have to do it. You were born to do it.

Health – both personal and for others – is still very much your mission, too.

But after the 27th your mission becomes your spouse, your lover, your significant other – to be there for this person. Also to be there for your friends. Like last month, 80 per cent to 90 per cent of the planets are in the West, so it is easy for you to perform this mission now. When you do for others, put their interests ahead of your own, you feel fulfilled – the cosmos smiles at you – good comes to you by grace and not so much through your personal talents or efforts.

Until the 21st, your financial planet is in the 6th House and many of the trends of last month are still in effect. Money comes from work. Perhaps you get a new job. Co-workers could bring interesting and profitable financial opportunities. You are a more productive worker and so you earn more – bonuses and overtime and the like.

After the 21st money comes through social contacts, spousal support, joint ventures or business partnerships. A new business partnership could happen this month too. You are spending more on social issues, too.

For professional investors, the health industry, publishing, long-distance transport and telecommunications, the travel industry and foreign stocks look interesting. After the 21st, the traditional, conservative blue-chip type stocks are good. Before the 21st you seem like a speculative investor, afterwards you are more value-oriented – more conservative and more risk-averse.

If you are buying big-ticket items, it seems best to wait until the 21st as the financial planet moves into conservative Capricorn. This might be difficult for you because of the season we're in, but if possible you should. For sure you will be a better shopper (and investor) – get more value for your money – after the 21st than before.

Health is very delicate after the 21st. Yes, the social life and social obligations are powerful – but when the car is out of petrol, there's nothing to be done – you have to fill the tank. Some 60 per cent of the planets arrayed in stressful aspect is not something to take lightly. If you feel tired, make a polite excuse and go rest. Have more massages or chiropractic treatments. Delegate tasks wherever possible. Try to work with a rhythm – alternate your activities. Happily, you probably took steps in previous months to ease things now.

Leo

♌

Personality Profile

LEO AT A GLANCE

Element – Fire

Ruling Planet – Sun
   Career Planet – Venus
   Love Planet – Uranus
   Money Planet – Mercury
   Planet of Health and Work – Saturn
   Planet of Home and Family Life – Pluto

Colours – gold, orange, red

Colours that promote love, romance and social harmony – black, indigo, ultramarine blue

Colours that promote earning power – yellow, yellow-orange

Gems – amber, chrysolite, yellow diamond

Metal – gold

Scents – bergamot, frankincense, musk, neroli

Quality – fixed (= stability)

Quality most needed for balance – humility

Strongest virtues – leadership ability, self-esteem and confidence, generosity, creativity, love of joy

Deepest needs – fun, elation, the need to shine

Characteristics to avoid – arrogance, vanity, bossiness

Signs of greatest overall compatibility – Aries, Sagittarius

Signs of greatest overall incompatibility – Taurus, Scorpio, Aquarius

Sign most helpful to career – Taurus

Sign most helpful for emotional support – Scorpio

Sign most helpful financially – Virgo

Sign best for marriage and/or partnerships – Aquarius

Sign most helpful for creative projects – Sagittarius

Best Sign to have fun with – Sagittarius

Signs most helpful in spiritual matters – Aries, Cancer

Best day of the week – Sunday

Understanding a Leo

When you think of Leo, think of royalty – then you'll get the idea of what the Leo character is all about and why Leos are the way they are. It is true that, for various reasons, some Leo-born do not always express this quality – but even if not they should like to do so.

A monarch rules not by example (as does Aries) nor by consensus (as do Capricorn and Aquarius) but by personal will. Will is law. Personal taste becomes the style that is imitated by all subjects. A monarch is somehow larger than life. This is how a Leo desires to be.

When you dispute the personal will of a Leo it is serious business. He or she takes it as a personal affront, an insult. Leos will let you know that their will carries authority and that to disobey is demeaning and disrespectful.

A Leo is king (or queen) of his or her personal domain. Subordinates, friends and family are the loyal and trusted subjects. Leos rule with benevolent grace and in the best interests of others. They have a powerful presence; indeed, they are powerful people. They seem to attract attention in any social gathering. They stand out because they are stars in their domain. Leos feel that, like the Sun, they are made to shine and rule. Leos feel that they were born to special privilege and royal prerogatives – and most of them attain this status, at least to some degree.

The Sun is the ruler of this Sign, and when you think of sunshine it is very difficult to feel unhealthy or depressed. Somehow the light of the Sun is the very antithesis of illness and apathy. Leos love life. They also love to have fun; they love drama, music, the theatre and amusements of all sorts. These are the things that give joy to life. If – even in their best interests – you try to deprive Leos of their pleasures, good food, drink and entertainment, you run the serious risk of depriving them of the will to live. To them life without joy is no life at all.

Leos epitomize humanity's will to power. But power in and of itself – regardless of what some people say – is neither good nor evil. Only when power is abused does it become evil. Without power even good things cannot come to pass. Leos realize this and are uniquely qualified to wield power. Of all the Signs, they do it most naturally. Capricorn, the other power Sign of the Zodiac, is a better manager and administrator than Leo – much better. But Leo outshines Capricorn in personal grace and presence. Leo loves power, where Capricorn assumes power out of a sense of duty.

Finance

Leos are great leaders but not necessarily good managers. They are better at handling the overall picture than the nitty-gritty details of business. If they have good managers working for them they can become exceptional executives. They have vision and a lot of creativity.

Leos love wealth for the pleasures it can bring. They love an opulent lifestyle, pomp and glamour. Even when they are not wealthy they live as if they are. This is why many fall into debt, from which it is sometimes difficult to emerge.

Leos, like Pisceans, are generous to a fault. Very often they want to acquire wealth solely so that they can help others economically. Wealth to Leo buys services and managerial ability. It creates jobs for others and improves the general well-being of those around them. Therefore – to a Leo – wealth is good. Wealth is to be enjoyed to the fullest. Money is not to be left to gather dust in a mouldy bank vault but to be enjoyed, spread around, used. So Leos can be quite reckless in their spending.

With the Sign of Virgo on Leo's 2nd House (of Money) cusp, Leo needs to develop some of Virgo's traits of analysis, discrimination and purity when it comes to money matters. They must learn to be more careful with the details of finance (or to hire people to do this for them). They have to be more cost-conscious in their spending habits. Generally, they need to manage their money better. Leos tend to chafe under financial constraints, yet these constraints can help Leos to reach their highest financial potential.

Leos like it when their friends and family know that they can depend on them for financial support. They do not mind – even enjoy – lending money, but they are careful that they are not taken advantage of. From their 'regal throne' Leos like to bestow gifts upon their family and friends and then enjoy the good feelings these gifts bring to everybody. Leos love financial speculations and – when the celestial influences are right – are often lucky.

Career and Public Image

Leos like to be perceived as wealthy, for in today's world wealth often equals power. When they attain wealth they love having a large house with lots of land and animals.

At their jobs Leos excel in positions of authority and power. They are good at making decisions – on a grand level – but they prefer to leave the details to others. Leos are well respected by their colleagues and subordinates, mainly because they have a knack for understanding and relating to those around them. Leos usually strive for the top positions even if they have to start at the bottom and work hard to get there. As might be expected of such a charismatic Sign, Leos are always trying to improve their work situation. They do so in order to have a better chance of advancing to the top.

On the other hand, Leos do not like to be bossed around or told what to do. Perhaps this is why they aspire so for the top – where they can be the decision-makers and need not take orders from others.

Leos never doubt their success and focus all their attention and efforts on achieving it. Another great Leo characteristic is that – just like good monarchs – they do not attempt to abuse the power or success they achieve. If they do so this is not wilful or intentional. Usually they like to share their wealth and try to make everyone around them join in their success.

Leos are – and like to be perceived as – hard-working, well-established individuals. It is definitely true that they are capable of hard work and often manage great things.

But do not forget that, deep down inside, Leos really are fun-lovers.

Love and Relationships

Generally, Leos are not the marrying kind. To them relationships are good while they are pleasurable. When the relationship ceases to be pleasurable a true Leo will want out. They always want to have the freedom to leave. That is why Leos excel at love affairs rather than commitment. Once married, however, Leo is faithful – even if some Leos have a tendency to marry more than once in their lifetime. If you are in love with a Leo, just show him or her a good time. Travel, go to casinos and clubs, the theatre and discos. Wine and dine your Leo love – it is expensive but worth it and you will have fun.

Leos generally have an active love life and are demonstrative in their affections. They love to be with other optimistic and fun-loving types like themselves, but wind up settling with someone more serious, intellectual and unconventional. The partner of a Leo tends to be more political and socially conscious than he or she is, and more libertarian. When you marry a Leo, mastering the freedom-loving tendencies of your partner will definitely become a life-long challenge – and be careful that Leo does not master you.

Aquarius sits on Leo's 7th House (of Love) cusp. Thus if Leos want to realize their highest love and social potential they need to develop a more egalitarian, Aquarian perspective on others. This is not easy for Leo, for 'the king' finds his equals only among other 'kings'. But perhaps this is the solution to Leo's social challenge – to be 'a king among kings'. It is all right to be royal, but recognize the nobility in others.

Home and Domestic Life

Although Leos are great entertainers and love having people over, sometimes this is all show. Only very few close friends will get to see the real side of a Leo's day-to-day life. To a Leo the home is a place of comfort, recreation and transformation; a secret, private retreat – a castle. Leos like to spend money, show off a bit, entertain and have fun. They enjoy the latest furnishings, clothes and gadgets – all things fit for kings.

Leos are fiercely loyal to their family and of course expect the same from them. They love their children almost to a fault; they have to be careful not to spoil them too much. They also must try to avoid attempting to make individual family members over in their own image. Leos should keep in mind that others also have the need to be their own people. That is why Leos have to be extra careful about being over-bossy or over-domineering in the home.

Horoscope for 2008

Major Trends

Though the early part of last year might have been challenging – especially in the area of self-esteem – 2007 should have ended as a fun kind of year. You learned how to enjoy yourself – enjoy life – in spite of physical challenges. This year, you seem more serious – more work-oriented and health-oriented. Of course Leo will never be in danger of being completely serious – but more serious than usual.

The challenge in the year ahead is to inject joy into your work – to make the humdrum tasks of everyday living into something enjoyable. More on this later.

The job situation (for those of you who are job-seekers) is very bright. There are dream jobs out there waiting for you.

Love has been important and unstable for many years, and the trend continues in 2008. It is certainly enjoyable, but filled with sudden and abrupt changes. More on this later.

Finance started to become important late last year and is still important in the year ahead. The main lesson this year is financial discipline. More on this later on.

Last year was sexually active, and the trend continues in the year ahead. Even older Leos have a stronger libido than usual.

Your most important areas of interest this year are health, work, finance, love and romance, sex, personal transformation, occult studies, past lives, death and rebirth, estates and other people's money.

Your paths of greatest fulfilment in the year ahead are health, work and love.

Health

(Please note that this is an astrological perspective on health and not a medical one. For the medical perspective, please consult your doctor.)

Now that Saturn is out of your own Sign (late last year), health and vitality seem much improved. Not only that, but with your 6th House of Health very strong this year – two long-term planets are there – you are focused here – you are not ignoring things – you are into healthy lifestyles and disciplined health regimes. I consider this a good health signal.

Pluto is making a major move from your 5th House to your 6th House this year. He is not yet established in your House of Health, but will flirt between these two Houses this year. He enters your 6th House permanently on November 27, where he will stay for the next 20 or so years.

This has profound health implications. For some of you, it shows a tendency to surgery – to see surgery as the solution to health problems. But many of you will opt for detox regimes, which in many cases can accomplish the same thing. You will start to see that good health is not so much about adding things to the body, but merely about removing things that shouldn't be there.

Pluto's move into your House of Health will also make you aware of the importance of emotional health, domestic harmony, harmonious family relationships. Good health for you is going to be more than just about how many miles you can run or bike, or how many pounds you can bench-press. It is more than just 'no physical symptoms' – it is also about feeling good emotionally – being in emotional harmony – being in a good mood. If health problems arise, this will be an area to check out and restore to harmony. (Pluto is the ruler of your 4th House, which rules these things.)

Pluto, generically, rules the sexual organs. So good health also means a healthy sex life. It also shows that safe sex is more important than usual. Now, Leo is perhaps (next to Scorpio) the sexiest Sign in the Zodiac. Sexual moderation is not easy here. But if you listen to your body, be aware, you will know when you've had enough. The abuse of the sex force can be a spiritual root-cause of problems now.

Pluto also rules the colon and bladder, so these organs are important this year and for many years to come.

Saturn is your health planet. In the physical body, Saturn rules the spine, knees, teeth, bone structure, gall bladder and overall skeletal alignment. These are always important – in any year. But this year, Saturn is in the Sign of Virgo, so the small intestine is also important. It needs more attention than usual.

This year Jupiter is in your House of Health, too. In the physical body, Jupiter rules the liver and thighs – and these organs, too, become important in overall health.

Regular back and thigh massage will be excellent this year. And there are many, many natural therapies that will strengthen all the areas mentioned above. But if you like you can work with our foot reflexology chart (opposite).

Jupiter rules your 5th House of Fun, Creativity and Children. This gives us many other health messages. You are concerned about the health of children – perhaps more than

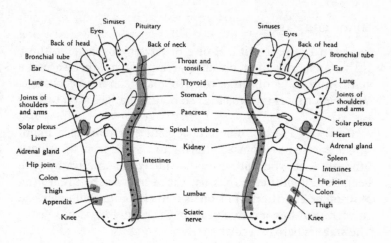

Reflexology
Try to massage the whole foot on a regular basis, but pay extra attention to
the points highlighted on the chart. When you massage, be aware of 'sore
spots', as these need special attention. It's also a good idea to massage the
ankles and top side (as well as the soles) of the feet.

your own health. A creative hobby – something you do for
the sheer fun of it – will be especially therapeutic this year.
Joy itself (something you already know about, but we're just
reminding you) is a great healing force. If you feel under the
weather, go out and have some fun. A night out on the town
will often do you as much good as a visit to a health professional. Laugh a lot and avoid depression like the plague.
Lack of joy can be another spiritual root-cause of health
problems.

Your ideas of health are becoming much more 'holistic'
than usual. Your health attitudes are broadening.

In general I expect health to be good; the above-
mentioned therapies are merely ways to make it even better.

Home and Family

Your 4th House is not a House of Power this year, so there isn't much emphasis on this area. Usually this shows a status-quo kind of situation. No major, dramatic change. You seem content in this area so major changes aren't called for.

However, Pluto (your family planet) is making a major move this year – from Sagittarius to Capricorn – from your 5th House to your 6th House. And while this transit will become established towards the end of the year (on November 27), there are signals of major change happening. It might not happen this year, but certainly in future years. The stage is being set for it now.

For many years you have been trying to make your home as much a 'place of entertainment' – a playground – as a home. By now you have succeeded. Most of you don't need to go out to have a good time – your house is filled with toys, sporting equipment, sports facilities, home theatres and games. But now you want to make the home more like a 'health spa'. It is going to be a place of healing and not just entertainment. So you will start installing exercise equipment and all sorts of health gadgets at home. You will probably be doing more work to clear up unhealthy factors – lead paint, asbestos and other things that could be involved in the construction. You will install air-purifiers and ozone machines. Some will install saunas and whirlpools. By the time you are finished you won't need to go out for exercise or to an outside health spa – everything will be right at home.

The second trend that we see is making the home more of a workplace. Many of you will be setting up home offices and doing more work from home. The home is not just a playground anymore, it is a place of work.

These trends won't happen immediately, but over many years. But the first stirrings are happening now.

The health of a parent or parent figure seems a concern this year, and perhaps this is the reason for the shift. This person might have special needs that need equipment to be installed in the home.

In the past, family conflicts or disputes could be settled by having fun, having a party, and through financial means. Now, good communication seems important. There needs to be a unity of thought within the family. Lacking that, there needs to be at least a good understanding of everyone's position. This won't be done through a party or more spending. You need to talk things out. Family unity can be fostered by attending classes or lectures as a family unit. The education of family members (not just children) seems a focus now.

If you are planning major construction or renovation of the home, October 4 to November 22 is a good time. If you are planning to redecorate or beautify the home – in cosmetic types of ways – September 24 to October 18 is a good time.

Finance and Career

Your 2nd House of Finance is an important House of Power this year – a major focus in the year ahead.

If you have been irresponsible in your financial life – living above your means, borrowing frivolously, not being honest in your financial dealings – this could be a very traumatic transit. Saturn abhors these kinds of things. His spiritual function is to set things in 'right order', and to get things in order he will create some crises. You are confronted with the consequences of your irresponsibility and the bill falls due – no way to avoid it. Once these things are taken care of, Saturn will rebuild your financial life on more firm and solid footing. His desire is to give you long-term and enduring wealth, but the obstacles to it have to be removed. New financial attitudes will have to be developed.

However, if you have been responsible in your financial life, you have nothing to fear from this transit. It will only make you richer. Many people achieve their greatest successes under a Saturn transit. But they earn it.

In general Leos are not dishonest. Their problem in finance is overspending. Life is to be enjoyed, and that always comes first. Rarely do they 'save for a rainy day'. So reining in the spending is going to be the challenge. Don't deprive yourself or punish yourself. Set up a budget that allows for 'having fun' – but keep these expenditures in proportion. Now is not the time to be dramatic in money matters – to make grand statements – to buy things you can't afford in order to show off.

Leos are grand speculators. I'd wager that if you took a poll of places like Las Vegas, Monte Carlo or Atlantic City, you would find a huge – disproportionate – percentage of Leos there. But this is not the year for that. (Last year was much better than this year.) This is a year for earning the 'hard way' – through work. The good news is that there are great jobs available – dream jobs – and this is a good financial signal.

Those of you who employ others will expand your workforce. But still the earnings are coming from work – either your work or the work of your employees. It is not a year for winning the lottery.

As investments, property (commercial), blue-chip type stocks, and the health care industry look very attractive. (These are interesting as business ventures, too.) This is a year where 'value investing' rather than momentum-type investing is called for.

In general (and this is another problem for the Leo mentality) there needs to be a long-term outlook on wealth. Avoid the seemingly quick money this year – quick money might not be as quick as you think. Build wealth over time, in evolutionary ways.

Sometimes a person prospers by expanding the income and sometimes by reducing waste – cutting costs. The latter road is better this year. Buy what you need, of course – Saturn is not trying to make you suffer – but avoid what you don't need. This is a year for breaking 'spending addictions'.

Your most prosperous periods (overall) this year will be August 6 to September 22.

With Mercury as your financial planet money, comes to you in a variety of ways and means. Mercury is a fast-moving planet – in a given month he can sometimes move through three Signs and Houses. So we will cover these short-term trends in the monthly reports.

Love and Social Life

This has been an important area of life for many years now. You are into one of the most exciting social periods of your entire life – especially for single Leos. Love can happen at any time – out of the blue – when you least expect it. It comes in shocking and sudden ways. It is always a love-at-first-sight kind of thing – like we see in the movies. It's like being hit by a bolt of lightning. Very magical. But alas, we can't live our lives – read a book, study, or function – by the brief but brilliant flash from lightning. Yes, this light is dramatic – but not long lasting. And this is how love has been. Dazzlingly brilliant for a time, and then a fade-out. But you still seem willing to undergo all, just to experience those few moments of brilliance. The fade-outs are soon forgotten, and you await the next flash.

Every flash reveals your ideal, until a new flash comes. Will this flash be 'the one'?

Many people enjoy this kind of love life. There is little commitment. Everything is now. The quest is everything – attainment is anti-climactic.

Marriage doesn't seem to be in the stars right now. If some of you have married in the past few years, the marriage is being tested. Even long-established marriages are being tested, and only the really strong ones will survive. Single Leos seem better off enjoying their freedom, enjoying serial-type love affairs than marrying – even though the opportunities are plentiful.

Marriage could work – but it would take effort on both sides. There would need to be a maximum of freedom on both sides. Both parties would have to get very creative – to create variety, change and experimentation – within the marriage. It is hard, but it could be done.

Marriages are being tested in other ways this year, too. There are two eclipses in your 7th House of Love and Marriage this year – a Solar Eclipse on February 7 and a Lunar Eclipse on August 16. When you consider that volatile Uranus is your love planet – love will have to be very strong to survive all this.

Everything we said refers to singles and to those in their first marriage. If you are in your second marriage, you are likely to remain married – the stresses are not severe. Those looking to marry for the second time need patience.

Those in or working towards their third marriage have a status-quo year.

Singles are allured most by the sexual chemistry and sexual performance of their partner. This, though important, is not enough to build a long-term relationship. Even the best sexual chemistry (if there is nothing else) has a life span of six to eight months. Spirituality seems important, too. If there is a good spiritual connection – a basic spiritual compatibility – the relationship can last a lot longer. But take care not to confuse lust with a spiritual connection. One feels a spiritual connection in different ways. We feel sexual chemistry in the body – usually in the belly or sexual organs – but a spiritual connection comes from 'over the head'.

There is a lot of experimentation going on in love and sexual matters. Nothing wrong with that *per se* – we often attain deeper knowledge through these means. But the experimentation should be kept legal and constructive.

Your love and social life will be active all year, but especially from January 20 to March 20.

Self-improvement

Your spiritual mission is ruled by Venus in your chart. And she is a fast-moving planet. Thus your mission involves other people, partners, teaching and education – but it will be expressed in various ways as the year progresses. We will deal with this in the monthly reports.

We discussed Saturn's move through your Money House in the financial section. But there's more to be said. And since this is a major area to be improved this year, we will discuss it now. When we talk of budgets, living within one's income, cutting costs and being creative about cost-cutting, we are not talking 'lack' – we are not advocating that you start thinking 'lack'. Saturn is not about lack or deprivation. Our lives should be beautiful. And this includes the financial life. Beauty is about 'right proportion'. So the person who spends more than he earns is creating ugliness and discord in his financial life. Likewise the person who under-spends – who deprives himself of good things even though he can afford them – this too is out of proportion – ugly. These behaviours create pictures in the psychic worlds, and clairvoyants can see them. Never mind the material consequences of these actions – on a spiritual level there is an increase of ugliness on the planet.

Even good things – like charitable giving – needs to be kept in the right proportion or that too will turn ugly and have negative consequences.

Saturn knows that wealth is unlimited and that every person has access to unlimited spiritual wealth. But at any given time the universe has supplied X amount for use – and that X amount should be used proportionately and beautifully.

A financial life that is inwardly beautiful will be a prosperous financial life. It will attract all the helpful forces of the universe to it.

Month-by-month Forecasts

January

Best Days Overall: 5, 6, 14, 15, 22, 23
Most Stressful Days Overall: 2, 3, 9, 10, 16, 17, 29, 30, 31
Best Days for Love: 2, 3, 5, 6, 9, 10, 12, 13, 14, 15, 20, 21, 23, 29, 30
Best Days for Money: 7, 9, 16, 18, 19, 24, 25, 26, 27, 28

The month begins with most of the planets below the horizon of the Horoscope – but this is short lived. By the end of the month the planets start to shift to the upper half of the Horoscope and, by next month, the upper half will be stronger than the lower half. So, the night cycle of your year is just about ending – symbolically speaking, it is dawn. The activities and methods of day will soon become more important than your 'night' activities. The outer life – career – will start to be important. In the meantime continue to focus on your emotional harmony, your family and being in the right state.

Your 6th House of Work is very powerful this month – it is the dominant interest for most of the month. This is very good news for job-seekers or those who employ others. Both jobs and workers are plentiful – and good. If you need cash, second jobs or overtime opportunities are plentiful.

You are all more productive workers, and in this chart it is hard to tell the difference between your work and your leisure and fun – they are so intertwined here. Work seems enjoyable – there are parties and gatherings at work. Many social opportunities. There is joy there – a good spirit.

Love is also important and happy this month. On the 20th the Sun enters your 7th House of Love, initiating a yearly social peak. You are personally very popular these days. You go out of your way for others – you put their interests ahead of your own – and others notice this. (Most of the planets – 70 to 80 per cent – are in the social, Western sector this month – and this adds to your popularity. You seem to be doing a good job in cultivating your social skills and graces.) You are socially confident and aggressive – not afraid to take risks – no fear of rejection. If you like someone, you let them know – you're not playing coy or hard to get. You are making social events happen, not waiting around for the phone to ring. Your tastes in love centre on physical attraction and sexual chemistry. But spirituality and creativity are also alluring. Wealth is not objectionable, either.

Finances are strong this month. In general, for this year, you are more conservative in your finances (very unlike you – but this is the kind of cycle you're into now). This month – and especially until the 8th – you are even more conservative. So, if you're buying big-ticket items, try to do it before the 8th – probably you will get a better deal – get more value for your money.

Overall health is good right now, but it won't hurt to rest and relax more after the 20th. Overall energy is not up to its usual standards then. Happily you are very health-conscious all month and are doing what needs to be done. You can enhance your health even more by paying attention to the heart, the spine, knees, teeth, bones and skeletal alignment. More sexual moderation (neither too much nor too little) will help after the 27th.

February

Best Days Overall: 1, 2, 10, 11, 19, 20, 28, 29
Most Stressful Days Overall: 6, 7, 12, 13, 26, 27
Best Days for Love: 3, 4, 6, 7, 8, 9, 13, 14, 17, 23, 26, 27
Best Days for Money: 3, 4, 6, 7, 12, 13, 14, 15, 21, 22, 23, 24

Two eclipses this month ensure that events will be dramatic – both personally and in the world at large.

The Solar Eclipse of the 7th (6th in the US) occurs in your 7th House of Love (which, by the way, is a dominant interest this month). This will test your marriage (if you are married) or current relationship. Either the current relationship will move forward or it dissolves – you can't sit on the fence anymore. Friendships will also get tested. The good relationships will survive and thrive – it is only the flawed ones that are in danger.

Every Solar Eclipse affects your image, personality and self-concept. There is nothing like a love or relationship issue for getting a person to upgrade and refine their image and personality. The only question for you is whether you will do this on your own – get a clear idea of who you are – or let others define you – and that isn't so pleasant. This eclipse also impacts on Mercury, your financial planet – bringing dramatic changes to your financial life – forcing you to make changes that long needed to be made. The disruptive events of the eclipse are not intended to punish you, only to make you aware of your financial vulnerabilities – this way you can correct them.

The Lunar Eclipse of the 21st (the 20th in the US) also affects finances. It occurs in your Money House. Anything that you didn't take care of during the previous eclipse will get taken care of now. These kinds of eclipses show all kinds of financial changes – people change their banks, brokers, accountants, financial planners, investments, investment managers, etc. In the end these changes are good. But they take up a lot of your time and energy. Every Lunar Eclipse affects the spiritual life – as the Moon is your spiritual planet. Your dream life will be hyperactive (and you shouldn't pay too much attention to it during this period – dreams now are merely reflecting the psychic flotsam and jetsam brought up by the eclipse). Many will change their spiritual regime and practice – try out new techniques, teachers or even teachings. There are shakeups in a spiritual or charitable organization that you belong to.

Once the dust settles from the eclipse your social life will return to normal – and will probably be better than it was before. Your yearly social peak is still very much intact.

On the 19th, as the Sun moves into your 8th House, you are more sexually active than usual (and that's saying something) – even older Leos will have a stronger libido than usual. As long as you don't overdo things, this is OK – if you overdo it, health (which still needs watching this month) can be affected.

The 19th onwards is excellent for detox (which will also enhance health) and for losing weight – if you need to. This is a time to get rid of all the 'effete' and useless material from your life – whether financial, possessions, mental and emotional patterns and the like. Clean house on all levels. Reduce the clutter on all levels. Allow space for the new and better that wants to come into your life.

March

Best Days Overall: 9, 17, 18, 27, 28
Most Stressful Days Overall: 4, 5, 11, 24, 25, 31
Best Days for Love: 4, 5, 6, 7, 15, 16, 24, 25, 31
Best Days for Money: 2, 3, 4, 5, 11, 14, 15, 19, 20, 24, 25, 29, 30

Most of the planets are above the horizon, so focus more on your career and de-emphasize home and family issues. You can enhance your career through social means – attending or hosting the right kinds of parties, through attracting the right kinds of friends who can help you, and through good communication and marketing. There seems to be some dramatic changes in your industry or corporate hierarchy after the 13th (on the 28th–29th something dramatic happens – you could be offered something new as well). Your spiritual mission this month involves your spouse, lover and other people – to be there for them. After the 13th it is about exploring past lives, life after death and occult studies. These things also clarify many career issues. Career can also be enhanced by focusing on the financial interests of the shareholders, ahead of your own. This will impress superiors. Have no fear, if you do this properly your own prosperity will come very naturally. No force in the universe can stop it.

We see job changes – instability at work – changes in the workplace and working conditions – in other ways, too. Saturn, your work planet starts to cross an eclipse point (the February 21 Lunar Eclipse) on the 30th and 31st. Those who employ others can experience employee turnover then.

Finances are good this month. Your financial planet is in its most 'exalted' position until the 15th. A business partnership or joint venture can manifest – and there are increased earnings in an existing partnership. Your spouse will be more generous all month – he or she is doing very well – and you seem personally involved in it. You're doing a good job of eliminating waste and excess expenses – plugging the 'leaks' in your financial body.

Professional investors should look at computers, high-tech industries, aeronautics and the beauty industry until the 15th. After the 15th, bonds, oil, natural gas, shipping and for-profit hospitals or retirement homes look interesting. After the 20th you are much more of a risk-taker – even more than usual – and you need to be careful. Speculations are not so favourable. Many of you won't be able to help yourself (the Sun in Aries is like being on a drug), so speculate with only a small percentage of your assets – allocate a certain amount and don't go over it.

Financial intuition is very strong until the 15th – and you can trust it. After the 15th it will be good to venture more deeply into the spiritual laws of wealth. This will bring you deeper and longer-lasting benefits.

Love is happy this month. There are many love opportunities for singles – in weird and wild ways – as described in the yearly report. A very important romantic meeting (and probably this applies more to singles than to marrieds) happens on the 8th–9th. This will be a sudden thing – unexpected – an out-of-the-blue experience. For marrieds or those involved in serious relationships, this can produce a sudden and dramatic social opportunity – an unexpected social invitation or party. An opportunity for a business partnership can also happen then.

April

Best Days Overall: 5, 6, 13, 14, 23, 24
Most Stressful Days Overall: 1, 2, 7, 8, 20, 21, 22, 28, 29
Best Days for Love: 1, 2, 3, 4, 11, 12, 13, 14, 21, 22, 24,
   28, 29, 30
Best Days for Money: 5, 6, 7, 8, 14, 15, 16, 17, 25, 26, 27

Your social life is not as active as it has been for the past few
months – perhaps this is a good thing, too – no one can
maintain that kind of pace for too long. The cosmos, in its
wisdom, gently shifts our attention to other things.

This month (and it really began last month on the 20th)
your 9th House of Religion, Higher Education, Philosophy,
Metaphysics and Foreign Travel is very powerful. A dominant interest that even rivals love. When the 9th House is
strong, people prefer a deep philosophical discussion to a
night out on the town. There are happy travel and educational opportunities now. Legal issues (if you are involved
in them) are favourable. Students hear good news from
colleges and universities. There is religious revelation available to those of you who want it. In general your mental
horizons are greatly expanded this month.

Health, too, is very good. Energy is abundant. Spring
fever is upon you with great force. Enjoy. With energy –
especially if it is directed properly – there is success. Also,
things that were not open to us when energy was low are
now suddenly available – doable – workable – reachable. If
you want to enhance your health even more, review our
discussion on this in the yearly report. After the 19th try and
rest and relax more (it won't be easy with your career so
busy, but you can try.) There is nothing serious amiss, only
energy is not what it was before the 19th.

The spiritual dimensions of wealth were important to
you last month, and this trend continues. This is another
month for going more deeply into these things. Your philosophy, your belief systems, your view of life have a great
effect on your finances (this is always true, but especially

and dramatically so this month). So if you can correct or enlarge these things (and you seem to be doing it) there is great prosperity. Like last month, you seem to be overly rash and speculative. You are an impulse-buyer, spender and investor. When intuition is on, you are very successful, but if intuition is off, you can get hurt. Be bold in financial matters when necessary – if you've thought something true, take direct and bold action – but avoid haste and impulsiveness. The urge this month is for financial independence. You don't want to be beholden to your spouse, partner or some outside authority. You want to be in charge of your own financial destiny. This is wonderful, but keep in mind that these things don't generally happen overnight. Take a long-range perspective on this. Finances become more conservative after the 18th. If you have to buy big-ticket items, do it after the 18th rather than before – you will get more value for your money. (There is speculative success or some important financial windfall on the 28th–29th.)

Career has been becoming ever more important for some months now. On the 19th, as the Sun crosses the Midheaven of your chart, you enter a yearly career peak. (Most of the planets are still above the horizon and your 10th House of Career is much stronger than your 4th House of Home and Family.) So, do right – succeed in the outer world – and you will feel right and serve your family better.

You are personally very elevated this month (your personal planet, the Sun, is the most 'elevated' in the Horoscope.) You are in charge, you are above everyone in your family and in your world. You are honoured, appreciated, acknowledged. You are the King on his throne (the way things are supposed to be). Probably this will lead to pay rises and promotions. This could be in your company or your industry or community. (Politics seems unusually interesting for you this month – and probably you are more politically involved than usual.)

May

  Best Days Overall: 2, 3, 11, 12, 20, 21, 30, 31
  Most Stressful Days Overall: 4, 5, 18, 19, 25, 26
  Best Days for Love: 1, 4, 5, 8, 9, 13, 14, 18, 19, 24, 25, 26,
    28, 29
  Best Days for Money: 4, 5, 6, 13, 14, 15, 16, 23, 24, 25,
    26

Your yearly career peak is still in full swing and the trends discussed last month are still in effect. Career is not only important from a worldly, financial or personal perspective – it seems to be your actual mission for the month. This is what Spirit wants from you now. Your commitment here is another factor in your success. It's as if a 'higher power' is just moving you around, and your moves are successful. The more you succeed, the more 'IT' becomes glorified.

After the 24th your spiritual mission seems to involve friends, groups and organizations. You need to be there for them – help them in some way – get involved more.

Last month (before the 18th) you were pretty reckless financially – and when a Leo gets reckless, it's really reckless. But happily, with your financial planet now in stable and conservative Taurus, you are more conservative. More careful both in spending and investing. There is something to be said about the 'safe and boring' financial life – which is the way I'd describe things now. There are no financial shocks, downswings or unhappy surprises. It's like life in a small town – boring, safe, predictable. Yet your conservatism brings you luck. Your speculative judgement now is far better than it was last month. Your financial planet will move out of Taurus on the 3rd and into Gemini. But still, conservative, safe and boring activity is still in effect until the 20th (50 to 60 per cent of the planets will be in Earth Signs). This is a good period (before the 20th) to make big-ticket purchases or investments. Your judgement is good, and you will get value for your money.

Love is happy until the 20th – it seems idyllic. This is not to say that there are NO problems – only that the easy things, the happy things seem more numerous than the problems. Your spouse, partner or current love seems supportive of the career. Your elevation brings honour to him or her as well. But after the 20th there are more challenges. Perhaps your involvement with friends is a problem – your lover or spouse feels 'second class'. For singles this transit shows that the focus on friendships and groups tends to distract from romance. Friendship seems more important than passion. There could also be some financial disagreements with your spouse or lover. These are short-term – not fundamental – problems. Perhaps they can't be solved immediately, but in coming months they will be.

Health still needs watching until the 20th. Review our discussion of last month.

This month Mars moves into your Sign (on the 9th). This increases energy levels – but can make you more of a risk-taker with your body. You excel at exercise and sport now. All of you will be more active and athletic than usual. Mind your temper now.

June

Best Days Overall: 7, 8, 16, 17, 18, 26, 27
Most Stressful Days Overall: 1, 2, 14, 15, 21, 22, 23, 28, 29
Best Days for Love: 3, 4, 5, 6, 14, 15, 21, 22, 23, 24, 25
Best Days for Money: 1, 2, 3, 4, 9, 10, 11, 12, 19, 20, 21, 22, 28, 29, 30

If there is any condition in your life that needs changing or transforming, this is the month to do it. Last month, towards the end, the planetary power shifted to the East from the West. Mars entered your own Sign. You are more independent now than you have been for months. So now is the time to have things your way. You have the power – you have the backing of the whole universe. This doesn't mean

that you get disrespectful to others or run roughshod over
them (with Mars in your Sign you need to be careful about
this – you don't know your own strength), only that you
know best what is right for you and what makes you happy
– and you have no need to compromise about these things.
If others don't go along with you, you can go it alone. You
have less of a need for others these days.

Some 40 per cent of the planets are Retrograde this
month – the pace of life is slowing down – but that is on a
world level. For you personally (with the exception of love)
there is rapid progress.

Your financial planet is Retrograde until the 19th (it
began to Retrograde on the 26th of last month) so do more
homework before making important purchases or financial
decisions. In fact, this period is best for reviewing your
finances – your products and services – to see where you can
improve things. Do a thorough financial analysis. Then,
when Mercury goes forward on the 19th, you'll be ready to
act. Mercury's Retrograde won't stop earnings, only slow
things down. Sales, marketing and communication are
important financially – but you will have to take extra care
when doing these things – take nothing for granted – spell
everything out – make sure you understand the other
person and that they understand you. Friends, groups and
organizations are important in finances now. Marketing to
groups or organizations seems good (better after the 19th
than before). Since your spiritual mission involves friends
(until the 18th) it seems to me that you will be more generous with them and financially helpful – your job is to be
there for them personally AND financially (to the best of
your ability).

Spirituality becomes very important after the 18th. Your
spiritual mission involves this. There is much that can be
written here, but it is beyond our scope. The highlights
include getting involved in some spiritual group (more
involved than usual) and with charitable organizations. Your
inner spiritual growth is most important now, too. For the
more you understand, the more you will be able to function

properly in the outer world. On a deeper level, spiritual growth is good for its own sake – it need have no 'practical value' as we understand it.

Health is much improved this month, and the trend gets better day by day.

July

Best Days Overall: 4, 5, 14, 15, 23, 24
Most Stressful Days Overall: 11, 12, 19, 20, 26
Best Days for Love: 2, 3, 11, 12, 13, 19, 20, 21, 22, 24, 30
Best Days for Money: 1, 6, 7, 10, 16, 17, 22, 26

Retrograde activity is still strong this month (the strongest period of the year) and there are many planets in your own Sign of Leo – a good month for a holiday. Not much happening in the world, and so you may as well have more fun.

Your personal independence is at its maximum in the month ahead (and next month, too) so this is a time to have life on your own terms and create the conditions of life the way you want them to be. Now it is easy to do these things – later on in the year it won't be so easy and you'll just have to adapt.

On the 22nd you enter one of your yearly personal pleasure peaks – something every Leo looks forward to – and uses to advantage. (The whole life is a personal pleasure peak – so these real peaks are even more special.)

This is also a good career month. Even though the planetary power shifts to below the horizon and it's time for you to get your family and emotional life in order – there are career opportunities – and happy ones – seeking you out. You are not pursuing them, they are pursuing you – especially after the 12th. But you can be more choosy now – and you don't want anything that will unduly disturb your family or overall emotional harmony. You can further your career by getting involved in charities and altruistic causes until the 12th. Watch your dream life then, too – there are career messages for you.

Your spiritual mission this month is spirituality – good for its own sake – and getting the body – the instrument of the spirit – in the right shape. Without the body, all the loftiest ideals will remain 'abstract' and 'unmanifest' – so take care of it. Enjoy all the sensual delights that are coming to you, but no need to overdo things.

Spirituality is good for other reasons, too – especially before the 22nd. With your birthday coming up – your personal New Year – the beginning of a whole new yearly cycle – it is good to spend more time alone – reviewing the past year objectively. See where you've succeeded, where you've failed, and where more work needs to be done. Correct the errors of the past, make your new year resolutions, and begin your year with a fresh slate. (Those of you born later in the Sign – who have their birthdays next month – still have time to do this all month.)

Family is starting to become more important, but with your family planet still Retrograde (it has been Retrograde for many months), avoid making major investments in the home or important family decisions. This is a time for review and analysis – a time for studying what can and can't be improved. Action can come later. Now is a time for getting mentally clear. Family unity is enhanced through having fun together as a family – through leisure activities.

Finances are strong and nice windfalls and opportunities are coming to you beginning the 26th. (You just need to show up.) Trust your intuition from the 10th to the 26th – it is sound and a short-cut to your goals.

Health is excellent.

August

Best Days Overall: 1, 2, 10, 11, 20, 28, 29

Most Stressful Days Overall: 7, 8, 9, 15, 16, 22, 23

Best Days for Love: 1, 2, 7, 8, 9, 15, 16, 17, 18, 21, 22, 23, 26, 27

Best Days for Money: 1, 2, 3, 4, 12, 13, 22, 23, 30, 31

There are two eclipses this month – one a Solar Eclipse on the 1st in your own Sign – this is a strong one – so take a reduced schedule. This will bring a redefinition of your image, personal appearance and self-concept. As you re-define your personality, you will think differently about yourself, and thus others will also think differently.

The second eclipse – a Lunar Eclipse on the 16th – occurs in your 7th House of Love and will test a marriage or serious relationship. Good to take a reduced schedule for this one, too.

Personal pleasure and finance (presumably to pay for these things) are the major focus this month. On the 22nd, you enter a yearly financial peak (actually you will feel it even before – beginning the 5th – but after the 22nd the prosperity is strongest). Financial windfalls and happy opportunities are still seeking you out until the 10th. You are spending on yourself now – investing in yourself – buying expensive personal items (but these can also come as gifts) and in general adopting an image of wealth. This image of wealth will attract all kinds of opportunities to you. Personal appearance seems more important on a financial level than usual. Money can come from pay rises, elders, parents and parent figures from the 5th onwards. In general these people are supportive of your financial goals and projects. If you're making important investments or purchases, you are better off doing them after the 10th when Mercury moves out of free-spending Leo and into Virgo. Before then you are apt to be too reckless – not care-ful enough. Afterwards, financial judgement will be sound. Speculations are favourable all month, but the 1st to the 10th is best. Professional investors have many, many oppor-tunities and industries to choose from – the problem is where to focus – sometimes too many opportunities are as bad as too few. Gaming, gold, energy, health, telecommu-nications, transport, military contractors, beauty and the beauty industry and blue chips all look interesting.

Job-seekers and those who employ others are all enjoying good fortune this month.

Serious love seems problematic this month. Both the planets involved with love are Retrograde. Not a time for serious love decisions. Also a current relationship could be moving backwards instead of forwards. (Your personal independence is one issue, but finance is also an issue here.) This is a time – whether you are single or married – to review your love life, relationships and marriage and see where things can be improved.

Singles are better off enjoying all the non-serious opportunities that are coming their way. Serious love might be on the back burner now, but you can still enjoy your life. You look great, magnetic and stylish – you have no problem attracting others.

Health is excellent this month.

September

Best Days Overall: 6, 7, 8, 16, 17, 24, 25
Most Stressful Days Overall: 4, 5, 11, 12, 18, 19
Best Days for Love: 1, 2, 4, 5, 11, 12, 14, 15, 21, 22, 23
Best Days for Money: 1, 2, 9, 10, 11, 12, 18, 19, 20, 21,
    27, 28, 29, 30

Most of the planets are below the horizon and your 4th House starts to get strong on the 24th. So this is a time to focus more on your internal life – your inner states, your moods, your feeling of emotional harmony – and your family life (these things are intimately related). From the right state, right mood and right feeling, career moves will be naturally successful. Also much better to work on the career by internal methods – visualizing, putting yourself 'in the mood' for success, setting goals, fantasizing and dreaming up the future. (These things are not enough to bring success – you will have to do the work to make these dreams come true – but that outer work will come later on – one thing at a time.)

In the meantime you can enhance your career through good marketing, communication and good use of the media until the 24th, and by working more from home – or through family connections – afterwards.

Your spiritual mission this month involves education – either learning or teaching (depending on what stage you are in life) and family. This is more than just being the 'good dad or mum' – it's the behest of a Higher Power.

Finances are still strong and your yearly financial peak continues until the 22nd. By then most goals are achieved and your interest shifts to other things – to education, intellectual interests and local travel.

You are still spending on and investing in yourself. You are taking a more personal interest in finance – not delegating these things to others. Thus you are more successful. Personal initiative and creativity are important this month.

Professional investors should continue to look at the health and beauty industries. Copper and sugar are interesting commodities to play.

Your financial planet goes Retrograde on the 24th, so try to wrap up important purchases, deals or investments before then.

Your family planet finally moves forward on the 9th – thus there is greater clarity (and better judgement) in this area. Family life can be improved through your personal attention – giving it priority in your life. Family members will feel – and feel deeply – if other things come before them. Doing social things together as a family, or entertaining from home, will also be good.

Health is good.

October

Best Days Overall: 4, 5, 13, 14, 22, 23, 31
Most Stressful Days Overall: 1, 2, 9, 10, 15, 16, 28, 29, 30
Best Days for Love: 1, 2, 9, 10, 11, 12, 19, 20, 21, 22, 23, 28, 29, 30
Best Days for Money: 6, 7, 9, 10, 15, 16, 17, 18, 24, 25, 26, 27

Your 4th House of Home and Family not only becomes powerful on the 23rd, but remains your actual spiritual mission for most of the month. This is the time to be there for family and children – to put your heart and soul into them. Also to get the home and the psychological state in order. (Curiously, as you do this you will find that your outer interests – career – are subtly enhanced. On the 4th Mars enters your 4th House – a wonderful period to make renovations or major repairs in the home (after the 15th is better than before – as Mercury goes direct on the 15th). This is also good for beautifying the home – buying art objects and the like (from the 15th to the 18th seems best for this).

Enhance family unity through education, attending religious services or courses as a family, family entertainments and leisure activities.

Aside from family, intellectual interests, communication and local travel are still important until the 23rd. Good to take courses in subjects that interest you, catch up on your reading – in general to give your mental body the nourishment and exercise it needs.

Spirituality seems unusually important from the 15th to the 23rd – your spiritual planet is the 'handle' of a 'bucket chart' during this period. This shows that it is through spirituality, spiritual discipline and understanding that you will be able to 'lift up' your whole life (the bucket).

Love seems easier than last month. But your two love planets are still Retrograde. Go slow and steady in love. Singles are meeting romantic interests this month (looks like in the neighbourhood, close to home) but shouldn't rush things. A current relationship is much improved.

Finances will get better after the 15th as Mercury goes forward. Financial judgement is much improved – and so is your confidence. Like last month, good marketing, media and communication skills are essential for profits. Professional investors should look at telecommunications, transport, media and the beauty industry. Keep trading to a minimum before the 15th.

Overall health is still good, but rest and relax more after the 23rd. Enhance health through maximizing energy and paying more attention to the heart, small intestine, liver and thighs.

November

Best Days Overall: 1, 10, 11, 18, 19, 27, 28
Most Stressful Days Overall: 5, 6, 12, 13, 25, 26
Best Days for Love: 1, 5, 6, 7, 8, 11, 12, 16, 17, 20, 21, 25, 26, 30
Best Days for Money: 2, 3, 4, 7, 12, 13, 16, 17, 20, 21, 25, 26, 30

Like last month your 4th House of Home and Family is a major House of Power, while your 10th House of Career is basically empty – only the Moon visits there temporarily on the 12th and 13th. Still a time to focus on home, family and domestic issues. This is still a good period for renovations and repairs – until the 16th. Family unity is enhanced through personal attention and focus – your physical presence at family gatherings and with family members, etc. – through educational and religious means (like last month) and through the expression of financial support.

Your financial planet moves into the 4th House on the 4th, so you are spending more on the home and family – and probably it is a good idea.

Finances look good this month. Mercury receives nice aspects from Jupiter and Uranus. This shows luck in speculations (the 16th and 17th seem very strong for that), good spousal support, and financial opportunities that come through friends, family and business partners. There is a joint venture or opportunity for a business partnership this month, too.

One of the problems with the financial planet in the 4th House is that you become moody when it comes to finances. You earn only when you're 'in the mood' – and if you're not in the mood, finances can go to pot. Also you need to be more careful of your mood when making investments or big purchases. Best to sleep on things until you feel at peace – then make your decision or purchases or investments.

Though finances are good, there are a few bumps on the road. Your financial planet re-stimulates eclipse points on the 10th–12th and the 18th–21st. This brings much-needed change to your financial thinking or strategy. We rarely make changes unless something dramatic happens, and this is the purpose.

Love, too, seems happy this month. First off, clarity is starting to come back on this subject – your love planet starts moving forward on the 27th. Also your personal planet is making fabulous aspects to your love planet until the 21st (but especially from the 9th to the 11th) – for singles, the unattached, this shows an important meeting – a meeting of someone special. For marrieds and those involved in relationships it shows a strong romantic period – a harmonious and loving period. Also there will be happy invitations to parties and things like that.

Students have some disruptions from the 6th to the 11th. They make important educational changes – perhaps a change of institutions or areas of study – or there is a dramatic shake-up at school. Teachers change, the administration changes, or the rules change. In the end these changes are for the good.

Health needs more watching until the 21st – refer to last month's discussion and the discussion in the yearly report. But health and energy improve dramatically on the 21st.

On the 21st you enter another yearly personal pleasure peak.

December

Best Days Overall: 7, 8, 15, 16, 24, 25, 26
Most Stressful Days Overall: 2, 3, 9, 10, 22, 23, 30, 31
Best Days for Love: 1, 2, 3, 5, 6, 11, 13, 14, 20, 21, 22, 23, 30, 31
Best Days for Money: 1, 7, 8, 9, 10, 17, 18, 27, 28

Most of the planets are still below the horizon, and though your 4th House of Home and Family is not strong this month, the focus should still be on home, family and psychological issues. Very soon now – in the next two months – the planetary power will shift. In the meantime keep your emotional batteries charged up.

There can be a major repair in the home from the 26th to the 30th. Students have more disruptions and changes in education. There is a power struggle in a religious organization you belong to. A legal issue reaches a climax.

You are still very much into a yearly personal pleasure peak. Enjoy. It would be nice if you could take a holiday now, but ALL – 100 per cent – of the planets are moving forward – and if you take off, you might miss out on a lot. Probably you will work hard and play hard – alternating between the two.

After the 21st you are in a serious work mode. The pace at work is hectic. Seldom have you worked this hard – yet it seems satisfying and happy. From a spiritual perspective, work is considered good for its own sake – not for the pay or material benefits. And this is something you are seeing first-hand right now. There is something ennobling about productive work – work that we love and can do well. The person who does an honest day's work has a healthy appetite and sleeps well at night. He or she might be working with the body, but the soul is at peace. They get more nourishment from their food – and nature herself ensures that they get the highest energies from her bounty.

Job-seekers have great success. Those who employ others have no shortage of workers. There is an expansion of the workforce now.

Health is good, yet you seem very focused on it this month. Part of the reason is vanity. When you are healthy (and into good health regimes) your physical appearance shines. There is a dramatic impact on the personal appearance. You seem into exercise and sport, too. With health, exercise and sport – as with anything else – the danger is in overdoing a good thing.

Love also seems very happy. The love planet is moving forward (both of them are) and Venus enters your 7th House on the 8th. Romance blooms. Current relationships deepen. It might be too soon to rush to the altar, but you're happy.

Finances are also good this month. This is a season for much spending. I would try to time it from the 12th onwards. Before the 12th you are likely to overspend and buy rashly. Afterwards you are more sober and conservative. Speculations are favourable all month (but the 30th and 31st seem most powerful). Money is earned through work as well – there are plenty of opportunities for overtime or second jobs. Co-workers have interesting financial ideas. Serious investors should look at the health industry and blue-chip type stocks after the 12th. Before that look at publishing, travel and foreign investments.

Virgo

♍

Personality Profile

VIRGO AT A GLANCE

Element – Earth

Ruling Planet – Mercury
    Career Planet – Mercury
    Love Planet – Neptune
    Money Planet – Venus
    Planet of Home and Family Life – Jupiter
    Planet of Health and Work – Uranus
    Planet of Pleasure – Saturn
    Planet of Sexuality – Mars

Colours – earth tones, ochre, orange, yellow

*Colour that promotes love, romance and social
    harmony* – aqua blue

Colour that promotes earning power – jade
    green

Gems – agate, hyacinth

Metal – quicksilver

Scents – lavender, lilac, lily of the valley, storax

Quality – mutable (= flexibility)

Quality most needed for balance – a broader perspective

Strongest virtues – mental agility, analytical skills, ability to pay attention to detail, healing powers

Deepest needs – to be useful and productive

Characteristic to avoid – destructive criticism

Signs of greatest overall compatibility – Taurus, Capricorn

Signs of greatest overall incompatibility – Gemini, Sagittarius, Pisces

Sign most helpful to career – Gemini

Sign most helpful for emotional support – Sagittarius

Sign most helpful financially – Libra

Sign best for marriage and/or partnerships – Pisces

Sign most helpful for creative projects – Capricorn

Best Sign to have fun with – Capricorn

Signs most helpful in spiritual matters – Taurus, Leo

Best day of the week – Wednesday

Understanding a Virgo

The virgin is a particularly fitting symbol for those born under the Sign of Virgo. If you meditate on the image of the virgin you will get a good understanding of the essence of the Virgo type. The virgin is, of course, a symbol of purity and innocence – not naïve, but pure. A virginal object has not been touched. A virgin field is land that is true to itself, the way it has always been. The same is true of virgin forest: it is pristine, unaltered.

Apply the idea of purity to the thought processes, emotional life, physical body, and activities and projects of the everyday world, and you can see how Virgos approach life. Virgos desire the pure expression of the ideal in their mind, body and affairs. If they find impurities they will attempt to clear them away.

Impurities are the beginning of disorder, unhappiness and uneasiness. The job of the Virgo is to eject all impurities and keep only that which the body and mind can use and assimilate.

The secrets of good health are here revealed: 90 per cent of the art of staying well is maintaining a pure mind, a pure body and pure emotions. When you introduce more impurities than your mind and body can deal with, you will have what is known as 'dis-ease'. It is no wonder that Virgos make great doctors, nurses, healers and dietitians. They have an innate understanding of good health and they realize that good health is more than just physical. In all aspects of life, if you want a project to be successful it must be kept as pure as possible. It must be protected against the adverse elements that will try to undermine it. This is the secret behind Virgo's awesome technical proficiency.

One could talk about Virgo's analytical powers – which are formidable. One could talk about their perfectionism and their almost superhuman attention to detail. But this would be to miss the point. All of these virtues are manifestations of a Virgo's desire for purity and perfection – a world without Virgos would have ruined itself long ago.

A vice is nothing more than a virtue turned inside out, misapplied or used in the wrong context. Virgos' apparent vices come from their inherent virtue. Their analytical powers, which should be used for healing, helping or perfecting a project in the world, sometimes get misapplied and turned against people. Their critical faculties, which should be used constructively to perfect a strategy or proposal, can sometimes be used destructively to harm or wound. Their urge to perfection can turn into worry and lack of confidence; their natural humility can become self-denial and self-abasement. When Virgos turn negative they are apt to turn their devastating criticism on themselves, sowing the seeds of self-destruction.

Finance

Virgos have all the attitudes that create wealth. They are hard-working, industrious, efficient, organized, thrifty, productive and eager to serve. A developed Virgo is every employer's dream. But until Virgos master some of the social graces of Libra they will not even come close to fulfilling their financial potential. Purity and perfectionism, if not handled correctly or gracefully, can be very trying to others. Friction in human relationships can be devastating not only to your pet projects but – indirectly – to your wallet as well.

Virgos are quite interested in their financial security. Being hard-working, they know the true value of money. They do not like to take risks with their money, preferring to save for their retirement or for a rainy day. Virgos usually make prudent, calculated investments that involve a minimum of risk. These investments and savings usually work out well, helping Virgos to achieve the financial security they seek. The rich or even not-so-rich Virgo also likes to help his or her friends in need.

Career and Public Image

Virgos reach their full potential when they can communicate their knowledge in such a way that others can understand it. In order to get their ideas across better, Virgos need to develop greater verbal skills and fewer judgemental ways of expressing themselves. Virgos look up to teachers and communicators; they like their bosses to be good communicators. Virgos will probably not respect a superior who is not their intellectual equal – no matter how much money or power that superior has. Virgos themselves like to be perceived by others as being educated and intellectual.

The natural humility of Virgos often inhibits them from fulfilling their great ambitions, from acquiring name and fame. Virgos should indulge in a little more self-promotion if they are going to reach their career goals. They need to push themselves with the same ardour that they would use to foster others.

At work Virgos like to stay active. They are willing to learn any type of job as long as it serves their ultimate goal of financial security. Virgos may change occupations several times during their professional lives, until they find the one they really enjoy. Virgos work well with other people, are not afraid to work hard and always fulfil their responsibilities.

Love and Relationships

If you are an analyst or a critic you must, out of necessity, narrow your scope. You have to focus on a part and not the whole; this can create a temporary narrow-mindedness. Virgos do not like this kind of person. They like their partners to be broad-minded, with depth and vision. Virgos seek to get this broad-minded quality from their partners, since they sometimes lack it themselves.

Virgos are perfectionists in love just as they are in other areas of life. They need partners who are tolerant, open-minded and easy-going. If you are in love with a Virgo do not waste time on impractical romantic gestures. Do practical and useful things for him or her – this is what will be appreciated and what will be done for you.

Virgos express their love through pragmatic and useful gestures, so do not be put off because your Virgo partner does not say 'I love you' day-in and day-out. Virgos are not that type. If they love you, they will demonstrate it in practical ways. They will always be there for you; they will show an interest in your health and finances; they will fix your sink or repair your video recorder. Virgos deem these actions to be superior to sending flowers, chocolates or St Valentine's cards.

In love affairs Virgos are not particularly passionate or spontaneous. If you are in love with a Virgo, do not take this personally. It does not mean that you are not alluring enough or that your Virgo partner does not love or like you. It is just the way Virgos are. What they lack in passion they make up for in dedication and loyalty.

Home and Domestic Life

It goes without saying that the home of a Virgo will be spotless, sanitized and orderly. Everything will be in its proper place – and don't you dare move anything about! For Virgos to find domestic bliss they need to ease up a bit in the home, to allow their partner and kids more freedom and to be more generous and open-minded. Family members are not to be analysed under a microscope, they are individuals with their own virtues to express.

With these small difficulties resolved, Virgos like to stay in and entertain at home. They make good hosts and they like to keep their friends and families happy and entertained at family and social gatherings. Virgos love children, but they are strict with them – at times – since they want to make sure their children are brought up with the correct sense of family and values.

Horoscope for 2008

Major Trends

For many years now you have been undergoing sudden and dramatic change. It seems that the cosmos is not satisfied with anything less than perfect for you (even though you might be satisfied). So, every time you settle into some pattern, it gets disrupted. This trend continues in the year ahead.

Last year, on September 3 Saturn made a major move into your own Sign. A long-term transit. It is going to reorganize your body and image. And since you are very health-conscious anyway, this reorganization will not be difficult. But self-esteem and self-confidence are not what they should be these days – and taking refuge in your innate humility is not a bad idea for the next few years. Oh, you are significant, you are a light, but shine silently.

Health is improving over last year, but is still delicate – more on this later on.

This year you are trying to achieve a balance between freedom and stability. Freedom is important to you, but you are willing to sacrifice some for a bit of stability – a feeling of being grounded. Getting just the right balance is the challenge. You can't go too far in either direction.

Marriages have been unstable for some years now. Many of you got divorced or had serious relationships break up in the past few years – and this area continues to be unstable in the year ahead. Love affairs, however, are plentiful and seem happy. More on this later.

Your most important areas of interest in the year ahead are the body, image and self-concept; home and family (from January 1 to January 27 and from June 14 to November 27); children, creativity, love affairs, fun; health and work; love and romance.

Your paths of greatest fulfilment this year are health and work; children, creativity, love affairs and the joy of life.

Health

(Please note that this is an astrological perspective on health and not a medical one. For the medical perspective, please consult your doctor.)

Health is always important to you, and with your 6th House of Health strong this area of life is even more of a focus than usual in the year ahead. This is good. You need to focus more on your health. Health, though much better than last year, still needs watching and attention. You can't take things for granted.

With two long-term planets stressing you full-time and with one stressing you part-time, you need to rest and relax more and focus on the important things in your life. I know the little details of life are important to you, but try to keep your focus on the big picture this year and let the unimportant things go. Pace yourself better and work more with a rhythm. Alternate different activities to maximize energy.

Also there are many other things that you can do to enhance health. Pay more attention to the ankles and feet. Wear sensible shoes – shoes that don't knock you off balance and that fit right. Keep your feet warm in winter. Massage your feet and ankles regularly (see the reflexology chart, overleaf). Give your ankles more support when exercising or engaged in sport.

If problems arise, the probable causes are low energy and 'inharmony' in the love and social life. So the first thing to do is just rest. This alone will do wonders for you. The second thing to do (and this has been a long-term trend) is examine your love life, your marriage and your relationships. Chances are that something is not in harmony there – there is some conflict going on – and this inharmony prevents the *chi*, the life-force, from flowing as it should. Restore the harmony, apologize where necessary, forgive others and yourself, and most likely the problem will either fade away of its own accord or, if the services of a health professional are needed, the healing will proceed more quickly.

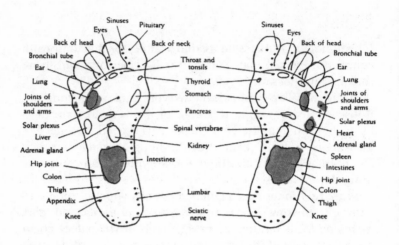

Reflexology

Try to massage the whole foot on a regular basis, but pay extra attention to the points highlighted on the chart. When you massage, be aware of 'sore spots', as these need special attention. It's also a good idea to massage the ankles and top side (as well as the soles) of the feet.

If this doesn't work, examine how you've used your love-force – this requires ruthless honesty. Has it been used positively, constructively? To help or harm or manipulate others? If you correct the mistakes here, healing should happen.

For many years now, spiritual healing has been very important in your life. By now many have learned a lot about this, and this year you will go into it more deeply. The depths to this subject are infinite – there is always more to learn.

Not only do you respond well to spiritually-oriented therapies – prayer, meditation, laying on of hands, reiki, the manipulation of subtle energies – but the causes of problems are probably in the spiritual realm, too. If you ignore the spiritual power within, you might receive a wake-up call in the form of a health problem. It might manifest as 'symptoms' but should not be viewed in the orthodox way. If you attend to this, the health problem will just fade away – or, even if healers are necessary, everything will go much faster.

Your most vulnerable periods this year – the periods where you need to pay extra attention to health issues – are from January 1 to 27; February 19 to March 20; May 21 to June 21; November 16 to December 22.

Home and Family

Your 4th House of Home and Family is still a 'part-time' House of Power this year, but definitely not as strong as last year. In 2007, as Jupiter moved through your 4th House most of you should have accomplished your major domestic goals. Many of you moved to bigger and better places. If you didn't move, the residence was expanded and made more comfortable in other ways (perhaps by buying big-ticket items for the home or by renovation of the home). Now you seem more or less content and have no need to make dramatic changes.

For many years now, the home, family (and especially the emotional life) have been undergoing a 'cosmic detox'. Pluto has been in your 4th House since November of 1995. He is very thorough. Anything that was impure in this area has come to the surface and been eliminated. At times this was painful and traumatic. Many of you suffered actual deaths of family members – parents or parent figures or other family members. Others saw the break-up and disintegration of the home and family pattern – perhaps through divorce and things of that nature. Homes could have been destroyed in other ways – through natural disasters or accidents. Emotionally, there was a separation from family members, too. The whole point was to 'give birth' to the ideal home and domestic situation. And all these things were like 'birth pangs'. The end result, which you're starting to see now (and last year, too) is a whole new domestic situation, family relationship and emotional life far superior to anything you ever knew in the past. Death and birth, both ruled by Pluto, are twins – two sides of the same coin. This detox is mostly over with now. You are in the last throes of it, and getting ready to move on. Pluto will move out of your 4th House on January 27, move back in on June 14 and leave permanently on November 27.

The focus this year seems more on children. Many of you are having children this year. (It could have happened last year, too.) Many of you are adopting children. And singles are certainly thinking along these lines in the year ahead. Whether or not you have children of your own, you are more involved with them this year. Virgos of childbearing age are very fertile right now.

Your family planet is in your 5th House in 2008. This is showing that you are working to make the home a place of entertainment – a fun place to be. Your home will be filled with both adults' and children's toys. You are investing in these things – probably also sports equipment and sports facilities.

If you are looking to do more renovation or heavy construction in the home (not likely) the best time is January 1 to January 27 and November 16 to December 27. If you're planning to redecorate in a cosmetic kind of way – or to buy objects of beauty for the home – the best time is from January 1 to January 24 and from October 18 to November 12.

Finance and Career

Your 2nd House of Finance is not a House of Power this year, Virgo. Not a major priority. Other things in your life are more important. But I'm reading this as a good thing. There is a basic contentment with the way things are – you have no need to make big changes.

The major financial danger with this condition is neglect. You could tend to overly ignore this area – not give it the attention it deserves – and thus get into trouble.

Your financial planet is Venus, which is a fast-moving planet. She will move through all the Signs and Houses of your Horoscope in any given year. Thus your financial fortunes will vary month to month based on where Venus is and what is happening to her in terms of aspects. We will cover these short-term trends in the monthly reports.

Venus rules partnerships, marriage, joint ventures and social connections. All these things tend to play a role in earnings. Some of you earn money from your marriage (spousal support), others through partnerships and joint ventures. You tend to have wealthy friends, and they are like money in the bank – not just in terms of material support when you need it, but also in terms of opportunity.

Venus rules the beauty industry – cosmetics, perfumes, hair-dressers, fashion and the like. All of these areas are interesting either as businesses, professions or investments.

The job situation seems very unstable this year. Like last year, there are changes going on in the workplace – both in a physical way and with co-workers. It is like musical chairs there. You could have job changes this year, too – and multiple ones. The freelance life seems best for you right now. If you employ others, this instability is still there. Workers will suddenly leave and suddenly come. Also it is difficult to know when who is available for what.

Your 10th House of Career is also not important this year. A status-quo year here as well. Children, creativity, love and health are more important interests this year. (With most of the long-term planets below the horizon, you don't seem very ambitious in an overall way – there will be periods in the year when ambitions will be stronger – but these will be temporary and we will discuss them in the monthly reports.)

With Jupiter in your 5th House of Speculations all year, you will be more interested in this. Also more fortunate. Family members also seem more speculative and also fortunate in this department.

Siblings had a banner financial year in 2007, but this year it is status quo. It looks like they've made their 'killing' and can now move on to other interests – like developing the mind, taking courses, pursuing intellectual interests. Intellectual interests will become ever more important to them as time goes on.

Love and Social Life

An active but challenging area for many years now. Married Virgos – especially if this is their first marriage – are having the marriages tested. Many have been divorced in recent years. Only the strongest love bonds can survive these kinds of transits – Uranus in the 7th House.

The best way to heal or save a troubled marriage right now is by giving your partner maximum space and freedom. So long as it isn't destructive, err on the side of freedom. It might be also good to try doing different things in your relationship. Avoid the routine and humdrum. Make the marriage more exciting. There is a need for variety here.

For singles, love is exciting – enjoyable – but highly unstable. You are meeting unconventional but very interesting people – computer engineers, doctors, healers, spiritual types, musicians, dancers and film people. But they come into your life and then they go. You don't know when you'll hear from them again. You don't know if you or they will still be in love a week from now – or even tomorrow. The mood-swings in love are very intense and very abrupt. Though you may have known the person for some time, have been intimate with them, you still don't know how a given date or evening will go.

Yes, it is exciting. In a way there is some good to all this. Every date is like a first date. Every intimacy like a first one.

As mentioned last year, there is a spiritual purpose behind all this: to learn to deal with social change and instability. To be calm, centred and happy in the middle of it. To learn to be happy within a relationship or outside one.

There is a lot of social and romantic change going on. For singles it has been a period of serial love affairs. The good thing about this is that you can learn what you want by experiencing what you *don't* want. Sort of a process of elimination. When Mr or Ms Right comes along, you'll know and appreciate him or her.

Many of you are now in the preparation stage for a serious relationship – and this preparation can last another few years.

Aside from the glamour kinds of people mentioned earlier, you also have the aspects for the office romance – co-workers or employees seem very alluring.

You are a service-oriented person and this is how you show love. This tendency is even stronger this year. But this is also how you feel loved. When someone is 'doing' for you – serving you in practical ways – you feel loved. Those involved with Virgos romantically should take note.

Virgos in or working towards their second marriage are having a lot less crisis. Marrieds will stay married and singles will tend to stay single. The same is true for those in or working towards their third marriage. Those working towards their fourth marriage probably shouldn't marry in the year ahead – enjoy others but keep your freedom. Those already in their fourth marriage are having many trials and tests.

Love will be active all year, but especially from February 19 to April 6.

Self-improvement

The main area of self-improvement in the year ahead will be personal – with the body, the image and self-concept. This is a great year for getting the body in shape, for losing weight and getting the right kind of image for yourself. (This is especially important for those of you who became or will become mums in the year ahead.)

A more conservative, traditional type of image seems best in the year ahead – and many are opting for this. Not a year to be flaunting your charms or dressing over-dramatically. Not a year for trying to attract too much attention to yourself. Dress elegantly, expensively if you can afford it, but modestly. You should be attractive, but not 'attracting'. The object is to attract the right people, rather than everyone. A low profile is called for now.

When Saturn moves through the 1st House people tend to feel their age. But even younger people are thinking of old age and future conditions. This can make you depressed or cold towards others. You will have to make special efforts to show warmth.

Self-esteem will get a reality check this year. If it is too low, Saturn will raise it up. If it is unrealistically high, reality will correct this. It is a time for being realistic about yourself and your abilities. This way you will make the right and sound judgements. The Lunar Eclipse of February 21 will shake things up a bit and will be part of the cosmic 'reality check'. If you have a healthy, realistic self-esteem, you have nothing to fear. If this area is out of order it can be traumatic.

Pluto moving into your 5th this year (and permanently towards the end of the year) is going to bring a detox in the area of children. We all have attitudes here that are imperfect – everyone basically loves their children, but we can't really love them properly if we don't understand who they are and who we are. Are we owners? Masters? Or are we merely caretakers for a higher power? Perhaps we see them as insurance for old age, or as investments. There's a lot more to this than meets the eye, and Pluto is going to reveal the deeper things here in coming years.

Month-by-month Forecasts

January

Best Days Overall: 7, 8, 16, 17, 25, 26
Most Stressful Days Overall: 5, 6, 12, 13, 18, 19
Best Days for Love: 1, 5, 6, 9, 10, 12, 13, 14, 15, 18, 19, 23, 27, 28
Best Days for Money: 1, 5, 6, 7, 14, 15, 16, 23, 24, 25, 27, 28

The year begins with most of the planets (70 to 80 per cent) in the social, Western sector of your chart. Even Mercury, your ruler, is in the West (for many months to come). So this is a strong social period. Other people are important to you. You get your way through popularity and likeability rather than self-assertion or independence. It is more difficult now to create conditions as you like them (it can be done, but with much more effort and at a high price), so better now to adapt as best you can. Let others have their way so long as it isn't destructive. The period of personal independence will come in due course – and that will be the time to make changes.

Most of the planets (70 to 80 per cent) are also below the horizon of the chart – the 'night' side of the Horoscope. Thus you need to focus on emotional and family issues – on attaining right state, right feeling and right mood, rather than on outer success. Seems to me that there are some big shake-ups going on in your corporate hierarchy – with bosses – parents and parent figures – and in your industry. Job changes can happen – either within your company or with another one. But don't get manoeuvred into some position that is not emotionally comfortable or that uproots the family relationship or pattern.

Family harmony can be enhanced through doing fun things together as a family unit – also through social gatherings and parties. Attending religious services together also seems important until the 24th (it is always important, but especially until the 24th).

Your spiritual mission this month involves children, creative projects and exploring the joy of life. A truly spiritual person is a joyous person. (This mission seems easy to achieve as your 5th House of Fun is very strong this month.) After the 8th your spiritual mission involves healing – the self and others – and your job.

You are in one of your yearly personal pleasure peaks right now. Enjoy. This is a time for leisure activities and getting in touch with your inner child and giving it some expression. Lighten up a little on life – you've been much too serious lately. Even your burdens can be enjoyed – let your inner child guide you.

This looks like a strong financial month, too. Speculations are favourable all month – but especially after the 24th (the 31st of this month and the 1st of next month seem especially fortunate). Your financial planet in Sagittarius until the 24th shows increases in earnings and large financial goals. You spend big and earn big. After the 24th you are more conservative – even when you speculate. The object this month is to earn and succeed in fun and enjoyable ways. Making money and being successful are not enough – it has to be fun – creative – happy.

Getting just the right balance between work and play is a challenge for the year. Too much work makes you a dull person. Too much play makes you frivolous. But this month the challenge is even more dramatic – both your 5th and 6th Houses are strong. (Virgo will generally err on the side of work over play.)

Health is excellent all month. Love is still very unstable. Infidelity is not going to help your marriage or overall happiness.

February

    Best Days Overall: 3, 4, 12, 13, 21, 22
    Most Stressful Days Overall: 1, 2, 8, 9, 14, 15, 28, 29
    Best Days for Love: 3, 4, 8, 9, 13, 14, 17, 23, 26, 27
    Best Days for Money: 3, 4, 12, 13, 21, 22, 23, 24

Speculations are favourable until the 17th, but especially on the 1st and 2nd. (A parent or parent figure is very prosperous then and generous with you, too.) Many of the financial trends of last month are still in effect. On the 17th your financial planet moves into your 6th House, and so money will come in the old-fashioned ways – through work. Prosperity is still strong, but the problem is lack of interest – your Money House has been basically empty for the past two months. You may not be giving this area enough attention.

On the 19th as the Sun moves into your 7th House of
Love, you enter a yearly social peak. (Your social life will
be active even before, but not at peak levels.) The 1st to
the 4th and the 9th to the 11th bring happy romantic
meetings for singles. These people look like creative or
spiritual types. Perhaps a co-worker or someone you meet
at the workplace or as you pursue your health goals. The
person could also be a healer or health professional. After
the 19th love opportunities come in spiritual settings –
retreats, spiritual seminars or workshops, at charity events,
as you pursue altruistic causes. But they can also happen in
the normal ways – at parties and the like. You are always
idealistic about love – always have ultra-high standards –
but this month (especially after the 19th) even more so.
This is a bit of a challenge – as few mortals could ever live
up to your standards – and this adds some instability to
your love life.

There are two eclipses this month. The Solar Eclipse of
the 7th (the 6th in the US) occurs in your 6th House and is
announcing job changes. This could be an actual job change
or changes that are going on in the workplace – the conditions of work are changing dramatically. The health regime
and diet will also undergo (now and in coming months)
dramatic change.

The Lunar Eclipse of the 21st (the 20th in the US) seems a
stronger one. It occurs in your own Sign. This eclipse will
test a friendship, bring shake-ups in organizations you
belong to, and cause a redefinition of the personality and
image. In coming months you will be adopting a new look.
Good to take a reduced schedule for both eclipses, but especially for this one.

Health needs more watching after the 19th, but you seem
to be on the case. Enhance health in the ways mentioned in
the yearly report (paying more attention to the ankles and
feet) and this month pay more attention to the heart,
kidneys and hips (after the 17th) and to the arms, shoulders,
lungs and small intestine. Air and water therapies are
powerful all month. Fresh air, windy places, soaking in hot

tubs, spas or whirlpools, being near or on water – all are natural tonics now.

March

Best Days Overall: 2, 3, 11, 19, 20, 29, 30
Most Stressful Days Overall: 6, 7, 13, 14, 27, 28
Best Days for Love: 4, 5, 6, 7, 13, 14, 15, 22, 23, 24, 25
Best Days for Money: 2, 3, 4, 5, 11, 15, 19, 20, 22, 23, 24, 25, 29, 30

Health and work are still major interests this month – especially until the 15th. The yearly social peak continues. Love might be unstable, unpredictable and volatile – but it is active and basically happy. Singles have a 'large menu' to choose from – spiritual types, creative types, money types, intellectuals, teachers and the like. Enjoy.

On the 15th – as your Ruler, Mercury, enters your 7th House – you become more socially aggressive. You go after what you want. You are not hard to get, if you like someone. No games. You are more personally popular as well. You are going way out of your way to please others – especially a current love or spouse. Their interests come first. (So long as it isn't destructive, there's nothing wrong with this. In fact, with so many planets in the West and your 7th House so strong – this is the way you should be right now. Go along with others so long as it isn't destructive. Continue to adapt to situations as best you can.)

This month there is a shift of planetary power to the upper half of the Horoscope. Now, because of the dynamic of your chart the upper half is not going to be dominant this year. Both halves are more or less equally balanced. However, you are starting to become more ambitious than you've been all year. And it is wise to shift some energy here. Home, family and domestic issues are important all year – now it is just a matter of emphasis and degree.

Health still needs watching all month. There will be some improvement in overall energy after the 20th, but you still need to rest and relax more and do things to enhance your health. Social harmony is very important to your health – it has been like that for some years now, but this month even more so. Pay more attention to the heart (all month), to the kidneys and hips (until the 13th), to the lungs, arms, shoulders and small intestine (until the 15th). The ankles and feet are important all year, and this hasn't changed.

On the 20th your 8th House becomes powerful. So this is a good period for detox regimes on all levels – physical, emotional and mental. This is a sexually active month for most of you, too. Libido is stronger than usual.

This is a period for personal transformation and reinvention – and these things can't happen without eliminating old patterns – mental and emotional – this is the whole key to personal transformation.

Your spiritual mission this month involves your job, health (and the health of others) and other people in general – especially your spouse or current love.

Finances are easier before the 13th than afterwards. Until the 13th it comes from work. Afterwards from social connections, spousal support (your spouse or partner is prosperous this month – prosperous and generous with you) or business partnerships. Professional investors should look at high technology (especially in the health field) until the 13th and at industries that involve water, shipping, shippers, oil and natural gas afterwards. Your financial intuition is very strong after the 13th, but there are challenges in implementing it. (Intuition sees directly and never sees obstructions, but we humans unfortunately have many obstructions to deal with.)

April

Best Days Overall: 7, 8, 16, 17, 25, 26, 27

Most Stressful Days Overall: 3, 4, 9, 10, 23, 24, 30

Best Days for Love: 1, 2, 3, 4, 9, 10, 13, 14, 18, 19, 24, 28, 29, 30

Best Days for Money: 4, 7, 8, 13, 14, 16, 17, 18, 19, 24, 26, 27

Saturn is camping out on an eclipse point all month (this began on the 30th of last month) and for some months to come. This is bringing dramatic and perhaps disruptive changes with children and your relations with them. These can be your own or other people's. A love affair (not a marriage) is getting severely tested now. Children are involved in dramatic events.

Health is improving dramatically. Your hard work here is paying off. Day by day it gets better and better. We see a steady progression of improvement (not something that happens all at once).

Your yearly social peak is starting to wind down, but it is still a sexually active month (like last month).

Your 8th House is still strong all month, so the interest in personal transformation and reinvention continues. Still a great period for detox regimes and for losing weight.

Like last month your partner, spouse or current love is prospering and generous with you. On a financial level (just as it is on other levels) you need to put the financial interests of others ahead of your own. As you do so, your own prosperity is guaranteed – it's as if you put the entire universe in your debt – nothing can stop the payment.

This is a month where you can earn by seeing value where others see only death – troubled properties or companies, for example – these can be very lucrative for professional investors. But there are other ways this can manifest: You clean out your attic (a very good thing to be doing this month anyway) and find a valuable collector's item. Or you pass by a junk shop and find a valuable antique.

Also, after the 19th the element of Earth – your native element – becomes very strong. And this tends to prosperity. You could be more rash than usual in financial matters after the 6th, so if you're buying big-ticket items or making important investments better to wait until the 19th.

After the 19th your 9th House becomes very strong. This is a happy House and a happy period. Your mental horizons are enlarged and there is more overall optimism. Happy travel and educational opportunities come – and you should take them. Students hear good news about university or graduate school. Also they seem successful in their studies. A legal issue takes a favourable turn.

This is also a period of greater interest in religion, philosophy, metaphysics and higher studies. There is much revelation available to those who desire it.

Your spiritual mission this month involves personal transformation (the removal of barriers to growth) and religion, philosophy and higher education. You are in a teaching mode now.

May

Best Days Overall: 4, 5, 13, 14, 23, 24
Most Stressful Days Overall: 1, 6, 7, 20, 21, 28, 29
Best Days for Love: 1, 4, 5, 6, 7, 13, 14, 15, 16, 24, 25, 26, 28, 29
Best Days for Money: 4, 5, 13, 14, 15, 16, 23, 24

The dominance of the Earth element continues this month and this is good for you. It is good health-wise and energetically. It is good financially. And it is good for your self-esteem and sense of self-worth. Your practical abilities – your down-to-earth attitudes – are prized and appreciated now.

You haven't been too ambitious this year, but on the 20th you begin a yearly career peak. First off you will have interest and enthusiasm for career and outer success. You want to be 'on top'– appreciated and respected for who you are. You want to be appreciated by the world and not just your family. And this is going to happen in the month ahead. You are very elevated now. If you work in a company you are likely to get promoted and receive more honour and recognition. After the 3rd you seem more elevated – of higher status – than anyone in your family. Succeeding in the outer world is not only for personal satisfaction – though this is one of the reasons for your ambition – but is also a good way to serve your family. You've been working on achieving emotional harmony this year (and it's right that you are) but emotional harmony is not complete without some worldly success, too. It seems part of your emotional harmony (at least for now).

You can further your career through personal involvement, personal effort, paying attention and personal commitment. Through a willingness to travel and take courses that help your career, and through charitable and altruistic activities. Charitable activities are not only good for their own sake – but you meet the right kind of people who can help your career. It has bottom-line benefits.

Your spiritual planet crosses the Midheaven on the 20th – thus these activities – meditation, inner growth, spiritual studies – are high on your agenda this month.

Career is important all month, but your 9th House of Religion, Philosophy, Metaphysics and Higher Education is still important until the 20th. Refer to last month's discussion.

Finances are good. The financial planet is very elevated from the 24th onwards. You have a stronger interest here (probably more than you've had all year) and this is 90 per cent of success. Earnings are increased. You will end the month richer than when you started. Financial opportunities come at educational or religious settings – perhaps you meet someone at school or worship service who helps you. After the 24th earnings come from your good professional reputation, from bosses, parents or parent figures – the authority figures in your life (and this includes the government) are very supportive this period. If you are in your own business, think about expanding or marketing to other countries. Government contracts seem interesting, too. Government help seems available in other ways.

Health is delicate after the 20th and needs watching. Pursue your ambitions by all means – but be rational about it – rest when tired and pace yourself more.

June

Best Days Overall: 1, 2, 9, 10, 19, 20, 28, 29
Most Stressful Days Overall: 3, 4, 16, 17, 18, 24, 25, 30
Best Days for Love: 3, 4, 11, 12, 14, 15, 21, 22, 23, 24, 25, 30
Best Days for Money: 1, 2, 3, 4, 9, 10, 11, 12, 13, 14, 15, 19, 20, 24, 25, 28, 29

Your yearly career peak continues, but the Retrograde of Mercury (which is both your personal and career planet) complicates things. This won't stop career success, but creates more confusion, indecision and delays. Try to wrap up important career projects or decisions before the 19th. Afterwards, it is better to review your career – subject it to analysis to see where improvements can be made. Then when Mercury moves forward again next month, you will be ready to move forward, too.

Continue to further your career in the ways mentioned last month – through education, willingness to travel, approaching your work with a spirit of idealism, through charitable involvements and personal attention and effort.

Children have been going through major changes and having dramatic events happen to them for some months now, and this trend continues in the month ahead. Happily most of the tumult is about over with. Things are starting to stabilize.

The two planets involved with your love life are now Retrograde. Neptune, your actual love planet, went Retrograde on the 26th of last month. Uranus (in your 7th

House of Love) goes Retrograde on the 27th. The social life is slowing down. You are getting a breather. If you are involved with someone, that person is getting a breather. This is not a time for making important love decisions one way or the other. It is a time for analysis, review and evaluation. This will take some time – a few more months at least – but in the end you will have clarity and know what to do. (Though the social life is slowing down, it doesn't mean that you won't have a social life – of course you will – but it 'lacks direction' at this time.) Love affairs are being tested this month – a continuation of a trend that has been going on for a few months. This is one of the periods where you learn to be calm in the middle of social instability.

Last month the planets shifted from the Western, social sector to the Eastern sector. Thus you are becoming more independent, capable of more independent action. And the timing of this is exquisite. This shift happened just as your love planets are going Retrograde. You can let go of social duties and responsibilities and focus on pleasing Number One. Now – and for the next few months – you will have more power to create conditions as you want them to be. No need for consensus or worrying about how others might feel (we're not talking about destructive things now – only making changes that make you happy). It is a time for building. (You're better off making these changes before the 19th. If not, wait until next month when Mercury starts to move forward.)

Health needs extra care until the 21st. Refer to the yearly report for specifics.

Finances are mixed this month. There's more work and effort involved – more challenges. Until the 18th you have the drive and the interest to overcome these challenges, but afterwards not. (You will have to force yourself.) Until the 18th money comes to you in the ways mentioned last month – through pay rises or promotions at work, through parents, parent figures or authority figures in your life. Through a good professional reputation. After the 18th it comes through networking, friends, social connections and involvement with organizations. Good to keep up to date technologically after the 18th – it seems important. Complicating the financial picture is a financial disagreement with family members – perhaps children as well – after the 18th. This is short term and will be resolved by the end of the month – or next month.

July

Best Days Overall: 6, 7, 16, 17, 26
Most Stressful Days Overall: 1, 14, 15, 21, 22, 28
Best Days for Love: 2, 3, 9, 10, 13, 19, 20, 21, 22, 24, 28, 29
Best Days for Money: 2, 3, 6, 7, 9, 10, 13, 16, 17, 24, 26

Most of the planets are in the East and your 1st House is strong now – as Mars enters on the 1st. Talk about independence! Now you won't listen to anybody! You will have your way no matter what!

If you use this Mars energy properly, you'll get a lot done this month. You will achieve objectives much faster than usual (especially if they are personal ones and don't involve other people – 40 per cent of the planets – a yearly high – are Retrograde this month, so things in the world are slowing down – but things that relate to you can be achieved quickly.) You will excel at sport and exercise regimes, too. Since Mars rules your 8th House, it is a great period to lose weight or detox the body or have cosmetic surgery. Many of you are thinking about this now. Of course spiritual methods are superior to this and should be explored first.

With Mars in your own Sign you need to drive more defensively and be more mindful and aware. You will take more risks this month – this goes with the territory – but do these things in an aware state. Many of you will have encounters with death – this doesn't mean that you will die, only that you will confront the dark angel in various ways – people close to you can have near-death type experiences, etc. Or you have to confront this issue on a psychological level. (These things are most likely from the 1st to the 8th). Death has many lessons to teach us about life – and this is the purpose of these encounters. It's not about taking you out of the picture, but showing you the fragility of life and how we need to make the most of it while we're around.

Mind your temper this month – especially with co-workers or at work. Focus your extra physical energy on constructive things. Under provocation, take a few deep breaths before answering.

This also happens to be a very spiritual month – especially beginning the 12th. Note how beautiful the timing is here – you are almost forced to think about the deeper things of life and gain more spiritual understanding.

Many of you are involved in personal transformation, and this is a month to make good progress here.

Finances are good – though there are some dramas and perhaps important changes from the 26th to the 29th. Until the 12th money comes through friends, organizations and your networking abilities. After the 12th it comes from 'spiritual sources' – actually it always comes from spiritual sources, only now you are more clear about it. Financial intuition is exceptionally good after the 12th. This is a period for gaining a deeper understanding of the spiritual laws of affluence and the supernatural supply. You are into 'miracle money' rather than natural money now.

The two love planets are still Retrograde, so the love life is slower than usual. But this is OK – focus on creating conditions as you desire them to be – make the personal changes that need to be made now. You have the power and the interest to make it happen. Love needs time to straighten out.

August

Best Days Overall: 3, 4, 12, 13, 14, 22, 23, 30, 31
Most Stressful Days Overall: 10, 11, 17, 18, 24, 25
Best Days for Love: 1, 2, 7, 8, 9, 17, 18, 21, 22, 23, 26, 27
Best Days for Money: 1, 2, 3, 4, 5, 6, 12, 13, 22, 23, 30, 31

A very active and tumultuous month, Virgo, but things will work out in your favour.

Mars is still in your Sign until the 19th, so keep in mind our discussion of last month.

You are still in a very spiritual period until the 22nd. A great period for going on spiritual retreats, being involved with spiritual people, sitting at the feet of the Guru, doing religious pilgrimages and being more involved in charities and altruistic activities. Though you are very self-willed and independent now, it is still better to accept the yoke of the Higher Power before your own will. The Higher Power wants nothing more than to give you what you need – but you need to let it have its way.

There are important spiritual changes happening now. The Solar Eclipse of the 1st occurs in your 12th House of Spirituality – not only that, but the Sun – the eclipsed planet – also happens to be your planet of spirituality. So you will, no doubt, change your teachers, practice or regime. Those not on a spiritual path will probably start on one this month. There are shake-ups in a spiritual or charitable organization you are involved in. These shake-ups affect your relationship with the organization.

There is another eclipse on the 16th that occurs in your 6th House of Health and Work. This eclipse announces job changes and changes in the conditions of the workplace. Many of you will also change health regime, doctors or diets as well. (With your health planet still Retrograde, do more homework before making the changes.)

In spite of all the shake-ups (both worldly and personal) you enter a yearly personal pleasure peak on the 5th and this will only get stronger as the month continues. All kinds of sensual pleasures and delights await you – your spirit is getting pleasured and so is the flesh.

As you trust your financial intuition – which is still very strong until the 5th – you will find that financial problems and worries just melt away. The wealth you desire is desiring you and on your pathway. Nothing much that you need to do. It has all been prepared. Financial windfalls come after the 5th. Personal items – clothing, jewellery, accessories – perhaps artistic objects – also come. Financial opportunities are pursuing you. Financial confidence and judgement are excellent now and if you need to make investments or important purchases this is a good period – especially from the 5th to the 30th. Speculations are very favourable on the 15th–16th. (Also you can have a job offer that pays a lot more.) You end the month a lot richer than when you began.

Health seems good in spite of the eclipse in your 6th House. If there is a problem there will be a best-case outcome. Personal energy is at a yearly high (of course with three long-term planets stressing you, you've had higher energy levels in your life – but for the year, this is a high). You look great: stylish, glamorous (more than usual). Self-esteem and self-confidence are very good.

September

Best Days Overall: 9, 10, 18, 19, 27, 28
Most Stressful Days Overall: 6, 7, 8, 14, 15, 20, 21
Best Days for Love: 1, 2, 3, 11, 12, 14, 15, 20, 21, 29, 30
Best Days for Money: 1, 2, 3, 9, 10, 11, 12, 18, 19, 21, 27, 29, 30

Your personal pleasure peak continues until the 22nd. Sensual fantasies are being fulfilled. You are still in a strong period of independence – so it is still a great period for making the changes that make you happy – for creating your life according to your personal specifications. This is a time to please yourself – if you are happy, others will be happy. You have to take responsibility for your own happiness now. Pretty soon it will be more difficult to take independent action – so act now.

Last month was a powerful financial month, and the trend is even stronger now. On the 22nd you enter a yearly financial peak. Some 40 to 50 per cent of the planets will either be in or moving through the Money House this month – this is a lot of financial fire-power. Mars in your Money House since the 19th of last month shows financial aggressiveness and risk-taking – but more important than that, it shows a financial detox – the elimination of waste, needless expenses and needless possessions – things that just clutter up your environment. Borrowing power is increased. Money can come from insurance claims, royalties, spousal support, trust funds and estates. Estate and tax issues are influencing many of your financial moves right now. With Venus in your Money House (her own Sign and House) your natural earning ability is enhanced – you radiate more 'wealth' inherently. Assets you own just naturally increase in value. But the most important factors in your success are your personal attention and personal involvement – this gives you the drive to overcome all obstacles. This is not a month for speculations. Investing is another story.

Professional investors should look at bonds, the beauty industry, gold, utilities, telecommunications, transport, military contractors and troubled companies. Mergers and acquisitions increase the value of your portfolio.

Love is improved this month, but still on the back burner. Singles find romantic opportunities as they pursue financial goals or with people involved in their finances. The workplace is still very much a venue for romance. There is better financial cooperation between you and your spouse or current love than last month.

Health is good this month, but energy is not as high as last month. Enhance health in the ways mentioned in the yearly report.

Last month the planetary power shifted to the lower half of the Horoscope. So home, family and emotional comfort are now more important than career and outer success. This month, the trend is even stronger as your career planet, Mercury, goes Retrograde on the 24th. Cultivate emotional harmony and right feelings, and outer success will just naturally follow – in due course. This month is more about money-making – the bottom line – than about status, prestige or the public image.

October

Best Days Overall: 6, 7, 15, 16, 24, 25
Most Stressful Days Overall: 4, 5, 11, 12, 17, 18, 31
Best Days for Love: 1, 9, 10, 11, 12, 17, 18, 21, 22, 23, 26, 27
Best Days for Money: 1, 6, 7, 11, 12, 15, 16, 21, 22, 24, 25, 26, 27, 31

Your yearly financial peak is still in full swing. Many of the trends of last month are still in effect. Even though Mars leaves your Money House on the 4th, financial detox is still a good idea (your financial planet is in Scorpio until the 18th). Get rid of the clutter. Get rid of investments that are not working out – or possessions you no longer need. Simplify your finances as much as possible. Cut waste and needless expense. You expand by cutting, much in the same way that grapes grow faster and more plentifully when the vine is pruned. Financial intuition is still very important, and so is charitable giving. You are still more interested in 'miracle' money – money that comes in supernatural ways – than you are in 'natural' money. Miracle money is much more interesting; the other kind is boring to you now. Bonds are still interesting for professional investors – likewise troubled or even bankrupt companies.

If you've done a good detox – good pruning – Venus' move into bullish Sagittarius brings increased earnings and wealth. Family support will be good. Parents or parent figures are more generous. And you seem to be spending more on the home and family – an important way to keep family harmony right now.

Like last month, attaining prosperity is not just something you do for personal fulfilment. It has a spiritual purpose behind it – it's actually your spiritual mission for the month. You need to attain a certain degree of financial security so that you can devote time to other worthy things. Once you have attained it you can teach or show others how it is done. With wealth you are more in a position to help others than without it – this is not always the case, but now it is.

Your 3rd House of Communication and Intellectual Interests is also powerful this month and will get even stronger as the month continues. So this is a good period to catch up on your reading, phone calls and e-mail. Good to take courses in subjects that interest you. Good to attend lectures and experience the pleasures of the mind. Sensual pleasure alone will degrade a person – if that's the only pleasure they know – but if you balance this out with giving the mind what it needs, you will be a more balanced person.

Health gets more delicate after the 18th, so rest and relax more and enhance health in the ways mentioned in the yearly report.

Love is more harmonious before the 23rd than afterwards – but basically status quo. Friendships seem very important from the 15th to the 23rd – and good friends will be instrumental in lifting up every aspect of your life.

November

Best Days Overall: 2, 3, 4, 12, 13, 20, 21, 30
Most Stressful Days Overall: 1, 7, 8, 14, 15, 27, 28
Best Days for Love: 1, 5, 6, 7, 8, 11, 12, 14, 15, 20, 21, 22, 23, 30
Best Days for Money: 1, 2, 3, 4, 11, 12, 13, 20, 21, 22, 23, 30

Avoid risk-taking or stressful activities from the 6th to the 12th and from the 18th to the 21st.

Health needs even more watching than last month – especially after the 21st. Be very vigilant about your energy levels – if you feel tired, rest or take a nap. If you feel a pain in your body, stop what you're doing and rest. This is not a time to test your physical limits or endurance. Enhance health by the methods mentioned in the yearly report. Also pay more attention to your heart. If you're on top of these things, you'll get through the month with flying colours.

Intellectual interests and communication are still an important focus until the 21st. It is good to study things that interest you, but also good to study things that will benefit your career – make you better at what you do. Career is not important this month – family and domestic issues are much stronger – but still you can prepare for the future.

Teaching others your skills or knowledge seems your spiritual mission until the 23rd. After that your mission is your family and their needs. With Mars moving into your 4th House of Home and Family on the 16th, tempers can flare at home. Emotions are high. Your personal presence and attention will be a big help. Spiritual understanding is also important for family unity and harmony after the 21st. And, until the 12th, financial support is important. But you will see (especially after the 12th) that not everything can be solved by just throwing money at it.

After the 16th there seems to be construction and renovation going on at home – perhaps a major repair. But if not, this is a good period to make needed repairs and renovations. (It might be wise to eliminate safety hazards or flammable or toxic materials from the home, too.) In general this is a good period for a deep kind of house-cleaning – not just on a superficial level – but the attic, basement, under-the-cupboards kind of cleaning.

With the Ruler of your 8th House in your 4th House this is an excellent period for psychological growth and progress – but on a deep level. Depth psychology – the psychology that explores past incarnations – is good. Many of the issues that are going on this month in the family are coming from these old patterns and it is good to understand them.

Finances are good all month, but will get even better after the 12th. Your financial planet starts to travel with Jupiter late in the month, bringing financial increase and luck in speculations. You will wind up richer at the end of the month than when you began.

Financial judgement is sound after the 12th and decision-making will be good. If you have to buy big-ticket items or make major investments, better to do it after the 12th than before. (Before, you are likely to overspend.)

December

  Best Days Overall: 1, 9, 10, 11, 17, 18, 27, 28
  Most Stressful Days Overall: 5, 6, 11, 12, 24, 25, 26
  Best Days for Love: 1, 2, 3, 5, 6, 11, 12, 20, 21, 30, 31
  Best Days for Money: 1, 9, 10, 11, 17, 18, 20, 21, 27, 28,
    30, 31

It's interesting how your Horoscope exactly mirrors the trends of the season. This is not so for many of the Signs, but for you definitely. The two important Houses this month are the 4th and the 5th – so the focus is on family (4th), children (5th House) parties, fun and entertainment (5th House). Traditionally this is what the coming season – Christmas and New Year – is all about. But I would wager that the partying this season will be more intense than usual – more than in previous seasons. Seldom have we seen your 5th House so powerful. Some 60 to 70 per cent (!) of the planetary power is either in or moving through your 5th House.

Last month the planets shifted (after the 21st) from the independent, Eastern sector to the Western, social sector of the Horoscope. So your period of independence is temporarily over with, now it's time to cultivate your people skills. It is more difficult now to change conditions your way – or to have things your way. In fact, your way is probably not the best way these days (uncomfortable though that fact is). Your good comes through others and through their good graces – and no amount of will-power or even talent will help you if you can't get on with others. So tone down self-will and self-assertion and let others have their way (so long as it isn't self-destructive). Younger Virgos are more subject to peer pressure, so it is important that they have the right kinds of friends.

You seem to be cultivating the social graces after the 12th. And love is improving as a result. Your two love planets are now moving forward (this began last month) and there is now clarity and good judgement in this department. After the 8th Venus starts to travel with Neptune, your love planet – a sure sign that love is in the air. As has been the case for many years, this love meeting (and it seems most likely to happen from the 26th to the 29th) happens at the workplace or with people you work with. It can also happen as you pursue your health goals or with people involved in your health. This meeting not only has romantic implications, but can lead to a business partnership or joint venture as well. (Perhaps this is how it begins.)

The problem with love now is not judgement or lack of confidence – it is your fun-loving spirit. You just want to have fun, and love is just another form of entertainment. Perhaps you are too light-hearted about it for anything serious to develop. In the meantime, though, you can have fun and enjoy the relationship for what it is.

Love is very idealistic now, too. Your ideals of perfection are always high – but this month even more. How can any mere mortal live up to those standards?

Speculations are still favourable this month, particularly before the 8th. After the 8th money comes from work, social connections, spousal support or joint ventures.

Financial judgement seems much better before the 8th than afterwards, and it seems advisable to get your holiday shopping done before the 8th.

Health is still delicate until the 21st, then it improves dramatically. You haven't felt this good all year.

Libra

♎

THE SCALES
Birthdays from
23rd September to
22nd October

Personality Profile

LIBRA AT A GLANCE

Element – Air

Ruling Planet – Venus
   Career Planet – Moon
   Love Planet – Mars
   Money Planet – Pluto
   Planet of Communications – Jupiter
   Planet of Health and Work – Neptune
   Planet of Home and Family Life – Saturn
   Planet of Spirituality and Good Fortune –
     Mercury

Colours – blue, jade green

Colours that promote love, romance and social
   harmony – carmine, red, scarlet

Colours that promote earning power –
   burgundy, red-violet, violet

Gems – carnelian, chrysolite, coral, emerald, jade, opal, quartz, white marble

Metal – copper

Scents – almond, rose, vanilla, violet

Quality – cardinal (= activity)

Qualities most needed for balance – a sense of self, self-reliance, independence

Strongest virtues – social grace, charm, tact, diplomacy

Deepest needs – love, romance, social harmony

Characteristic to avoid – violating what is right in order to be socially accepted

Signs of greatest overall compatibility – Gemini, Aquarius

Signs of greatest overall incompatibility – Aries, Cancer, Capricorn

Sign most helpful to career – Cancer

Sign most helpful for emotional support – Capricorn

Sign most helpful financially – Scorpio

Sign best for marriage and/or partnerships – Aries

Sign most helpful for creative projects – Aquarius

Best Sign to have fun with – Aquarius

Signs most helpful in spiritual matters – Gemini, Virgo

Best day of the week – Friday

Understanding a Libra

In the Sign of Libra the universal mind – the soul – expresses its genius for relationships, that is, its power to harmonize diverse elements in a unified, organic way. Libra is the soul's power to express beauty in all of its forms. And where is beauty if not within relationships? Beauty does not exist in isolation. Beauty arises out of comparison – out of the just relationship between different parts. Without a fair and harmonious relationship there is no beauty, whether it be in art, manners, ideas or the social or political forum.

There are two faculties humans have that exalt them above the animal kingdom: their rational faculty (expressed in the Signs of Gemini and Aquarius) and their aesthetic faculty, exemplified by Libra. Without an aesthetic sense we would be little more than intelligent barbarians. Libra is the civilizing instinct or urge of the soul.

Beauty is the essence of what Librans are all about. They are here to beautify the world. One could discuss Librans' social grace, their sense of balance and fair play, their ability to see and love another person's point of view – but this would be to miss their central asset: their desire for beauty.

No one – no matter how alone he or she seems to be – exists in isolation. The universe is one vast collaboration of beings. Librans, more than most, understand this and understand the spiritual laws that make relationships bearable and enjoyable.

A Libra is always the unconscious (and in some cases conscious) civilizer, harmonizer and artist. This is a Libra's deepest urge and greatest genius. Librans love instinctively to bring people together, and they are uniquely qualified to do so. They have a knack for seeing what unites people – the things that attract and bind rather than separate individuals.

Finance

In financial matters Librans can seem frivolous and illogical to others. This is because Librans appear to be more concerned with earning money for others than for themselves. But there is a logic to this financial attitude. Librans know that everything and everyone is connected and that it is impossible to help another to prosper without also prospering yourself. Since enhancing their partner's income and position tends to strengthen their relationship, Librans choose to do so. What could be more fun than building a relationship? You will rarely find a Libra enriching him- or herself at someone else's expense.

Scorpio is the ruler of Libra's Solar 2nd House of Money, giving Libra unusual insight into financial matters – and the power to focus on these matters in a way that disguises a seeming indifference. In fact, many other Signs come to Librans for financial advice and guidance.

Given their social grace, Librans often spend great sums of money on entertaining and organizing social events. They also like to help others when they are in need. Librans would go out of their way to help a friend in dire straits, even if they have to borrow from others to do so. However, Librans are also very careful to pay back any debts they owe, and like to make sure they never have to be reminded to do so.

Career and Public Image

Publicly, Librans like to appear as nurturers. Their friends and acquaintances are their family and they wield political power in parental ways. They also like bosses who are paternal or maternal.

The Sign of Cancer is on Libra's 10th House (of Career) cusp; the Moon is Libra's Career Planet. The Moon is by far the speediest, most changeable planet in the Horoscope. It alone among all the planets travels through the entire Zodiac – all 12 Signs and Houses – every month. This is an important key to the way in which Librans approach their careers, and also to what they need to do to maximize their career potential. The Moon is the Planet of Moods and Feelings – Librans need a career in which their emotions can have free expression. This is why so many Librans are involved in the creative arts. Libra's ambitions wax and wane with the Moon. They tend to wield power according to their mood.

The Moon 'rules' the masses – and that is why Libra's highest goal is to achieve a mass kind of acclaim and popularity. Librans who achieve fame cultivate the public as other people cultivate a lover or friend. Librans can be very flexible – and often fickle – in their career and ambitions. On the other hand, they can achieve their ends in a great variety of ways. They are not stuck in one attitude or with one way of doing things.

Love and Relationships

Librans express their true genius in love. In love you could not find a partner more romantic, more seductive or more fair. If there is one thing that is sure to destroy a relationship – sure to block your love from flowing – it is injustice or imbalance between lover and beloved. If one party is giving too much or taking too much, resentment is sure to surface at some time or other. Librans are careful about this. If anything, Librans might err on the side of giving more, but never giving less.

If you are in love with a Libra, make sure you keep the aura of romance alive. Do all the little things – candle-lit dinners, travel to exotic locales, flowers and small gifts. Give things that are beautiful, not necessarily expensive. Send cards. Ring regularly even if you have nothing in particular to say. The niceties are very important to a Libra. Your relationship is a work of art: make it beautiful and your Libra lover will appreciate it. If you are creative about it, he or she will appreciate it even more; for this is how your Libra will behave towards you.

Librans like their partners to be aggressive and even a bit self-willed. They know that these are qualities they sometimes lack and so they like their partners to have them. In relationships, however, Librans can be very aggressive – but always in a subtle and charming way! Librans are determined in their efforts to charm the object of their desire – and this determination can be very pleasant if you are on the receiving end.

Home and Domestic Life

Since Librans are such social creatures, they do not particularly like mundane domestic duties. They like a well-organized home – clean and neat with everything needful present – but housework is a chore and a burden, one of the unpleasant tasks in life that must be done, the quicker the better. If a Libra has enough money – and sometimes even if not – he or she will prefer to pay someone else to take care of the daily household chores. However, Librans like gardening; they love to have flowers and plants in the home.

A Libra's home is modern, and furnished in excellent taste. You will find many paintings and sculptures there. Since Librans like to be with friends and family, they enjoy entertaining at home and they make great hosts.

Capricorn is on the cusp of Libra's 4th Solar House of Home and Family. Saturn, the Planet of Law, Order, Limits and Discipline, rules Libra's domestic affairs. If Librans want their home life to be supportive and happy they need to develop some of the virtues of Saturn – order, organization and discipline. Librans, being so creative and so intensely in need of harmony, can tend to be too lax in the home and too permissive with their children. Too much of this is not always good; children need freedom but they also need limits.

Horoscope for 2008

Major Trends

For many years now the lower half of your Horoscope has been much stronger than the upper half. Home, family and emotional issues have been very important – more important than outer achievement. This year, the trend is even stronger as two long-term planets are in your 4th House of Home and Family. Jupiter will be there all year. Pluto is making a major move into this House after many years in your 3rd House. More on this later.

For the past two years your social genius got quite a workout. Saturn in your 11th House of Friends was testing friendships – and even you had a hard time here. (If a Libra is having a hard time, that means other Signs would be having an even harder time.) This whole area of life was re-organized and re-structured. As far as friendships are concerned, you are leaner but healthier. You may not have as many friends as you used to, but the ones you have are good ones.

This year (and this trend will continue into next year as well) there is a big focus on your spiritual life.

Your most important interests this year will be communication and intellectual interests; home and family; children, creativity and fun; health and work; spirituality.

Your paths of greatest fulfilment this year are home, family and psychological growth; children, creativity and fun.

Health

(Please note that this is an astrological perspective on health and not a medical one. For the medical perspective, please consult your doctor.)

For many years (since 1995) Pluto was in harmonious aspect to you. Now he is moving into Capricorn and inharmonious aspect. There he joins Jupiter – another long-term planet – in a stressful aspect. So, health is basically good, but energy is not as high as last year. In coming years you will have pay more attention here.

The good news is that your 6th House of Health is strong and thus you ARE giving health the attention it needs. Two planets making stressful aspects are not enough to cause major problems – especially if you are taking care of yourself. But when the planets start to 'gang up' on you (such as from January 1 to January 20, March 20 to April 19, June 21 to July 22 and December 21 to 31) then you have to be more careful. These are periods to reduce activity, rest and relax more, and let go of inessential things.

The good news is that there is much you can do to enhance your health and prevent problems from developing. First off, pay more attention to the ankles and feet. Wear shoes that fit right and don't pinch you or throw you off balance. Better from a health perspective to sacrifice fashion for comfort – but you Librans aren't likely to sacrifice fashion. Perhaps, though, you can find both – comfort *and* fashion. Give your ankles more support when exercising or indulging in sport. Regular foot and ankle massage will do wonders for you. You respond very well to these kinds of things. Foot massage is not only good for the feet themselves, but benefits the whole body – the feet contain reflexes to the entire body. (See the chart opposite.)

Let's go deeper. Neptune is your health planet. In the physical body he rules the feet – thus the importance of the feet in overall health. Neptune rules your health from the Sign of Aquarius. In the physical body, Aquarius rules the ankles – hence their importance in overall health. (Uranus, the planet that rules the ankles, is also in your 6th House of Health – reinforcing what we are saying.)

Neptune also happens to be the most spiritual of all the planets. (And Uranus in your House of Health is in the spiritual Sign of Pisces.) Thus, as has been the case for many years now, the spiritual aspects of health are very important for you. You have by now made a lot of progress in this area, and this year you will go more deeply into it. The depths here are infinite, and no matter how much we know there is always more to learn.

The main thing is to be open to intuition if a health problem occurs. And of course, number one when it comes to spiritual healing is to know who the real Healer is – the Divine within you. (Other people can get away with giving healing power to health professionals or drugs or herbs or therapies – but you cannot.)

There is another important health trend that has been going on for some years now – also ultimately positive. You are in a period where you need to throw out all the rule books and learn how you personally function – how you respond to certain diets, foods, therapies, exercises, etc. What works for other people might not work for you. You are wired up in a very unique way and your health needs are very personal.

Reflexology

Try to massage the whole foot on a regular basis, but pay extra attention to the points highlighted on the chart. When you massage, be aware of 'sore spots', as these need special attention. It's also a good idea to massage the ankles and top side (as well as the soles) of the feet.

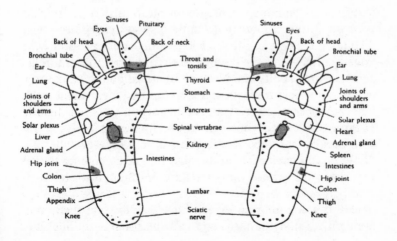

Home and Family

This is a very important area in the year ahead – and for many years to come.

This year things look very happy. Jupiter in your 4th House is bringing great family support – both financial and in other ways. Many of you will move this year, and the move looks very happy. The move will be to a bigger (and probably fancier) home. Some of you might not actually move but buy additional homes. Many of you will be buying big-ticket items for the home (again, making the home 'like new'). Renovations or expansions of the present home are other possible scenarios. Generally with this transit the family as a whole prospers. There is a fortunate sale or purchase of a home. The value of your home and your furnishings increases.

Librans of childbearing age are more fertile this year and next year. The family circle will expand either through births or marriage. Many of you will meet new people who are 'like family' to you.

Fancy and high-end communication gadgets are being installed in the home this year. Perhaps you are creating a family 'network' to link all family members together in a high-tech way.

Jupiter is your planet of communication. His position in your 4th House shows that family disputes can be resolved through good communication. Talk things out in a calm way. Wait until passions die down and then discuss things intelligently. Family unity can also be enhanced by taking courses or attending lectures together as a family. There need to be more intellectual interests in common.

Pluto flirts with your 4th House in the year ahead. He won't really be established in this House until November 27. Those of you born early in the Sign of Libra are going to feel this the most. Those born later in the Sign will feel it in coming years.

This is going to bring a cosmic detox to bear on the home, family life, family patterns and your personal emotional life.

Impurities in these things – ideas or patterns not in harmony with universal truth – will be brought up, revealed and then disposed of. It will be a long-term period of great (and very profound) psychological growth. I won't say this will be pleasant or pretty – at times it will be messy – but the end result will be the home and family life of your dreams. The family patterns (especially if they are unhealthy or dysfunctional) might have to die, so that a new pattern can be installed.

The best time to do construction or major renovation of the home will be from January 27 to June 14 and from December 21 to 31. If you are redecorating in a cosmetic way or buying art objects for the home, the best time will be from January 1 to 24.

Finance and Career

Your 2nd House of Finance is not a House of Power this year. Usually this denotes a status-quo kind of year. But this year I'm not so sure about that.

Pluto, your financial planet, is making a major move from Sagittarius into Capricorn this year. Keep in mind that Pluto has been in Sagittarius since 1995 – about 13 years. For Pluto this is not a long time – his average transit is between 20 to 35 years. But still this is a very long-term trend.

This move signifies a shift in your financial thinking, strategy and investments. While Pluto was in ebullient Sagittarius you had a certain attitude to finance. Your goals were huge. You weren't interested in just 'getting by' – you wanted BIG wealth. By now many of you have attained it. Your financial planet in Sagittarius made you a risk-taker *par excellence*. You believed in 'quick money'. Many of you were hurt by this attitude, too. But even so, your optimism has been unquenchable. You've believed in the 'Infinite Supply' – in limitless wealth – and losses were only temporary.

Pluto in Capricorn is a whole different mindset. Where formerly you were a risk-taker – a speculator – now you are becoming more conservative in financial matters. Formerly you spent big (and probably impulsively). Now you are a more careful spender. Oh you will spend, but you will want value for money. You will start to take on more of Capricorn's financial attitudes. You will have a long-term perspective on wealth. You will want to conserve your wealth (and for many of you who got rich this past cycle, this is definitely so). But even if you are too young to have participated in the Pluto-in-Sagittarius cycle, you will be taking a long-term perspective on wealth. Instead of focusing on 'quick money' you will see that wealth is built up over time, little by little, consistently. It is an evolutionary rather than revolutionary process. You will start to think about what an investment will be worth 20 or even 30 years down the road. You will make long-term financial goals and be more able to stick to them.

The free-spending days of Pluto in Sagittarius seem about over (by the end of the year they will be over). Now the cosmos wants you to have more control over your spending. Budgeting might be in order these days.

We also see changes in investments and investment strategy. Serious investors leaned towards the 'momentum' investing style for many years. Now they will become 'value' investors. There are even changes in the nature of the investments (for serious investors). Previously telecommunications (local and long distance), transport, publishing and the travel business were profitable. Now the focus will be more on conservative companies – the large blue-chip stocks – the traditional companies. Property – both commercial and residential – will become very interesting.

Bonds and the bond market have always been interesting for Libran investors, and this trend continues in the year ahead. But we see changes in the kinds of bonds you are buying. Less speculative. And perhaps in the industries mentioned above. (Also, government bonds seem interesting now and for years to come.)

There is prosperity in the year ahead, but more of an 'evolutionary' kind.

Job-seekers have much job instability. There could be multiple job changes in the year ahead. Your most important consideration is whether the job is enjoyable or not. Your challenge this year (as it has been for many years now) is to truly enjoy your work.

Those who employ others also have great instability in the workforce. There is constant employee turnover. (If you can do things to make work more enjoyable – to make the workplace more of a fun place – it might be easier to hold on to employees.)

Your 10th House of Career is not a House of Power this year. Thus I expect a status-quo kind of year. As mentioned earlier, home and family seem much more important to you than outer, worldly success. During the course of the year there will be periods where you are more ambitious than usual. We will discuss these short-term trends in the monthly reports.

Your most important financial periods will be from October 23 to November 22 and from December 21 to 23. (This latter period looks like a nice payday.)

Love and Social Life

Your 7th House of Love and Romance is not a House of Power this year, Libra. And though you are always interested in these things, this year this is less so than other times. I expect that marrieds will stay married and singles will stay single.

Your 11th House of Friendship is much easier these days, now that Saturn has left that House. But this too seems status quo. Friendships have been tested for two years now and many of them went down in flames. This year there is another testing – but short term – by the Solar Eclipse of August 1.

The main action this year is in the 5th House of Love Affairs. This seems very exciting and constantly changing. No stability whatsoever. Yet you don't seem to mind – since you are not serious about these things. Lovers come and go.

The workplace is the major scene for these things. Either with co-workers or superiors. Opportunities for love affairs also happen as you pursue your health goals – at the gym, aerobics or yoga studio, doctor's surgery and the like. And of course they will happen in the usual ways – at parties, the theatre, sporting events, outings to gaming arenas or resorts.

You seem to want to experiment in sexual matters this year. If you keep the experiments legal and non-destructive, you will have fun and gain much new knowledge.

Librans in or working towards a second marriage have a status-quo year. Librans in their third marriage have just gone through a very difficult period. The marriage might not have survived. (But a sound marriage will have.) If you are still married you can breathe a little more easily. If you are single, it will probably be a status-quo year. Those working towards or in their fourth marriage also have a status-quo year.

Your most active social period will be from March 20 to April 30.

Self-improvement

Spirituality *per se* has not been important for many years. It has been important from a health perspective, but not much else. This year, the 12th House of Spirituality is very important. A whole re-organization is going on there. Your whole regime and practice is getting re-organized and put into 'right order'.

For a long time you've practised haphazardly, when you've had time or were in a crisis. But now you seem more willing to take on a more disciplined daily regime – and it is important that you do. You need to create the right kind of spiritual habits.

When the 12th House is strong, people tend to seek more seclusion. So this is a greater need in your life right now. Now most people have a terrible fear of this – a fear of being cut off from others, from society and from friends. And Libra has this fear more than most. Their social life is the most important thing for them. To deprive them of this is like depriving a fish of water.

Yet, seclusion these days will be healthy for you, Libra. We're not talking total seclusion, but spending more time (than usual) with yourself. Many wonderful things will happen as you do this. First off, you will lose your fear of being 'cut off' from others. (It is wonderful to have a good social life, but it should come from joy and genuine pleasure in the company of others – not from fear of being alone.) Secondly, you will learn to enjoy your own company – and this, ultimately, will help your love life. If you don't enjoy your own company, how can you expect others to enjoy it?

Ultimately you have one true friend. Death will eventually end them. But you – your True Self – will always be there for you. Isn't it worthwhile to spend some time with this friend?

Spirituality is often seen as something 'vague and nebulous' – intangible. Yet there is a science and a knowledge behind it that is as exact as physics or mathematics. Yes, spirituality deals with the so-called 'intangibles' – but the results are very tangible. This is a good period to explore the scientific side of these things.

Spiritual success requires many of the same qualities that 'worldly success' requires. There is a need for discipline, order, focus and persistent practice. These are the qualities that need to be developed in coming years.

Month-by-month Forecasts

January

Best Days Overall: 1, 9, 10, 18, 19, 27, 28
Most Stressful Days Overall: 7, 8, 14, 15, 20, 21
Best Days for Love: 1, 6, 10, 14, 15, 18, 19, 23, 24, 28
Best Days for Money: 2, 3, 6, 7, 15, 16, 24, 25, 29, 30, 31

Your year begins with 70 to 80 per cent of the planets below the horizon. You are in the 'night' phase of your year. Not only that, but your 4th House of Home and Family is very powerful – 50 to 60 per cent of the planets are either there or moving through there this month. Your 10th House of Career, by contrast, is empty (only the Moon visits there on the 20th and 21st). A very clear message: This is a period for de-emphasizing the career and paying attention to the home, family and emotional life in general. You are in a period (and this month even more so) where what you achieve and do are not so important. It's how you feel, your inner state, your mood that is important. Under these kinds of aspects people often pass up lucrative career opportunities – opportunities that others would kill for – if they interfere with the family or overall emotional harmony. It is hard for others to understand this, but for you it is logical.

This is a month of great psychological progress – and this brings great inner joy and satisfaction. If you are involved in therapy, there are important breakthroughs this month. Professional therapists will have a banner month – and are unusually good at what they do.

Family unity is enhanced in many ways this month – through good communication and religious observance (as a family unit) – through education (as a family unit, attending lectures together or school) and through spiritual understanding. Later on in the month, your personal attention – just your presence – seems important. And (as your financial planet moves into the 4th House on the 27th) financial support becomes important.

Family is the major headline and focus of the month ahead. Moves, renovations, redecorations, big-ticket items for the home are all likely in the month ahead.

Finances are excellent this month. Happy windfalls or opportunities happen from the 23rd to the 25th and on the 31st. You will end the month richer than when you began it. You are becoming a more conservative and shrewd investor and spender now. Financial judgement is much enhanced as your financial planet moves into Capricorn on the 27th. If you are making important financial decisions or buying big-ticket items, better to do it after the 27th than before.

Love is on hold this month. Your love planet is Retrograde until the 30th. Your usually excellent social judgement is not up to its usual standards. You are still in a period (until the 30th) where a review and analysis of your love life is in order. Review your present relationship and see where improvements can be made.

Further complicating your love life is that you are going way out of your usual bounds in the search for love.

Health needs more watching all month but especially until the 20th. Happily you seem focused on health and are on the case. The main thing is to rest and relax more and maximize your energy. Enhance health in the ways described in the yearly report, but this month pay more attention to the heart (all month), the lungs, arms, shoulders and small intestine (from the 8th onwards).

February

Best Days Overall: 6, 7, 14, 15, 23, 24
Most Stressful Days Overall: 3, 4, 10, 11, 17
Best Days for Love: 3, 4, 7, 10, 11, 13, 14, 15, 16, 23, 24
Best Days for Money: 2, 3, 4, 11, 12, 13, 20, 21, 22, 26, 27

Two eclipses shake up the world this month but you seem relatively unaffected.

The Solar Eclipse of the 7th (the 6th in the US) occurs in your 6th House and announces job changes and changes in the health regime. Sometimes this produces health scares, but overall health is basically good now, so these will only be 'scares' and nothing more. Friendships will get tested. The good ones will survive and thrive, but the weak ones will probably dissolve. There is a shake-up in the hierarchy of an organization you belong to. There are changes in the physical workplace itself. Those who employ others will have employee turnover now (and in coming months). However there seems no problem in getting new workers – they seem plentiful. And jobs also seem plentiful. There are shake-ups – dramatic changes – in the financial lives of parents or parent figures – perhaps with children, too.

The Lunar Eclipse of the 21st (20th in the US) occurs in your 12th House of Spirituality. This announces changes in your spiritual regime and practice. For those on the spiritual path these changes are coming from interior revelation – and are good. Those not on a spiritual path might begin now (and in coming months). Every Lunar Eclipse brings career shake-ups. This doesn't mean that you actually change your career (though this could happen) but that you make important changes that have long needed to be made – in your approach and strategy and thinking. There are dramatic events with parents, parent figures or authority figures in your life. There are shake-ups in the corporate hierarchy or industry (and this is part of the reason you are changing your strategy and approach).

Even though eclipses are shaking things up, you are still well into one of your yearly personal pleasure peaks. It began on the 20th of last month and is in full swing all month. Enjoy. This is a time for exploring the 'rapture' side of life – for leisure and creative activities. Children are a major focus. (They may be hard to care for, but they have a lot to teach us about enjoying life.) It might be good – if possible – to schedule some holiday time now. If you can't, try to incorporate fun into your everyday life. When you make your budget – both financially and with time – make sure to include time and money for fun.

A part of you is very speculative now (and in truth, the 1st and 2nd are good days for this) – but your financial planet still in Capricorn is not comfortable with speculations. It enjoys a calculated kind of risk, but not wild casino-type ones. Take a long-term perspective on wealth – build it gradually, step by step. Job-seekers are successful after the 19th. Likewise those who employ others. Overall prosperity is good now – the only financial weakness is the empty Money House. You might not be giving this area enough attention or respect.

Love is much improved this month. Singles are travelling far and wide – to exotic and unknown places off the beaten path – in search of love. And this month the search is successful. Mars receives beautiful aspects all month. Love is in the air. Work obligations stress a current relationship after the 19th, but this is short term. Love opportunities are at educational or religious settings – at school or worship services or in foreign lands. Good philosophical compatibility will enhance a current relationship. Also attending worship services or lectures together.

March

Best Days Overall: 4, 5, 13, 14, 22, 23, 31
Most Stressful Days Overall: 2, 3, 9, 15, 16, 29, 30
Best Days for Love: 4, 5, 6, 9, 15, 24, 25
Best Days for Money: 1, 2, 3, 10, 11, 18, 19, 20, 24, 25, 28, 29, 30

Most of the planets are still below the horizon of your Horoscope. Continue to focus on your family and emotional well-being. Keep your emotional batteries charged. Enhance family unity through material gifts and financial support, good communication and spiritual understanding. Being on the same page religiously and philosophically is very important all year. And attending worship services – together as a family unit – seems like a good idea. Also good to develop some common intellectual ground – common intellectual interests – by attending lectures or courses together as a family.

Mars moves into your 10th House of Career on the 4th. Thus you can advance your career by social means – hosting and attending the right kinds of parties – and through the intervention of friends in the right places.

Mars' move into your 10th House has important implications for your love life, too. You are mingling with the high and mighty – people of power and prestige – people above you in status. Status is like an aphrodisiac for singles this month. Marriage or a serious relationship is seen as another 'career move'. There are romantic opportunities at work or with people involved in your career. Love is challenging, but your strong interest this month – Mars is the most elevated planet in the chart – and the power in your 7th House (after the 20th) – shows success. There is a financial disagreement with your current love from the 4th to the 8th – it threatens the relationship. Perhaps the family is not accepting of your current love as well.

On the 20th you begin a yearly social peak. You are working hard this month and also playing hard. Job-seekers still have success. Those who employ others likewise.

Finances are easier before the 20th than afterwards – afterwards there is more work and challenge involved. But financial judgement is sound and investments are shrewd.

On the 6th and 7th you have profound spiritual experiences – a vivid dream or synchronistic type of experience. (It also brings a happy job opportunity to you.) If there have been health problems, this is a time to get a miraculous (supernatural) kind of healing. In general you will have an increase of spiritual experiences – encounters with supernatural phenomena – after the 13th. (You are more sensitive during this period, and more easily hurt in love, too. Be more patient with lovers – they might not realize that they're hurting you.)

Health, though, is basically good. After the 20th it needs a lot more attention. The main thing is to rest and relax more. Maximize energy. Be aware of the messages that your body is giving you – if there is a pain somewhere, stop what you're doing. Don't try to ignore it or force your way through. Pay more attention to the heart after the 20th.

April

Best Days Overall: 9, 10, 18, 19, 28, 29
Most Stressful Days Overall: 5, 6, 11, 12, 25, 26, 27
Best Days for Love: 3, 4, 5, 6, 11, 12, 13, 14, 20, 21, 22, 24
Best Days for Money: 6, 7, 8, 15, 16, 17, 20, 21, 22, 25, 26, 27

Most of the planets have been in the Western, social sector of the Horoscope for many months now. Your 7th House of Love is very powerful (40 per cent of the planets are either there or moving through there) while your 1st House of the Self is empty (only the Moon visits there on the 18th and 19th). This is about as close as one gets to 'Libra Heaven' – it's all about cultivating social skills, getting your way through charm and grace rather than through self-assertion or personal independence.

You are well into your yearly social peak. Love is happy and successful.

This month the planetary power makes an important shift from the lower, night side, of your Horoscope to the upper, day side. Mars is still in your 10th House of Career all month. It is time to start paying more attention to your career. Sure, home, family and emotional issues are still important – they will be important all year – but now shift some attention to your career. Most of you will be doing a 'juggling' act this month – shuttling between home and career. But you can serve your family best by succeeding in the world. (Focusing on your career is lot better for your social life, too.)

Singles have many options this month. A large menu to choose from. The main problem for singles is making a choice. Too many opportunities are as difficult as too few. Love opportunities happen in the usual places this month – at parties, social gatherings or group activities. With Venus, your ruler, entering into the 7th House on the 6th you are personally very popular. You are going way out of your way both for friends and your current love. Like last month you are still socializing with prominent people – people of status and position. These are people who can help your career and in other ways. The issue for you is, what do you want? Real passion? Or just a good provider?

The month ahead also seems an unusually sexually active month – from the 19th onwards. No matter what your age or stage in life, libido will be stronger than usual.

Health is stressful until the 19th. Like last month, pay more attention to your heart. Detox regimes are powerful from the 19th onwards. Another issue here is that you seem to be losing your focus. Until the 6th you're paying attention, afterwards your social urges overpower you. Force yourself to pay more attention to health this month.

Your financial planet begins a multi-month Retrograde period on the 2nd. Of course this will not stop earnings, only slow things down. Since this Retrograde lasts so long (until September 9) you will not be able to refrain from all economic activity or decision-making. But you will need to do more homework and study things more carefully than usual. Take your time in decision-making – resolve all doubts – read the small print in all your contracts and make sure, if you're buying big-ticket items, that the shop has a good returns policy. Still, even with the Retrograde this is a prosperous month – especially from the 18th to the 20th.

May

Best Days Overall: 6, 7, 15, 16, 25, 26
Most Stressful Days Overall: 2, 3, 8, 9, 23, 24, 30, 31
Best Days for Love: 1, 2, 3, 4, 5, 10, 13, 14, 20, 24, 25, 30, 31
Best Days for Money: 3, 4, 5, 12, 13, 14, 18, 19, 22, 23, 24, 31

A parent or parent figure, an authority figure in your life, is having tumultuous and dramatic experiences. This has been going on for over a month, and the trend continues in the month ahead. The domestic life in general seems shaky. Perhaps there are problems with the physical house you live in. It might need major repairs. Just keep as calm as possible and take one day at a time.

With all this excitement going on at home and with family, it is a little harder to focus on your outer life. Yet you should. The upper half – the career half – of your Horoscope is still stronger than the lower half.

Power in the 8th House shows a strong interest in personal transformation and reinvention. Your ideal self is not something that you will create but rather something that already exists – has been already created, and has merely been covered over with all kinds of false patterns – thoughts and feelings which have collected 'substance' and are merely 'obscuring' your ideal. So, the focus has to be on removing this effete material to reveal the perfection that you always were. This is done through mental, emotional and physical detox regimes.

Power in the 8th House shows that your spouse, partner or current love is prospering. He or she is more generous with you. You have good access to outside money this month – through borrowing or attracting investors. Estate and tax issues are influencing many financial decisions. With your own financial planet still Retrograde, you might be better off working to help others prosper – putting their interests ahead of your own. This is also a good month, if you have spare cash, to pay off debts or to refinance existing debt on more favourable terms.

Love and romance seem less important now than they have been the past two months. Your 7th House is empty and your love planet moves away from its prominent position in your 10th House. Until the 9th you are still interested and allured by lovers who have status and power, but afterwards you want a more 'equal' relationship – a relationship of peers. Friendship is important in love. You want friendship as much as you want romance. With your love planet in Leo after the 9th you also want a 'good time' – fun. The person who can entertain you, show you a good time, is the one who is alluring. Status and position are nice – but you want to laugh nowadays.

By now many of you have achieved your social or romantic goals, and your interests lie elsewhere, but if you are still unattached, groups and organizations seem a scene of romance. Resort areas – the playgrounds of your country or world – are also scenes for romance.

Health is much improved this month – after the 9th it will get even better. And after the 20th even better than that. Watch how 'miraculous' – magical – healings happen for you now. Perhaps some healer or health professional will get the credit – perhaps some herb, pill or medication – but the truth is your energy returned. Your immune function is strong. No sickness can stand against it.

June

Best Days Overall: 3, 4, 11, 12, 13, 21, 22, 23, 30
Most Stressful Days Overall: 5, 6, 19, 20, 26, 27
Best Days for Love: 3, 4, 7, 8, 14, 15, 17, 18, 24, 25, 26, 27
Best Days for Money: 1, 2, 8, 9, 10, 14, 15, 18, 19, 20, 27, 28, 29

This month the planetary power is shifting from the Western, social sector (your favourite place) to the Eastern, independent sector. The shift is not yet fully established – this will happen next month. It is time – very soon – to create your own happiness. To design your life as you desire it to be. Of course you will always love and be respectful of others, but you know best what's right for you. If others don't go along, then you have the power to go it alone. This 'going it alone' is perhaps the greatest fear that a Libra has. So long as you are true to yourself and following your path of bliss, you will always have companions along the way.

Career is very important this month. On the 21st you enter a yearly career peak. Great progress will be made. Again we see you shuttling back and forth between family and career responsibilities. This is the main obstacle to the success that you seek – your attention is divided. On the other hand, this divided attention will bring other benefits. You will have a career AND a happy family life. You will have outer success AND emotional harmony.

You are very elevated this month – not just for your career achievements but for who you are as a person. This elevation often brings pay rises and promotions – but also honours and recognition. You are above everyone in your family in terms of power and status this month (especially after the 18th).

Career is furthered through personal attention and personal presence – being there at the job when needed. Career is also furthered through your natural talents – social skills, networking skills, the ability to attract the right kind of people. Friends seem very helpful. Being involved with organizations – professional or social – also seems a help. (Being involved in organizations also has other side benefits – it seems good for your love life, too.)

There are still dramas at home and with parent figures. But as the month progresses, these issues begin to resolve. The worst is over with.

Health needs more watching beginning the 21st. Refer to the discussion in the yearly report. Also pay more attention to your heart now.

Your 9th House of Religion, Metaphysics, Higher Education and Philosophy is powerful until the 21st. This brings success for university students or those applying to university. There are happy travel and educational opportunities – which should be taken. There is a general expansion of the mental horizons – and this leads to optimism, happiness and success. Power in the 9th House also brings religious revelation and experience to those who desire it.

July

  Best Days Overall: 1, 9, 10, 19, 20, 28
  Most Stressful Days Overall: 2, 3, 16, 17, 23, 24, 30
  Best Days for Love: 2, 3, 6, 13, 16, 23, 24, 25, 26
  Best Days for Money: 5, 6, 7, 11, 12, 15, 16, 17, 25, 26

With 40 per cent of the planets Retrograde, the pace of events, on a worldly level, is slowing down – but for you things are heating up. You seem little affected by this slowdown. You are still in a yearly career peak and making much progress – working hard – advancing – succeeding. For many this seems a good time for a holiday – but not for you. You need to be at your post. Like last month, the challenge is balancing family life with career – a tall order but a good lesson.

You can advance your career in various ways this month. Like last month, cultivating the right friends and getting involved in organizations is a big help. Your personal presence and attention are very important now. A willingness to travel and to take courses or otherwise educate yourself is also helpful – a big plus.

By the 22nd you seem to have achieved your major goals, and your interest shifts to friends, groups, group activities and organizations.

You seem more interested in friendship than in love and romance this month. Serious love seems like a bumpy ride. A marriage or current relationship is getting tested. Real love will always weather these tests – but the flawed relationships will be in trouble. Dramatic events are happening with your spouse or lover as well – they should drive defensively and avoid risk-taking or stressful activities. They should do whatever has to be done, but reschedule the non-essential.

Both you and your lover seem more perfectionist this month. And while this attitude comes from good motives (it is good to want perfection), it can lead to destructive criticism and general dissatisfaction. Just remember that perfection is a process, and though we are all far from the goal, just getting closer to it every day is success.

Health needs more watching this month – especially until the 22nd. Keep in mind the discussion in the yearly report. Also pay more attention to your heart. Rest and relax more and delegate tasks wherever possible. Health and energy improve dramatically after the 22nd.

Avoid stressful or risk-taking activities from the 26th to the 29th.

Finances should be good this month – in spite of the continued Retrograde of your financial planet. You are in a period of career success, but continue to do more homework with regard to major purchases or investments. You are still in a period of financial review. If you do this properly, you will be in great shape when Pluto starts to move forward. You will have clear plans and goals.

August

Best Days Overall: 5, 6, 15, 16, 24, 25
Most Stressful Days Overall: 12, 13, 14, 20, 26, 27
Best Days for Love: 1, 2, 3, 4, 12, 13, 14, 20, 21, 22, 23, 24
Best Days for Money: 2, 3, 4, 7, 8, 9, 11, 12, 13, 21, 22, 23, 29, 30, 31

Some 40 per cent of the planets are still Retrograde – yet you are making rapid personal progress. Venus, your ruler, moves exceptionally fast this month – moving through three Signs and Houses of your Horoscope. You have confidence and cover a lot of territory. The general slowdown seems to be helping you.

Most of the planets are still in the Eastern sector of the self, and dynamic Mars moves into your own Sign on the 19th. This is definitely the time to take decisive action to change undesirable conditions. Happiness depends on personal initiative now – and you seem to realize this. Create your own happiness and the world will conform to you, rather than vice versa.

There are two eclipses this month. The first is a Solar Eclipse on the 1st that occurs in your 11th House of Friends. This eclipse will test friendships pretty severely (keep in mind that the eclipsed planet, the Sun, is also the ruler of friendships). There will be dramatic events in the lives of your friends and in organizations that you belong to – big shake-ups there. Parent or parent figures are making dramatic changes in their financial life. Your spouse or lover should avoid speculations during this period.

The Lunar Eclipse of the 16th occurs in your 5th House of Children, Love Affairs and Speculations. You should avoid speculations during this period. There are dramas in the lives of children. A love affair (not a serious relationship) will get tested. (But have no fear, there is serious love in the stars for singles.) Again there are financial changes for parents or parent figures. This eclipse has an impact on Neptune, your work planet, so there are job changes and changes in the physical workplace. Those who employ others will have employee turnover. There will be long-term – and dramatic – changes in your health regime, too. Children of appropriate age are making dramatic financial changes, too.

Love is pursuing you, and beginning the 19th will find you. For singles or the unattached this is a happy new romance. Nothing you need to do, he or she will come to you. This person seems very devoted and you are having

love on your terms. For marrieds or those in a serious relationship, this shows that your spouse or lover is going way
out of his or her way to please you. Your interests – your
happiness – come before their own.

Health is good this month. Almost all the planets are kind
to you. And with Mars in your own Sign you have the
energy of 10 people. You have all the fire-power you need to
achieve any goal. The only health danger now is 'burnout' –
being overactive or pushing the body beyond its limits. Still,
you look great – charismatic, with that certain energy which
is something deeper than just beauty – personal magnetism.
Others take notice – in fact you might have to beat them
away with a stick right now. Spirituality becomes very
important after the 22nd.

September

    Best Days Overall: 1, 2, 3, 11, 12, 20, 21, 29, 30
    Most Stressful Days Overall: 9, 10, 16, 17, 22, 23
    Best Days for Love: 1, 2, 11, 12, 16, 17, 20, 21, 29, 30
    Best Days for Money: 4, 5, 8, 9, 10, 17, 18, 19, 25, 27

Personal independence was very strong last month; this
month it is even stronger. This is still a period to please yourself – to create the conditions that you desire – to achieve
your goals through direct action and personal initiative. You
have all the energy to do it. The world will conform to you.
It is good to have life on your terms, but there is a downside,
too. Freedom to create also means that you will – eventually
– have to live with your creations – and if you build
unwisely, it won't be very pleasant. However, after a brief
period of digesting these lessons, you will again have more
freedom to create anew.

On the 22nd you enter another of your yearly personal
pleasure peaks – a time for indulging the senses and pleasures of the flesh. Finances will improve over last month –
but after the 22nd – and thus you seem well able to afford all
these delights.

Spirituality is still important until the 22nd. (It has been important all year, but even more so now.) This is a time for more seclusion (probably you won't be able to have total seclusion, you have too much going on in your personal life – but more seclusion than usual). Good to reconnect with the Higher Power within you – to clear the channels and get into a state of grace. Good to get more acquainted with yourself – your true self, the best and most loyal friend you will ever have. Good to review your past year and analyse your achievements. Correct past mistakes and set goals for the future. Also good to involve yourself in charities or altruistic activities. This is good period for spiritually-oriented retreats, too. You should come out of this period with great clarity of mind and purpose – ready to jump into the swing of life again on the 22nd.

Finances are improving. On the 9th your financial planet finally starts to move forward again. Financial judgement will be sound. Also after the 22nd the Sun will start to make good aspects to your financial planet. Venus, your ruler, moves into the Money House on the 24th. This shows personal interest and involvement – more interest than you've had all year. So there is prosperity now. You are spending on yourself, your image and appearance, and personal things. You are investing in yourself. Until the 24th it is good to buy clothing or personal accessories that you need – your sense of style, always good, is even better now than usual. Personal appearance plays a bigger role in finance than it has all year.

Health is good, too. Like last month, the only danger is hyperactivity – burnout. You are making fast progress this month, but try to avoid the sense of rush or impatience. One can achieve much without rushing. Mind your temper, too. You are less likely to suffer fools gladly.

Love is still happy. You are still having it on your terms. Lovers are seeking you out and ready to do anything for you. Singles who are still unattached are likely to meet someone this month, too. (Last month was also very good for this.)

October

Best Days Overall: 9, 10, 17, 18, 26, 27
Most Stressful Days Overall: 6, 7, 13, 14, 19, 20
Best Days for Love: 1, 11, 12, 13, 14, 19, 20, 21, 22, 23, 28, 29
Best Days for Money: 1, 2, 5, 6, 7, 14, 15, 16, 23, 24, 25, 28, 29, 30, 31

Last month the planets made an important shift from the top half – the day side – to the bottom – night side – of the Horoscope. Ambitions have been more or less achieved for the year. Now it is time to give almost total focus to the home, family, domestic and emotional situation. Your inner life is more important than your outer life. How you feel is more important than 'how you do'. Your state of mind – your mood – is more important than glory or status. This doesn't mean that you lack ambition totally – many of you are involved in outer careers – only that certain things come first. If you can find – and maintain – your point of emotional harmony, you can enjoy great career success from that point. But if some company or person offers you an opportunity that violates your emotional comfort zone, or uproots your family, it's probably wiser to pass on it right now.

Also it is good to work on your career in the ways of the night rather than the ways of the day. The ways of the day are overt, direct outer action. The ways of the night are more interior – through creative dreaming, fantasizing, setting goals, putting yourself in the 'emotional state' of the goal you desire. As you succeed in this, you will find – at the right time – that career goals are achieved naturally and spontaneously.

You are still well into a yearly personal pleasure peak. So enjoy. Pamper yourself. You are much more than your body, but it's good to give the body its due, when it is the season for that. This is also a good time (until the 23rd) for getting your body in shape – the way that you want it to be. You have been doing a good job of this for the past two months. You've been athletic and exercising more. Athletes have been at their 'personal best'. And even though Mars leaves your Sign on the 4th – the month ahead (until the 23rd) is still good for these things. You still look great and charismatic. Perhaps not as stylish as last month – you favour action wear, sportswear, over glamour wear this month. Good to accessorize with gold, reds, yellows and oranges. Agate, yellow diamonds and rubies are nice gems to accessorize with, too.

On the 23rd you enter a yearly financial peak. With 30 per cent of the planets in your Money House, your interest is stronger than it has been all year. And this is the primary reason for the success you enjoy. Financial goals will be attained rapidly and rather easily now. Pluto, your financial planet, is moving forward – so your financial judgement is good. You will make wise decisions. Earnings are coming in the ways that they have been coming for many years now – through communication, teaching, writing, sales, marketing, the media or good use of the media. This month networking and social contacts seem important. If you are in your own business, think about marketing to trade or professional organizations. It is important to keep up to date with the latest technology in your field. (Investments in this area in order this month.) A business partnership or joint venture could happen. If a project is too big to be handled alone, enlist a partner – this seems easy to do now. Professional investors should look at gold, utilities, military contractors, bonds and the beauty industry.

Love is happy this month, but seems more practical and less 'romantic' – love is shown through material support and gifts. This is how you feel loved as well. The wealthy person – the good provider – is more alluring than the 'romantic'. Sexual chemistry is more important than usual. Love opportunities for singles come as they go about achieving their financial goals – or with people involved in their finances.

Love passions are unusually intense this month, and while this makes the highs of love 'breathtaking' – if the passion goes negative, it can lead to undue temper and even violence (hopefully not physical). These passions need to be handled 'just so' – avoid jealousy and possessiveness.

November

Best Days Overall: 5, 6, 14, 15, 22, 23
Most Stressful Days Overall: 2, 3, 4, 10, 11, 16, 17, 30
Best Days for Love: 1, 7, 8, 10, 11, 12, 18, 20, 21, 27, 30
Best Days for Money: 1, 2, 3, 4, 11, 12, 13, 19, 20, 21, 25, 26, 29, 30

Your yearly financial peak is very much in full swing – until the 21st. After that the focus shifts to intellectual interests, communication and local travel. Home, family and emotional issues are growing in importance day by day. Most of the planets (80 to 90 per cent – a huge percentage) are below the horizon this month. On the 12th, Venus, your ruler, enters the 4th House. On the 27th, Pluto moves back into it – this time permanently.

The family situation still seems happy – not perfect – but more happy than stressful (especially after the 21st). Many things will change in the family over the next 15 years or so, but for now it seems idyllic. Family unity can be enhanced first and foremost by your personal presence and attention. People often don't realize how important this is. Financial support and material gifts are again becoming more important (and for many years to come). Good communication and common religious and philosophical ground has been important all year, and this month is no different.

So the path of success now is definitely in the realm of 'inner life' – your moods and emotional states. Feel right and everything else will fall into place. Those of you in therapy will enjoy important breakthroughs this month. But there will be increased psychological growth for all of you.

Love still seems happy, but there is a mood shift after the 16th. Until then, you still seem very practical about love – material things and sexual chemistry seem the most important things. But after the 16th (and I'm sure the tests that are happening in love from the 6th to the 11th have a lot to do with this) mental compatibility and good communication become important. Money and sex are important, but with nothing else it is doubtful whether the relationship can last. There are the pleasures of the body – and they are wonderful – but there are also pleasures of the mind, which are, in certain ways, even more wonderful. And you need to explore these things as a couple. Singles still find love as they pursue their financial goals until the 16th; after that love happens in educational settings – at schools or lectures, or even at the post office. Love is in the neighbourhood – though you would be attracted to neighbours who are of foreign origin and who are 'exotic'.

Finances are excellent this month – a prosperous month. Pluto, your financial planet, is receiving strong stimulation all month. An important financial windfall or opportunity happens from the 11th to the 13th. There's another one on the 29th and 30th. (Speculations are very favourable on the 29th and 30th – and it might be wise to invest a harmless sum on a lottery ticket or other form of speculation). You are very lucky then (Venus is travelling with benefic Jupiter) and your natural instincts are good. (Keep in mind that the cosmos can bring you luck in many other ways and not necessarily through a lottery.) This is an important shopping season, and in your case it will be wiser to shop – to buy big-ticket items – after the 27th than before. Your judgement will be better and you will get more value for your money.

Health is good.

December

Best Days Overall: 2, 3, 11, 12, 20, 21, 30, 31
Most Stressful Days Overall: 1, 7, 8, 13, 14, 27, 28
Best Days for Love: 1, 7, 8, 11, 15, 16, 20, 21, 26, 27, 30, 31
Best Days for Money: 1, 9, 10, 17, 18, 22, 23, 27, 28

If last month was good for psychological breakthroughs and growth, this month is going to be even better. Some 60 to 70 per cent of the planets are either in or moving through your 4th House of Home, Family and Emotional Life. This is really the major headline of the whole month. We can dispense with everything else and just talk about this.

First off, moves can easily happen this period. The home can be sold or bought in fortunate ways. Big-ticket items are coming for the home. Many people are coming to visit – more than usual – and there is much entertaining from the home. After the 27th it is a good period for doing construction or major repairs in the home. Tempers are flying high at home and with family members – this is only to be expected, with so much going on – but overall family life is happy.

Love is happy this month, but you can expect a period of testing from the 26th to the 30th. Money can be an issue. But this period is also likely to bring an opportunity for a business partnership or joint venture. Your spouse or partner has a financial windfall. Love is still about mental compatibility and communication most of the month. But after the 27th emotional compatibility becomes important. You want to be able to share feelings – to have emotional intimacy. You want to be emotionally nurtured – and this is how you show love. You are attracted to people with strong family values. Romantic opportunities for singles are still in educational settings until the 27th; after that they happen at family gatherings or through the introduction of family members. In some cultures, these aspects often show an 'arranged' marriage.

Speculations are very favourable on the 1st and 2nd and, like last month, it might be wise to invest a small sum on a lottery ticket. You are very lucky then and you should take advantage of this. (Again, remember that the cosmos can bring you luck in many other ways, too.) Profitable financial ideas come to you from the 12th to the 14th. These look like trading ideas, but are not limited to that. Important financial information comes that period – information that clarifies many things.

You and your spouse or partner are spending big on each other this month.

Avoid risky or stressful activities from the 12th to the 14th. Do what needs to be done (and only you can decide this) but re-schedule the inessential.

Health needs more – a lot more – watching this month – especially after the 21st. Things are basically going well if you can keep your energy levels high. But 50 to 60 per cent of the planets in stressful alignment with you is not something you can ignore. Enhance health in the ways mentioned in the yearly report – but also pay more attention to your heart. Don't be embarrassed to take a nap if you feel tired.

Scorpio

ﷲ

Personality Profile

SCORPIO AT A GLANCE

Element – Water

Ruling Planet – Pluto
   Co-ruling Planet – Mars
   Career Planet – Sun
   Love Planet – Venus
   Money Planet – Jupiter
   Planet of Health and Work – Mars
   Planet of Home and Family Life – Uranus

Colour – red-violet

*Colour that promotes love, romance and social
   harmony* – green

Colour that promotes earning power – blue

Gems – bloodstone, malachite, topaz

Metals – iron, radium, steel

Scents – cherry blossom, coconut, sandalwood, watermelon

Quality – fixed (= stability)

Quality most needed for balance – a wider view of things

Strongest virtues – loyalty, concentration, determination, courage, depth

Deepest needs – to penetrate and transform

Characteristics to avoid – jealousy, vindictiveness, fanaticism

Signs of greatest overall compatibility – Cancer, Pisces

Signs of greatest overall incompatibility – Taurus, Leo, Aquarius

Sign most helpful to career – Leo

Sign most helpful for emotional support – Aquarius

Sign most helpful financially – Sagittarius

Sign best for marriage and/or partnerships – Taurus

Sign most helpful for creative projects – Pisces

Best Sign to have fun with – Pisces

Signs most helpful in spiritual matters – Cancer, Libra

Best day of the week – Tuesday

Understanding a Scorpio

One symbol of the Sign of Scorpio is the phoenix. If you meditate upon the legend of the phoenix you will begin to understand the Scorpio character – his or her powers and abilities, interests and deepest urges.

The phoenix of mythology was a bird that could recreate and reproduce itself. It did so in a most intriguing way: it would seek a fire – usually in a religious temple – fly into it, consume itself in the flames and then emerge a new bird. If this is not the ultimate, most profound transformation, then what is?

Transformation is what Scorpios are all about – in their minds, bodies, affairs and relationships (Scorpios are also society's transformers). To change something in a natural, not an artificial way, involves a transformation from within. This type of change is a radical change as opposed to a mere cosmetic make-over. Some people think that change means altering just their appearance, but this is not the kind that interests a Scorpio. Scorpios seek deep, fundamental change. Since real change always proceeds from within, a Scorpio is very interested in – and usually accustomed to – the inner, intimate and philosophical side of life.

Scorpios are people of depth and intellect. If you want to interest them you must present them with more than just a superficial image. You and your interests, projects or business deals must have real substance to them in order to stimulate a Scorpio. If they haven't, he or she will find you out – and that will be the end of the story.

If we observe life – the processes of growth and decay – we see the transformational powers of Scorpio at work all the time. The caterpillar changes itself into a butterfly, the infant grows into a child and then an adult. To Scorpios this definite and perpetual transformation is not something to be feared. They see it as a normal part of life. This acceptance of transformation gives Scorpios the key to understanding the true meaning of life.

Scorpios' understanding of life (including life's weaknesses) makes them powerful warriors – in all senses of the word. Add to this their depth, patience and endurance and you have a powerful personality. Scorpios have good, long memories and can at times be quite vindictive – they can wait years to get their revenge. As a friend, though, there is no one more loyal and true than a Scorpio. Few are willing to make the sacrifices that a Scorpio will make for a true friend.

The results of a transformation are quite obvious, although the process of transformation is invisible and secret. This is why Scorpios are considered secretive in nature. A seed will not grow properly if you keep digging it up and exposing it to the light of day. It must stay buried – invisible – until it starts to grow. In the same manner, Scorpios fear revealing too much about themselves or their hopes to other people. However, they will be more than happy to let you see the finished product – but only when it is completely wrapped up. On the other hand, Scorpios like knowing everyone else's secrets as much as they dislike anyone knowing theirs.

Finance

Love, birth, life as well as death are Nature's most potent transformations; Scorpios are interested in all of these. In our society, money is a transforming power, too, and a Scorpio is interested in money for that reason. To a Scorpio money is power, money causes change, money controls. It is the power of money that fascinates them. But Scorpios can be too materialistic if they are not careful. They can be overly awed by the power of money, to a point where they think that money rules the world.

Even the term plutocrat comes from Pluto, the ruler of the Sign of Scorpio. Scorpios will – in one way or another – achieve the financial status they strive for. When they do so they are careful in the way they handle their wealth. Part of this financial carefulness is really a kind of honesty, for

Scorpios are usually involved with other people's money – as accountants, lawyers, stockbrokers or corporate managers – and when you handle other people's money you have to be more cautious than when you handle your own.

In order to fulfil their financial goals, Scorpios have important lessons to learn. They need to develop qualities that do not come naturally to them, such as breadth of vision, optimism, faith, trust and, above all, generosity. They need to see the wealth in Nature and in life, as well as in its more obvious forms of money and power. When they develop generosity their financial potential reaches great heights, for Jupiter, the Lord of Opulence and Good Fortune, is Scorpio's Money Planet.

Career and Public Image

Scorpio's greatest aspiration in life is to be considered by society as a source of light and life. They want to be leaders, to be stars. But they follow a very different road than do Leos, the other stars of the Zodiac. A Scorpio arrives at the goal secretly, without ostentation; a Leo pursues it openly. Scorpios seek the glamour and fun of the rich and famous in a restrained, discreet way.

Scorpios are by nature introverted and tend to avoid the limelight. But if they want to attain their highest career goals they need to open up a bit and to express themselves more. They need to stop hiding their light under a bushel and let it shine. Above all, they need to let go of any vindictiveness and small-mindedness. All their gifts and insights were given to them for one important reason – to serve life and to increase the joy of living for others.

Love and Relationships

Scorpio is another Zodiac Sign that likes committed, clearly defined, structured relationships. They are cautious about marriage, but when they do commit to a relationship they tend to be faithful – and heaven help the mate caught or even suspected of infidelity! The jealousy of the Scorpio is legendary. They can be so intense in their jealousy that even the thought or intention of infidelity will be detected and is likely to cause as much of a storm as if the deed had actually been done.

Scorpios tend to settle down with those who are wealthier than they are. They usually have enough intensity for two, so in their partners they seek someone pleasant, hardworking, amiable, stable and easy-going. They want someone they can lean on, someone loyal behind them as they fight the battles of life. To a Scorpio a partner, be it a lover or a friend, is a real partner – not an adversary. Most of all a Scorpio is looking for an ally, not a competitor.

If you are in love with a Scorpio you will need a lot of patience. It takes a long time to get to know Scorpios, because they do not reveal themselves readily. But if you persist and your motives are honourable, you will gradually be allowed into a Scorpio's inner chambers of the mind and heart.

Home and Domestic Life

Uranus is ruler of Scorpio's 4th Solar House of Home and Family. Uranus is the planet of science, technology, changes and democracy. This tells us a lot about a Scorpio's conduct in the home and what he or she needs in order to have a happy, harmonious home life.

Scorpios can sometimes bring their passion, intensity and wilfulness into the home and family, which is not always the place for these qualities. These traits are good for the warrior and the transformer, but not so good for the nurturer and family member. Because of this (and also because of their need for change and transformation) the Scorpio may be prone to sudden changes of residence. If not carefully constrained, the sometimes inflexible Scorpio can produce turmoil and sudden upheavals within the family.

Scorpios need to develop some of the virtues of Aquarius in order to cope better with domestic matters. There is a need to build a team spirit at home, to treat family activities as truly group activities – family members should all have a say in what does and does not get done. For at times a Scorpio can be most dictatorial. When a Scorpio gets dictatoral it is much worse than if a Leo or Capricorn (the two other power Signs in the Zodiac) does. For the dictatorship of a Scorpio is applied with more zeal, passion, intensity and concentration than is true of either a Leo or Capricorn. Obviously this can be unbearable to family members – especially if they are sensitive types.

In order for a Scorpio to get the full benefit of the emotional support that a family can give, he or she needs to let go of conservatism and be a bit more experimental, to explore new techniques in child-rearing, be more democratic with family members and to try to manage things by consensus rather than by autocratic edict.

Horoscope for 2008

Major Trends

You are coming off a very strong financial year, Scorpio. In fact the past two years have been very prosperous. You have worked hard – for sure – many have achieved career peaks – your material desires seem sated – achieved. Now you want to explore other areas of life. Prosperity is a wonderful blessing – but surely there is more to it? This year you are going to explore the intellectual pleasures – the pleasures of the mind. In fact, we could make a very strong case that this is the whole purpose of 'material security' – to buy a person some time to explore the mind.

Home, family and children have been a focus for some years now, and the trend continues. Most of the trends that we wrote of last year are still very much in effect. More on this later.

Career was very important last year, but now the interest is shifting to friendships and group organizations. We can make a very strong case here, too – that the whole purpose of career success is to bring you in contact with the right kinds of people.

Your most important interests this year are finance (from January 1 to January 27 and from June 14 to November 27); communication and intellectual interests; home, family and psychological issues; children, creativity and fun; friends, groups, group activities and organizations.

Your paths of greatest fulfilment this year are home, family and psychological growth; communication and intellectual interests.

Health

(Please note that this is an astrological perspective on health and not a medical one. For the medical perspective, please consult your doctor.)

When Saturn moved out of Leo late last year, it was a significant health turning-point. Overall energy started to improve. Illnesses or problems began to 'mysteriously' vanish. Many of you experienced 'miraculous' healings. From the perspective of astrology, though the healings may well have seemed miraculous, Saturn's move out of Leo had a lot to do with them. Life-force is the strongest medicine there is.

Another signal of good health this year is the empty 6th House. Most of the planets are being kind to you (only one long-term planet, Neptune, is in stressful aspect) and so you have no need to pay undue attention to health. You sort of take good health for granted.

Health is good. But, of course, during the year there will be periods where health and energy are not up to their usual standards – these come from the transits and are not trends for the year. When the difficult transits pass, your normal good health returns. This year, these difficult periods are from January 20 to February 19, April 19 to May 20 and

July 22 to August 22. These are periods to rest and relax more and pay more attention to health issues.

You can make your good heath even better that it is by paying more attention to the colon, bladder, sexual organs, head and adrenal glands.

With Mars as your health planet, vigorous physical exercise is also very good. Good health for you means much more than just the absence of symptoms – it means physical fitness (the ability to run or jog X number of laps or lift X amount of pounds) and good sexual health. Since you tend to be more sexually active than most Signs, sexual moderation and safe sex are more important for you than for most.

Mars will move through a few Signs in the year ahead. And this will show other health needs and other therapies that might be important. We will cover these short-term trends in the monthly reports.

Reflexology

Try to massage the whole foot on a regular basis, but pay extra attention to the points highlighted on the chart. When you massage, be aware of 'sore spots', as these need special attention. It's also a good idea to massage the ankles and top side (as well as the soles) of the feet.

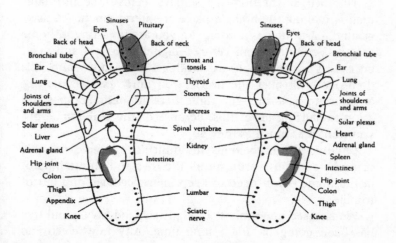

Most of our readers understand that diseases always have spiritual root causes. And the Horoscope shows us very clearly what they tend to be. Thus, if problems arise, check out your anger and its source. Also check if you have been abusing the sexual forces.

Pluto, your ruling planet, is moving out of Sagittarius into Capricorn this year – by November 27 it will be a permanent move. Thus there are important image changes. You will start to dress more conservatively. You will be less 'flaunting' of your wealth and charms. You will keep a lower profile. You will work to 'look smart' rather than 'rich'.

Home and Family

An important area of life for many years. Many of the trends written of in previous years are still in effect.

The main challenge – and also joy – is the domestic adjustments you are making because of children. Children seem very important – and have been for some years now. Single Scorpios are thinking of having them (and are very fertile these days). Married Scorpios are actually having them and are into raising them. Many are adopting children.

The focus in the home these days seems to be entertainment – making the home a place of entertainment – a playground – as much as a home. So you are investing in home theatres, entertainment centres, digital recorders and players, sports equipment, sports facilities. Toys (adults' and children's) are all over the house. You don't need to go out anymore to have fun – it's right there at home. Perhaps you are rationalizing all of this 'because of the children' – but you want it as much as they do.

Children seem rebellious and difficult to handle – so this could be another reason for all the toys and entertainment in the home – you need to keep them occupied and out of trouble.

We also see investments in high-tech gadgetry – and this has been going on for a long time. Any new electronic gadget that can make life easier (i.e. robots that hoover, networking your appliances so that you can operate them by remote control, video cameras that record all visitors, video wallpaper – things of this nature) is alluring and irresistible. Also the home is a continuous 'work in progress' – continuously 'upgraded' – continuously being renovated, changed or redecorated.

There have been moves in recent years – probably a few of them – and there could be more in the future. You are searching for the ideal home, and every time you think you've found it – something new and better is revealed.

All of this can be expensive and time consuming, to be sure. But perhaps this is what life is all about – a continuous progression into ever greater perfection. Some people explore this 'infinite perfection' in their career or finances or love lives – but you are doing it in the home.

Your family planet, Uranus, is in a water Sign – Pisces. Neptune, a watery planet, is in your 4th House of Home and Family – a clear message: Those of you looking to move, should move near water. On the water would be best – most comfortable – but lacking that, get as close as you can. You have the kind of chart of someone who would be very happy living on a houseboat – actually on the water!

There is a downside to this as well. Flooding or problems with water can be more of a problem in the year ahead. (Chances are that this has been a problem in previous years, too.) Check your pipes and plumbing. If you move near water, try to live on higher ground.

There are two eclipses in your 4th House this coming year – a Solar Eclipse on February 7 and a Lunar Eclipse on August 16. This is going to reveal any hidden flaws in the home so that you can make corrections. Also it will bring dramas with family members – in their personal lives. Family members will be more temperamental during those periods. Some of you might opt to move during those periods, too.

There is also a spiritual dimension to all of this, which we'll discuss in the Self-improvement section.

Construction or serious renovation is best done from October 4 to November 16. Beautification of the home – from a cosmetic perspective – is good from February 17 to April 6.

Finance and Career

Pluto, your ruling planet (a most important planet in your Horoscope) has been in your Money House for many years – since November of 1995. So there has been an intense interest in finance – and no one gets more intense about anything than you do. When you pursue something it is with your whole heart and mind – your whole strength. Thus success happens. Last year was an especially prosperous year – but so was 2006. By now you have attained your financial goals and are looking for new worlds to conquer.

This year Pluto is making a major move out of your Money House and into your 3rd House of Communication and Intellectual Interests. Most of the year Pluto will flirt with your 3rd House, but by November 27 he will move in permanently. Your drive and interest in wealth (just for the sake of wealth) are waning.

In previous years you were spending on yourself – investing in yourself – investing in your image and appearance. 'Looking wealthy' seemed just as important as actually 'being' wealthy. You were working the 'wealth magic'. But now you will spend more on communication equipment, cars and education. You will buy more books and magazines and spend more on lectures and seminars. This is a happy area of life this year.

Of course you're not going to just 'cease' all economic activity now. But you will shift the emphasis.

Your financial planet is also in the Sign of Capricorn this year – your 3rd House. Thus your interest in communication and education will probably enhance your income. I like these fields as investments, jobs or actual businesses. Also the media business.

Professional investors should look at the blue-chip, traditional type stocks – the big, established, old-line companies. The approach to investing should be conservative – not aimed at making big money fast – but more at making money over the long term. Momentum-investing seems out of favour for you – value-investing, buying good-quality companies at fair or undervalued prices will work better. (The industries mentioned above seem best.)

Property – both commercial and residential – also seems good.

If you have teaching or writing ability, this is the year to launch out and spread your wings. Whatever business or work you are involved with, communication will play a greater than usual role. It's not so much about the quality of your work, service or product – but about letting people know about it. Good use of the media is very important.

Job-seekers have a status-quo year. Likewise those who employ others. There will be job changes – sudden ones – from July 1 to August 19. And for those who employ others, that period brings turnover with the staff.

Although you seem very speculative this year (and have been that way for some years), this is not a year to make money that way. The conservative, tried-and-true approaches work best. (If you speculate, see it more as a form of entertainment rather than as a money-making proposition.)

Career doesn't seem important this year. There are various reasons for this. Number one, your 10th House is empty this year. Number two, all the long-term planets (with the exception of Saturn) are below the horizon of the Horoscope – showing that you are more concerned with emotional harmony and domestic tranquillity than you are with outer achievement. Psychological progress and growth are more important than promotions and glory.

A Solar Eclipse on August 1 will bring career changes or changes in your corporate hierarchy. But aside from this, career seems basically status quo.

Your most active and prosperous financial periods will be from January 1 to 20 and from October 18 to December 31.

Love and Social Life

Your 7th House of Love and Romance is not a House of Power this year, Scorpio. I read this as basically a good thing. You seem basically satisfied with your romantic life as it is, and have no need to make dramatic changes. Contentment leads to status quo. Singles will probably remain single, marrieds will stay married.

Your 5th House of Love Affairs (outside of marriage) is very active, however – and has been active for many years. An exciting area of life for singles. You have the aspects for 'serial' love affairs. They don't last very long but it is exciting while they do. None of these relationships seems likely to lead to commitment – however, they could lead to pregnancy as mentioned earlier. A word to the wise is sufficient.

Probably we will be seeing a lot more Scorpio 'single mums' in the year ahead.

For singles it is a year of experimentation and learning. You sort of find out what you really want by experiencing different things. A clear concept of Mr or Ms Right is forming in your mind.

It is the area of friendships that seems most challenging in the year ahead. Friendships are getting reorganized and restructured. Saturn in your 11th House is setting this area into 'right order'. It is very important for a person's happiness and well-being to know who his or her real friends are. It is important to mix with the right people. Positive people will lift you up, energize you and help you. Negative people will drag you down. So you are in a multi-year process of weeding out the true friends – the desirable ones – from the false, the lukewarm and the undesirable. Yes, it can be traumatic at times. Yes, there can be disillusionments. But it is still better than living in 'la la land'. Reality therapy doesn't always taste good, but in the end it *is* good.

This transit is also introducing a healthy caution in this area. Take your time making friends. Don't rush things or push things. Let friendship develop over time, in natural ways. The events of life will reveal who is who.

With Venus as your love planet, love and social opportunities come to you in a variety of ways and through a variety of means – Venus is a very fast-moving planet. So we will deal with these short-term trends in the monthly reports.

Love affair opportunities are close to home and perhaps with old flames. Friendship opportunities are also close to home – in the neighbourhood or with neighbours. There are friendship opportunities at school, lectures and seminars – as you pursue your intellectual interests.

Scorpios in their second marriage will have the marriage tested by the Solar Eclipse of August 1. But a good marriage will survive. It will bring up some dirty laundry for clearing. Singles working towards their second marriage are having a status-quo year.

Those involved in their third marriage are having their marriage tested – and this is another multi-year trend. This doesn't mean that it will dissolve, but that the going is rough – there are duties and burdens involved here that you didn't count on. Singles working towards their third marriage will probably not marry this year.

Self-improvement

Saturn, as mentioned, is testing friendships in the year ahead. It won't always be pleasant, but in the end it will be good. Basically you will learn that it is better to have a few really good friends – true friends – than hordes of lukewarm ones. Also you will see that a real friend is something to be treasured and appreciated. We don't meet many of these kinds of people very often in life – and when we do, we should honour the relationship.

Your 11th House also rules 'fondest hopes and wishes'. So Saturn is going to do a reorganization of that, too. Understand that the cosmos wants nothing better than to fulfil your Heart's Desire. However, if these 'fondest hopes and wishes' are not realistic – or if they are damaging to other people – they will need some revision on your part. This is a year to look at these things.

Those on the spiritual path are working to bring their highest spiritual ideals into everyday life – the home and family. Instilling these values in children is perhaps the greatest thing you can do. Parenting, from the spiritual perspective, is more powerful than any other activity – there is no outer career – even in politics or government – that more surely shapes and changes the future than parenting.

There are other things happening, too. Many of you are looking at the past-life connections between you, the children and family members. This seems part of your spiritual path this year (and for the past few years).

The path of love and devotion – exalting the feelings – seems like the most powerful spiritual path this year. You don't seem interested in intellectualizing the Divine, but more about actually 'feeling' it on an experiential level. Bhakti Yoga should be explored.

Month-by-month Forecasts

January

Best Days Overall: 2, 3, 12, 13, 20, 21, 29, 30, 31
Most Stressful Days Overall: 9, 10, 16, 17, 22, 23
Best Days for Love: 5, 6, 14, 15, 16, 17, 23
Best Days for Money: 5, 6, 7, 16, 24, 25

Your year begins with most of the planets (70 to 80 per cent) below the horizon. You are in the 'night' period of your year. Your 10th House of Career is empty; only the Moon is there on the 22nd and 23rd, while your 4th House of Home and Family is very strong all month – but especially after the 20th. A very clear message: Home and family – and especially psychological growth – are more important than career. This doesn't mean that you quit your job, only that you give more focus to the home and family. Even your spiritual mission (after the 20th) involves being there for family members. Inner growth is more important than outer growth. 'Right feeling' and the right state are more important than 'right doing'. Inner success is more important than outer success (and will lead to outer success later on).

The month begins with most of the planets in the independent East, but this is changing. By the end of the month, the East and West (in your chart) will be balanced. And next month the Western, social side of your Horoscope will become dominant. So, if there are things in your life that need changing, early in the month is the time to do so. Later on it will become more difficult to make these changes.

The main interests this month are home and family (especially after the 20th) and communication and intellectual interests (all month). Your 3rd House of Communication is very powerful (and this is really the main headline of the month ahead) – 60 per cent of the planets are either there or moving through there this month – a huge, huge percentage. Writers, teachers and lecturers are going to have a banner month – very productive and financially profitable. But even those who don't do these things for a living will find that they are more involved in writing and communication. The mind will be especially sharp and students will learn more easily and quickly – they will 'inhale' information. Communication skills will also be much enhanced. A great period to catch up on your reading and letter writing, to take courses (or teach) in subjects that interest you, and to give your mental body good feeding and exercise.

This is a prosperous month as well, but by the end of the month your interest in finance is not very strong. I read this as a good thing – you have attained your most important financial goals and now you can move on to other interests. This, as we mentioned in the yearly report, is a long-term trend. You spent many years developing your wealth and material success, now it is time to develop the mind.

You can enhance family unity and harmony through doing fun things together as a family this month. But your personal presence – your personal attention – being there – seems most important.

Love also seems happy, though not such an important focus. Singles will find love opportunities as they pursue their financial goals until the 24th (also people involved in their finances are alluring). After the 24th love opportunities happen in educational settings – schools, lectures, seminars. Intellectual compatibility becomes very important. A current relationship can be enhanced through material gifts and support until the 24th, and afterwards through good communication and common intellectual interests.

Rest and relax more after the 20th.

February

    Best Days Overall: 8, 9, 17, 26, 27
    Most Stressful Days Overall: 6, 7, 12, 13, 19, 20
    Best Days for Love: 3, 4, 12, 13, 14, 23
    Best Days for Money: 1, 2, 3, 4, 12, 13, 21, 22, 28, 29

A very happy love and financial opportunity is happening on the 1st and the 2nd (it could have happened on the 31st of last month as well). Your spouse or partner or current love seems very fortunate on a financial level and is generous with you.

There are two eclipses this month. The 1st a Solar Eclipse on the 7th (the 6th in the US) occurs in your 4th House and is very strong on you. Do take a reduced schedule – a few days before and after – and avoid risky, stressful activities. Those of you who are more sensitive will feel this eclipse even a week or two before it actually happens – and when you start feeling it, that is the time to start taking it easy. This eclipse brings changes in the home and the family pattern. If there are flaws in the home, now you find out about them so you can correct them. There are dramas in the lives of parents, parent figures or bosses. There are career changes as well – and shake-ups in your corporate hierarchy. Solar Eclipses have tremendous impact on the world at large, and tend to be tumultuous periods – just read the newspapers now.

Health needs more watching until the 19th anyway. But especially around the period of the Solar Eclipse.

The Lunar Eclipse of the 20th is a milder eclipse on you, but it won't hurt to take a reduced schedule anyway. This eclipse occurs in your 11th House and will test a friendship (around the period of the eclipse, but also over the course of the next six months). For students (especially in university or above, or those applying to university) it brings changes in educational plans. These are disruptive, but in the end they are good (often we only see this good in hindsight). For non-students it shows the turning-point in a legal issue – which starts to move forward one way or another. There are shake-ups in the religious institution that you are involved with – and sometimes 'crises of faith' – your belief systems get tested.

Prosperity is still good this month; the only weakness is your lack of interest. Sales, marketing, communication and social contacts seem important in finances. The social dimension seems more important early in the month.

Love opportunities for singles are still in educational settings – or in the neighbourhood or even with neighbours. Love is close to home all month. Intellectual compatibility is still alluring and necessary until the 17th, after that you crave more of an emotional connection. You want more nurturing and sharing of feelings.

After the 19th your spiritual mission involves your children and certain creative projects that you know you must do – perhaps you've had them on the back burner and now it's time to work on them. On the 19th you enter one of your yearly personal pleasure peaks – a time for fun and leisure activities.

March

Best Days Overall: 6, 7, 15, 16, 24, 25
Most Stressful Days Overall: 4, 5, 11, 17, 18, 31
Best Days for Love: 4, 5, 11, 15, 24, 25
Best Days for Money: 2, 3, 11, 19, 20, 27, 28, 29, 30

Most of the planets are now in the Western, social side, of your Horoscope. If conditions are uncomfortable, adjust to them as best you can. Make note of the discomforts as, later on in the year, you will more easily be able to change them. You are in a period where you need to cultivate your social skills. You are more in need of the good graces of others and it is best to let them have their way – as long as it isn't destructive. Personal initiative is not so much a factor in success or happiness – but likeability is.

Most of the planets are still below the horizon and your 4th House is still strong (until the 15th). Your 10th House of Career is still basically empty (only the Moon visits there on the 17th and 18th – your monthly career peak). So continue to give your family the attention they need and cultivate the right state and right feeling. Find, and then function from, your own (very unique) point of emotional harmony. Family harmony and unity can be enhanced through group activities (especially of the fun and leisure sort – going to the theatre, cinema, concert, football match or sporting event as a family) and through good communication – common intellectual interests. Until the 15th it is good to do a thorough housecleaning – get rid of excess possessions or household items and make room for the new and good that wants to come in. (This too can be done as a family and will enhance family unity.)

Though career is not a big issue this month, there can be some sudden changes on the 8th and 9th. Parents or parent figures experience personal dramas. An unmarried parent or parent figure can meet a special someone then.

You are still well into a yearly personal pleasure peak – especially until the 20th. You seem well able to afford these pleasures, too. There is prosperity now (but stronger before the 20th than afterwards). Speculations are favourable (the 6th to the 8th especially) and money seems to come in happy ways. Your personal happiness seems to release the cosmic abundance. Worry and stress were actually blocking it.

Love also seems happy. Emotional, tender and idealistic. Your lover, spouse or current relationship is very sensitive from the 13th onwards, so be more patient. Be more aware of your gestures, tone of voice and body language. It might seem like nothing to you, but to them it can be devastating. Until the 13th love is about emotional support and nurturing – the sharing of feelings is very important. But afterwards it is about fun and entertainment. The one who can show you a good time is the one you are attracted to. But this is only one dimension of it. Many of you will also experience a spiritual dimension to love – you will have transcendent love experiences. In many cases there will be an idealistic desire for perfect love – and if you look in the wrong places, there is disappointment. If you look in the right places – within – to the spirit that always loves you – you will have fulfilment, and not just on a spiritual level but on a tangible, material level. There is a need to worship the source of love – the power that produces it – rather than the outer symbol of it.

April

  Best Days Overall: 3, 4, 11, 12, 20, 21, 22, 30
  Most Stressful Days Overall: 1, 2, 7, 8, 13, 14, 28, 29
  Best Days for Love: 4, 7, 8, 13, 14, 24
  Best Days for Money: 7, 8, 16, 17, 23, 24, 26, 27

Your 6th House of Health and Work is the main headline of the current month. Job-seekers have been looking in strange and out-of-the-way places for work in the past few months. Some of you have found it. In many cases the job itself involved being in strange places – outside of your normal bounds. This trend continues in the month ahead. Job-seekers will have good success now, but they need to 'think out of the box' and be willing to do unusual things and go to unusual places – off the beaten path. There are other ways, too – parents and elders seem very helpful. Social connections – friends or your current love or spouse likewise. The government is either a potential employer or has resources that can help the job-seeker. Success looks good. Those who employ others also need to look in 'out of the way' places.

The party period of the past two months is winding down. Your focus is on health and work. A serious work-oriented month now. This is a time to catch up on your accounting and detail-oriented (and usually boring) tasks – cleaning the garage, manicuring the lawn, repairing appliances or tools, etc.

Health is good – especially until the 20th. Part of the reason is your strong focus on it. You seem to be doing all the right things regarding diet and exercise. Many of you are trying out far-fetched or unusual kinds of regimes now. But after the 19th you will discover that even the best diet and exercise regime is often not enough – there are times when you just need to rest and relax more. The batteries need to be recharged. Continue with your regime, just spend more time resting. Also health can be enhanced through more attention to the stomach, breasts and to overall emotional health. Emotional instability can be VERY draining. After one of these episodes (even a short one) you can feel as if you've been on a 'chain gang' for a few days. Mood control and emotional equilibrium will be very helpful for your health.

Health, healing (both of the self and others), being of practical service to others and doing your job properly are all part of your main spiritual mission until the 19th. After that your spiritual mission involves your spouse, current love and other people – to be there for them.

On the 19th, as the Sun enters your 7th House, you enter a yearly social peak. You are successful socially and romantically – mainly because you have a strong interest here. But kind planetary aspects are also helping. This is a period where you socialize with people of power and prestige. You can further your career (which is starting to become important) though social means, networking, attracting just the right people who can help you and having friends in the right places. Hosting and attending the right kinds of parties also is helpful.

Love can be very rash and impetuous this month – especially after the 6th. You seem fearless and risk-taking here.
You are in a 'love-at-first-sight' mood. Caution is thrown to
the winds. Though this can produce many adventures in
love – and some hurtful experiences – it also has some
psychological and spiritual value. You learn to overcome
social fears and inhibitions. When you fall, you pick yourself
up, dust yourself off and throw yourself back into the social
swing – and this is the right attitude. Singles find love at the
workplace, with co-workers, or as they pursue their health
goals. Love this month is about service – doing for one
another.

May

Best Days Overall: 1, 8, 9, 18, 19, 28, 29
Most Stressful Days Overall: 4, 5, 11, 12, 25, 26
Best Days for Love: 4, 5, 13, 14, 24, 25
Best Days for Money: 4, 5, 13, 14, 20, 21, 23, 24

Your yearly social peak is in full swing now. Singles have
significant romantic opportunities (and happy experiences) on the 1st and 2nd (the 30th of last month was also
powerful) and from the 16th to the 20th. If you are
unattached, these periods are good for meeting a special
someone – someone who is 'marriage material'. If you are
attached, these periods are romantically special with your
spouse or current love. Love is romantic now and seems
stable. Marrieds might want to enhance the current relationship by going on a second honeymoon or doing
honeymoon-ish kinds of things. Social opportunities are
happening in the expected places – at parties, weddings,
social gatherings. Friends are playing Cupid. Your parents
or parent figures likewise. Like last month, your spiritual
mission now involves your current love or spouse – to be
there for him or her. From a spiritual perspective, we
cannot measure – from a human level – the ultimate
consequences of your help. Your actions now could affect

the destiny of millions of people in the future – even those unborn.

On the 20th your interests shift to favourite Scorpio interests – sex, life and death, personal transformation, personal reinvention, the deeper things of life, occult studies, depth psychology – being 'born again'. Love becomes more passionate, more sexual than earlier in the month. Love is less romantic and flowery and more about a mutual exploration into sexual passion.

Finances also seem good. Speculations are very favourable until the 24th (but especially from the 16th to the 20th). A business partnership or joint venture could happen. Your spouse, partner or current love is prospering all month – but especially from the 16th to the 20th. There is a nice windfall there and he or she is generous with you. Spousal support seems important all month. A good month to pay off debt, but also to take out a loan if you need to. Good for attracting outside investors to your projects.

Personal earnings are slowing down a bit as your financial planet starts to go Retrograde on the 9th – but as mentioned, your spouse or partner picks up the slack. This is a month where you need to put the financial interests of others ahead of your own – to work to help others prosper. This will be more profitable than just focusing on your own financial interests.

Health improves after the 20th. Until then, try to rest and relax more. Enhance health through more attention to the heart, stomach and breasts. After the 9th as your health planet changes Signs, just focus on the heart. Health seems especially delicate from the 9th to the 20th.

There seem to be dramas in the lives of siblings. There can be big changes in your neighbourhood – construction and the like. Old neighbours can move out and new ones move in. Relations with siblings and neighbours get more delicate after the 20th.

Last month the planets started to shift from the lower to upper half of your Horoscope. From the night side, to the day side. This month the shift is complete. With 50 (and sometimes 60) per cent of the planets above the horizon it is time to start focusing on career and your outer goals in life. Career is enhanced through your social activities and social connections. You have a knack for attracting just the right friends who can help you. After the 20th enhance career through a purification and detox – get rid of the wasted effort or erroneous thoughts or emotional patterns connected with your ambitions. Focus on the essentials of your career and let the trivial things go.

June

Best Days Overall: 5, 6, 14, 15, 24, 25
Most Stressful Days Overall: 1, 2, 7, 8, 21, 22, 23, 28, 29
Best Days for Love: 1, 2, 3, 4, 14, 15, 24, 25, 28, 29
Best Days for Money: 1, 2, 9, 10, 16, 17, 18, 19, 20, 28, 29

There are still many dramas with siblings and neighbours. The neighbourhood seems unstable. Cars and communication equipment are getting tested as well. (If they pass through this test you know you have quality.) You should drive more defensively this month as well – especially until the 21st.

Health is much improved. You can enhance it further by paying more attention to the heart – like last month.

Though your financial planet is still Retrograde (all month), Pluto is moving back into the Money House (until November 27th). This slowdown is forcing you to pay more attention to finance and get more actively involved – more personally involved. Your strong interest will be a big factor in your financial success. However, do more homework when it comes to major purchases or investments. You are in a period of financial review and analysis. As you do this you will see which areas can be improved – either your product or service – and will be ready to move forward on these ideas later on when Jupiter starts to move forward again.

In the meantime, continue to focus on the prosperity of other people – but especially your spouse or partners. They are prospering and being generous with you – picking up any slack in personal earnings. Money can come to you in various ways this month – through insurance payments, royalties or inheritance (no one need actually die, but you can be named in a will or receive an inheritance while the principals are still alive).

Your 8th House (your favourite House) is still powerful until the 21st. So continue to pursue your favourite subjects – personal transformation, occult studies, life after death, past lives and depth psychology.

The whole period (until the 21st) is good for detox and purification. With Venus in this House until the 18th it is good to detox your love life (in fact it is good to do this with your social life in general). Remove emotional or mental patterns that block you from romance or friendship. Perhaps there are character traits that are undesirable and only caus-ing social havoc – this is the time to get rid of them. Also it is time to review some of your friendships – both of the heart and mind – and perhaps weed out the true from the untrue – the good from the bad.

Your 9th House of Foreign Travel, Religion, Philosophy, Metaphysics and Higher Education becomes strong after the 21st. So these are important interests then. Under these aspects people often have happy travel and educational opportunities. In your chart these seem related to your career. Either you are travelling on business or the company is sending you for study, or you are studying on your own. This is a period of mental expansion. And, for those who want it, a period of religious and philosophical revelation.

Love is still sexual and passionate until the 18th. After that there is a need for philosophical compatibility. You want someone you can learn from – someone who can expand you mentally and philosophically. Singles have the aspect for love with professors or ministers – people of this calibre. Romantic opportunities happen in foreign lands or in educational or religious settings. An existing relationship can be enhanced through a foreign trip – some really exotic locale.

July

    Best Days Overall: 2, 3, 11, 12, 21, 22, 30
    Most Stressful Days Overall: 4, 5, 19, 20, 26
    Best Days for Love: 2, 3, 13, 24, 26, 27
    Best Days for Money: 6, 7, 14, 15, 16, 17, 26

This month the planets make a decisive shift from the Western, social side of the Horoscope to the Eastern, independent side. It starts on the 12th, gets stronger on the 22nd and by the 26th, 60 per cent of the planets will be in the East. You are entering a period of personal independence. You will have the power to have life on your terms – to have things your way. If conditions are irksome or uncomfortable, change them to your liking. You have less of a need for others or their approval. The truth is that you know best what's right for you. You will be in this cycle for the rest of the year. The only problem here is that Pluto, your ruler, is Retrograde. So give more thought to the changes you want to make. You will have to live with the consequences. Take your time and resolve all doubts.

On the 22nd, you begin a yearly career peak. Career is going to get stronger from the 12th onwards, but on the 22nd you begin to peak. With most of the planets above the horizon, this is a time to let go (to a degree) of family and home issues and focus on your outer, professional life. Outer success will help you achieve emotional harmony and family unity. You serve your family best by being successful.

Like last month, it is still good to detox the career attitudes and strategies – to eliminate the frivolities and hone in on the essential. This focus will lead you to the heights. Like last month getting the education you need and a willingness to travel are also important. After the 12th career is enhanced by social means, too – through networking with the right people, having the right social connections, and through the friends that you already have. By all means attend the parties and gatherings that can help your career. The social dimension is very important. (Of course, the social dimension by itself is not enough, eventually you have to perform, but it does open doors.)

Until the 22nd, your 9th House (like last month) is strong. Thus there are still happy travel and educational opportunities. Legal issues seem very favourable (especially if they involve homes, family issues or property) until the 22nd. There is probably a desire to move this month or enlarge the residence – but with your family planet still Retrograde, best to give this more thought. Those who want it still have access to religious and philosophical revelation.

Things are turbulent at the workplace from the 1st to the 7th. There could be job changes this period. But have no fear, your career looks bright now – these changes couldn't have happened at a better time. Job-seekers should of course consult social connections – friends and the like – but should also look to professional or trade organizations. These can be helpful in finding you work, or they themselves could have a position for you.

Your love life is basically happy. On the 12th Venus, your love planet, crosses the Midheaven. This shows that your spouse, partner or current love is also experiencing a career peak (a pay rise or promotion now wouldn't be a surprise) but professional elevation can happen for him or her in other ways, too. After the 12th you are mingling with people of power and prestige – people above you in status. And these aspects often indicate an office romance – but not with co-workers, but with bosses or superiors. Singles are allured by professorial and ministerial types until the 12th – but afterwards seem more allured by power and status. Power is the great aphrodisiac then.

Health needs more watching after the 22nd. The situation doesn't look serious (though you could have a health scare from the 1st to the 7th) – it seems mainly a question of energy. The immune system is less efficient when overall energy is low – so make sure to rest and relax more then.

August

Best Days Overall: 7, 8, 9, 17, 18, 26, 27
Most Stressful Days Overall: 1, 2, 15, 16, 22, 23, 28, 29
Best Days for Love: 1, 2, 21, 22, 23
Best Days for Money: 3, 4, 10, 11, 12, 13, 22, 23, 30, 31

There are two eclipses this period, ensuring a month of
drama and long-term change – both personally and for the
world. These eclipses are particularly strong on you, Scorpio,
so do take a reduced schedule then (a few days before and
after each eclipse). Actually you need to rest and relax more
over the whole period until the 22nd – but especially around
the eclipse periods.

The Solar Eclipse of the 1st occurs in your 10th House
and this has stronger career implications than usual – it not
only occurs in your 10th House of Career, but the eclipsed
planet is also your career planet. So this eclipse for sure is
bringing career changes. This could be with another
company, or within the same company but in radically
different conditions (and rules). There are dramas in the
lives of parents, parent figures, bosses and authority figures
in your life. The career is at a dramatic turning-point. You
can't sit on the fence – you have to make a decisive move
one way or another.

From a spiritual perspective it is time to gain clarity on
your overall mission in life and make the changes that need
to be made. From a short-term perspective your mission is
your career until the 22nd and friends afterwards – being
there for friends is very important.

The Lunar Eclipse of August 16 occurs in your 4th House
of Home and Family – and this again indicates a drama in
the life of a parent or parent figure. But it also shows a
possible move (better to delay it for a while if you can), a
renovation or major repair in the home. Children and
family members are more temperamental this period, so be
more patient with them. Children, especially, seem affected
by this eclipse – and this can bring dramas and important

changes in their lives and in your relationship with them. This eclipse will also test a love affair or a creative project you are involved with. Students make important educational changes (especially those at university level or above – but college applicants are also affected). There are shake-ups in a religious organization you are involved with. Religious beliefs get tested by reality. Nothing like a reality check to detox the higher mind. This is the purpose of this eclipse.

Health needs watching. Enhance health in the ways mentioned in the yearly report, but also pay more attention to the heart (until the 22nd), small intestine (until the 19th) and the kidneys and hips (after the 19th). If problems arise, check any social in-harmonies you might have and bring them into harmony.

For singles love is still at work – or with people involved in your career until the 5th. After the 5th, it can happen as you engage with organizations or group activities. Friends are playing Cupid then. The main obstacle to love after the 5th is a critical, judgemental attitude. Avoid this like the plague. Keep in mind that perfection is a process, and work to get closer to the ideal. Perfection is rarely handed to us on a silver platter.

Finances look good this month. Financial judgement is sound. Speculations are favourable from the 5th onwards but especially from the 15th to 19th. Unattached singles meet significant people during this period – these people are marriage material.

September

Best Days Overall: 4, 5, 14, 15, 22, 23
Most Stressful Days Overall: 11, 12, 18, 19, 24, 25
Best Days for Love: 1, 2, 6, 7, 8, 11, 12, 21
Best Days for Money: 9, 10, 18, 19, 27

Hopefully you've been using the past few months to review and study the changes that you want to make in your life. For this month, after the 9th, Pluto will start to move forward. Also, 70 per cent to 80 per cent of the planets will be in the independent East. This combination is unstoppable. You will easily create conditions as you like them and face little opposition from others. In fact, it might surprise you to find that others are perfectly willing to conform and adjust to you – rather than vice versa. You are the Master of your Destiny now – clear minded and confident. Master, go forth and create your universe. The cosmos is with you.

Your 11th House of Friends is very strong this month – until the 22nd. In fact, like last month, it seems to be your spiritual mission on a short-term basis. To be there for friends and to involve yourself in organizational-type activities. (Career, which is much less in focus this month, can be enhanced in these ways, too – through networking, organizations and group activities. It is also helpful to take a 'team' attitude when it comes to your career – in personal matters your are independent, but in your career you need team spirit.)

Spirituality becomes very important after the 22nd. It has been important from a health perspective since the 19th of last month. But now it becomes important from a love, social and career perspective, too. Many of the important things in life depend on good spiritual understanding. The solutions to career or love problems lie within – in the Spirit. Working in overt ways will basically be a waste of time. You need the guidance and wisdom of a Higher Power now. Ask and it will gladly help you – either directly or through dreams or messengers – spiritual channels, psychics, astrologers, ministers or gurus. Those on a spiritual path and well grounded in their path will experience the direct action of the Spirit. Those new to the path and not yet fully established will probably get their answers indirectly – through messengers.

Scorpios are naturally very psychic people, but this month even more so. ESP and the dream life will be more active than usual. The invisible world will be very real to you – as real as the most matter-of-fact reality.

Charities, altruistic kinds of activities and volunteer work will enhance both your career and public status this month. Though these things seem to have no 'practical' value, there will be real bottom-line consequences.

If you are a nightclub or disco person, this is not a month for this – not if you're looking for love. Love will find you in spiritually-oriented retreats or weekends, at meditation seminars, at the feet of the guru or master, or as you get involved in charitable activities. After the 24th, love pursues you and will find you. Nothing much you need to do. You are having life AND love on your terms. Enjoy.

Health is good and can be made even better with spiritually-oriented therapies. There will be much progress made in understanding the power of the spirit to heal.

October

Best Days Overall: 1, 2, 11, 12, 19, 20, 28, 29, 30
Most Stressful Days Overall: 9, 10, 15, 16, 22, 23
Best Days for Love: 1, 11, 12, 15, 16, 21, 22, 23
Best Days for Money: 4, 5, 6, 7, 15, 16, 24, 25, 31

Spirituality continues to be a major interest until the 23rd. Keep last month's discussion in mind. Since you are all having birthdays – either this month or next – this is a great period to withdraw from the outer world and review the past year. You are entering your personal new year soon (your birthday – technically speaking, your Solar Return) and you want to start it fresh, with a clean slate. So look at the past year, analyse your failures and correct your errors, pat yourself on the back for your successes and set new goals for the year ahead.

A little 'other worldliness' is a healthy thing. It is curious, yet true, that we can only understand the world by getting out of it periodically. (We do this every night when we sleep.) But 'other worldliness' was never intended to be a permanent condition. We are here in the world for a purpose, and we must fulfil this purpose. So, by the 23rd (and you will feel it even earlier) you are more or less back in your body, back in the world, back into outer life – but hopefully with more understanding.

On the 23rd you enter a yearly personal pleasure peak. It is interesting how you are now just the opposite of what you were for the past month. You were more ascetic in the past month, now you are into all the pleasures of the flesh. This is how nature works – she is always alternating between opposites.

Health, energy, personal charisma, personal appearance, self-confidence and self-esteem are now at yearly highs. With Mars in your own Sign after the 4th you have the energy of 10 people. Goals are achieved rapidly (Retrograde activity in the world is also reduced this month). Mars in the Sign of Scorpio makes him most intense and powerful. Your desires are intense – white hot – and obstacles just melt before them. Libido is even stronger than usual (and that's saying something) and the month ahead seems more sexually active.

The major health danger comes from too much of a good thing – over-indulgence in the good life, and pushing the body beyond its limits. You are very independent and self-willed this period – you can be impatient if your desires are blocked – you are not in the mood for delays. Mind your temper and avoid violent people and situations.

You seem focused on health this period from the 4th onwards. It seems that the 'vanity component' of health makes it interesting. You see that when you feel good, when you exercise and eat right, you look good. There is a dramatic improvement in personal appearance. So health is interesting from a cosmetic perspective.

This is one of those months where you just need to be who you are, just be yourself, just enjoy life, and everything you want or need comes to you. (This is not always so, but you are in one of these phases.) Job and career opportunities are seeking you out. Love is pursuing you. Amazing.

Finances are good this month, but much better after the 23rd than before. Your financial planet started to move forward last month and there is good financial confidence and judgement. Long-stalled financial projects or plans now start moving forward.

November

Best Days Overall: 7, 8, 16, 17, 25, 26
Most Stressful Days Overall: 5, 6, 12, 13, 18, 19
Best Days for Love: 1, 11, 12, 13, 20, 21, 30
Best Days for Money: 1, 2, 3, 4, 12, 13, 20, 21, 27, 28, 30

On the surface you seem very ambitious. You dress for success, to show your status and position (or the status and position you aspire to). You have the look of ambition – but on the inside, not so much. Last month (and this month it gets even stronger) the planetary power shifted from the upper, day side of your Horoscope to the night side. It is time to focus on your inner life, your emotional life, your domestic happiness and the needs of your family.

Career opportunities are still pursuing you, still seeking you out, but you will probably (and wisely) be more choosy now. There are many opportunities coming to you; choose the ones that don't disturb your emotional comfort zone. The less family upheaval in a career move, the better. Enhance the family life in the ways mentioned in the yearly report. Make the home more of a fun place. Do fun things together as a family unit. Bring more joy into the home.

Job opportunities are also pursuing you. Job-seekers don't need to do anything special, just show up.

Career is very much enhanced by your sense of independence and your 'can do' attitude. Your self-confidence and good personal appearance (unusually good this month) are also a big help.

You are still very much into a yearly personal pleasure peak. Enjoy. This is a time for the fulfilment of all constructive sensual fantasies.

On the 21st you enter a yearly financial peak – the most prosperous period of your year. Your personal interest in finance is still very powerful – and this is the most important factor in your success. As mentioned, your personal interest will soon wane – you are moving to other interests in life – but in the meantime it is strong.

A business partnership can materialize this month. This can happen all month, but the 29th and 30th seem the most likely time. Your spouse or partner has a windfall and seems very generous with you. Speculations are favourable from the 12th onwards, but the 29th and 30th seem best for that, too. (Keep in mind that the cosmos is not limited in the way it brings good to you – it can happen in other ways, too.)

Love is happy now and will get even better as the month progresses. The unattached have very significant meetings from the 11th to the 14th. More serious opportunities come on the 29th and 30th. These meetings may or may not lead to marriage – but these are people who are 'marriage material' – the opportunity is there. Those who are already married or in a serious relationship will experience a deepening of the love during these periods. Also there are likely to be more social invitations – happy ones.

December

Best Days Overall: 5, 6, 13, 14, 22, 23
Most Stressful Days Overall: 2, 3, 9, 10, 15, 16, 30, 31
Best Days for Love: 1, 9, 10, 11, 20, 21, 30, 31
Best Days for Money: 1, 9, 10, 17, 18, 24, 25, 26, 27, 28

Your yearly financial peak continues in full swing all month. (Your financial peak extends for a longer period than for most of the Signs – for when the planetary power leaves the Money House they start to stimulate your financial planet, Jupiter.) A very prosperous month.

The 1st to the 3rd seems especially happy both socially and financially. If a business partnership or joint venture didn't materialize last month, it could still happen now. You may or may not take this opportunity (the planets never take away your free will), but the opportunity will be there for you. Your spouse or partner is still very hot financially and still unusually generous with you. Serious love opportunities and happy social experiences happen from the 1st to the 3rd.

But really the main headline of the month ahead is the unusual power in your 3rd House of Communication and Intellectual Interests. This House has been strong all year. But this month 60 to 70 per cent of the planets (a huge, huge percentage) are either here or moving through here this month. This House is not only strong quantitatively (no other House comes close to it in terms of numbers) but qualitatively as well. The most important planets in the chart, the Sun, your career planet, your ruler (which moved in late last month), your love planet and your financial planet are all in this House. This is the centre from which you direct all the activities in your life.

Thus money, career and love (also personal fulfilment) happen as you pursue your intellectual interests – as you take courses or attend lectures or seminars in the subjects that interest you. Also, all these things – money, love and career success – are close to home – in your neighbourhood. No need to travel far and wide for these things.

Students should do exceptionally well. Seldom has the mind been this strong, this acute. You absorb information like a sponge.

Those of you involved in sales, marketing, journalism, teaching, lecturing or media activities are having a banner month. You are sharp and effective. You have the gift of the gab (Scorpio is not noted for this, but this month you have it). Even if you are not involved in these fields on a professional level, they are still important for love, money, career and personal fulfilment.

Many of you are buying new cars or communication equipment – or receiving these things as gifts – and they look like good-quality items.

Health is good this month and you can enhance it further by paying more attention to the liver and thighs (until the 27th) and to the spine, knees, teeth, bones and skeletal alignment afterwards. Too much of a good thing can be a danger to health as well – the mind is very sharp, sensitive and easily stimulated. Thus you run the danger of thinking too much or talking too much, and this can deplete your energy. Use your mind by all means, but don't abuse it.

Sagittarius

↗

Personality Profile

SAGITTARIUS AT A GLANCE

Element – Fire

Ruling Planet – Jupiter
   Career Planet – Mercury
   Love Planet – Mercury
   Money Planet – Saturn
   Planet of Health and Work – Venus
   Planet of Home and Family Life – Neptune
   Planet of Spirituality – Pluto

Colours – blue, dark blue

*Colours that promote love, romance and social
   harmony* – yellow, yellow-orange

Colours that promote earning power – black,
   indigo

Gems – carbuncle, turquoise

Metal – tin

Scents – carnation, jasmine, myrrh

Quality – mutable (= flexibility)

Qualities most needed for balance – attention to detail, administrative and organizational skills

Strongest virtues – generosity, honesty, broad-mindedness, tremendous vision

Deepest need – to expand mentally

Characteristics to avoid – over-optimism, exaggeration, being too generous with other people's money

Signs of greatest overall compatibility – Aries, Leo

Signs of greatest overall incompatibility – Gemini, Virgo, Pisces

Sign most helpful to career – Virgo

Sign most helpful for emotional support – Pisces

Sign most helpful financially – Capricorn

Sign best for marriage and/or partnerships – Gemini

Sign most helpful for creative projects – Aries

Best Sign to have fun with – Aries

Signs most helpful in spiritual matters – Leo, Scorpio

Best day of the week – Thursday

Understanding a Sagittarius

If you look at the symbol of the archer you will gain a good, intuitive understanding of a person born under this astrological Sign. The development of archery was humanity's first refinement of the power to hunt and wage war. The ability to shoot an arrow far beyond the ordinary range of a spear extended humanity's horizons, wealth, personal will and power.

Today, instead of using bows and arrows we project our power with fuels and mighty engines, but the essential reason for using these new powers remains the same. These powers represent our ability to extend our personal sphere of influence – and this is what Sagittarius is all about. Sagittarians are always seeking to expand their horizons, to cover more territory and increase their range and scope. This applies to all aspects of their lives: economic, social and intellectual.

Sagittarians are noted for the development of the mind – the higher intellect – which understands philosophical, metaphysical and spiritual concepts. This mind represents the higher part of the psychic nature and is motivated not by self-centred considerations but by the light and grace of a Higher Power. Thus, Sagittarians love higher education of all kinds. They might be bored with formal schooling but they love to study on their own and in their own way. A love of foreign travel and interest in places far away from home are also noteworthy characteristics of the Sagittarian type.

If you give some thought to all these Sagittarian attributes you will see that they spring from the inner Sagittarian desire to develop. To travel more is to know more, to know more is to be more, to cultivate the higher mind is to grow and to reach more. All these traits tend to broaden the intellectual – and indirectly, the economic and material – horizons of the Sagittarian.

The generosity of the Sagittarian is legendary. There are many reasons for this. One is that Sagittarians seem to have an inborn consciousness of wealth. They feel that they are rich, that they are lucky, that they can attain any financial goal – and so they feel that they can afford to be generous. Sagittarians do not carry the burdens of want and limitation – which stop most other people from giving generously. Another reason for their generosity is their religious and philosophical idealism, derived from the higher mind. This higher mind is by nature generous because it is unaffected by material circumstances. Still another reason is that the act of giving tends to enhance their emotional nature. Every act of giving seems to be enriching, and this is reward enough for the Sagittarian.

Finance

Sagittarians generally entice wealth. They either attract it or create it. They have the ideas, energy and talent to make their vision of paradise on Earth a reality. However, mere wealth is not enough. Sagittarians want luxury – earning a comfortable living seems small and insignificant to them.

In order for Sagittarians to attain their true earning potential they must develop better managerial and organizational skills. They must learn to set limits, to arrive at their goals through a series of attainable sub-goals or objectives. It is very rare that a person goes from rags to riches overnight. But a long, drawn-out process is difficult for Sagittarians. Like Leos, they want to achieve wealth and success quickly and impressively. They must be aware, however, that this over-optimism can lead to unrealistic financial ventures and disappointing losses. Of course, no Zodiac Sign can bounce back as quickly as Sagittarius, but only needless heartache will be caused by this attitude. Sagittarians need to maintain their vision – never letting it go – but must also work towards it in practical and efficient ways.

Career and Public Image

Sagittarians are big thinkers. They want it all: money, fame, glamour, prestige, public acclaim and a place in history. They often go after all these goals. Some attain them, some do not – much depends on each individual's personal horoscope. But if Sagittarians want to attain public and professional status they must understand that these things are not conferred to enhance one's ego but as rewards for the amount of service that one does for the whole of humanity. If and when they figure out ways to serve more, Sagittarians can rise to the top.

The ego of the Sagittarian is gigantic – and perhaps rightly so. They have much to be proud of. If they want public acclaim, however, they will have to learn to tone down the ego a bit, to become more humble and self-effacing, without falling into the trap of self-denial and self-abasement. They must also learn to master the details of life, which can some-times elude them.

At their jobs Sagittarians are hard workers who like to please their bosses and co-workers. They are dependable, trustworthy and enjoy a challenge. Sagittarians are friendly to work with and helpful to their colleagues. They usually contribute intelligent ideas or new methods that improve the work environment for everyone. Sagittarians always look for challenging positions and careers that develop their intellect, even if they have to work very hard in order to succeed. They also work well under the supervision of others, although by nature they would rather be the supervisors and increase their sphere of influence. Sagittarians excel at professions that allow them to be in contact with many different people and to travel to new and exciting locations.

Love and Relationships

Sagittarians love freedom for themselves and will readily grant it to their partners. They like their relationships to be fluid and ever-changing. Sagittarians tend to be fickle in love and to change their minds about their partners quite frequently.

Sagittarians feel threatened by a clearly defined, well-structured relationship, as they feel this limits their freedom. The Sagittarian tends to marry more than once in life.

Sagittarians in love are passionate, generous, open, benevolent and very active. They demonstrate their affections very openly. However, just like an Aries they tend to be egocentric in the way they relate to their partners. Sagittarians should develop the ability to see others' points of view, not just their own. They need to develop some objectivity and cool intellectual clarity in their relationships so that they can develop better two-way communication with their partners. Sagittarians tend to be overly idealistic about their partners and about love in general. A cool and rational attitude will help them to perceive reality more clearly and enable them to avoid disappointment.

Home and Domestic Life

Sagittarians tend to grant a lot of freedom to their family. They like big homes and many children and are one of the most fertile Signs of the Zodiac. However, when it comes to their children Sagittarians generally err on the side of allowing them too much freedom. Sometimes their children get the idea that there are no limits. However, allowing freedom in the home is basically a positive thing – so long as some measure of balance is maintained – for it enables all family members to develop as they should.

Horoscope for 2008

Major Trends

Last year was a prosperous year, and the trend is getting even stronger in the year ahead. Money and career are really the main headlines and focus for the year ahead. We will deal with this in more detail later on.

Pluto's move out of your Sign and into Capricorn is another important headline. Pluto has been in your Sign since November of 1995. It has been a bittersweet kind of transit. On the one hand, many of you grew on a spiritual level (Pluto is your spiritual planet) and were able to give birth to your ideal of self – your ideal self-image and body. On the other hand, birth rarely comes easy – there are birth pangs – and many of you underwent many a life-and-death crisis – and near-death experiences. Sometimes the obstructions to our goals – and they are always within us – need dramatic treatment.

So Pluto's move out of your Sign is, first off, a good health signal. Your spiritual gifts – especially intuition – will now be used in the financial realm. But health still needs watching this year. More on this later.

Communication and intellectual interests have been important for many years, and the trend continues this year. Spiritual studies seem the most interesting.

Home and family have been important for many years, and this trend also continues.

As written in previous years, your main challenge is in dealing with dramatic change – sudden and dramatic. It seems dangerous for you to get too secure in any pattern – it can be uprooted in a second. There is a need to sit loose to life and make change your friend.

Your most important interests this year are finance; the body, image and self-concept (from January 1 to 27 and from June 14 to November 27); communication, intellectual interests, short-term travel and siblings; home, family and psychological growth; career.

Your paths of greatest fulfilment this year are finance, communication and intellectual interests.

Health

(Please note that this is an astrological perspective on health and not a medical one. For the medical perspective, please consult your doctor.)

As mentioned, Pluto leaving your Sign (and it will be permanent November 27) is a good health signal for you. Health should be much better than late last year, but still it needs watching. Two powerful long-term planets – Saturn and Uranus – are still in stressful aspect. Pluto will still be in your own Sign from January 1 to 27 and from June 14 to November 27. (When this happens there will be three long-term planets impacting on you.)

The problem this year is that your 6th House of Health is empty and you are probably not paying as much attention as you should. You sort of have to force yourself to pay attention to health.

There are many positive things you can do to improve your health. With Venus as your health planet, you need to always pay more attention to your kidneys and hips. Hips should be regularly massaged. The heart, too, needs more attention this year. There are many natural and drugless ways to strengthen these parts of the body – hosts of them – but if you like you can work with the foot reflexology chart overleaf.

When energy is not up to its usual standards there is a need to rest and relax more – to live in such a way that energy is maximized and not frittered away on frivolities. Delegate tasks where possible. Work with a rhythm and vary the activities. Think less and talk less. Keep your focus on the essentials in your life and let the lesser things go.

When a person faces stressful aspects it doesn't mean that he or she will get sick or will fail in life. It only means that they are facing more resistance to their goals, and that more energy is needed (and often more material resources) to

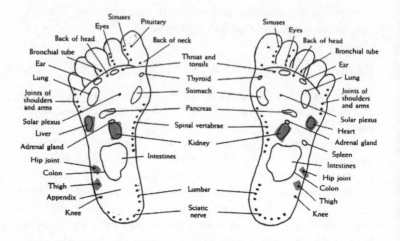

Reflexology

Try to massage the whole foot on a regular basis, but pay extra attention to the points highlighted on the chart. When you massage, be aware of 'sore spots', as these need special attention. It's also a good idea to massage the ankles and top side (as well as the soles) of the feet.

achieve them than normal. The car driving up a steep mountain will get to the top eventually, but it will take longer and use more petrol. (But you have to make sure that you have the petrol.)

Also very important not to compare yourself to others (who might be driving downhill and making faster and easier progress) or to judge yourself. Everyone exists in a different 'inner environment'. The person who walks a half-mile in a blizzard might be more heroic and strong than the person who walks 15 miles on a sunny day. This removal of judgement will eliminate a lot of stress – and add more energy.

Since your health planet is a very fast-moving planet – during the year, she (Venus) will move through all the Signs and Houses of your Horoscope – there are many short-term health trends, needs and therapies in your chart. These will be dealt with in the monthly reports.

Two (and sometimes three) long-term planets arrayed against you is stress enough, but when the short-term planets also start to gang up on you, then you need to pay special attention. This year these periods are January 1 to March 20, May 20 to June 21, and July 1 to September 22 (this latter period seems the most challenging). So be sure to rest and relax more during these periods. Listen to your body. If you feel a pain somewhere, stop what you're doing and rest. No need to be a hero. Your body has a wisdom of its own.

The health of your spouse or love can be improved through detox and sexual moderation. The spine, knees, teeth and bone structure need special attention. Children, too, need to pay more attention to these parts of the body. Parents or parent figures benefit from detox. Let them get second opinions regarding surgery.

Home and Family

An important and challenging area for some years now. Uranus has been in your 4th House since 2002, and this is creating dramatic changes both at home – in the physical home – and in relations with family members.

On a physical level – the worldly level – this shows many moves and changes of residence. Sometimes it doesn't manifest as a 'move' but as living in different places for long periods of time (it is like multiple moves, but not literally so). It indicates constant renovations of the home – a constant upgrading going on. It shows investments in communication equipment and high-tech gadgetry in the home.

On a psychological level it shows volatile personal emotions and moods. The emotions of family members are also very volatile. There are great – and extreme – mood shifts, both personally and with family members – and this is very difficult to deal with. The whole family pattern – the domestic routine – seems exploded. There are often divorces in the family that cause these things. Fights for custody of children and the like.

The main challenge – and spiritual lesson – is to cultivate emotional equilibrium. This has been the lesson for some years now. This is not something that we learn in a day, a week or a year. It can take many years and much persistent practice. But every step forward is good. Also, these volatile emotions and family dramas are putting a stress on overall health. Another good reason to learn 'inner peace'.

There are two ways that you can enhance – improve – a very volatile domestic situation. Both are related. One is to improve communication between family members (but keep in mind, shouting and being emotional is not communicating). Two, a spiritual understanding of what is going on will also help. Personal spiritual growth and the spiritual growth of family members will be a big help. You can foster family unity by attending spiritual lectures, praying, meditating and studying as a family. Also by attending courses or school as a family. This will give a lot of common ground – give a common interest – upon which to build more unity.

Moves are still likely in the year ahead.

Family members seem very rebellious and freedom-loving. Give them space – as much as possible – the maximum freedom so long as it isn't destructive.

Engaging family members in scientific pursuits – such as electronics or automobile repair – or setting up a scientific lab – is another way that tensions can be eased. There needs to be some creative outlet for the emotional energy and rebelliousness.

If you're doing serious construction in the home, August 19 to November 16 seems the best time to do it. If you are redecorating in a cosmetic way, February 17 to April 6 is good.

Finance and Career

Both your 2nd House of Finance and your 10th House of Career are Houses of Power this year. And here, really, we have the whole story of the year ahead. This is where most of the focus will be. This is a serious work and career year.

Last year was prosperous, and this year will be even more. Jupiter is in the Money House all year. Jupiter is not only the planet of wealth and abundance, but in your chart he is also the ruler of the Horoscope – thus his normal benevolent qualities are magnified. When he visits your Money House (as he is doing) it's as if you have a visit from two Father Christmases.

Also, your Money House is very strong all year, and your financial planet is right on the Midheaven – the highest point of the chart. This shows an intense drive – an intense interest – that is even more important than easy aspects. Where there is strong interest a person is not cowed by the various challenges that arise in finance. He or she is willing to overcome anything. And this always leads to success – sooner or later. It must.

But here's what's really interesting. Usually you are one of the most speculative, risk-taking people in the Zodiac. You and Leo vie for this honour. But this year, both of the planets involved in your finances are in Earth Signs – Jupiter is in Capricorn and Saturn, your financial planet, is in Virgo. So this year you are much more conservative and thoughtful in financial matters than usual. You take the step-by-step approach. You build wealth slowly, over time. You take the long-range – long-term perspective – on wealth.

This is not a year for winning the lottery, but for earning your wealth.

Assets you own will be worth more by the time the year is over. There will be promotions and pay rises at work. (Keep in mind this will bring more work and responsibility – it is not a free ride. You will have to perform.) Elders, parent figures, authorities, the government and bosses all seem sympathetic and helpful to your financial goals. As you work and earn and produce, they smile on you.

Those in your own business should solicit government contracts – as this seems a viable path to profits. Good relations with the government in general are vital to financial success – government regulators and agencies seem very involved with you.

From an investment perspective, the blue-chip, traditional types of stocks seem good. Property, government bonds, government contractors and the health industry all seem profitable. (This doesn't mean that you run out and buy these things, but that you watch them, watch the prices, and then you will know – intuitively – when to buy, when to sell and when to hold.)

Sagittarius generally likes to project an image of wealth, but this year more than usual. You are dressing very expensively. You impress others with your appearance. And this seems important in the way you earn. Sometimes, when we have to negotiate with banks or government agencies, the affluent look – the affluent appearance – is very useful.

On a deeper level, you are investing in yourself – in what you need – in things that make you more than you were. Not just clothing and accessories – but in education and training, too. You correctly understand that you are the earner, and the more you ARE, the more you can earn.

There is no freer (or more impulsive) spender in the Zodiac than Sagittarius (again, Leo vies for the honour). But this year you are much less so. You want value for money. You think things over more carefully. Your purchases and investment decisions will tend to be good this year.

Also helping matters this year (and for years to come) is Pluto's move into your Money House. Since Pluto is your spiritual planet, this indicates that intuition will start playing more of a role in decision-making. And this is the true short-cut to wealth.

As the years go by – you will feel it more next year than now – the spiritual dimensions of wealth are going to become more important than the 'worldly' ones. You are going to explore the 'supernatural' supply, rather than the natural. This is a great and exciting adventure. There is always more to learn.

Saturn, your financial planet, is camping out on an eclipse point for many months early in the year – and this is showing major and dramatic financial change. You long needed to do this, but now you are forced to. The changes will be good – but very dramatic.

Love and Social Life

This is not an important social year. Some years are like that. It was designed that way by the Creator. Some years are for psychological growth, some are for spiritual growth, some for career, some for finance. The cosmos wants a well-rounded development for us.

So, just because your 7th (Love and Romance) and 11th (Friendships) Houses are empty doesn't mean that you won't have a social life. Of course you will, only it is more on the back burner now than at other times.

I read this in a good way. In most cases this indicates a 'contentment' with things as they are. No need to make major changes. Marrieds will tend to stay married and singles will tend to stay single.

With Mercury as your love planet you are the type of person who finds social opportunities in many ways and through many kinds of people. Your needs in love constantly change as well. This might be a mystery to those involved with you (and perhaps even to yourself) but it's not a mystery to the astrologer. It all depends on where Mercury is at a given time and what kinds of aspects he is receiving. These short-term trends are best dealt with in the monthly reports.

In general, you can enhance your marriage or serious relationship with good communication. Talk problems out – but in a calm and loving way. It is important in love to have a good heart relationship – that is probably number one – but there needs to be a good head relationship, too – especially for you. If the marriage or relationship is feeling stale or 'blah', try taking courses together as a couple or go to school together. Develop some common intellectual interests. (This is good for family unity, too.)

Mercury, your love planet, goes Retrograde three times a year. And these are times when love can seem to go backwards instead of forwards. These are times, from a spiritual perspective, to review your relationship and your social life and see where you can improve things. This can be done whether you are married or single. Not good to make important love decisions during these periods – one way or another. Just review, get clear, and then when Mercury starts to move forward you can act.

This year Mercury will be Retrograde from January 28 to February 19, May 26 to June 19, and September 24 to October 15.

Everything we've written seems to apply to all Sagittarians, whether you are on your first, second or third marriage. Basically status quo.

Your most active (and happy) social periods this year will be from May 20 to June 21 and from November 23 to December 27.

Self-improvement

There are two main areas of life that will get improved in the coming year – family and the career.

We discussed the need for emotional equilibrium earlier. But this is a lot easier said than done. Basically there are two ways to go about this – medication, or true spiritual development. Sometimes – especially if there are no spiritual interests – medication is the only way to go. There are many problems with this. There are side-effects. The medication doesn't solve the problem at the root – but does give a temporary feeling of emotional tranquillity. However, you become dependent on the medication – and if you forget to take it, you are worse off than before.

The path of spiritual development is harder, will take longer, but will have permanent results. Here we look to cure the problem at the root. We confront the issues that disturb us – we observe them objectively – and a time comes – not right away – when we can do things about it.

Regular periods of meditation – of focusing on a higher power within you – will also do wonders for the emotional life. Little by a little a feeling of peace will enter – as if by magic. This peace is not something that is manipulated by the human mind. It is not created. It already exists, and we can contact it in meditation. As this peace comes in, you become more and more immune to emotional volatility. Even if some major emotional event is happening, you can always turn within and contact the peace.

The second area of improvement is in the career. As mentioned, there is strong focus here. There are likely to be promotions. There is more responsibility on you. Also, it is a year (and next year, too) for succeeding through real and honest achievement. Friends in the right places, political connections, scheming and manipulating will be of little avail. You just have to achieve and do the job properly. You have to earn your way to the top. There are no short-cuts this year. The seeming short-cut is going to be much longer than you thought. It will actually set you back. Slow and steady as she goes – this is the road.

Those of you who have this attitude will enjoy great career success. But if not, you can expect demanding bosses who will force you to achieve – who might stretch you beyond your limits.

The best way to handle this type of situation is to give the boss even more than what is demanded. Watch how fast you rise. Watch how fast the stern demeanour becomes a smile.

Month-by-month Forecasts

January

Best Days Overall: 5, 6, 14, 15, 22, 23
Most Stressful Days Overall: 12, 13, 18, 19, 25, 26
Best Days for Love: 5, 6, 9, 14, 15, 18, 19, 23, 27, 28
Best Days for Money: 7, 8, 16, 24, 25

The year begins with most (70 to 80 per cent) of the planets below the horizon of the Horoscope. You are in the 'night' time of your year and it is good to focus on home, family and domestic issues. However, in your case the 10th House of Career is very strong – just as strong as your 4th House of Home and Family – and it might be difficult for you to shift your focus – the demands of the career are very strong on you. You might not have the luxury to cultivate 'right' feeling and the right state. It will be tougher to do. But you can shift some emphasis off the career (it is a matter of degree). Probably you will be alternating back and forth between family and career.

You are well into a yearly financial peak this month. (It began last month on the 21st.) A very prosperous month now. Some 50 to 60 per cent of the planets are either in or moving through your Money House. Your financial planet is the most elevated in the Horoscope. Your drive for wealth is incredible and unstoppable – even the Retrograde of your financial planet will not stop it – only introduce some glitches or delays. This interest – this personal involvement – is the main factor in your success. You will let nothing stop or obstruct you. You go around, above or underneath any barrier. You will end the month richer than when you began. (You will be spending more, too – buying big-ticket personal items, health items or gadgets, art objects and communication equipment.)

Job-seekers have good success all month, but especially until the 24th. Jobs are seeking you and there's nothing special that you need to do – a nice position to be in. Something very interesting comes to you on the 31st. Employers will also have applicants seeking them, rather than vice versa.

Health is reasonable. There are three dynamic planets in stressful aspect, but most of the planets are in good aspect to you. Still, it won't hurt to avoid risky, stressful activities – no need to go bungee-jumping or try to break athletic records now. Drive more defensively. Enhance health by paying more attention to the liver and thighs (until the 24th) and to the spine, knees, teeth, bones and skeletal alignment afterwards.

Love seems challenging this month. A love affair is getting tested and will probably not make it. Your love planet is going Retrograde on the 23rd, so after the 23rd you should be reviewing and analysing your love and social life to see where improvements can be made. This is not a time for making important love or social decisions one way or another. Power struggles in love seem the major challenge this month.

On the 20th, your 3rd House becomes powerful. Finances are still important, but you have a greater urge to pursue intellectual interests – to read books and magazines, take courses, attend lectures and feed your mind.

February

Best Days Overall: 1, 2, 10, 11, 19, 20, 28, 29
Most Stressful Days Overall: 8, 9, 14, 15, 21, 22
Best Days for Love: 3, 4, 6, 7, 13, 14, 15, 23, 24
Best Days for Money: 3, 4, 12, 13, 21, 22

Up to now most of the planets have been in the independent East – and this trend continues for the month ahead. But pretty soon – by next month – this will change. Thus if there are conditions or circumstances that don't suit you, make the changes now while you have the power to do it. Later on it will be more difficult. You will need other people more – their consent or approval.

Finances continue to be important and basically successful this month. Your yearly financial peak is about over – but there is still prosperity happening. Last month – on the 27th – your spiritual planet entered your Money House. This shows a need to explore the spiritual dimensions of wealth. Your financial intuition is exceptional now. The only problem is the Retrograde of your financial planet. Try to resolve all doubt before making important investments, purchases or financial decisions. Intuition is wonderful – the short-cut to wealth – but do your homework as well. (There is no contradiction here – one will help the other.)

Your 3rd House is still very powerful all month – but especially until the 19th. A great period for taking courses, catching up on your reading, letter-writing and phone calls. Generally when the 3rd House is strong it is good for mass-mailings and advertising campaigns – but Mercury is Retrograde until the 19th. After the 19th is better for these things than before.

There are two eclipses this month. One a Solar Eclipse on the 7th (the 6th in the US) and the other (and stronger) Lunar Eclipse on the 21st (the 20th in the US). You need to take a reduced schedule from the 19th onwards, but especially around the period of the Lunar Eclipse.

The Solar Eclipse occurs in your 3rd House and brings dramatic events with siblings or neighbours. Important changes – major changes – are happening in your neighbourhood. Old neighbours move, new ones come in. The rules of the neighbourhood change. Communication equipment gets tested. There can be communication snafus this period (keep in mind that Mercury is also Retrograde now). There are dramatic events with parents or parent figures. And a move or renovation or repair could happen in the home. Family members are more temperamental. (Family is affected here because your family planet is impacted by this eclipse.)

The Lunar Eclipse occurs in your 10th House of Career and announces career changes. Also shake-ups in your corporate hierarchy and power structure. Often there are shake-ups in an entire industry under this aspect, and thus the overall 'game' is being played differently. Over the next few months you will be making dramatic and important financial changes – I feel for the good – but you are sort of 'pushed into' them. Again, there are dramas with parent or parent figures.

March

> Best Days Overall: 9, 17, 18, 27, 28
> Most Stressful Days Overall: 6, 7, 13, 14, 19, 20
> Best Days for Love: 4, 5, 13, 14, 15, 24, 25
> Best Days for Money: 2, 3, 10, 11, 19, 20, 29, 30

The planetary power has now shifted to the Western, social sector of your Horoscope. So this is a time to tone down self-will and self-assertion and begin cultivating the social graces and skills. In the past six months you had the power to create conditions as you liked them and to more or less have things your way – now, for the next six months or so your creations will get 'road tested'. You're more or less stuck with what you've created and it is best to adjust to conditions as best you can. Make note of the discomforts and the things that can be improved. You'll have another chance in about six months.

Your 4th House of Home and Family is the most important House of Power this month – the dominant interest. Career is still important and you won't be able to ignore it, but you can pay more attention to family issues. Cultivate emotional harmony. Career demands are strong, but work to integrate them with family interests. Try to pursue your career goals from a point of emotional harmony – from the right inner state. Work on the career by the methods of the night – through dreaming, fantasizing and visualizing. A solid career needs a solid psychological foundation. The higher you want to go, the deeper and stronger this foundation needs to be. So this is a time for working on the foundation, rather than the building itself.

Family unity and harmony (a challenge for some years now) can be enhanced through good communication and common intellectual interests; through common religious and philosophical interests – general philosophical compatibility; through entertaining from home and entertaining family members and through making the home more beautiful.

Finances are basically good this month, though not as important as they've been for the past few months. Perhaps you are spending more on the home and family, and this temporarily puts a dent in the budget. But these problems are short term – overall prosperity is very much intact.

Later in the month your financial planet starts to re-stimulate last month's Lunar Eclipse point, and this suggests dramatic financial changes. Perhaps you are forced into them. Your financial thinking is perhaps unrealistic.

Job-seekers get interesting job opportunities from family or through family connections on the 6th and 7th. A family member could find a job during this period, too.

Love is improving. Mars leaves the 7th House of Love on the 4th – and reduces the need for power struggles. Mercury, your love planet, is forward all month – so your social judgement and confidence are good. For singles, love opportunities are close to home all month. Until the 15th they are in the neighbourhood or with neighbours – perhaps at school, or lectures or as you pursue your intellectual interests. After the 15th love is actually at home – through family or family connections – or at family gatherings. (Family plays a role in romance on the 9th, too.) Love is intellectual until the 15th; afterwards it becomes more emotional and idealistic. Until the 15th singles are allured by mental brilliance. Afterwards by sensitivity and emotional nurturing.

Health needs more watching this month – especially until the 20th. Enhance health by paying more attention to the heart (all month), the ankles (until the 13th) and the feet (after the 13th). Emotional health becomes very important after the 13th – keep moods constructive and avoid depression.

April

Best Days Overall: 5, 6, 13, 14, 23, 24
Most Stressful Days Overall: 3, 4, 9, 10, 16, 17, 30
Best Days for Love: 4, 5, 6, 9, 10, 13, 14, 15, 24, 25, 26
Best Days for Money: 7, 8, 15, 16, 17, 25, 26, 27

On the 20th of last month you entered a yearly personal pleasure peak; this carries on in full swing this month. This is a month for parties, leisure activities and exploring the 'rapture' side of life. If there is anyone in the Zodiac who knows how to party it's you, Sagittarius – only Leo can give you a run for your money. Enjoy.

This is also a period for dealing with children and getting on with them. You are more able to connect with children now as you have more of the child within you. Also a great period for exploring your personal creativity. Anyone who has ever been seriously involved in this will testify that this is one of the most joyous experiences of life. This might be a good month to take up a creative hobby, too. With your health planet in the 5th House you will find that it is not only joyous in its own right but therapeutic – it enhances your health.

Health is much, much improved over last month. Energy is back to normal levels. You also have a greater interest in health from the 18th onwards (and so does your spouse, partner or current love). You can enhance your already good health even further by paying more attention to the feet (until the 6th) and to the face, scalp and adrenal glands afterwards. Emotional health (like last month) is important until the 6th. If there is a problem, check out family relationships – past or present – and bring them back into harmony. After the 6th health is enhanced by having fun. Many of you will be more interested in the health of children than in your own personal health – and problems or in-harmonies with children can impact on your personal health. If a problem arises, work to bring your relations with children back into harmony.

Job-seekers have good success all month, but especially after the 20th. Part of the reason is that you have a stronger interest in work – and that is generally 90 per cent of success. There could be interesting openings for you in colleges, universities, religious institutions and foreign countries this month. A willingness to travel seems an important job consideration (and Sagittarius loves to travel, so this is not a problem). Social connections also play a role here.

From the 20th onwards wealth increases dramatically. (The 19th to the 23rd seems especially prosperous – and there is luck in speculations that period – your intuition is right on target.) You are entering another yearly financial peak. The dramatic financial changes you are making all month seem to come from prosperity and how to handle it properly rather than financial difficulties (these are nice problems to have.) You are a shrewd buyer and investor all year – but now your financial judgement is at yearly and perhaps lifetime highs. But if I had to choose a period for making a major purchase or investment (big-ticket items), after the 20th is better than before. There will be more Earth in the Horoscope and you will get more for your money.

For singles love seems mostly fun and games – not serious – until the 18th. Love is just another form of entertainment, and marriage doesn't seem on your mind. You like the honeymoon aspects of love, but not much else. After the 18th you get more serious. There are opportunities at the workplace, with co-workers, or as you pursue your health goals (or with people involved in your health).

May

Best Days Overall: 2, 3, 11, 12, 20, 21, 30, 31
Most Stressful Days Overall: 1, 6, 7, 13, 14, 28, 29
Best Days for Love: 4, 5, 6, 7, 13, 14, 15, 16, 24, 25, 26
Best Days for Money: 4, 5, 13, 14, 22, 23, 24

Incredible prosperity is forcing more financial changes upon you. One of the downsides of wealth – as you are discovering now – is that one must pay attention to it – manage it – invest it – deal with myriad little details that the less wealthy have no clue about. There are tax issues to weigh and consider – estate issues – and most importantly, how to protect against loss. Your financial planet starts to move forward on the 3rd after many months of Retrograde motion, so your changes should be good. Financial judgement is good now. This is still a wonderful period – until the 20th – to make those investments or buy those big-ticket items. Speculations are favourable until the 20th, but especially from the 11th to the 14th. Job-seekers have good fortune from the 17th to the 20th.

Love is happy and becoming ever more active. On the 20th you enter a yearly social peak. Many singles met someone special last month (the 27th to the 29th was a likely time) and the relationship gets deeper and more romantic in the month ahead. If you haven't met anyone special yet, this is still a good month for it to happen. Love and love opportunities happen in the usual places – at parties, weddings, celebrations and social gatherings. Existing relationships can be enhanced through mutual service – being of practical service to each other – through foreign trips, and through developing common religious, philosophical and educational interests.

On the 26th the love planet will go Retrograde and this will test new relationships. Give space to the beloved. Don't rush things. Let love develop as it will – naturally and organically. You are in another period (after the 26th) where you can improve your love life by reviewing and analysing it – this will show the areas that can be worked on. The Retrograde of your love planet is not going to stop love (you are still in the yearly social peak) but introduces some caution.

This month the planets make an important shift. The planetary power moves to the upper, 'day' side of your Horoscope, after many months on the night side. It is time to shift more attention to your blooming and blossoming career. Home and family are still very important, but with the family planet starting to go Retrograde on the 26th (and the other family planet getting set to Retrograde next month) family issues will need time to resolve. You may as well focus on your outer life and goals. This is a time to review and analyse the family situation with an eye to making improvements in the future. Not a good time for making important family decisions.

Health is good until the 20th but gets more delicate afterwards. Be sure to rest and relax more then. Also enhance health through paying more attention to the neck and throat (until the 24th) and to the arms, shoulders and lungs afterwards. Earth-based therapies – mud baths, soaking in mineral heavy springs or waters, being in mountainous places or very old forests – are powerful until the 26th. After that the air-based therapies – breathing exercises, wind-bathing, wind-surfing, fresh air – are powerful.

June

    Best Days Overall: 7, 8, 16, 17, 18, 26, 27
    Most Stressful Days Overall: 3, 4, 9, 10, 24, 25, 30
    Best Days for Love: 3, 4, 11, 12, 14, 15, 21, 22, 24, 25, 30
    Best Days for Money: 1, 2, 9, 10, 19, 20, 28, 29

You are still in a yearly social peak and social opportunities abound, but the Retrograde of your love planet until the 19th suggests caution in love. Enjoy the social rounds, but don't make important commitments or decisions until after the 19th. By then your thinking will be clearer – judgement will be better – decisions should also be better.

Most of the planets are still in the social West and your 7th House of Social Activities is much stronger (for most of the month anyway) than your 1st House of Self. Further, your personal planet has been Retrograde for the past few months (perhaps this is a good thing – it makes it easier to tone down self-will and self-assertion). Continue to adjust to conditions as best you can – now is not the time to make important personal changes. (In finance you don't seem to have a choice, but in other issues, such as personal desires, personal conditions, it is best to review and study rather than to act.) Let others have their way so long as it isn't destructive. Continue to cultivate your social skills.

Your home and family planets are Retrograde, too (Neptune, your actual family planet, went Retrograde last month, and Uranus – the occupant of your 4th House of Home and Family – goes Retrograde on the 27th). Continue to review the family and home situation with an eye to making future improvements. Avoid important family decisions now.

Health still needs watching until the 21st. The main thing is to rest and relax more and keep overall energy as high as possible. Enhance health by paying more attention to the arms, shoulders and lungs (arm and shoulder massage seems a good idea). After the 18th pay more attention to the stomach and breasts. Diet will be more of a health issue after the 18th as well. Good emotional health – keeping moods constructive and upbeat – is also important. Detox regimes become more powerful after the 18th.

With your 8th House becoming powerful after the 21st, you are in an excellent period for losing weight and getting rid of 'excess' in your life. Now this excess is not necessarily evil. It's just material for which there is no need. Perhaps at one time it served a purpose, but not now. So this is a good month to clean the attic or basement and get rid of the things that you don't need. Good to eliminate financial waste, too – expenses that you don't need – or to pay off debt. Those of you into therapy or a spiritual path will have success in getting rid of mental and emotional patterns that aren't needed any more – some of these were perhaps necessary at a certain age, but not now.

July

Best Days Overall: 4, 5, 14, 15, 23, 24
Most Stressful Days Overall: 1, 6, 7, 21, 22, 28
Best Days for Love: 1, 2, 3, 10, 13, 22, 24, 28, 29
Best Days for Money: 6, 7, 16, 17, 25, 26

Mars re-stimulates February's Lunar Eclipse point from the 1st to the 8th. Avoid risky or stressful activities then. Drive more defensively and avoid arguments. This is important for you, but even more important for children. Keep them close to home. This transit will also test a love affair and bring dramatic changes in a creative project. There is luck in speculations this month, but better after the 8th than before.

Venus' re-stimulation of February's Solar Eclipse from the 26th to the 29th brings job changes and changes in the workplace. Important changes will happen in your health regime, too. Job changes can only be for the better, as you are soon to enter a yearly career peak – the stage is being set for career advancement. This transit also brings dramatic events in the lives of friends and shake-ups in organizations you belong to.

Mars moves from the Western, social sector of the Horoscope to the Eastern, personal sector. And this is a 'cuspy' – borderline – kind of month. Neither the East nor the West dominates. The planets are equally dispersed between the two sectors. Thus, you are neither as dependent as you have been in past months, nor are you overly independent. At times you can be independent and initiate actions and changes; at other times you must have the approval of others. At times you can have things your way; at other times you must adapt and adjust to circumstances. (This will start to change next month.)

Your 8th House is still powerful until the 22nd. A sexually active period. But also a period for getting involved in personal transformation and reinvention. Refer to last month's discussion, as this month continues a trend.

After the 22nd the planetary power shifts to the 9th House of Religion, Foreign Travel, Metaphysics and Higher Education. This is Sagittarius heaven. The planets are pushing you to do the things that you most love to do. So there is going to be foreign travel – and happy foreign travel. Some of it looks like business, but there is pleasure involved, too. Happy educational opportunities are also coming. A true Sagittarius loves a deep philosophical discussion as much as a night out on the town – and these kinds of things are happening this month. There is much religious and philosophical revelation. Your normally expanded mind gets even more expanded.

Health is basically good. You might be overworking. Things look very hectic in that department – you are defending your turf, staving off competition – ready to fight all comers.

Parents or parent figures need to mind their temper this month. They seem rash and impatient.

August

Best Days Overall: 1, 2, 10, 11, 20, 28, 29
Most Stressful Days Overall: 3, 4, 17, 18, 24, 25, 30, 31
Best Days for Love: 1, 2, 12, 21, 22, 23, 24, 25
Best Days for Money: 3, 4, 12, 13, 14, 21, 22, 23, 30, 31

We have two eclipses this month and they seem powerful for the world at large, but for you they seem benign. (Of course your actual personal chart, cast for your actual time and place of birth, could modify this – you could have planets in your Horoscope that are impacted by these eclipses.)

The Solar Eclipse of the 1st occurs in your 9th House. For students (especially at university level, or about to enter university) this shows dramatic changes in their education or educational plans. Sometimes a disruption – a freakish occurrence – is actually a good thing. A person can fail an important examination, be disappointed, but afterwards be led to a career that is much better and more lucrative. Sometimes one is rejected by one institution (which their heart was set on) and thus is forced (by the cosmos) to go to one that turns out to be better for them. We have our plans and the cosmos has its plan. The function of the eclipse is get us close to the true plan for our lives. Often, there are major administrative changes at the university and this changes all the rules, planning and strategy. Often students change their primary area of study under such an eclipse. The eclipse will reveal flaws in educational thinking so that they can be corrected. In general, for students or non-students, this eclipse brings shake-ups in religious organizations you belong to. Also your religious and philosophical beliefs get tested. Those that are not true, or only partially true or sometimes true, get revised. A good thing, too. This is a period for more foreign travel – but try to schedule around the eclipse. Avoid travel a few days before and after the eclipse.

The Lunar Eclipse of the 16th occurs in your 3rd House. This too affects students – but those who are below university level. There are changes at school, or an actual change of schools, or changes in educational plans. Students and non-students alike can expect that their cars and communication equipment will get tested. There can be moves or repairs in the home (Neptune, the family planet, is involved in this eclipse). There are dramatic events in the lives of parents, parent figures, siblings and neighbours.

Though these eclipses are basically benign, it won't hurt to take a reduced schedule anyway.

Health becomes more delicate after the 10th, so try to rest and relax more. It would be wonderful if you could go on holiday during this period. But if not, just pace yourself better. Enhance health by paying more attention to the heart (all month), the small intestine (from the 5th to the 30th) and the kidneys and hips (after the 30th). The important thing is to keep energy levels as high as possible.

You are in a powerful career period all month, but especially after the 22nd. There is much progress now. There are pay rises and promotions. Your work is appreciated. Finances are super.

Love also seems happy. There are opportunities for office-type romances from the 10th to the 19th. With both the love planets in the Sign of Virgo (from the 10th to the 29th) the main obstacle to romance is a critical and judgemental attitude. (You might not even be aware you're doing it – you will have to force yourself to be warm and loving towards others.)

September

Best Days Overall: 6, 7, 8, 16, 17, 24, 25
Most Stressful Days Overall: 14, 15, 20, 21, 27, 28
Best Days for Love: 1, 2, 11, 12, 20, 21, 29, 30
Best Days for Money: 9, 10, 18, 19, 27, 28

Last month the planets shifted (this time decisively) to the Eastern sector of the Horoscope, and the trend continues even more strongly now. Further, your personal power and personal initiative are even stronger as Jupiter, your ruler, finally moves forward on the 8th – after many months of Retrograde motion. You have clarity. You have confidence. You know what you want and how things should be – and most importantly you have the power and the independence to achieve. From this point of clarity it is actually desirable to make the changes – create the conditions – that you want in life. You have nobody to answer to. Even those close to you seem willing to make the adjustments. The world is ready to adjust to you instead of vice versa. With overall planetary momentum (80 per cent) now forward, you should see fast progress towards your goals. The pace of general events, on a worldly level, is also much faster now.

Last month was a banner financial month – one of your yearly peaks. And finances are still good this month – especially until the 22nd. Also your yearly career peak is still very much in effect, until the 22nd. Then the focus shifts to the social arena – friendships, organizations and group-oriented activities. Fondest hopes and wishes start to manifest.

Career is enhanced through social skills, hosting and attending the right parties, networking and getting involved with or marketing to professional or trade organizations – clubs, fraternities and sororities.

Your spiritual mission for the month involves friends, groups and organizations – contributing to them in some way. Love, too, is in these places. There are romantic opportunities with someone you considered 'just a friend' or through the introduction of friends.

Love gets more complicated after the 29th as Mercury starts to Retrograde (career gets more complicated then, too). This will be a time to make an internal review of both your love life and career with a view to improving things. There is some temporary dispute with a current love or your spouse. It doesn't seem serious, but you are not seeing eye to eye.

Health improves after the 22nd. In the meantime enhance health through rest and relaxation, keeping high energy levels, and paying more attention to the heart (until the 22nd), the kidneys and hips (until the 24th – regular hip massage would be good) and to the colon, bladder, and sexual organs (after the 24th).

October

Best Days Overall: 4, 5, 13, 14, 22, 23, 31
Most Stressful Days Overall: 11, 12, 17, 18, 24, 25
Best Days for Love: 1, 9, 10, 11, 12, 17, 18, 21, 22, 23, 26, 27
Best Days for Money: 6, 7, 15, 16, 24, 25

Mars re-stimulates the Solar Eclipse point of August 1, from the 17th to the 20th. Keep the children close to home and advise them to avoid risk-taking activities. The normal activities of life – things that need to be done – should be done. But the risky, stressful things can be rescheduled. This is a dynamic transit for the world at large, too.

Venus re-stimulates eclipse points twice this month – from the 1st to the 3rd and from the 12th to the 15th. On a worldly level this creates love disturbances, and you will probably hear more about these things during that period. On a personal level, it brings job changes or disruptions at the workplace. Those who employ others can have abrupt or surprising employee turnover. There are changes to the health regime as well.

But with Venus (your work planet) moving into your own Sign on the 18th, job changes need not be feared. There are many opportunities awaiting you – in fact they are pursuing you. You seem in demand as a worker.

Love is still complicated this month – especially until the 15th, as Mercury is still Retrograde then. Things will clear up more after the 15th. For singles there is love as they get involved in groups, organizations and group activities. Friends – and perhaps high-tech type dating services – are important in love.

Your spiritual mission will get more clarified this month, too – after the 15th. But it still involves friends, groups and organizations. Career is furthered in these ways, too. (Good use of technology and staying up to date technologically will also enhance the career.)

Though your 8th House is not strong this month, the 8th House ruler, the Moon, is highlighted from the 15th to the 23rd. Thus personal transformation – your ability to reinvent yourself – is the way you will lift up your whole life that period. Also, it is important to help your spouse, current love or partner to prosper.

Spirituality becomes important after the 23rd. Those on a spiritual path can enhance it through creativity – doing creative things. This is a valid way for getting closer to the Creator of all – the same laws that you use to paint a picture or write a song are the same laws the Creator uses to shape the universe. Spirituality is very important in health this month, too – especially until the 18th. You will respond very well to spiritually-oriented therapies and to the techniques of spiritual healers.

This period, after the 23rd (actually all month is good, but especially then) is good for spiritual retreats, bible or scripture study, meditation or involvement in selfless causes – causes that benefit the whole world and not just you personally.

A new friend is coming into your life after the 18th. It could also be that a current friend is coming to stay and you deepen your relationship.

Health is good and can be improved even further through spiritual means, as mentioned, and by paying more attention to the colon, bladder and sexual organs (until the 18th) and to the liver and thighs afterwards.

November

Best Days Overall: 1, 10, 11, 18, 19, 27, 28
Most Stressful Days Overall: 7, 8, 14, 15, 20, 21
Best Days for Love: 1, 7, 11, 12, 14, 15, 16, 17, 20, 21, 27, 28, 30
Best Days for Money: 2, 3, 4, 12, 13, 20, 21, 30

Spirituality is still a major interest until the 21st. Like last month this is a wonderful time to go on retreat or spiritual-type weekends or workshops, to get involved in meditation and to volunteer your services to altruistic types of causes – things that you believe in. It's the kind of period where you want to drop everything and sit at the feet of the Guru. Sagittarians are renowned travellers – ready to go to the other side of the world at the drop of a hat. Just give them an excuse (even the most tenuous one) and they are ready to travel. So here's your excuse: a religious-type pilgrimage would be powerful now. Even those not on a spiritual path will benefit from more seclusion this month. Good now to review your past year and rationally assess how you've done and where you want to go in the future. You are having a birthday (a personal new year) this month or next month, and it is good to start your new year – your new cycle – with a clean slate.

On the 21st you enter a yearly personal pleasure peak. You've just come out of a very intensely spiritual period – you've fed and developed your soul and spirit – now it's time to indulge the physical body. A period of sensual delights and the fulfilment of sensual fantasies are in order – and will happen. Enjoy.

Health is fabulous this month. Your energy is now at a yearly high. Some 50 to 60 per cent of the planets are either in or moving through your own Sign. And with increased energy, all kinds of possibilities open up to you. Personal independence, which has been strong for a few months, is even stronger now and you are having life on your terms. You should continue to change conditions to your liking – and to design them according to your specifications. Everything is coming to you (you have no need to pursue things – not money, not love, not travel or educational opportunity). Job opportunities are still seeking you out until the 12th. But there is an exceptionally happy opportunity – and it looks lucrative – on the 29th and 30th. You look great. Mars in your own Sign gives you personal magnetism and sex appeal. Love is happy all month. Until the 4th love opportunities are at organizations and group activities. After the 4th it is at spiritual environments. (For singles this is a good period to formulate your ideal of love.) After the 23rd love finds you, and not the other way around.

Finances are strong all month and will get even stronger next month. Speculations are favourable from the 12th onwards, but especially on the 29th and 30th.

Mars re-stimulates an eclipse point (the Lunar Eclipse of August 16) from November 6 to 11 – a dynamic transit for the world at large. Keep the children away from risky kinds of activities. Keep them close to home as much as possible. Avoid anger, temper and impatience (this will be more difficult now with Mars in your own Sign – but it is a good spiritual lesson). Walk away from tense situations.

Mercury, your love and career planet, will re-stimulate eclipse points twice this month – from the 10th to the 12th and from the 18th to the 21st. This will test a current love relationship (the good ones will survive and get even better) and brings career changes. There are dramas in the lives of bosses, parents and parent figures.

December

Best Days Overall: 7, 8, 15, 16, 24, 25, 26
Most Stressful Days Overall: 5, 6, 11, 12, 17, 18
Best Days for Love: 1, 7, 8, 11, 12, 17, 20, 21, 27, 28, 30, 31
Best Days for Money: 1, 9, 10, 17, 18, 27, 28

You are still very much into a yearly personal pleasure peak until the 21st – enjoy. But really, the main headline for the month ahead is the financial life. This is where the action is. With 60 and sometimes 70 per cent of the planets either in or moving through your Money House, you are in a yearly – and probably lifetime – financial peak. You will remember the events of this month for years to come. It will be the basis upon which you compare future earnings.

So, the month ahead is about finances – earning and spending – investing – counting your money (and there's a lot to count here). You really have a golden touch now. It's as if there is a cosmic conspiracy to make you rich, and there is nothing that can stand in the way of it. Almost everything and everyone is cooperating on a financial level. Speculations are favourable all month, but especially until the 12th.

Many of you are seeing the downside of wealth now. Wealth is a great blessing, but perhaps it is not all it's made out to be. Wealth has to be managed. There are myriad little details attached to it. There are tax issues, estate issues, accountants, brokers and financial consultants to deal with. You are buried under a mountain of paperwork. Still and all, it is infinitely better to have these kinds of problems than the problems of poverty or lack.

Interesting business partnerships or joint ventures are likely this period. There is good spousal support. Lucrative job opportunities are coming on the 1st and 2nd. Employers will attract good types of employees as well. And with very little effort. But Venus' re-stimulation of the Lunar Eclipse point of August 16 will test these jobs and workers. Perhaps the job (or the worker) has hidden flaws that you weren't aware of – and this is when you find out. Truth is always healthy, even if it is sometimes unpleasant – with truth we can always make corrections. Reality therapy is the best therapy there is. (It could be that these flaws are negligible – but it's good to understand them anyway.)

The Sun will travel with Pluto from the 20th to the 23rd. This is a peak travel period – but see if you can schedule around it.

Mars will travel with Pluto – a very dynamic transit – from the 26th to the 30th. Keep children close to home and away from stressful, risky activities. Drive more defensively.

Love seems happy (though there is a brief testing from the 12th to the 14th). Singles are interested in the practical side of love after the 12th – they are allured by wealth and the good provider. For singles there is a liaison with someone very wealthy. Love is shown in material ways – through material gifts and financial support.

Capricorn

♑

Personality Profile

CAPRICORN AT A GLANCE

Element – Earth

Ruling Planet – Saturn
   Career Planet – Venus
   Love Planet – Moon
   Money Planet – Uranus
   Planet of Communications – Neptune
   Planet of Health and Work – Mercury
   Planet of Home and Family Life – Mars
   Planet of Spirituality – Jupiter

Colours – black, indigo

Colours that promote love, romance and social
   harmony – puce, silver

Colour that promotes earning power –
   ultramarine blue

Gem – black onyx

Metal – lead

Scents – magnolia, pine, sweet pea,
    wintergreen

Quality – cardinal (= activity)

Qualities most needed for balance – warmth,
    spontaneity, a sense of fun

Strongest virtues – sense of duty, organization,
    perseverance, patience, ability to take the
    long-term view

Deepest needs – to manage, take charge and
    administrate

Characteristics to avoid – pessimism,
    depression, undue materialism and undue
    conservatism

Signs of greatest overall compatibility – Taurus,
    Virgo

Signs of greatest overall incompatibility – Aries,
    Cancer, Libra

Sign most helpful to career – Libra

Sign most helpful for emotional support – Aries

Sign most helpful financially – Aquarius

Sign best for marriage and/or partnerships –
    Cancer

Sign most helpful for creative projects – Taurus

Best Sign to have fun with – Taurus

Signs most helpful in spiritual matters – Virgo,
    Sagittarius

Best day of the week – Saturday

Understanding a Capricorn

The virtues of Capricorns are such that there will always be people for and against them. Many admire them, many dislike them. Why? It seems to be because of Capricorn's power urges. A well-developed Capricorn has his or her eyes set on the heights of power, prestige and authority. In the Sign of Capricorn, ambition is not a fatal flaw, but rather the highest virtue.

Capricorns are not frightened by the resentment their authority may sometimes breed. In Capricorn's cool, calculated, organized mind all the dangers are already factored into the equation – the unpopularity, the animosity, the misunderstandings, even the outright slander – and a plan is always in place for dealing with these things in the most efficient way. To the Capricorn, situations that would terrify an ordinary mind are merely problems to be managed, bumps on the road to ever-growing power, effectiveness and prestige.

Some people attribute pessimism to the Capricorn Sign, but this is a bit deceptive. It is true that Capricorns like to take into account the negative side of things. It is also true that they love to imagine the worst possible scenario in every undertaking. Other people might find such analyses depressing, but Capricorns only do these things so that they can formulate a way out – an escape route.

Capricorns will argue with success. They will show you that you are not doing as well as you think you are. Capricorns do this to themselves as well as to others. They do not mean to discourage you but rather to root out any impediments to your greater success. A Capricorn boss or supervisor feels that no matter how good the performance there is always room for improvement. This explains why Capricorn supervisors are difficult to handle and even infuriating at times. Their actions are, however, quite often effective – they can get their subordinates to improve and become better at their jobs.

Capricorn is a born manager and administrator. Leo is better at being king or queen, but Capricorn is better at being prime minister – the person actually wielding power.

Capricorn is interested in the virtues that last, in the things that will stand the test of time and trials of circumstance. Temporary fads and fashions mean little to a Capricorn – except as things to be used for profit or power. Capricorns apply this attitude to business, love, to their thinking and even to their philosophy and religion.

Finance

Capricorns generally attain wealth and they usually earn it. They are willing to work long and hard for what they want. They are quite amenable to foregoing a short-term gain in favour of long-term benefits. Financially, they come into their own later in life.

However, if Capricorns are to attain their financial goals they must shed some of their strong conservatism. Perhaps this is the least desirable trait of the Capricorn. They can resist anything new merely because it is new and untried. They are afraid of experimentation. Capricorns need to be willing to take a few risks. They should be more eager to market new products or explore different managerial techniques. Otherwise, progress will leave them behind. If necessary, Capricorns must be ready to change with the times, to discard old methods that no longer work.

Very often this experimentation will mean that Capricorns have to break with existing authority. They might even consider changing their present position or starting their own ventures. If so, they should be willing to accept all the risks and just get on with it. Only then will a Capricorn be on the road to highest financial gain.

Career and Public Image

A Capricorn's ambition and quest for power are evident. It is perhaps the most ambitious Sign of the Zodiac – and usually the most successful in a worldly sense. However, there are lessons Capricorns need to learn in order to fulfil their highest aspirations.

Intelligence, hard work, cool efficiency and organization will take them a certain distance, but will not carry them to the very top. Capricorns need to cultivate their social graces, to develop a social style, along with charm and an ability to get along with people. They need to bring beauty into their lives and to cultivate the right social contacts. They must learn to wield power gracefully, so that people love them for it – a very delicate art. They also need to learn how to bring people together in order to fulfil certain objectives. In short, Capricorns require some of the gifts – the social graces – of Libra to get to the top.

Once they have learned this, Capricorns will be successful in their careers. They are ambitious hard workers who are not afraid of putting in the required time and effort. Capricorns take their time in getting the job done – in order to do it well – and they like moving up the corporate ladder slowly but surely. Being so driven by success, Capricorns are generally liked by their bosses, who respect and trust them.

Love and Relationships

Like Scorpio and Pisces, Capricorn is a difficult Sign to get to know. They are deep, introverted and like to keep their own counsel. Capricorns do not like to reveal their innermost thoughts. If you are in love with a Capricorn, be patient and take your time. Little by little you will get to understand him or her.

Capricorns have a deep romantic nature, but they do not show it straightaway. They are cool, matter of fact and not especially emotional. They will often show their love in practical ways.

It takes time for a Capricorn – male or female – to fall in love. They are not the love-at-first-sight kind. If a Capricorn is involved with a Leo or Aries, these Fire types will be totally mystified – to them the Capricorn will seem cold, unfeeling, unaffectionate and not very spontaneous. Of course none of this is true; it is just that Capricorn likes to take things slowly. They like to be sure of their ground before making any demonstrations of love or commitment.

Even in love affairs Capricorns are deliberate. They need more time to make decisions than is true of the other Signs of the Zodiac, but given this time they become just as passionate. Capricorns like a relationship to be structured, committed, well regulated, well defined, predictable and even routine. They prefer partners who are nurturers, and they in turn like to nurture their partners. This is their basic psychology. Whether such a relationship is good for them is another issue altogether. Capricorns have enough routine in their lives as it is. They might be better off in relationships that are a bit more stimulating, changeable and fluctuating.

Home and Domestic Life

The home of a Capricorn – as with a Virgo – is going to be tidy and well organized. Capricorns tend to manage their families in the same way they manage their businesses. Capricorns are often so career-driven that they find little time for the home and family. They should try to get more actively involved in their family and domestic life. Capricorns do, however, take their children very seriously and are very proud parents, particularly should their children grow up to become respected members of society.

Horoscope for 2008

Major Trends

Last year was an unusually spiritual kind of year, Capricorn. Your 12th House of Spirituality was the most important of the Houses. Though there is no one more practical and down to earth than you, somewhere deep inside – in the deeps of the deeps – you knew that the solution to your problems – even your practical, material kinds of problems – was a spiritual breakthrough. Not a practical breakthrough – but something much deeper. Many of you spent more time in meditation or prayer. A good many of you got into prayer and fasting. Others got into altruistic kinds of activities. Others just spent more time in the 'silence' of the soul. And, from this chart, it looks like you achieved your break-through and now you are in the outer world with renewed gusto and enthusiasm. You haven't lost your spirituality, but are merely bringing it into expression in the outer world. Spirituality is still an important interest in the year ahead.

Pluto, which has been in Sagittarius since 1995, is making an important move into your own Sign this year. Most of the year it will flirt between Sagittarius and Capricorn, but on November 27, it enters the latter for good. This will have major implications for you for many years to come. (More on this later).

Finance is always important to you. It was very important last year, and the trend continues. And spirituality is, again, the key that unlocks the doors to prosperity.

Late last year, your ruling planet (Saturn) made an important move from Leo into Virgo. From your 8th House to your 9th House. This again emphasizes the 'higher' life – religion, higher education, philosophy and metaphysics. In light of your recent spiritual breakthroughs it is time for you to bring your personal philosophy of life into the right order – it needs some adjustments and fine-tuning. More on this later.

Your most important interests this year are finance; communication and intellectual interests; religion, philosophy, metaphysics, higher education, foreign travel; spirituality.

Your paths of greatest fulfilment this year are finance, the body, image and personal pleasures.

Health

(Please note that this is an astrological perspective on health and not a medical one. For the medical perspective, please consult your doctor.)

The long-term planets are either making harmonious aspects or leaving you alone this year. Health should be good. Energy is high. Of course there will be periods during the year when energy is not up to par – but these periods come from stressful short-term transits – they are temporary – and when they pass your normal good health returns.

With such basically beautiful aspects, your empty 6th House is another positive health indicator. You are not too involved here, as you have no need to be involved. Health is basically good and you don't need to focus on it overmuch.

In the past few years you seem to have undergone detox – some of you have had surgeries. But these procedures did their job and things are OK now. (Many of you had near-death experiences, too.)

Pluto moving into your Sign from January 21 to June 14 and then again on November 27 has important health implications for you. Many of you will be considering cosmetic-type surgery – not for health purposes but for image purposes. But it shows the importance of detox, on a regular basis, not just for health but for your general appearance. Many of you will start to practise fasting – perhaps spirituality plays a role in this, but there is another motive – it cleans out the body.

You will be in an excellent period – especially after November 27 – to lose weight (if you need to). Pluto is a master at this kind of thing. Now and for many years to come you will be working at personal transformation and reinvention. You want to give birth to the ideal body and image – the ideal personality – the person that you truly want to be. It will be a long process – Pluto stays in a Sign for many years – but in the end you will succeed. This is an excellent year for it, too.

With Mercury as your health planet, in general you need to pay more attention to the lungs, arms, shoulders and small intestine. There is nothing especially wrong with them *per se*, but keeping them fit has a powerful impact on the whole body. Arms and shoulders can be regularly massaged. The lungs and small intestine can be strengthened in many natural ways – and, if you like, you can work with the chart below.

Mercury is a very fast-moving planet, as our steady readers know. In a year he will move through all the Signs and Houses of your chart. In some months he will move through

Reflexology
Try to massage the whole foot on a regular basis, but pay extra attention to the points highlighted on the chart. When you massage, be aware of 'sore spots', as these need special attention. It's also a good idea to massage the ankles and top side (as well as the soles) of the feet.

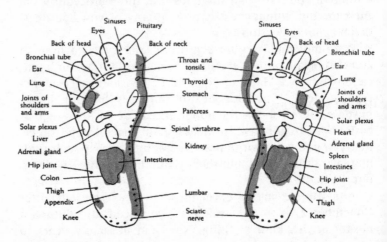

as many as three Signs and Houses. So your health needs are rarely static. They change all the time. Likewise with the therapies and parts of the body that need more care. These short-term issues will be dealt with in the monthly reports.

With Mercury as your health planet, if problems arise look at the way you may be abusing your powers of thought and speech. Also it is good to purify the mind of all error – the major pathology of the intellect. Once these things are corrected, the health problem should more or less dissolve.

Your spiritual planet is in your own Sign all year. This has many messages, but from a health perspective it shows a need to be careful of drugs and alcohol. Your physical body is becoming more refined – more spiritualized – more sensitive. And so these kinds of things are not good. Looks to me like many of you are involved in yoga, tai chi and spiritual kinds of exercises. And this is good. These are good, natural ways to transform your body. The right diet will also be a help.

Your most vulnerable health periods this year are from March 20 to April 20, June 21 to July 22, and September 23 to October 23. These are times to rest and relax more and listen to your body.

Your health planet, Mercury, will go Retrograde three times this year – from January 28 to February 19, May 26 to June 19, and September 24 to October 15. These are times to review your health regimes and overall health and see where you can make improvements. These are not specially good for making dramatic changes to the health regime.

Home and Family

Your 4th House of Home and Family is not a House of Power this year. Not a major focus. On one level this gives you more freedom to shape this area as you wish – the planetary forces are not pushing one way or the other. But people seldom make major changes when they lack interest in something – and this is the situation here. A status-quo kind of year.

With Jupiter in your own Sign there could be an enlargement or renovation of the room where you spend most of your time – not so much the home, but your personal space.

With Mars as your family planet, family unity and harmony can be maintained by doing things together as a family – through activities. Sports, construction projects, DIY projects – done as a family unit – will do much to keep the family harmony.

Mars is a fast-moving planet. Not as fast as Mercury, the Moon, the Sun or Venus – but much faster than the long-term planets. In a given year he will move through six to eight Signs and Houses of your Horoscope. This will bring short-term family developments best dealt with in the monthly reports.

Children were depressed the past few years, but there is much improvement this year. The emotional situation began improving late last year. They have been feeling cramped in the home for some years now, and this year might be the time they make a move. (There is a Solar Eclipse on August 1 that forces the issue.)

Grandchildren of appropriate age could have moved last year (and if they didn't they bought big-ticket items for the home and perhaps enlarged their home). This year things seem status quo. Capricorns of appropriate age seem much more involved and engaged with grandchildren this year.

If you are planning major construction or renovation – June 14 to August 19 is a good time to do it. If you are planning redecorating or beautifying the home – on a cosmetic level – April 6 to April 30 is a good time for it.

Finance and Career

Your Money House has been strong for many years now (and even if it weren't – this is always a major issue for you). You have been in a prosperity cycle for many years now. This year, the prosperity will be even stronger. And 2009 will be more prosperous than 2008. Enjoy.

Many of the financial trends of past years are still very much in effect. On a worldly level, it is sales, marketing and PR that are most important. Your skill in getting the word out about your product or service seems most essential. There is a need to stay very up to date with the latest technology, both on a communication level, and in your work or the manufacturing of your product.

The conditions of your industry are always changing and you have to be nimble, flexible and adaptable. Conditions will not allow you to get into a 'rut'.

Earnings are rarely stable (this year they are a little more stable than the last few years). They can go extremely high and then vanish for a time. There is a need to 'smooth out' your earnings. This can be done through setting aside reserves from the strong months, to cover the weaker months.

On a deeper level, the lesson has been to cope with financial change and insecurity. For many years it has been difficult to make long-range financial plans, as you could never predict what you would earn. So handling all this change and insecurity with calm is an important achievement.

The spiritual aspects of wealth have been important for a long time. This year they are even more important. Your spiritual planet is now in your own Sign. Neptune, the most spiritual of all the planets, is in your Money House (and has been there for many years). Uranus, your actual financial planet, is in the spiritual Sign of Pisces. So this is a period where you delve more deeply into the spiritual nature of wealth – into the supernatural sources of supply – and work with them. For a down-to-earth Capricorn this is some lesson and some experience! But very worthwhile. When we work with the 'natural' ways of earning there is always limitation, frustration and stress. By definition we are working from a world where resources are limited. But the spiritual perspective is totally different. Supply is spiritual – unlimited and infinite. We can never exhaust the resources of the spirit. Nor do we need to compete with other people. There is as much there as anyone could want. Accessing this supernatural supply, however, requires new attitudes and new ways of thinking. Rarely does a person do it overnight. It is a process – and you seem well into it.

Accessing the supernatural supply requires more giving. And this you are doing. You seem very charitable and generous lately – and especially this year.

Intuition has been important for many years, and this is especially true this year.

From an investment perspective, oil, natural gas, energy, high-tech industries, communications, media (both electronic and print) and telecommunications are all good areas to focus on.

Job-seekers and those who employ others are having a status-quo year. The trends here will be short term, so we will cover them in the monthly reports.

The earnings of your spouse or partner are much improved over last year. Children are having a status-quo financial year. Likewise grandchildren. Parents or parent figures are prospering and travelling more.

Your most active and prosperous financial period this year will be from January 20 to March 20.

Love and Social Life

Your 7th House of Love and Romance is not a House of Power this year. There is a basic contentment this year. No need to make major changes. Marrieds will tend to stay married and singles will tend to stay single.

Though your 11th House of Friendships is empty, there are major changes happening there. Pluto, the planet that rules these things, is moving into your Sign this year. Most of the year it will be 'in and out' of your Sign, but on November 27 it will move in permanently. This shows that friends are seeking you out. They are coming to you. Nothing special that you need to do. Also these new friends seem very devoted to you – they put your interests ahead of their own.

Also you are going to be more friendly to others – you are going to project this kind of image. Being surrounded by friends is as much a fashion statement as a new suit, dress or jewellery.

Those of you in your second marriage will have the marriage tested. Financial issues seem to be a problem. You are working hard to make it work, and this is a good sign. True love will survive any test.

Those working towards a second marriage seem very aggressive about it – you are out there looking – but you need patience. A second marriage is not likely.

Those working towards their third marriage could have got married (or seriously involved) in 2006. This year seems status quo.

Those working towards their fourth marriage will have good fortune. Wedding bells are likely.

The Moon is your love planet, Capricorn, and she is the fastest-moving planet in the Horoscope. She shifts from day to day. And this is how your love life tends to be. It can happen in many different ways and places. These short-term trends will be dealt with in the monthly reports.

In general your social magnetism is stronger when the Moon waxes than when she wanes. If you understand this you can schedule yourself accordingly.

In general you favour mates with strong family values. Capricorn males like very feminine women. Capricorn women like their men to be emotionally supportive and devoted to family. The planetary aspects are indicating that family and family members like to play Cupid.

Your happiest and most active social period will be from June 18 to July 22.

Self-improvement

With Pluto moving into your own Sign (permanently on November 27 – but you will be feeling the effects before then), personal transformation and reinvention is becoming a major, long-term interest.

Your body and image are going to undergo a detox on very deep levels. You are going to redefine your image and self-concept in coming years – a continuous process. St Paul said 'I die daily,' and this is how it will seem to you. You die daily to old notions and concepts of yourself. You die to old ideas. A dead person cannot respond – so it is with you, you won't 'respond' – won't resonate – to certain undesirable things anymore. It will be as if you had 'died' to them.

With your spiritual planet now in your 1st House, these tendencies are greatly magnified. You are spiritualizing your image. You are going to see yourself as 'more' than just a 'mortal personality' with a certain history and lineage – but as a child of the Divine – eternal and immortal. You will work to incarnate this 'perfect image and likeness' in the flesh. A big job. A lot of junk will have to go. This perfect image of you already exists, but it is covered over – concealed, as it were. You have to peel away all the concealments. Pluto is a master of this kind of thing and he will help you. (It is not an issue of 'creating a new you' but more about rediscovering the you that has always been there.)

As mentioned, some people will opt for cosmetic types of surgery under these aspects. But the best way – the longest-lasting way – is by spiritual means, through meditation, eating right and spiritual kinds of exercises (like yoga or tai chi). The main revelation that will help you in your process is to understand that the body is not a 'thing' – not a static object. It is an energy system – dynamic and changing. Our five senses cannot register the speed of the vibrations of the body, and so they 'manufacture' an image. But the reality is that the body is constantly being renewed and regenerated. It is highly responsive to thoughts and feelings. It can be changed through spiritual means.

Spirituality has been very important in finances for many years now. And now, spirituality will also help you create a new body and image – a temple of the most high.

Transformation can be messy business. It is more akin to childbirth than anything else. So there will be traumas and adventures as old effete material (thought and emotional

patterns) surface, kick up a fuss, and then pass out. But the
end result will be good – a new you.

New friends are coming to you who are experts in this
sort of thing and they will guide you along. Also a spiritual
guru is coming into the picture this year. (It could have
happened already, but if not, it will happen this year.)

Month-by-month Forecasts

January

Best Days Overall: 7, 8, 16, 17, 25, 26
Most Stressful Days Overall: 1, 14, 15, 20, 21, 27, 28
Best Days for Love: 5, 6, 7, 8, 14, 15, 16, 17, 20, 21, 23,
    27, 28
Best Days for Money: 2, 3, 7, 9, 10, 12, 13, 16, 20, 21, 24,
    25, 29, 30

You are in a yearly personal pleasure peak as your year
begins. A period for indulging the senses and enjoying all
the (constructive) delights of the flesh. The whole year
ahead is going to be about personal pleasure, but right now
this is most intense. The good food, good wine, gourmet
restaurants, fine resorts are all calling to you. The only
danger now is overindulgence – there will be a price to pay
later on. Enjoy but don't overdo things.

Last month (of last year) the planetary power shifted
from the upper half – the 'day' side – to the lower half – the
'night' side of your Horoscope. This month the shift is intensified. Between 80 and 90 per cent of the planets are below
the horizon after the 24th. (Even your career planet is below
the horizon – beginning the 24th.) Career should not be
abandoned, but worked on in the ways of the night rather
than the ways of the day. Night is for sleeping, resting,
recharging the physical and emotional batteries – for dreaming, fantasizing and setting goals. Just as a good night's sleep

lays the groundwork for a successful day, so too a good night's 'career sleep' will leave you refreshed and enthusiastic when your career day begins. The focus should be on family, home, the emotional life and recharging your emotional batteries. Feeling right is more important than doing right. Attending the school play or soccer match outweighs the next deal or corporate manoeuvre. Family unity can be enhanced through good communication, doing sport or exercise as a family unit, and through group DIY projects at home. Common health interests – such as going to the gym or yoga studio together – or running or jogging as a family unit – will also enhance family harmony.

The year ahead is very prosperous, and this month is one of the most prosperous months in a prosperous year. You enter a yearly financial peak on the 20th. Money comes through work, spousal support, fabulous intuition and through borrowing or from outside investors if necessary. After the 20th, as the ruler of your 8th House moves through the Money House, it is good to 'detox' on a financial level. Pay off or refinance debt (at more favourable rates), eliminate unnecessary expense, calculate (more carefully) the tax consequences of your financial moves, and get rid of excess – no longer needed – personal possessions. It is a time to prosper by cutting back.

If you have insurance claims pending this is a good month to hear a happy result.

Though career is not as important as usual, nevertheless career opportunities are seeking you out. You can afford to be choosy, you seem in demand. Ensure that your family and emotional harmony are not violated by these career offers.

Health is excellent. Energy is at a yearly high now. Personal independence is strong. Now is the time to make the changes that will increase personal happiness – now is the time to create and design things according to your wishes.

Your health planet goes Retrograde on the 23rd, so avoid making important changes to your diet or health regime then. This will be a period for a health review and analysis but not for making changes.

February

Best Days Overall: 3, 4, 12, 13, 21, 22
Most Stressful Days Overall: 10, 11, 17, 23, 24
Best Days for Love: 3, 4, 6, 7, 13, 14, 15, 16, 17, 23, 25, 26
Best Days for Money: 3, 4, 6, 7, 8, 9, 12, 13, 17, 21, 22, 26, 27

Another happy and very prosperous month. Financial intuition is super on the 1st and 2nd, and there is luck in speculations then. Singles have happy love opportunities then (but these don't look like 'marriage material' – just enjoy them for what they are).

You are still well into your yearly financial peak. Enjoy. Many of the financial trends of last month are still in effect. On the 17th Venus moves into your Money House which shows earnings from creative projects or from your personal creativity. Perhaps you are spending more on children and entertainment then, too. But keep in mind that these so-called expenses can also be profitable – children can have interesting and profitable financial ideas – out of the mouths of babes ... Your spouse, partner or current love has an interesting financial intuition on the 10th. Drive defensively on the 10th – make sure you are not 'dreamy' or 'in another world' – be mindful and aware.

There are two eclipses this month and both seem relatively benign to you. The Solar Eclipse of the 7th (the 6th in the US) occurs in your Money House. This brings major and dramatic financial changes. I read this as a good thing – you are so prosperous that all your former financial thinking and strategies just don't apply any more. You need to adjust to your prosperous reality. Every Solar Eclipse brings changes in the financial situation of your spouse, partner or current love, and this one is no different – you are both making important changes. (As this point gets re-stimulated by other planets in the course of the next few months, these changes will become even more apparent.) Since this eclipse occurs very near to Neptune, your planet of communication, there will be tests of your car or communication equipment. There are dramatic events in the lives of siblings and neighbours, and perhaps important changes in the neighbourhood as well. Students (below university level) will make important educational changes.

The Lunar Eclipse of the 21st (the 20th in the US) occurs in your 9th House and again affects students – but this time on the university level (or entering university). This brings changes in areas of study, or changes in the university. Often there are changes in the administration or changes of the rules and requirements that cause a shift of plan and strategy. In the end it works out. These eclipses often bring crises of faith – a testing of religious and philosophical beliefs – and those found wanting are revealed for what they are. One of the hardest things to do is to let go of some core belief or value that we have – but if it is not adequate or true, it is best that we let it go. Every Lunar Eclipse will test the marriage or current relationship, and this one is no different. Good relationships will certainly survive (these eclipses occur twice a year and most of you involved in relationships have already weathered a few of these). But faulty relationships can dissolve now. Business partnerships also get tested by Lunar Eclipses.

March

Best Days Overall: 2, 3, 11, 19, 20, 29, 30
Most Stressful Days Overall: 9, 15, 16, 22, 23
Best Days for Love: 4, 5, 6, 7, 15, 16, 24, 25, 27
Best Days for Money: 2, 3, 4, 5, 6, 7, 11, 16, 20, 24, 25, 29, 30, 31

Most of the planets are still in the independent East – but this situation will not last for too much longer – so make the personal changes that you need to make. Continue to create conditions as you desire them to be. Later on – by next month – it will be more difficult to do this.

Your financial life is still important until the 15th, but your financial peak is winding down. Have no fear, overall prosperity is very good, but now you shift attention to your intellectual interests and to home and family.

Good marketing and good use of the media have been important in finances for some years now, but now even more so. This is an excellent month for doing those mass-mailings, advertising campaigns or telemarketing. On a general level it is good for catching up on your reading, taking courses in subjects that interest you, attending lectures and in general feeding the mind. The proper care and feeding of the mind is very neglected in our culture. The mental body is a body (though more subtle than the physical body) – it is real – it has its needs. We neglect it at our own risk.

A parent or child, or both, have fabulous financial intuition on the 6th or 7th – it is worth exploring. Interesting marketing ideas come too.

The 8th and 9th bring happy experiences with bankers or investors. You and your spouse or partner cooperate very well financially – and it is in both your interests to do so.

There could be some important repair or renovation in the home from the 4th to the 8th. Perhaps a family member contemplates a surgery or has some brush, some encounter with, death. (This doesn't necessarily mean a literal death – but some psychological encounter.) This is just a message to pay more attention to the home and family situation.

Love is stormier this month. Mars moves into the 7th House of Love. A current relationship will get tested. If you can manage to avoid power struggles and just come from the heart – from love – you will get through with flying colours. There is more entertaining from home during this period.

And singles will find that family – either subtly or not so subtly – is trying to engineer a marriage. Love opportunities come at family gatherings or through the introduction of family members.

With the ruler of your 8th House moving into your 4th House of Home and Family (on the 20th) this is a great period to detox your home – clean it out, get rid of excess furniture or possessions that you no longer need. Streamline the home. Good to clean out the attic and basement. On another level, this is good for detoxing the emotional life – and emotional patterns.

April

Best Days Overall: 7, 8, 16, 17, 25, 26, 27
Most Stressful Days Overall: 5, 6, 11, 12, 18, 19
Best Days for Love: 4, 5, 6, 11, 12, 13, 14, 24, 25, 26
Best Days for Money: 1, 2, 3, 4, 7, 8, 11, 12, 15, 16, 17, 25, 26, 27, 28, 29

By the 6th the Western, social sector of the Horoscope will become stronger than the independent Eastern sector. So this is a time for toning down self-will and self-assertion and to start cultivating the social skills, seeing other people's positions on things, and in general letting others have their way if it isn't destructive. By now you have made the changes you needed to make and you are in a period of 'road testing' – how well did you build? So, this is a period for 'paying karma', by which we mean experiencing the consequences of your creations, either positively or negatively. Good creations will bring happy circumstances. Miscreations will bring discomfort – and you will have to adjust as best you can. But have no fear: in six months or so you will again have more power to create and you can make corrections.

There are two important areas of interest this month – home, family and emotional issues (the 4th House) and children, creativity and fun (the 5th House).

Even your career planet will be in the 4th House from the 6th onwards – and this shows that even bosses and superiors are supporting your family goals and your attention there. Focusing on the family could even help your career – not hurt it. With Venus in the 4th House this is a good time to redecorate, repaint or buy art objects for the home. Seems like you are also investing in toys, entertainment or sports equipment. The home seems as much as a playground as any outside place of entertainment. Many of you are doing more work from home these days. The whole idea now – the whole intent of the cosmos – is to get you into your emotional comfort zone. When you are feeling right, outer things will happen in the right way, too.

Like last month it is still good to do a major – and deep – house-cleaning. Both of the physical home and of the emotional life. Before new good can come to you, you need to make some room for it. If you're redecorating now, empty space seems elegant. Sure, you should have everything you need in the home – but there should be some accent on spaciousness – emptiness. There is something beautiful about that.

On the 19th the Sun moves into Taurus, an Earth Sign. From that point onwards there will always be 50 per cent (and sometimes 60 per cent) of the planets in the Earth element – your native element. This is very good for you. Your practical abilities – always strong – get stronger. Your management abilities (always awesome) get stronger. Further, you are more comfortable – your natural talents are appreciated more by the world.

Health needs watching until the 19th. Enhance health through more attention to the feet (until the 2nd), the head and face (from the 2nd to the 18th – scalp massage and facials will be beneficial) and the neck and throat afterwards (neck massage will be good). Pay more attention to the heart until the 19th. Overall health is good, but this is not one of your best periods.

Last month's love trends are still very much in effect. Avoid power struggles. The good point of Mars in your 7th

House is that you become more socially aggressive and you learn to overcome social fears and inhibitions.

May

  Best Days Overall: 4, 5, 13, 14, 23, 24
  Most Stressful Days Overall: 2, 3, 8, 9, 15, 16, 30, 31
  Best Days for Love: 4, 5, 8, 9, 13, 14, 24, 25
  Best Days for Money: 1, 4, 5, 8, 9, 13, 14, 18, 19, 23, 24,
    25, 26, 28, 29

Health is much improved now and you can enhance it even further by paying more attention to the neck and throat (until the 8th) and to the arms, shoulders and lungs afterwards. Also there is a greater focus on health this month – you will feel it all month but the focus is most intense after the 20th. You are into disciplined health regimes and healthy lifestyles. Saturn, your ruling planet, is camping out on an eclipse point all month. This shows big changes in your physical body and appearance. You are redefining your personality – how you think of yourself – how you want others to see you. (The possible power struggles going on in love or with partners might have something to do with this.) But this is a healthy thing to do. There will be wardrobe changes (changes of the hairstyle and the like) this month and next month. If you haven't been careful in dietary matters, there could be a detox of the physical body. Drive more defensively this month.

With the Earth element still strong you are in a prosperous period. Financial judgement – which is always good with you – is razor-sharp now. A good period for making investments or big purchases (try to wrap up these things before the 26th). In general prosperity comes easier with less muss, fuss and bother before the 20th than afterwards.

On the 19th of last month you entered another yearly personal pleasure period. It continues in full swing this month. By the 20th you enter a more serious work period. It would be great if you could go on holiday before the 20th. If it is not possible, try to spend more time in leisure activities – as if you were on holiday. Pursue creative interests as much as possible.

Job-seekers have good success. The main reason is personal interest. Seek and ye shall find is a law of the universe. But job offers and openings will need more study and review after the 26th as Mercury goes Retrograde. Read all the small print and do all the homework; things might not be as they seem. Employers, too, should do more research on applicants after the 26th.

Again we see more repairs or renovations of the home after the 9th. Passions are high at home. It might be wise to invest in accident-proofing the home – installing more safety features.

Love is starting to get happier. Mars leaves the 7th House on the 9th. The conflicts in love have been settled one way or another. The month ahead seems sexually active. In general there is more social energy and enthusiasm from the 5th to the 20th as the Moon waxes. Your social magnetism is stronger then.

June

Best Days Overall: 1, 2, 9, 10, 19, 20, 28, 29
Most Stressful Days Overall: 5, 6, 11, 12, 13, 26, 27
Best Days for Love: 3, 4, 5, 6, 11, 12, 14, 15, 24, 25
Best Days for Money: 1, 2, 5, 6, 9, 10, 14, 15, 19, 20, 21, 22, 23, 24, 25, 28, 29

The personality changes you've been going through are winding down this month. By the 14th Saturn moves away from the eclipse point and you have settled into your new image and self-concept.

On the 21st you enter a yearly social peak. And though singles will probably not marry now (unless this is in your actual personal Horoscope cast personally for you) you will meet more 'marriageable' kind of people. You will date more, go out more, attend more parties. It looks like a lot of fun.

Until the 21st the focus is on work. You want to be productive – to serve others in practical ways. Work is good for its own sake. There is something very cosmic about it – especially when it is work that is honest and for which we are well suited. The honest worker sleeps well at night. He or she might be tired after a day's work, but there is mental and emotional peace. For honest work – work that we are designed to do – is the universe's work – the cosmos achieves its ends through us.

This is a still a good period for job-seekers (and employers) but, like last month, job offers (and job applicants) need more scrutiny – more attention – more homework. Don't just look at the surface of things. Go deeper.

Health is good until the 21st. (It is good afterwards, but less so; overall energy is not up to its usual standards.) Detox seems powerful all month. There is more sexual activity and more libido this month, but try to keep things in moderation. Joy and creative hobbies are therapeutic (more than usual) until the 18th. After the 21st enhance health through keeping energy levels high, paying more attention to the heart, and paying more attention to the arms, shoulders and lungs. Your health planet is still Retrograde until the 19th, so avoid making important changes to the diet or health regime then. This is a period (until the 19th) for reviewing your health, diet and health regimes and seeing where improvements can be made.

A detox of the love life might be in order after the 21st. Just as a tree grows better and stronger after it has been pruned, so too your social life will get better and happier if you weed out the 'effete material' – friends who are not truly friends, who bring you down instead of lift you up, social activities that you just do to keep up appearances or to show off or to avoid boredom or loneliness. Social activities should be meaningful and joyous. There should be mutual nourishment there. Better to go out less but to quality events, than just to go out for the sake of it.

July

Best Days Overall: 6, 7, 16, 17, 26
Most Stressful Days Overall: 2, 3, 9, 10, 23, 24, 30
Best Days for Love: 2, 3, 11, 12, 13, 23, 24, 30
Best Days for Money: 2, 3, 6, 7, 11, 12, 16, 17, 19, 20, 21,
    22, 26, 30

Last month the planets made an important shift from the lower – night side – of the Horoscope to the upper – day side. This month the shift gets even stronger as Mercury crosses into the upper half on the 10th. So this produces a new attitude and focus in you. Your outer life, your career, your outer achievements are becoming more important. It is as if you have just woken up from a six-month sleep – it is dawn in your Horoscope. You are ready to face the world, conquer all career challenges with renewed energy. Your internal work is over with and now you work in the normal external ways.

You are still very much into a yearly social peak. Many of last month's social trends are still in effect. You are mixing with the high and mighty this month – with people of power and prestige – with people above you in status. For singles this shows romantic opportunities at the workplace, with co-workers or superiors. (These are the aspects of the office romance.) But there are opportunities that come in the normal ways too – at parties, entertainments, sporting events and nightclubs. Still a good idea to detox the social life now – until the 22nd. Get rid of the dross so that the gold can come in.

Career is enhanced through social means as well – especially until the 12th. This means attending or hosting the right kinds of parties. Taking important clients or people to dinner or a show. Entertaining them.

The planetary power is now pretty much at the maximum Western power now. So continue to avoid personal assertion, self-will and power struggles. Go along with others so long as their way isn't destructive. Your way is probably not the best way this period. Attain your ends (and especially your career ends) through grace and charm.

Mars re-stimulates the Lunar Eclipse of February 21 from the 1st to the 8th. Parents or parent figures should be encouraged to 'play it safe' that period, avoid risky kinds of activities (surgery and the like) and to drive more defensively. It wouldn't hurt to increase the safety standards in the home, either. Repairs might be necessary in the home.

Venus re-stimulates the Solar Eclipse point of February 7 from the 26th to the 29th. This brings career changes and perhaps some dramatic events in the lives of parents, parent figures or bosses. This is short term, though.

Health needs more watching until the 22nd. Enhance health through more attention to the arms, shoulders and lungs (until the 10th), the stomach and breasts (from the 10th to the 26th) and to the heart all month. If health problems arise, check out your love life and friendships and do what is needed to restore harmony – this is a likely cause. This is a sexually active month, and overdoing it (especially after the 26th) could also impact on your health.

August

Best Days Overall: 3, 4, 12, 13, 14, 22, 23, 30, 31
Most Stressful Days Overall: 5, 6, 20, 26, 27
Best Days for Love: 1, 2, 10, 11, 21, 22, 23, 26, 27, 30, 31
Best Days for Money: 3, 4, 7, 8, 9, 12, 13, 15, 16, 17, 18, 22, 23, 26, 27, 30, 31

Your 8th House became very strong on the 22nd of last month and is still strong until the 22nd of this month. Thus the focus now is on sex, paying off debt (or borrowing), helping others to prosper and being involved in personal transformation and reinvention. Detox – on all levels – is good now. It is good from a purely health perspective – until the 10th – and from a psychological perspective until the 22nd. Even the career – which is becoming ever-more important – would benefit from a detox – a detox of attitudes, or of the 'side issues' that cloud your main purpose. Another good month to do a thorough house-cleaning, get rid of excess possessions, excess expenses and excess 'foreign material' in your body and mind.

There are two eclipses this period which ensure that there will be plenty of excitement in the world – and for you personally.

The Solar Eclipse of the 1st occurs in your 8th House (and the eclipsed planet is the ruler of your 8th House). Take a reduced schedule. Your spouse or partner is forced to make dramatic – and long-term – financial changes. There could be sudden expenses – or sudden happenings that expose the fallacies of the current thinking. Things can't go on as they are. This eclipse could bring psychological encounters with death – perhaps through recurrent dreams, or through near-death experiences of people you know (or on a personal level) or through dramatic events in the world. Older, infirm Capricorns on the edge of life and death could decide to make transition now. Not one of you is leaving before your time, but encounters with the dark angel help us to understand how to live – he shows us the 'fragility' of the outer life – how a human is 'like grass' in the reckoning of Eternity. And this helps us to get our values and priorities in order. The dark angel is only feared by those who lack knowledge. Those who understand him understand his functions and come to terms with him. If you are involved in estate issues or insurance claims, there is now a dramatic turning-point – things will start to move forward now. Those of you involved in personal transformation will make changes in your approach to it.

The Lunar Eclipse of the 16th occurs in your Money House. This shows personal financial changes (not just with your spouse or partner). Financial thinking and strategy need revision. (Probably you have been underestimating yourself and your abilities.) Every Lunar Eclipse tests the marriage, current relationship or current business partnership – and this one is no different. Twice a year the cosmos gives you the opportunity to fine-tune your relationship by bringing up the flaws and the 'dirty laundry' – this way you know what the problems are and you can correct them once the dust settles. Neptune, the ruler of your 3rd House, is once again impacted by this eclipse (just as he was on February 7). So again this shows a testing of your car and communication equipment, and important educational changes for students (below university level). There are dramatic events in the lives of siblings and neighbours.

September

Best Days Overall: 9, 10, 18, 19, 27, 28
Most Stressful Days Overall: 1, 2, 3, 16, 17, 22, 23, 29, 30
Best Days for Love: 1, 2, 9, 10, 11, 12, 18, 19, 21, 22, 23, 27
Best Days for Money: 4, 5, 9, 10, 11, 12, 14, 15, 18, 19, 22, 23, 27

Between 60 and 70 per cent of the planets are above the horizon of your Horoscope and your 10th House of Career becomes very powerful after the 22nd. You enter a yearly career peak. You are working hard, probably over-working, but you are seeing the results of your efforts. This is a period of success, advancement and achievement. It would be criminal to divert energy or attention to mundane domestic matters now. Maintain your focus. Go for the heights. Happily, family seems supportive of your efforts. In fact, family members also seem very ambitious (and are perhaps even involved in your career this month). The family as a whole is very elevated this month. It is as if the family as a whole is succeeding. When you are lifted up, they are lifted up. Also, the company you are with seems more 'family friendly' this period.

Again we see a need for 'detox of the career' – this means eliminating the frivolities and inessentials and maintaining a clear focus on the essence. Your spouse, partner or current love is investing financially in your career. Your spouse seems very prosperous until the 22nd and has interesting financial windfalls and luck in speculations (especially from the 4th to the 6th). Your spouse or partner seems especially generous from the 2nd to the 4th (does one thing have something to do with the other? Something to think about). If you are interested in borrowing, refinancing, or attracting outside investors – the 4th to the 6th looks like a powerful time.

Your 9th House has been important all year, but was especially strong last month and is still very strong until the 22nd. This is a successful period for students – especially at university or post-graduate level. It is a period of religious and philosophical revelation for those of you who want it. Probably you are travelling more, too. Even non-students are attracting happy educational opportunities. Legal issues seem fortunate now.

Both of your financial planets are still Retrograde. You are still in a very prosperous year – the trend is up – but this month and last month have been more difficult. There is more work involved in earnings. College or travel expenses crimp the bottom line. Financial judgement is not up to your usually high standards, and confidence could be better. Things will improve after the 22nd, but only slightly – the real improvement will happen next month.

Love is status quo this month. In general you will have more social grace and magnetism (and more enthusiasm for social activities) from the 1st to the 15th and on the 29th and 30th as the Moon waxes.

October

Best Days Overall: 6, 7, 15, 16, 24, 25
Most Stressful Days Overall: 13, 14, 19, 20, 26, 27
Best Days for Love: 1, 9, 10, 11, 12, 17, 18, 19, 20, 21, 22, 23, 28, 29
Best Days for Money: 1, 2, 6, 7, 9, 10, 11, 12, 15, 16, 19, 20, 24, 25, 28, 29, 30

Health needed more watching since the 22nd of last month. The demands of the career have been taxing and it is difficult for you to slow down. Overwork seems the main health danger now. Enhance health by paying more attention to the heart, kidneys and hips all month. With your health planet Retrograde until the 15th, avoid making important health decisions now (such as surgery, or major changes of diet and regime). This is a time (until the 15th) for analysis and review. Later you will have the clarity to make better decisions.

Career is still going great guns – and you are working very hard. Your spouse or partner, too, seems successful – but more in a financial than a personal way. He or she is investing in your career.

You can enhance your career by social means, by networking and getting involved in groups and organizations. You have the help of friends as well.

Your hard work is producing the desired career changes – but they can happen suddenly and disruptively – a seeming negative event on the 1st–3rd and on the 12th–15th can have very positive consequences. These are blessings in disguise – actual signals of success. (There can be dramas in the lives of the children – or those who are like children to you – during these periods, too.)

Career is enhanced through involvement in charities and volunteer-type activities from the 18th onwards.

On the 23rd the focus shifts from the career to friendships, groups and group activities and involvement with organizations.

Finances are getting better day by day. After the 23rd you enter another yearly financial peak. But still, with both your financial planets Retrograde be more cautious – especially with major purchases or investments. Family or parents or parent figures seem very supportive after the 4th. There are opportunities for the fortunate purchase or sale of a home. Your involvement with organizations is not only helping your status and reputation, but also the bottom line.

Love is status quo. Social enthusiasm and magnetism are strongest from the 1st to the 14th and from the 28th onwards – as the Moon is waxing.

Mars' re-stimulation of the Solar Eclipse of August 1 from the 17th to the 20th is a dynamic transit for the world at large. On a personal level, parents or parent figures in your life are advised to stay close to home and avoid risky, high-stress activities. There could be sudden repairs in the home. Avoid tempestuous type people then.

November

Best Days Overall: 2, 3, 4, 12, 13, 20, 21, 30
Most Stressful Days Overall: 10, 11, 16, 17, 22, 23
Best Days for Love: 1, 7, 8, 11, 12, 16, 17, 20, 21, 27, 28, 30
Best Days for Money: 2, 3, 4, 5, 6, 7, 8, 12, 13, 16, 17, 20, 21, 25, 26, 30

Personal independence is growing day by day – and this isn't even the maximum. You will be even more independent next month. Some 80 to 90 per cent of the planets are in the independent East and your 1st House of Self is getting ever stronger. This is a time to chart your own course in life, to create conditions as you desire them to be and to take personal responsibility for your own happiness. It's all up to you. You have the energy and the backing to have your way in life. If others don't go along with your plans, go your own way. But chances are that true friends will eventually adjust to you. With the planetary momentum overwhelmingly forward now (90 per cent forward beginning the 2nd, and 100 per cent forward after the 27th) you will see rapid progress towards your goals.

Career goals seem basically achieved. There's not much you need to do now – career opportunities are seeking you out after the 12th – and people of importance are coming to visit. You can enhance your career through volunteer or charitable activities until the 12th. Personal appearance –

overall demeanour – plays a huge role in career after the 12th. You are dressing for success – dressing to show your actual or desired status. A very happy career opportunity (perhaps even a pay rise or promotion) is happening towards the end of the month (on the 29th and 30th).

Finances are a little rocky after the 21st – probably because of overwork, too much going on – but overall prosperity is very much intact. These problems are very short term. Earnings come more easily (and probably in a big way) before the 21st than afterwards. The good news this month is that the two planets involved in your finances are starting to move forward after many months of Retrograde motion. Neptune, the Occupant of your Money House, moves forward on the 12th; Uranus, your actual financial planet, starts to move forward on the 27th. Many stuck or delayed deals and projects start moving forward again. And there is a new sense of financial clarity, purpose and direction now. (Many of you were rather drifting for the past few months.)

Serious love seems status quo. Yet you look good. Venus in your own Sign gives beauty and a sense of style. A natural grace. Pluto (which moves into your Sign permanently on the 27th) gives a subterranean kind of sex appeal – which others respond to no matter how you try to hide it. You are attractive, but the opportunities are not serious ones – just fun, games and entertainment. Singles have many opportunities for love affairs – and there's nothing much that they need to do – these opportunities pursue them.

You have been enjoying the good life this year. And now with Pluto moving into your own Sign, it will be easier to shed those pounds.

Friendships, groups and organizations are still a focus until the 21st; after then the focus shifts to spirituality.

December

Best Days Overall: 1, 9, 10, 11, 18, 27, 28
Most Stressful Days Overall: 7, 8, 13, 14, 20, 21
Best Days for Love: 1, 7, 8, 11, 13, 14, 15, 16, 20, 21, 27, 28, 30, 31
Best Days for Money: 1, 2, 3, 5, 6, 9, 10, 13, 14, 17, 18, 22, 23, 27, 28, 30, 31

Spirituality became important on the 21st of last month and will be important until the 21st of this month. This is a period for spiritual revelation, for those who want it. A great period for attending spiritual workshops, meditation seminars or spiritual retreats. A behind-the-scenes conflict can only be resolved by spiritual means – the intervention of a Higher Power. Also good to get involved in charities, altruistic activities – activities that are 'selfless'. Aside from the fact that these kinds of things are good for the world in general, there are many personal benefits to them – the most important being that they burn off negative karma – this is one of the fastest ways to do it.

This period of 'selflessness' will not last for ever. By the 21st you enter another yearly personal pleasure peak. In fact, with 60 and sometimes 70 per cent of the planets either in or moving through your own Sign, this could be a lifetime peak as well. Now you are into 'pleasuring yourself' – you were selfless for a while and this was good – now you're taking care of number one. This is a period for all the pleasures and delights of the senses. For good food, fine wine, gourmet restaurants, travel, love affairs and the fulfilment of fantasies of the flesh (hopefully these will be constructive – with the aspects you have, everything you ask for will be given).

Personal pleasure, having things your way, having life on your terms, is what the month ahead is all about. At times like these it is good to understand why all this power, energy and good is happening. You are more than your body, and you, more than most, understand that life is not just about the pursuit of pleasure – yet here you are indulging in all these things. From the astrological perspective, it seems that you have to go through the pleasures of the flesh – to experience all of them – to see their good points and limitations – before you can really transcend the flesh. As long as there are lingering longings, it is difficult to truly move into a 'purpose-driven' life. The pleasures of the flesh need to be understood and comprehended – with all their consequences – before you can move on. You are being given this opportunity now.

Having things your way sounds wonderful – and you should enjoy it. But if you abuse this power – use it in harmful ways – you will soon experience the negative consequences of it. If one is driving a slow-moving old car, an accident can't cause too much damage. But if one is flying in a jet plane, an accident has more serious consequences. You are in a jet planet now. So be a responsible pilot.

A very happy career opportunity can still happen on the 1st and 2nd. A pay rise or promotion or some other very interesting offer.

Singles are having all the love they want and don't need to do much to have it. It comes to them.

Health is fabulous and you have all the energy you need to succeed in anything you set your mind on.

Aquarius

~~~

THE WATER-BEARER

Birthdays from
20th January to
18th February

Personality Profile

AQUARIUS AT A GLANCE

Element – Air

Ruling Planet – Uranus
   Career Planet – Pluto
   Love Planet – Venus
   Money Planet – Neptune
   Planet of Health and Work – Moon
   Planet of Home and Family Life – Venus

Colours – electric blue, grey, ultramarine blue

Colours that promote love, romance and social
   harmony – gold, orange

Colour that promotes earning power – aqua

Gems – black pearl, obsidian, opal, sapphire

Metal – lead

Scents – azalea, gardenia

Quality – fixed (= stability)

Qualities most needed for balance – warmth, feeling and emotion

Strongest virtues – great intellectual power, the ability to communicate and to form and understand abstract concepts, love for the new and avant-garde

Deepest needs – to know and to bring in the new

Characteristics to avoid – coldness, rebelliousness for its own sake, fixed ideas

Signs of greatest overall compatibility – Gemini, Libra

Signs of greatest overall incompatibility – Taurus, Leo, Scorpio

Sign most helpful to career – Scorpio

Sign most helpful for emotional support – Taurus

Sign most helpful financially – Pisces

Sign best for marriage and/or partnerships – Leo

Sign most helpful for creative projects – Gemini

Best Sign to have fun with – Gemini

Signs most helpful in spiritual matters – Libra, Capricorn

Best day of the week – Saturday

Understanding an Aquarius

In the Aquarius-born, intellectual faculties are perhaps the most highly developed of any Sign in the Zodiac. Aquarians are clear, scientific thinkers. They have the ability to think abstractly and to formulate laws, theories and clear concepts from masses of observed facts. Geminis might be very good at gathering information, but Aquarians take this a step further, excelling at interpreting the information gathered.

Practical people – men and women of the world – mistakenly consider abstract thinking as impractical. It is true that the realm of abstract thought takes us out of the physical world, but the discoveries made in this realm generally end up having tremendous practical consequences. All real scientific inventions and breakthroughs come from this abstract realm.

Aquarians, more so than most, are ideally suited to explore these abstract dimensions. Those who have explored these regions know that there is little feeling or emotion there. In fact, emotions are a hindrance to functioning in these dimensions; thus Aquarians seem – at times – cold and emotionless to others. It is not that Aquarians haven't got feelings and deep emotions, it is just that too much feeling clouds their ability to think and invent. The concept of 'too much feeling' cannot be tolerated or even understood by some of the other Signs. Nevertheless, this Aquarian objectivity is ideal for science, communication and friendship.

Aquarians are very friendly people, but they do not make a big show about it. They do the right thing by their friends, even if sometimes they do it without passion or excitement.

Aquarians have a deep passion for clear thinking. Second in importance, but related, is their passion for breaking with the establishment and traditional authority. Aquarians delight in this, because for them rebellion is like a great game or challenge. Very often they will rebel strictly for the fun of rebelling, regardless of whether the authority they defy is right or wrong. Right or wrong has little to do with the rebellious actions of an Aquarian, because to a true Aquarian authority and power must be challenged as a matter of principle.

Where Capricorn or Taurus will err on the side of tradition and the status quo, an Aquarian will err on the side of the new. Without this virtue it is doubtful whether any progress would be made in the world. The conservative-minded would obstruct progress. Originality and invention imply an ability to break barriers; every new discovery represents the toppling of an impediment to thought. Aquarians are very interested in breaking barriers and making walls tumble – scientifically, socially and politically. Other Zodiac Signs, such as Capricorn, also have scientific talents. But Aquarians are particularly excellent in the social sciences and humanities.

Finance

In financial matters Aquarians tend to be idealistic and humanitarian – to the point of self-sacrifice. They are usually generous contributors to social and political causes. When they contribute it differs from when a Capricorn or Taurus contributes. A Capricorn or Taurus may expect some favour or return for a gift; an Aquarian contributes selflessly.

Aquarians tend to be as cool and rational about money as they are about most things in life. Money is something they need and they set about acquiring it scientifically. No need for fuss; they get on with it in the most rational and scientific ways available.

Money to the Aquarian is especially nice for what it can do, not for the status it may bring (as is the case for other Signs). Aquarians are neither big spenders nor penny-pinchers and use their finances in practical ways, for example to facilitate progress for themselves, their families or even strangers.

However, if Aquarians want to reach their fullest financial potential they will have to explore their intuitive nature. If they follow only their financial theories – or what they believe to be theoretically correct – they may suffer some losses and disappointments. Instead, Aquarians should call on their intuition, which knows without thinking. For Aquarians, intuition is the short-cut to financial success.

Career and Public Image

Aquarians like to be perceived not only as the breakers of barriers but also as the transformers of society and the world. They long to be seen in this light and to play this role. They also look up to and respect other people in this position and even expect their superiors to act this way.

Aquarians prefer jobs that have a bit of idealism attached to them – careers with a philosophical basis. Aquarians need to be creative at work, to have access to new techniques and methods. They like to keep busy and enjoy getting down to business straightaway, without wasting any time. They are often the quickest workers and usually have suggestions for improvements that will benefit their employers. Aquarians are also very helpful with their co-workers and welcome responsibility, preferring this to having to take orders from others.

If Aquarians want to reach their highest career goals they have to develop more emotional sensitivity, depth of feeling and passion. They need to learn to narrow their focus on the essentials and concentrate more on the job in hand. Aquarians need 'a fire in the belly' – a consuming passion and desire – in order to rise to the very top. Once this passion exists they will succeed easily in whatever they attempt.

Love and Relationships

Aquarians are good at friendships, but a bit weak when it comes to love. Of course they fall in love, but their lovers always get the impression that they are more best friends than paramours.

Like Capricorns, they are cool customers. They are not prone to displays of passion or to outward demonstrations of their affections. In fact, they feel uncomfortable when their mate hugs and touches them too much. This does not mean that they do not love their partners. They do, only they show it in other ways. Curiously enough, in relationships they tend to attract the very things that they feel uncomfortable with. They seem to attract hot, passionate, romantic, demonstrative people. Perhaps they know instinctively that these people have qualities they lack and so seek them out. In any event, these relationships do seem to work, Aquarius' coolness calming the more passionate partner while the fires of passion warm the cold-blooded Aquarius.

The qualities Aquarians need to develop in their love life are warmth, generosity, passion and fun. Aquarians love relationships of the mind. Here they excel. If the intellectual factor is missing in a relationship an Aquarian will soon become bored or feel unfulfilled.

Home and Domestic Life

In family and domestic matters Aquarians can have a tendency to be too non-conformist, changeable and unstable. They are as willing to break the barriers of family constraints as they are those of other areas of life.

Even so, Aquarians are very sociable people. They like to have a nice home where they can entertain family and friends. Their house is usually decorated in a modern style and full of state-of-the-art appliances and gadgets – an environment Aquarians find absolutely necessary.

If their home life is to be healthy and fulfilling Aquarians need to inject it with a quality of stability – yes, even some conservatism. They need at least one area of life to be enduring and steady; this area is usually their home and family life.

Venus, the Planet of Love, rules the Aquarian's 4th Solar House of Home and Family as well, which means that when it comes to the family and child-rearing, theories, cool thinking and intellect are not always enough. Aquarians need to bring love into the equation in order to have a great domestic life.

Horoscope for 2008

Major Trends

The same major trends that we saw last year are pretty much still in effect in 2008. Spirituality is the major headline. Not only is Neptune, the most spiritual planet, still in your 1st House, but your Horoscope ruler is in the spiritual Sign of Pisces. And if this weren't enough, Jupiter will be in your 12th House of Spirituality all year. Even your career planet, Pluto, is making a major long-term move into your 12th House of Spirituality. This is what the year ahead is basically about – spirituality and spiritual growth.

Love has been stressful for the past two years. Marriages have been severely tested, but the worst is over. Any marriage that survived the past two years is likely to survive this year. Saturn is now out of your 7th House of Marriage. More on this later.

Saturn's move out of Leo, last year, not only improved your love life, but health started to improve as well. More on this later.

Your most important interests this year are spirituality; finance; the body, image and sensual pleasures; sex, personal transformation, estates, taxes, debt and debt issues, the deeper things of life – past lives, reincarnation, occult studies (spirituality but from another perspective), friendships (from January 1 to 27 and from June 14 to November 27).

Your paths of greatest fulfilment this year are spirituality and the body, image, and personal pleasures.

Health

(Please note that this is an astrological perspective on health and not a medical one. For the medical perspective, please consult your doctor.)

Health is much improved over last year. Saturn's move out of Leo and into Aquarius did wonders for your overall energy, self-confidence and self-esteem. This year there are NO – zero – *nada* – long-term planets in stressful aspect to you. Perhaps they could be in better alignment with you – we are not saying that the aspects are perfect – but they are more or less leaving you alone. Health looks good.

Your empty 6th House is reinforcing the good that we see. You are not paying too much attention here because you have no need to. You sort of take good health for granted.

During the course of a year there will be periods where health is less easy than usual. This is in the natural order of things. These things come from the transits and are temporary. They don't show long-term trends. When the difficult transits pass, your normal good health returns.

These periods will be from April 19 to May 20, July 22 to August 22, and October 23 to November 22. Be sure to rest and relax more then.

There are ways that you can make your good health even better. Pay more attention to the ankles, stomach and breasts. Ankles should be regularly massaged and given more support when exercising. Diet is more of an issue for you than for most people. There are hosts of natural therapies that can strengthen these organs, too – and most of you know about them – acupuncture, acupressure, shiatsu, kinesiology, herbology, massage and others. But if you like you can work with the foot reflexology chart opposite.

Because your health planet, the Moon, is such a fast-moving planet, your health needs vary almost daily (actually every two to three days). You respond well to different therapies at different times. When it comes to your health there are almost no rules. At one time one thing works, at another something else.

Good health for you also means good emotional health – good family relationships and a harmonious domestic life. It means 'feeling good'. You can go to the doctor, take batteries of tests and they are all negative – yet you still don't believe you are well. And, the contrary is also true: Pathology reports can give you all kinds of scary results, but if you feel good – you are healthy as far as you are concerned.

If problems arise, there is a need to do more than just deal with symptoms – there is a need to deal with the spiritual root causes – and these lie in your emotional life (the Moon). First check out your family relationships and work to bring them back into harmony. Second, look into early traumas from childhood, and especially with your mother – release and clear these things. Third, work to keep your moods constructive and positive (this is done through spiritual means). Chances are, if you do these things your health problem will dissolve – and even if you need the

Reflexology

Try to massage the whole foot on a regular basis, but pay extra attention to the points highlighted on the chart. When you massage, be aware of 'sore spots', as these need special attention. It's also a good idea to massage the ankles and top side (as well as the soles) of the feet.

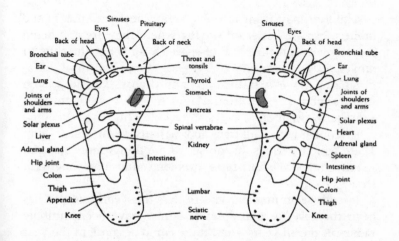

services of a health professional, the healing will go much more quickly.

Home and Family

Your 4th House of Home and Family is not a House of Power this year. While you have more freedom in this area, there is also less interest. You seem content with things as they are – hence the year ahead seems status quo.

There will be periods in the year when family interests – duties and obligations – will be more important – but these are temporary. April 19 to May 20 is such a period.

Major construction or renovations are best done during that period. If you are beautifying the home, the above period is also good – but April 30 to May 20 is even better.

Parents or parent figures would be happier living near water – perhaps they already do – this aspect has been in effect for many years. But if not, it is something for them to think about. They too seem to be investing in a lot of entertainment equipment and sports facilities in the home. They would be happy in a resort-type location, where all these facilities are readily available. A Solar Eclipse on August 1 will test the home and bring up any hidden flaws there.

Children may want to move – they feel cramped in the home – but are better off staying where they are and being more creative in their use of space. Now is not the time to move.

Siblings have a status-quo family year. Relations with siblings seem stressed from May 9 to July 1 – but this is a short-term situation.

Relations with children and parents seem status quo. There will be periods, of course, where things more stressful – but they are short-term problems and not long-term trends.

Friends seem nomadic and restless this year (and this has been the case for many years). There have been multiple moves in recent years – and there could be more in the year ahead. Moving around a lot might not be the solution for them – they need to cultivate more inner peace. It's the feeling of restlessness that is the root cause here.

Finance and Career

A very important area of life for many, many years now, and this year as well.

The trends written of last year are still very much in effect. The planets involved in your finances are long-term planets that stay in a Sign for many years.

This is another year of prosperity and record-breaking earnings. Not only do you have good financial aspects, but your personal interest in finance is very strong. This personal interest – this drive – helps you to overcome the various challenges that arise. A strong interest is more important than easy aspects or even good luck, in my opinion.

Like last year you are investing in yourself. You understand that ultimately, you are the 'earner' and 'creator of wealth' – the more you ARE, the more you earn. You are the best investment there is. You are dressing expensively. Donning and projecting the image of wealth. Personal appearance and overall demeanour play a big role in earnings.

Also we see a great degree of financial independence. You understand that it is all 'up to you'.

There is still a great degree of experimentation going on in finances. All the rule books have been thrown out the window and you are learning what works through trial and error. You have been a great risk-taker in recent years and the trend continues. It is these 'leaps into the unknown' that make your financial life so interesting and creative. With you it is never the 'same old, same old' routine. Something new and exciting is always in the works.

Earnings fluctuate wildly and uncontrollably. When they are high, they are sky-high. But when they are low they are very low. Learning to deal with this financial roller-coaster ride has been one of your main spiritual lessons these past few years.

From an investment perspective, oil, natural gas, energy, high technology (especially in the oil and natural gas industry), retirement homes, assisted living centres and the makers of certain types of pharmaceuticals (painkillers, opiates and mood-enhancers) are all good. Shipping and makers of ships and industries involving water also seem good.

But the main development is the learning of the spiritual dimension of wealth and the application of these laws. You have been very involved in this for many years, and this year you delve more deeply into it.

Intuition – an inner faculty – is more important to your wealth than hordes of outside investors, customers or bank accounts. More on this later.

Debt seems more of a problem in the year ahead. It seems a burden. You will succeed in paying it off, but in a step-by-step way.

Issues involving estates, taxes, royalties and insurance payments also seem a burden. You just need to be patient and settle in for the long haul – these things are not likely to be resolved quickly.

This is not a year for soliciting outside investors. Work to generate your own cash and use that.

The income and earnings of your spouse or partner seem challenging this year. There is a need for a long-term financial reorganization. They need to bring the 'right order' in their finances – and probably it won't happen overnight. He or she seems to be spending more on health issues, but the field of health, the health industry, could also become a source of income.

Job-seekers and those who hire others are having a status-quo year.

Career is not a major interest in the year ahead. Your 10th House of Career is mostly empty. But we do see more dramatic changes – not only this year – but for many years to come. Your career planet, Pluto, is changing Signs – and this is a big deal. He doesn't do that very often. The last time he changed Signs was in 1995.

Pluto moves from your 11th House to your 12th House of Spirituality. This has many meanings. On a worldly level, it shows that you further your career through involvement in charities and altruistic causes. But in many cases it will go further than that – many of you will actually choose a spiritual type of career. More on this later.

Love and Social Life

Your 7th House of Love and Marriage is not a House of Power this year. Love and romance are not such big issues for you. In most cases this shows a contentment with the status quo and you have no need – no pressing urge – to make dramatic changes this year.

However, the past two years were very challenging. Many of you are coming out of a divorce and you don't seem in a hurry to re-marry. Those of you who are still married have gone through the worst of it, and things are much better now. Even a Solar Eclipse in your 7th House on August 1 is not going to be as serious as you've experienced for two years. Yes, the marriage will be re-tested, but if you've got this far, you'll get through that too. Not advisable to make drastic changes this year.

Though friendships are always important to you, Pluto's move out of your 11th House shows that even here your interest is waning. Again, you seem content with your present social circle – your present friends – and have no need to make big changes. Money and spirituality are much more important this year than your social life.

Though your 7th House is not strong, you will still have a social life. Singles will be dating and having fun. But there is nothing really serious in store. Your most active love period will be from July 22 to August 22. Your most active period for friendships will be from November 16 to December 21.

With the fast-moving Sun as your love planet, your love needs and opportunities will change month to month.

We will cover these short-term trends in the monthly reports.

Romantically you are drawn to strong kinds of people – they have to have 'star quality'. You like actors, entertainers, celebrities or sports heroes. You like a 'dramatic' kind of love life.

With friends, it is the spiritual types – also very creative types – who draw you. Your planet of friends will be in the spiritual 12th House all year. By the way, it is at spiritual type of events – spiritual retreats, meditation seminars or lectures, charitable events – that you make new and interesting friends.

Spiritual compatibility seems the most important element in friendship this year. You need to be on the same spiritual wavelength – share the same spiritual ideals – with your friends.

Those working towards (or in) their second marriage are having a status-quo year. Singles will tend to stay single and marrieds will tend to stay married.

Those involved in their third marriage could have been widowed or divorced in recent years. Marriage opportunities were more likely in 2007 than in 2008. If you didn't marry or remarry last year, this year seems status quo.

Those working on their fourth marriage need patience this year – next year, 2009, is your year.

Self-improvement

As mentioned earlier, spirituality is the major focus this year. I mean major.

With your career planet also starting to move into your 12th House, it is actually your mission in life for many years to come. Spiritual growth is number one – everything else in life revolves around that.

Once you understand your priorities – and apply them – growth and progress will be breathtakingly rapid. And as this happens, watch your financial life start to soar. For, in truth, there is ONE and ONLY ONE source of supply, ONE and

ONLY ONE prospering power. All the things that happen in your business or investments are only side-effects of the action of this ONE. You will discover that it has always been this way. That even your parents or spouse were only the instruments that this ONE used to supply you.

The idea you had for a business or investment, or to make that purchase, came from the ONE.

As long as you acknowledge this, strive to remain close to it – in a state of connection – your life will go well. You will prosper beyond your wildest dreams – and with harmony and peace of mind. (You probably will have to work, but your work will be interesting and something that you can easily do.) Your career – your standing in the public eye – will also sky-rocket. It will be as if you have crossed some invisible boundary and have the 'license of a Higher Order of Being' as Thoreau says.

This year, financial problems, career problems, problems with friends are merely signals that somehow, in some way, you've got disconnected. The solution is to get reconnected as quickly as you can. It's that simple.

You are a scientifically-oriented person. An intellectual. The right spiritual path is something practical and scientific – something rational. Now spirit itself is beyond all human rationality – but the path to it is rational. Things like jnana yoga or hermetic science will help you this year. Something that engages your intellect. Astrology is always an important interest, but this year the spiritual side of astrology (another form of jnana yoga and very related to hermetic science) will draw you. The planet that rules astrology, Jupiter, is your 11th House.

Your spiritual planet is in the 8th House. Pluto, which is the natural ruler of the 8th House, is in your 12th House of Spirituality. So this is a year where you explore life after death, past lives and the fact that death as we understand it is an illusion. Your spiritual growth will conquer the fear of death.

But there is another reading of this, too. Your spiritual understanding and intuition will not only help you to prosper, but your spouse or partner as well. You will be getting spiritual messages about their finances.

Pluto and the 8th House are associated with death – elimination. So there will be a detox of many of your spiritual attitudes this year. The false ones will go. Also patterns in you that obstruct growth will also 'die' – and good riddance.

Month-by-month Forecasts

January

Best Days Overall: 1, 9, 10, 18, 19, 27, 28
Most Stressful Days Overall: 2, 3, 16, 17, 22, 23, 29, 30, 31
Best Days for Love: 5, 6, 7, 8, 14, 15, 16, 17, 22, 23, 27, 28
Best Days for Money: 1, 7, 9, 10, 12, 13, 16, 18, 19, 24, 25, 27, 28

Your year begins with 70 and often 80 per cent of the planets in the independent, Eastern sector of your Horoscope. Your 1st House of Self is strong all month (but gets very strong after the 20th) while your 7th House of Others is basically empty – only the Moon visits there on the 22nd and 23rd. A very clear message: You are in one of the most independent periods of your year. (Next month will be even stronger.) This is a time to have life on your terms and to take personal action to create conditions as you desire them to be. No need now for compromising, consensus and people skills (of course you should always be polite and respectful to others) – it is a time for direct action. Personal initiative matters now. As you create your own happiness, the world will adapt to you.

Spirituality is the main headline of the month ahead. The spiritual power and revelation coming to you are absolutely incredible. It's as if you live more in the spiritual world than in the material, concrete world. This is the chart of someone who leaves all and travels to some distant land to sit at the feet of the Guru, or who is on a religious pilgrimage to some holy place. All of you are going to experience interior revelation this period – but how much depends on how far along you are on the path. All of you are going to have more spiritual-type experiences – dreams, visions, synchronistic experiences, experiences with beings of other dimensions. Also you will be more involved with ministers, gurus, spiritual channels and psychics. You will be attracting spiritual kinds of people in your life.

But while in incarnation we were never intended to live in the other worlds. We were sent here to Earth for a purpose. And while these other worlds are very beautiful, after the 20th you start to get more involved in your body. You enter one of your yearly personal pleasure periods. You've experienced the pleasures of the spirit, and now you are going to experience the pleasures of the flesh. Spirit wants you to experience those things, too – so that you will know how one rates with the other – and so that you get a true perspective on the two types of pleasures.

Love is very happy this month. Until the 20th singles find love opportunities in spiritually-oriented settings: at pilgrimages, ashrams, meditation seminars or workshops, spiritual retreats or as they involve themselves in charities or causes. Until the 20th only the most idealistic kind of person appeals to you – the poet, the prophet, the artist, musician or spiritual channel. The more otherworldly he or she is, the better. Romantic experiences can happen at poetry readings to fund the homeless or at drumming or fire ceremonies. After the 20th love is more physical, more worldly. The physical chemistry seems to matter most. The good news is that love pursues you and there's not much you need to do – in fact it is hard to see how you could escape it.

Both health and finances are good all month – but you don't seem to care much about these things.

February

Best Days Overall: 6, 7, 14, 15, 23, 24
Most Stressful Days Overall: 12, 13, 19, 20, 26, 27
Best Days for Love: 3, 4, 6, 7, 13, 14, 15, 16, 19, 20, 23, 25, 26
Best Days for Money: 3, 4, 6, 7, 8, 9, 12, 13, 14, 15, 21, 22, 23, 24

Your yearly personal pleasure peak is still in full swing – and from the 17th to the 19th is even stronger than last month. Like last month, this is a strong period of personal independence. So make the most of it. Make the changes in your life that need to be made and design your life for personal happiness. Others are more than happy to please you and cooperate with you.

Basically a happy month, but two eclipses this month show that there are bumps along the way. The Solar Eclipse of the 7th (the 6th in the US) is very strong on you. And even though health is good this month, take a reduced schedule for this eclipse – a few days before and after. Do the things that you need to do, but let the inessential (especially if risky or stressful) go. This eclipse occurs in your own Sign and thus produces a redefinition of your personality (this is a good thing to do now, considering the strong spiritual period you've been through in the past two months – you are a different person and now you have to bring your mind and emotions into adjustment with this new reality). The eclipses have ways of forcing you into this – better to do it voluntarily. Usually this produces a new wardrobe, a new way of dressing, a new hairstyle and a new overall image and demeanour. A new you is coming into being. Every Solar Eclipse will test the marriage and the love life, and this one is no different. But the good relationships will survive (keep in mind that Solar Eclipses happen twice a year, so long relationships have weathered these things many times – it is merely an opportunity to confront problems in the relationship and correct them). Since your financial planet,

Neptune, is impacted by this eclipse, there will be dramatic and long-term financial changes, too.

The Lunar Eclipse of the 21st (the 20th in the US) occurs in your 8th House. This eclipse is more friendly to you, but it won't hurt to take a reduced schedule anyway. People in general are not up to par during eclipse periods. Your partner, spouse or current love is also making dramatic financial changes. There are job changes or changes in the conditions of the workplace. Employers are experiencing employee turnover. There are long-term changes in health attitudes, diet and the health regime. Sometimes these aspects bring near-death experiences or encounters with the dark angel – this is to help us overcome the fear of death, and to learn how to live better.

Love, once the dust settles from the eclipse, should still be happy. You seem to be getting your way in love and your spouse, partner or current love goes way out of his or her way to please you. Your interests come first. Singles still find love opportunities pursuing them. After the 19th love opportunities come as you pursue your financial goals.

It is a prosperous month – in spite of the shake-ups caused by the eclipse. The changes you make will be positive. Overall prosperity is still very much intact. Continue to trust your intuition.

March

Best Days Overall: 4, 5, 13, 14, 22, 23, 31
Most Stressful Days Overall: 11, 17, 18, 24, 25
Best Days for Love: 4, 5, 6, 7, 15, 16, 17, 18, 24, 25, 27
Best Days for Money: 2, 3, 4, 5, 6, 7, 11, 13, 14, 19, 20, 22, 23, 29, 30

Last month the planetary power shifted from the upper – 'day' side of the Horoscope to the 'night' side – the lower half. Thus you are in a period where it is important to find your point of emotional harmony and to function from there. Feeling right is more important than doing right. The most prestigious job will be meaningless to you if you are not emotionally comfortable. Many of you are into careers, and this shift will not stop things, but it is good now to work on the career by more interior means – through visualizing, dreaming, fantasizing (in a controlled way), rather than by objective methods. Though a person is 'idle' at night when he or she sleeps, the night is still very important – one awakes ready and refreshed for the day ahead. It is said that the 'night is mother to the day' – and what happens in the dream world of the night is what will happen during the day. This how it is with your career. You are in the night period of your year. It has a purpose – what you dream about for the next few months (provided you don't deny your dreams) is what will happen in your career when your yearly day begins.

Family harmony and unity can be enhanced by your personal presence and personal attention (until the 13th) and through material support – practical means – afterwards. Family seems supportive financially, but you are also spending more on them – and also the home. A parent figure is visiting this month (this could have happened last month, too).

On the 19th of last month you entered a yearly financial peak and this is now in full swing. A very prosperous month. There is a nice windfall on the 6th or 7th. A parent or parent figure is generous with you then (and they in turn experience a nice financial increase). There is good spousal support all month, but especially on the 8th or 9th. A business partnership or joint-venture opportunity is likely this period. Social connections in general are very important financially. Speculations are favourable from the 15th onwards – the 9th, 27th and 28th are favourable for this, too. On the 9th you receive a fabulous financial intuition – a trading idea or creative idea. (This intuition could be delivered to you via messengers – a psychic, astrologer or spiritual channel.) In general you are experiencing the supernatural sources of supply – and these far transcend the natural ones – and are much more fun, too.

Love is happy. Your spouse or lover shows love through
material support. Singles are allured by the wealthy – the
good providers (but even so, they need to have a spiritual,
idealistic side to them), There is a happy (and unexpected)
romantic experience or opportunity on the 8th or 9th.

April

Best Days Overall: 1, 2, 9, 10, 18, 19, 28, 29
Most Stressful Days Overall: 7, 8, 13, 14, 20, 21, 22
Best Days for Love: 4, 5, 6, 13, 14, 24, 25, 26
Best Days for Money: 1, 2, 3, 4, 7, 8, 9, 10, 16, 17, 18, 19,
    26, 27, 28, 29, 30

Finances are less important this month and the focus (especially after the 6th) is on communication and intellectual
interests – among your favourite activities. Now Aquarius,
almost more than anyone, doesn't need prodding to feed
and exercise the mind – you are always doing that. But this
month the interest is stronger. Your always sharp mind is
even stronger in the month ahead – especially until the
19th. (By then you have probably read every book in the
library and every current magazine.)

Your 4th House of Home and Family becomes very
powerful after the 19th. Most of the planets are below the
horizon. Your 10th House of Career is basically empty, with
the exception of the Moon's visit there on the 20th, 21st and
22nd. So give home and the family some attention. You'll
achieve more by being at the school play or sports day than
by making another deal (which may or may not materialize). Besides, your career planet, Pluto is Retrograde beginning the 2nd, and you are in a period of career review and
analysis. So you may as well focus on the family. Enhance
family harmony through social activities – entertaining from
home or entertaining family members. Or through attending
social events together as a family unit. Entertainments also
create good energy – going to the theatre or theme park
or match as a family. It might also be wise to invest in

entertainment equipment for the home. Family life needs to be taken out of the 'humdrum' and made fun and socially exciting.

Finances, though less important, are still basically good. But after the 19th there is more challenge involved. These challenges won't interfere with your overall prosperous outlook – nothing long term has changed – but these are short-term bumps on the road. There could be financial disagreements with your spouse, current love or business partners. Perhaps with children as well. Speculations are mixed this month.

There is another issue here, too. With many planets in the practical Earth Signs after the 19th – a whopping 50 to 60 per cent – you could allow 'appearances' or a 'matter-of-fact' attitude to obstruct your intuition. Intuition is always practical, but we generally only see this in hindsight. While it is happening it often seems impractical and impossible (and this is the situation after the 19th) and thus you might go against it.

Your spiritual life has been important for many years. It is very important this year, too. But now your spiritual planet, Saturn, is re-stimulating an eclipse point all month – it practically camps out there. (This began on the 30th of last month.) This shows great change and disturbance in a spiritual organization (or charity or cause) that you are involved with. Also it shows that you are making very important changes in your spiritual regime. Perhaps because of some spiritual crisis. In the end this will all work out, but keep your faith and trust in the Higher Power.

Health needs more watching after the 19th. Happily you seem on the case – focused on health issues. Enhance health through vigorous physical exercise and keeping good muscle tone. Pay more attention to the stomach, breasts, heart, colon, bladder, sexual organs and adrenal glands.

May

Best Days Overall: 6, 7, 15, 16, 25, 26
Most Stressful Days Overall: 4, 5, 11, 12, 18, 19
Best Days for Love: 4, 5, 11, 12, 13, 14, 24, 25
Best Days for Money: 1, 4, 5, 6, 7, 13, 14, 15, 16, 23, 24, 25, 26, 28, 29

Retrograde activity increases dramatically this month. By the end of the month 40 per cent of the planets will be Retrograde – including Neptune, your financial planet. Forty per cent is the high we will have for the current year. The maximum percentage. So the pace of events in the world, in your career and in your financial life is slowing down. Certain issues – especially financial and career issues – will only be resolved with time and not by personal action. Earnings will still happen – you will see dramatic improvement after the 20th – but slowly and with more delays. When Neptune goes Retrograde on the 26th you enter a period of financial review and analysis. Avoid (where possible) important purchases (big-ticket items) or major investments. However, since this Retrograde lasts a long time (many months) there are times when you have little choice – in those cases, do more homework and study all the details. These Retrogrades are like the 'pause that refreshes' – if they are used properly, the new ideas and plans that you evolve will increase prosperity down the road.

Saturn, your spiritual planet, is still camping out on the eclipse point of February 21. He camps out there all month – so refer to our discussion of this last month.

Home, family and domestic concerns are still the main focus until the 20th. This is as it should be. Most of the planets are still below the horizon and your 10th House is still basically empty. Your career planet, like last month, is still Retrograde. You can safely downplay the career and focus on the home. This is a great period for buying art objects for the home or for redecorating. Making the home more beautiful as well as entertaining will enhance family unity and harmony. Studies have shown that the right colours in the home reduce tempers and cure sleep problems. This is something to consider now.

Those of you undergoing therapy will have important breakthroughs. But all of you will be making more psychological progress – there will be growth this month.

On the 20th you enter another yearly personal pleasure peak. This is a period for all the delights of the senses, for love affairs (if you are single), for going on holiday (and this is a great time, because things have slowed down at work and with your career) and for leisure activities. Life was meant to be enjoyed, and this is a time for exploring this dimension. Artists will be unusually creative. You will get on better with children, either your actual children or those who are like children to you.

Health (though good overall) still needs more watching until the 20th. Try to rest and relax more. Listen to your body and avoid pushing it beyond its limits. Enhance health through more exercise (until the 9th) and by paying more attention to the heart (until the 20th), stomach and breasts (all month), colon, bladder, sexual organs, head and adrenals (until the 9th).

June

Best Days Overall: 3, 4, 11, 12, 13, 21, 22, 23, 30
Most Stressful Days Overall: 1, 2, 7, 8, 14, 15, 28, 29
Best Days for Love: 3, 4, 7, 8, 11, 12, 14, 15, 24, 25
Best Days for Money: 1, 2, 3, 4, 9, 10, 11, 12, 19, 20, 21, 22, 23, 24, 25, 28, 29, 30

Your personal pleasure peak is in full swing. The party is on and the band is playing. Enjoy. Love is mixed this period. On the one hand it seems very honeymoon-ish, but on the other there is some personal disagreement or conflict with the beloved until the 21st. You just don't see eye to eye. (Perhaps a second honeymoon might be the ticket to harmony now.) You seem focused on finances, but the beloved is focused on fun and games. With most of the planets in the Western sector now, downplay self-will and self-assertion. Let others, especially the beloved, have their way (so long as it isn't destructive) – in this matter, the beloved might be right. Get your way through social skills, compromise and consensus now. Your good comes to you through others.

Fun is important and so is work. But work becomes more important after the 21st, when you are all 'partied out'. Job-seekers will have better success then. Social connections, your spouse or current love, or family members seem to have the best job leads.

For singles, love is at the usual places until the 21st. At parties, clubs, at the hot spots, resorts or places of entertainment. After the 21st, the workplace is the scene of romance. The reason for the shift of venue is that two philosophies of love are playing out in you. One philosophy says love has to be fun, it is all about fun. If a relationship isn't joyous it's time to get out. The other philosophy says fun is very ephemeral, love is about practical service to the beloved. We show love not by partying, but by serving them. So in the beginning you have the first philosophy (which often leads to frivolity and irresponsibility) and later you have the second philosophy.

Health is good this month. You can make it even better by paying more attention to the stomach and breasts (all month), the heart (after the 21st) and the kidneys and hips (after the 18th). Diet is always important for you, but this month especially so. With your 6th House of Health very strong after the 21st you are more focused here, more into healthy lifestyles and health regimes. Your interest in health could even lead to romance, as this could happen as you pursue your health goals or regime – at the gym, yoga studio or doctor's surgery. Healers and health professionals have a special allure for singles.

Finances are much improved. Speculations should be avoided until the 19th – afterwards they seem more favourable. But your financial planets are Retrograde and so continue doing your financial review and analysis.

July

Best Days Overall: 1, 9, 10, 19, 20, 28
Most Stressful Days Overall: 4, 5, 11, 12, 26
Best Days for Love: 2, 3, 4, 5, 11, 12, 13, 23, 24
Best Days for Money: 6, 7, 9, 10, 16, 17, 19, 20, 21, 22, 26, 28, 29

With your personal planet, Uranus, Retrograde all month – and self-confidence a bit weaker than usual – it is good that you are into a yearly social peak beginning the 22nd. With most of the planets in the Western, social sector to boot, you need to tone down your self-will and personal preferences anyway. Uranus' Retrograde makes this easier to do. Go along with others so long as it isn't destructive. Your way is probably not the best way these days (and many of you are not even sure what your way is). Cultivate the social skills and graces, and let your good come to you through others.

Mars re-stimulates an eclipse point from the 1st to the 8th – drive defensively. Communication equipment gets tested. There are dramas in the lives of siblings and neighbours. Parents or parent figures also experience dramas from the 26th to the 29th. They should avoid risk-taking activities then. The 26th to the 29th could also bring repairs in the home.

Love is happy and active this month – the primary reason is your personal interest. This is always 90 per cent of success. You have the drive and the urge – and this enables you to overcome whatever challenges confront you. Existing relationships should deepen, become more romantic this month – especially after the 22nd. For the unattached there are significant meetings all month (but especially from the 13th to the 15th). Because your personal planet is Retrograde your lover or current love interest has trouble figuring out how to please you. But the important thing is that he or she does want to please you. Until the 22nd love is at the workplace, with people you work with, or with people involved in your health. After the 22nd love is in the usual places – parties, weddings, engagement parties, social events, places of entertainment, resorts and the like. There will be more family-type gatherings, too. Singles have many options this month – they can opt for the fun-and-games type of relationship or the more serious kind. Both are available. Love is expressed through service – doing for the other – until the 22nd, but afterwards it is more romantic. An old flame from your past comes into the picture after the 12th – but you have many other options. For marrieds, this is a good time for a second honeymoon.

Health needs more watching after the 22nd. But you have been focused here this past month and this is a help. Still, try to rest and relax more. Pay more attention to the heart. Laughter is the best medicine this month.

Job-seekers still have good success – especially until the 22nd.

Finances are more challenging after the 22nd – but overall prosperity is intact. This is a short-term trend. You just need to work harder for earnings than usual – go the extra mile for your clients or boss.

August

Best Days Overall: 5, 6, 15, 16, 24, 25
Most Stressful Days Overall: 1, 2, 7, 8, 9, 22, 23, 28, 29
Best Days for Love: 1, 2, 10, 11, 21, 22, 23, 28, 29, 30, 31
Best Days for Money: 3, 4, 5, 6, 12, 13, 15, 16, 17, 18, 22, 23, 24, 25, 30, 31

There are two strong eclipses on you this month, so take a reduced schedule during these periods. Actually you should take a reduced schedule from the 1st until the 22nd, but even more reduced around the eclipse periods. You just have to analyse your schedule. Do you really have to make that foreign trip, or have that elective surgery, or get involved in that soccer match around the eclipse? The things you need to do, you must do, but electives should be rescheduled.

The Solar Eclipse of August 1 occurs in your 7th House and this will severely test your marriage or serious relationship. Your relationships get tested pretty regularly – twice a year. But this testing seems stronger than usual. A faulty or weak relationship is in danger. The same is true for business partnerships. Since Mercury is involved in this eclipse there are dramatic events with children, too. A love affair will also get tested (not just a marriage or serious relationship). Keep the kids close to home during this eclipse – a few days before and after. There can be encounters or brushes with death (we don't mean this in a literal way – it is most often on a psychological level) – and there is a need to confront and understand these things.

The Lunar Eclipse of the 16th occurs in your 1st House. This announces a redefinition of your personality and image – your concept of yourself – how you think of yourself. My feeling is that you are forced to do this because of the testing of your marriage or current relationship. The other party has very different ideas about you than you have about yourself, and lets you know. So now you have to give more thought to these things. The end result will be a new you – a new hairstyle, new wardrobe, a new look. This eclipse also impacts on Neptune, your financial planet (this is practically a repeat of the Solar Eclipse of February 7). And again you are forced to make more financial changes – and dramatic ones. The only difference now is that your financial planet is Retrograde and so you need think these changes through more thoroughly. But the need for change is very apparent. Because the eclipsed planet is the Moon, your health planet, there will be long-term changes in your diet and health regime – people often change doctors or therapists under these aspects. Job changes are in the works. If you employ others, there is staff turnover now.

Once the dust settles from the eclipse, love seems happy – the eclipse is merely purifying your love life – afterwards there will be more clarity here. Good relationships survive,

bad ones dissolve, and singles are ready to move on to the
new and better.

Last month the planets shifted from the lower to the
upper half of the Horoscope – from the night side to the day
side. This month the shift is even stronger. Dawn is breaking
in your chart. It is time to focus on the outer world and
leave the night behind. Ambitions and outer success are calling to you. It is time to make the dreams of the night practical, concrete realities.

September

Best Days Overall: 1, 2, 3, 11, 12, 20, 21, 29, 30
Most Stressful Days Overall: 4, 5, 18, 19, 24, 25
Best Days for Love: 1, 2, 9, 10, 11, 12, 19, 21, 24, 25, 29
Best Days for Money: 1, 2, 3, 9, 10, 11, 12, 14, 15, 18, 19,
   20, 21, 27, 29, 30

There is some very beautiful timing going on in your
Horoscope (and thus your life). Most of the planets are
above the horizon of your Horoscope and your 10th House
will start to get strong on the 24th – and all of this is
happening as Pluto, your career planet, starts to move
forward after many months of Retrograde motion. By now
you have clarity about your plans, and most importantly
you have the power and drive to execute them. You lost
nothing by focusing on home and family while Pluto was
Retrograde – in fact you probably advanced your career by
this. Very soon – next month – you will enter a yearly
career peak and the stage is being set for it. You can
enhance your career through social means and through
family connections (and perhaps intervention) after the
24th. Family is very important in spite of your career interests, but they are supporting your outer activities. The
family as a whole seems more ambitious, too – and there is
elevation for the family as a whole (and particularly a
parent or parent figure) this period. Career is also advanced
through social networking, having friends in the right

places, and being up to date with the latest technology – things you love anyway.

Your spiritual mission this month (and since June) is your friends – to be a friend and to be there for them.

Your 8th House was very strong last month and is still strong this month – until the 22nd especially. This shows prosperity for your spouse or partner, strong spousal support, the ability to pay off (or to incur) debt (according to your need) and a strong interest in estate and tax issues.

This is a strong period for personal transformation and reinvention – to give birth to the you that you want to be. But before resurrection there is death (psychological death) – that is, old patterns of thinking and feeling die – and when this happens you start to soar like an eagle.

A great period to detox yourself on all levels – financially, materially, emotionally, mentally and physically. Also a good period for weight-loss regimes.

After the 22nd the focus shifts to religion, philosophy, higher education, metaphysics, delving into the meaning of life, and foreign travel. This is a nice period for students (either university or below-university level) – they seem successful this month. There will be happy travel opportunities, too.

Love is happier after the 22nd. Before that there is too much criticism and ultra-perfectionism. Also you and your beloved seem at opposite ends of the spectrum – you just don't see eye to eye. The truth is that both of you are right – in certain cases your lover is right and in certain cases you are right. There is a path in the middle that can bridge your differences. A foreign trip will enhance a current relationship after the 22nd. Also, common religious or educational interests will help. There is a need to build common ground on a philosophical level.

Finances improve dramatically after the 22nd.

October

Best Days Overall: 9, 10, 17, 18, 26, 27
Most Stressful Days Overall: 1, 2, 15, 16, 22, 23, 28, 29,
   30
Best Days for Love: 1, 9, 10, 11, 12, 17, 18, 21, 22, 23, 28,
   29
Best Days for Money: 6, 7, 9, 10, 11, 12, 15, 16, 17, 18,
   24, 25, 26, 27

You are now in a very powerful career period. Mars crosses
the Midheaven on the 4th and stays in your 10th House all
month. This shows a lot of work – perhaps even conflict and
competition – in your career – either within your company
or in your industry (or both). Yet you will be successful.
Hang in there; by the 22nd friends or partners are strongly
supportive. You make good alliances or partnerships that
enhance your career. You attract just the right people who
can help your career. Your spouse or partner also seems very
ambitious both on a personal level and for you.

All this career activity takes a toll on your energy, so try
to rest and relax more after the 22nd and delegate tasks
wherever possible. Pay more attention to the heart, stomach
and breasts.

The pace at the career is fast this month, but it is also
speeding up in the world at large. Retrograde activity is
reduced again. By the 15th 80 per cent of the planets will be
moving forward.

Finances are excellent until the 23rd. Your spouse, partner or current love is very supportive. Foreigners are helpful. There is prayer on your behalf going on. But your
financial planet is still Retrograde and you are still in a
period of financial review and analysis. After the 23rd
finances are more challenging. You just need to work harder
for earnings and be more patient with delays. A financial
disagreement with your spouse, partner or current love is
not helping matters. But this disagreement is short term.
Your overall prosperity is not affected by any of this.

Love is in foreign lands, with foreigners or in religious or educational settings until the 23rd. A foreign trip will enhance a current relationship (like last month). Singles have the aspects of love with a teacher, professor or mentor. University students find love while at their studies. After the 23rd love opportunities come as you pursue your career goals or with people involved in your career. For singles you have the aspects of the office romance, but not with co-workers, with superiors. In general you are mixing with people who are above you in status. And this seems alluring to you. Power turns you on. For some, love is seen as just another career move – there is a very practical way of thinking here. Those in existing relationships will have to be patient with their spouse or partner as he or she has a need to be 'on top' – in charge. Above everyone. This is not malicious – in truth, he or she is enjoying success and elevation this period. This behaviour is merely one of the 'perks' of success.

November

Best Days Overall: 5, 6, 14, 15, 22, 23
Most Stressful Days Overall: 12, 13, 18, 19, 25, 26
Best Days for Love: 1, 7, 8, 11, 12, 16, 17, 18, 19, 20, 21, 27, 28, 30
Best Days for Money: 2, 3, 4, 5, 6, 7, 8, 12, 13, 14, 15, 20, 21, 22, 23, 30

Your yearly career peak is still in full swing. But there are important changes going on. By the 23rd the 10th House empties out – the interest shifts to your favourite activity – friends, groups and organizations – group activities. I read this as career goals being more or less fulfilled and now you can move on to other things. But on the 27th Pluto makes a move (permanent this time) into Capricorn, your 12th House. This is indeed a major career shift. You will be more idealistic about your career. It will have to be something that fits in with your spiritual values and ideals – just being successful for the sake of it is not enough for you – your success has to happen in spiritually correct (not politically or financially correct) ways. Also as mentioned in the yearly report, career is enhanced through involvement in charities and causes – causes you believe in.

Spirituality has been strong in your Horoscope for many years. This year it has become even more important and this month even more important. Many of you will be thinking about a spiritual-type career – making spiritual activities your actual career. Many of you will juggle a worldly career with a spiritual career. These trends are only getting stronger as time goes on.

Though there are some bumps in the road, love is basically happy this month – especially until the 21st. For singles, love is still with people involved in their career – 'power people' – or as they pursue career goals. The aspects for the office romance are still very much in effect until the 21st. The new love (or current love) still seems elevated over you, and this can be hard for some of you to handle. The relationship doesn't seem 'equal'. Perhaps this why you change your philosophy after the 21st. You want friendship – a peer kind of relationship – as well as love. The platonic aspects of love – the similarity in ideas – being of like mind – are more important than just power and position. Love gets tested from the 1st to the 3rd and from the 18th to the 21st. There are dramatic events in the life of your spouse, partner or current love then – perhaps with friends, too.

Health still needs watching until the 21st. Like last month, pay more attention to the heart, stomach and breasts. Above all, rest and relax more. Listen to your body. After the 21st there is a dramatic increase in energy and health starts improving.

Finances are improving day by day. On the 2nd your financial planet starts moving forward after many months of Retrograde motion. By now you have a clear plan, good judgement, and you know where you're going. And, by the 21st, the aspects to your financial planet start to improve as well. (Until then there seem to be financial disputes with a current love or business partner.)

December

Best Days Overall: 2, 3, 11, 12, 20, 21, 30, 31
Most Stressful Days Overall: 9, 10, 15, 16, 22, 23
Best Days for Love: 1, 7, 8, 11, 15, 16, 20, 21, 27, 28, 30, 31
Best Days for Money: 1, 2, 3, 5, 6, 9, 10, 11, 12, 17, 18, 20, 21, 27, 28, 30, 31

This month we have a repeat performance of your January Horoscope. Only this month it is even stronger. Your 12th House of Spirituality is the main headline of the month ahead. Between 60 and 70 per cent of the planets are either in this House or moving through there. It is a month of spiritual growth, attainment and realization. It is a month of living in the reality of the invisible world – and it seems more real to you – more vivid, more powerful – than the concrete matter-of-fact world that we perceive with our five senses.

As we saw in January, this is a time for going on spiritual retreats or religious pilgrimages. In some religions it is obligatory to do this once in a life time – and this would be a good year – and good month – to do this.

It is a month where the supernatural is the norm and the natural is abnormal – just the reverse of what most people experience. The natural is seen as just another form of 'miracle' and not a fixed reality. Many of you are going to witness and experience all kinds of miraculous events now – for the invisible world is letting you know that it exists. You will see miraculous types of healings – the healing of incurable diseases through the power of spirit. Many of you will have experiences with angels, masters and other supernatural beings. The dream life will be vivid and hyperactive. And prophetic. Your already strong ESP powers will be even stronger. Someone will call you and you will know who it is before you pick up the phone – you will even know that they are calling before they call. You will know what's in the post before you open it. Your financial intuition has been ultra-strong for some years, and now with Neptune moving forward and all this power in your 12th House it will be uncanny. I feel the month ahead will be very prosperous – more than you imagine – because of this. Supernatural financial experiences will happen – and these, by the way, are the most fun kind. You don't worry about your next pay-packet or whether a client is coming back to you. It is all in the hands of the supernatural – and it is acting on your behalf. Usually the supernatural supplies in 'natural' ways – you almost don't realize that something miraculous is happening – but this month I feel the miracles will be dramatic. Flamboyant-type events will happen. Nullifications of the laws of nature. You will remember the events of this month all your life. For singles, even love will happen in miraculous, supernatural ways. For marrieds, problems in the relationship can be cured instantly through the intervention of Spirit. In fact, the best way to enhance a current relationship is through spiritual understanding and through getting involved in spiritual activities as a couple.

You have the aspects of the person who wants to leave the world – all the glamour and entertainment and pleasures of the world – and sit at the feet of the Guru. A meditation seminar is more alluring to you than the hottest new film or play.

Pisces

)(

Personality Profile

PISCES AT A GLANCE

Element – Water

Ruling Planet – Neptune
   Career Planet – Pluto
   Love Planet – Mercury
   Money Planet – Mars
   Planet of Health and Work – Sun
   Planet of Home and Family Life – Mercury
   Planet of Love Affairs, Creativity and Children
      – Moon

Colours – aqua, blue-green

*Colours that promote love, romance and social
   harmony* – earth tones, yellow, yellow-
   orange

Colours that promote earning power – red,
   scarlet

Gem – white diamond

Metal – tin

Scent – lotus

Quality – mutable (= flexibility)

Qualities most needed for balance – structure and the ability to handle form

Strongest virtues – psychic power, sensitivity, self-sacrifice, altruism

Deepest needs – spiritual illumination, liberation

Characteristics to avoid – escapism, keeping bad company, negative moods

Signs of greatest overall compatibility – Cancer, Scorpio

Signs of greatest overall incompatibility – Gemini, Virgo, Sagittarius

Sign most helpful to career – Sagittarius

Sign most helpful for emotional support – Gemini

Sign most helpful financially – Aries

Sign best for marriage and/or partnerships – Virgo

Sign most helpful for creative projects – Cancer

Best Sign to have fun with – Cancer

Signs most helpful in spiritual matters – Scorpio, Aquarius

Best day of the week – Thursday

Understanding a Pisces

If Pisces have one outstanding quality it is their belief in the invisible, spiritual and psychic side of things. This side of things is as real to them as the hard earth beneath their feet – so real, in fact, that they will often ignore the visible, tangible aspects of reality in order to focus on the invisible and so-called intangible ones.

Of all the Signs of the Zodiac, the intuitive and emotional faculties of the Pisces are the most highly developed. They are committed to living by their intuition and this can at times be infuriating to other people – especially those who are materially-, scientifically- or technically-orientated. If you think that money or status or worldly success are the only goals in life, then you will never understand a Pisces.

Pisces have intellect, but to them intellect is only a means by which they can rationalize what they know intuitively. To an Aquarius or a Gemini the intellect is a tool with which to gain knowledge. To a well-developed Pisces it is a tool by which to express knowledge.

Pisces feel like fish in an infinite ocean of thought and feeling. This ocean has many depths, currents and undercurrents. They long for purer waters where the denizens are good, true and beautiful, but they are sometimes pulled to the lower, murkier depths. Pisces know that they do not generate thoughts but only tune in to thoughts that already exist; this is why they seek the purer waters. This ability to tune in to higher thoughts inspires them artistically and musically.

Since Pisces is so spiritually-orientated – though many Pisces in the corporate world may hide this fact – we will deal with this aspect in greater detail, for otherwise it is difficult to understand the true Pisces personality.

There are four basic attitudes of the spirit. One is outright scepticism – the attitude of secular humanists. The second is an intellectual or emotional belief, where one worships a far-distant God figure – the attitude of most modern church-going people. The third is not only belief but direct personal spiritual experience – this is the attitude of some 'born-again' religious people. The fourth is actual unity with the divinity, an intermingling with the spiritual world – this is the attitude of yoga. This fourth attitude is the deepest urge of a Pisces, and a Pisces is uniquely qualified to pursue and perform this work.

Consciously or unconsciously, Pisces seek this union with the spiritual world. The belief in a greater reality makes Pisces very tolerant and understanding of others – perhaps even too tolerant. There are instances in their lives when they should say 'enough is enough' and be ready to defend their position and put up a fight. However, because of their qualities it takes a good deal of doing to get them into that frame of mind.

Pisces basically want and aspire to be 'saints'. They do so in their own way and according to their own rules. Others should not try to impose their concept of saintliness on a Pisces, because he or she always tries to find it for him- or herself.

Finance

Money is generally not that important to Pisces. Of course they need it as much as anyone else, and many of them attain great wealth. But money is not generally a primary objective. Doing good, feeling good about oneself, peace of mind, the relief of pain and suffering – these are the things that matter most to a Pisces.

Pisces earn money intuitively and instinctively. They follow their hunches rather than their logic. They tend to be generous and perhaps overly charitable. Almost any kind of misfortune is enough to move a Pisces to give. Although this is one of their greatest virtues, Pisces should be more careful with their finances. They should try to be more choosy about the people to whom they lend money, so that they are not being taken advantage of. If they give money to charities they should follow it up to see that their contributions are put to good use. Even when Pisces are not rich, they still like to spend money on helping others. In this case they should really be careful, however: they must learn to say no sometimes and help themselves first.

Perhaps the biggest financial stumbling block for the Pisces is general passivity – a *laissez faire* attitude. In general Pisces like to go with the flow of events. When it comes to financial matters, especially, they need to be more aggressive. They need to make things happen, to create their own wealth. A passive attitude will only cause loss and missed opportunity. Worrying about financial security will not provide that security. Pisces need to go after what they want tenaciously.

Career and Public Image

Pisces like to be perceived by the public as people of spiritual or material wealth, of generosity and philanthropy. They look up to big-hearted, philanthropic types. They admire people engaged in large-scale undertakings and eventually would like to head up these big enterprises themselves. In short, they like to be connected with big organizations that are doing things in a big way.

If Pisces are to realize their full career and professional potential they need to travel more, educate themselves more and learn more about the actual world. In other words, they need some of the unflagging optimism of the Sagittarius in order to reach the top.

Because of all their caring and generous characteristics, Pisces often choose professions through which they can help and touch the lives of other people. That is why many Pisces become doctors, nurses, social workers or teachers. Sometimes it takes a while before Pisces realize what they really want to do in their professional lives, but once they find a career that lets them manifest their interests and virtues they will excel at it.

Love and Relationships

It is not surprising that someone as 'otherworldly' as the Pisces would like a partner who is practical and down to earth. Pisces prefer a partner who is on top of all the details of life, because they dislike details. Pisces seek this quality in both their romantic and professional partners. More than anything else this gives Pisces a feeling of being grounded, of being in touch with reality.

As expected, these kinds of relationships – though necessary – are sure to have many ups and downs. Misunderstandings will take place because the two attitudes are poles apart. If you are in love with a Pisces you will experience these fluctuations and will need a lot of patience to see things stabilize. Pisces are moody, intuitive, affectionate and difficult to get to know. Only time and the right attitude will yield Pisces' deepest secrets. However, when in love with a Pisces you will find that riding the waves is worth it because they are good, sensitive people who need and like to give love and affection.

When in love, Pisces like to fantasize. For them fantasy is 90 per cent of the fun of a relationship. They tend to idealize their partner, which can be good and bad at the same time. It is bad in that it is difficult for anyone to live up to the high ideals their Pisces lover sets.

Home and Domestic Life

In their family and domestic life Pisces have to resist the tendency to relate only by feelings and moods. It is unrealistic to expect that your partner and other family members will be as intuitive as you are. There is a need for more verbal communication between a Pisces and his or her family. A cool, unemotional exchange of ideas and opinions will benefit everyone.

Some Pisces tend to like mobility and moving around. For them too much stability feels like a restriction on their freedom. They hate to be locked in one location for ever.

The Sign of Gemini sits on Pisces' 4th Solar House (of Home and Family) cusp. This shows that the Pisces likes and needs a home environment that promotes intellectual and mental interests. They tend to treat their neighbours as family – or extended family. Some Pisces can have a dual attitude towards the home and family – on the one hand they like the emotional support of the family, but on the other they dislike the obligations, restrictions and duties involved with it. For Pisces, finding a balance is the key to a happy family life.

Horoscope for 2008

Major Trends

For many years now you have been in a cycle of 'breaking barriers' – breaking with old patterns and traditions – old habits – old ways of doing things. Compared with 2002, when Uranus first entered your Sign, you are in dramatically different conditions and circumstances. Practically unrecognizable. You want change, but don't exactly know what you want – so you go from one thing to the next. There is a passion for personal freedom – a desire to be free of every kind of obligation. These trends are continuing in 2008.

Last year was a very strong career year. For many it was a lifetime peak. (Younger Pisces will have many future lifetime peaks – but last year was one of them.) This year, career is gradually becoming less important and the focus will be more on friendships and group activities. One of the fruits of career success is that one meets the right kinds of people – and this is what is happening now.

Love has been stressful for various reasons for some years now. This trend continues in the year ahead. Marriages are getting tested – pretty severely. More on this later.

The spiritual life is always important to you, but for the past 15 to 20 years even more so. Like last year you are in a period of intense spiritual growth and change. There is great personal experimentation going on here – many break-throughs – infinite possibilities are opening up to you. The spiritual life, and spiritual phenomena, are more real to you than the so-called real world. More on this later.

Your most important interests in the year ahead are spirituality; the body, image and personal pleasure (also redefining the image); love and romance; career (from January 1 to January 27 and from June 14 to November 27); friendships, organizations and group activities.

Your paths of greatest fulfilment this year are friendships and group activities; spirituality.

Health

(Please note that this is an astrological perspective on health and not a medical one. For the medical perspective, please consult your doctor.)

Health became very delicate late last year as there were three long-term planets stressing you out. Now that Pluto is moving away from its stressful aspect to you, there is some improvement (at least for parts of the year), but health still needs watching. Health will start to improve on a more permanent basis from November 27 onwards. And it will get even better next year when Saturn moves out of Virgo. In the meantime you need pay more attention to health and respect the limits of your body.

There are three periods this year where you seem most vulnerable – if you can schedule holiday time or trips to a health spa or spiritual retreat during these times it would be wonderful. If not, try to rest and relax more. These periods are May 20 to June 21, August 22 to September 22, and November 22 to December 21.

Health can be enhanced (and problems prevented) by paying more attention to the feet (always important to you) and the heart. Pay more attention to the shoes you wear and make sure they fit right and don't knock you off-balance. Keep the feet warm in the winter. Regular foot massage is wonderful for you – not just for the feet themselves, but as a way to energize the entire body. (See the chart opposite.) Foot baths and foot whirlpools are also very good. There are many natural ways to strengthen the heart and I'm sure you know about them. But the heart can also be strengthened through the feet.

Blood pressure can now be checked at home, and this is advisable for older Pisces. But more important than that is to be aware of the body. If you are working and feel a pain or strain – just stop what you're doing and rest – don't try to be a hero.

Spiritual healers affirm that the root spiritual cause of heart problems is worry. So work to eliminate worry from your mind. This can be done in spiritual ways. If there is something positive you can do about a situation, then of course take the appropriate action. But if there's nothing positive that can be done, how does worrying help? It just wastes your energy. There is no point to it. Also worry is a symptom of lack of faith. Strengthen your faith in the Laws of the Universe – in the power of the Spirit – and worry will just disappear.

Energy levels need to be kept high. This is the main bulwark against disease. With high energy, the immune system can handle anything that is thrown at it. But when energy is low, the immune system is less functional and problems can happen.

As mentioned last year, focus on priorities and let lesser things go. Delegate tasks wherever possible. Work with a rhythm and alternate your activities. Take naps when tired. When the car is out of petrol, there's nothing much that can be done – the tank just needs to be filled.

One of the problems that we see this year is the empty 6th House of Health. Your tendency will be to ignore things when you shouldn't. You will have to force yourself to focus on health issues.

The health of your spouse or partner can also be enhanced through the feet – foot and ankle massage is powerful this year. Also there is a need to explore spiritual and alternative healing modalities. Your spouse or partner

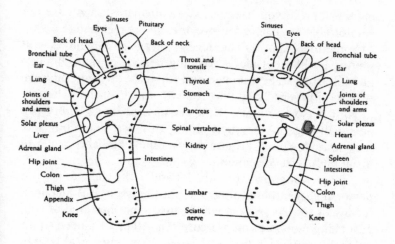

Reflexology

Try to massage the whole foot on a regular basis, but pay extra attention to the points highlighted on the chart. When you massage, be aware of 'sore spots', as these need special attention. It's also a good idea to massage the ankles and top side (as well as the soles) of the feet.

may have a few health scares this year – brought on by the two eclipses in his or her 6th House. But if they pay attention to health all year – they will be just that – scares and nothing more. However, they are making major changes to their health regime this year.

Health of children can be enhanced through detox and better care of the colon, bladder and sexual organs. The health of one of your parents or parent figures likewise. The other parent figure needs to take better care of the kidneys and hips.

Home and Family

Your 4th House of Home and Family is not a House of Power this year. Family relationships seem status quo.

Though your 4th House is empty, Uranus in your own Sign is showing great restlessness – and this often indicates moves. It's like you have 'ants in your pants' – you are not comfortable anywhere for too long. You crave change.

Sometimes this transit doesn't bring actual moves, but staying in different places for long periods of time. Being a nomad. One can be a nomad and still have the same address.

Also, it is very likely that you will make constant changes in your personal room – the space in your home where you personally spend the most time. This will get renovated, redecorated, shifted around many times. Probably you will instal high-tech equipment or gadgetry here.

Though you move around a lot and make changes in your personal space, these things are not the issue. It is a general feeling of restlessness – a wanderlust – that has hold of you. Just being nomadic will not cure this – there is a need to see what the purpose of this restlessness is and then deal with it. Basically, from the Horoscope, it comes from a desire for freedom to fulfil your spiritual mission. Also, big changes are going on in your body and this also makes you feel restless. (The Archangel of the Presence is stirring things up – leading you into your deeper purpose in life.)

If you plan to do heavy construction or renovation in the home, February 19 to March 4 is a good time. If you plan to beautify the home – in a cosmetic kind of way – May 2 to July 10 is a good time (do it before or after the Mercury Retrograde of that period).

From the short-term perspective, family relationships and trends in the home will vary greatly from month to month. Mercury, your financial planet, is a fast-moving planet – sometimes moving through three Signs and Houses in a given month. We will deal with these things in the monthly reports.

Mercury goes Retrograde three times this year – from January 28 to February 19, May 26 to June 19, and September 24 to October 15. These are not times to make important purchases for the home or important family decisions. These periods are for reviewing the domestic and family situation and seeing where you can make improvements. You can put your plans in action when Mercury starts to move forward.

Finance and Career

Your 2nd House of Finance is not a House of Power this year, thus the status quo seems in effect. Since you are coming off a very strong career year, I expect that you are prospering and more or less satisfied with the way things are. No major need to change your financial thinking, plans, strategies or investments. Just keep doing what you've been doing.

Job-seekers and those who employ others are also having a status-quo year – most of the year anyway. A Solar Eclipse in your 6th House of Work on August 1 can shake things up – bring job changes, changes at the workplace and employee turnover. But this is a short-term disruption.

Most of you have made great career strides over the years – especially since 1995. Last year, as mentioned, was a peak year. You are still riding the afterglow of it. But Pluto, which has been in your 10th House of Career since 1995, is getting ready to move out of that House. It will be in and out of your 10th House most of the year and then leaves – for good – on November 27. Ambitions and outer success are becoming gradually less important. Friendship is important.

But there are other readings of these changes, too. The power in your 11th House (your career planet is there, and Pluto is there part time) shows that you can advance your career through having friends in the right places (and this is one of the reasons you're so involved with friends), through getting involved in organizations – professional or trade organizations – and through networking.

It would also be helpful to keep yourself up to date on the latest, cutting-edge technologies in your field. This will assist your career no end.

Those of you just starting out in a career might want to investigate the electronic media – radio, TV, the Internet. Those of you already in a career can further your career through good use of electronic media.

The 11th House rules 'fondest hopes and wishes'. With the career planet there, the obvious message is that 'fondest career hopes and wishes' are coming to pass. There is another reason why this needs to happen: It is very difficult to move on in life until we have fulfilled our original urge. So, your original (and righteous) career urges are coming to pass now. Then you will be ready to move on. (There is more to life than just worldly success, but you need to experience that for yourself.)

Your most active and prosperous financial period this year will be from March 20 to April 30. Your most active career periods will be from January 1 to January 20 and from November 22 to December 31.

Your spouse or partner is having a status-quo financial year. One of your parents or parent figure is prospering greatly and very personally involved in finance. He or she is spending heavily on personal items – clothing, jewellery, things that enhance the image. The other parent figure is having a status-quo year.

You Pisces are spiritual people – and lately more than ever. Often this spirituality brings confusion when it comes to finances. People think that the Divine will do it and that they don't have to do anything. In your case, there is work involved. The divine will supply opportunities, customers, insights, etc. – but you need to do the work. You have to satisfy the customer or boss. You have to take action on the insights and intuitions that are given to you. Often manifestation can happen strictly though spiritual, interior work – but still you have to do the interior work that is necessary. Spiritual work is also considered work – from the cosmic perspective.

Pisces will understand what is being said here.

Mars, your financial planet, will pass through eight Signs in the coming year and these will show the short-term trends in finances – we will cover these in the monthly reports.

Love and Social Life

Your 7th House of Love and Romance is an important House of Power this year – a major focus in the year ahead.

On one level, Saturn's move through your 7th House of Love and Marriage is bringing great challenges and tests. Saturn is going to bring 'right order' into your marriage or love life.

If you have been irresponsible in this department, if your attitudes have not been right, this can be a traumatic transit. It will probably show the break-up of a marriage or serious relationship.

If your attitudes have been correct – cosmically correct – and your marriage or relationship is fundamentally sound, you will come through with flying colours.

We see the testings going on here in many ways. First off, Saturn is moving through your 7th House. Secondly, there is a Lunar Eclipse on February 21 in your 7th House. (Saturn will more or less camp out on this point for a few months early in the year.) Mars – also a tester of relationships – will move through the 7th House from July 1 to August 19. So even good marriages are being tested. If they can withstand this kind of stress, they can probably withstand anything. If you come through this, give yourself and your spouse a nice hug, pat on the back, and congratulations – you've earned it.

(What we say here also applies to business partnerships.)

Part of the problem with the marriage or serious relationship is your restlessness and need for personal freedom. This generally doesn't go with committed kinds of relationships. If you want freedom you must also grant it to your partner.

Infidelity also seems like a problem. (It doesn't have to happen, but the potential is there.)

Your spouse might want children and you want to be free – this is another potential source of conflict.

Singles probably will not marry this year. Perhaps it is better to cultivate a friendship with a prospect, and let that friendship grow into something over time. Also you seem to be weeding out serious prospects – serious suitors – from the unserious ones.

Singles are gravitating to older, more established types of people. You are so restless personally that you feel some comfort with someone who is stable. Organizations and group activities are not only good for your career, but are also the scene of romantic opportunities.

Singles want stability and friendship. They don't want just a lover – they want to be friends with their beloved as well.

Singles might tend to marry for convenience – as another kind of career move. These are seldom happy – though they can last a long time. Duty is seen as the purpose of marriage – not romantic love. Duty is a higher form of love – but it is not commonly associated with our notions of it.

The feeling of romantic love is lacking this year – it's as if you no longer believe in the concept. Those involved with Pisces on a romantic level will have to work very hard to make believers out of them.

The happiest and most active love period this year will be from August 23 to September 23. The most active period for friendships will be from January 1 to January 20.

The main headline socially, is friendships. This area of life looks very happy. Your circle of friends is expanding. Also, the quality of these new friends is high – these are people of status and position – people able to help you – significant kinds of friends.

Self-improvement

In a general way, your spiritual mission for this life involves higher education, ministry and metaphysics – natural Pisces interests. Though you are mystical by nature, there is a need to teach others about your mystical experiences. Many Pisces teach through the arts, film or poetry. The medium can vary, but the end result is the same – higher education.

Many of you think or believe you are in a worldly career – but underneath that you are really educating your customers or your industry.

This year your mission involves friends, groups and organizations – perhaps giving talks to them, or supporting their educational activities. Also you are supposed to be there for your friends this year – to be helpful to them – to be a friend in need. There is no better way to attract friends than to be one.

Bringing the marriage and love life in order is a major challenge in the year ahead. The cosmos isn't satisfied with 'just anything' for you – it wants you to have the best. If the current relationship is not of that calibre – though you should strive to make it work it will probably fail – not because you are being punished but because you deserve the best – and the cosmos has a higher perspective on what is best than you do.

You deserve the best in friendships, too. (And these are getting tested this year, too – the friendships of the heart – the friendships of the mind, ruled by the 11th House, are OK.)

So the current testing period is serving a good purpose. In the end you will know where you stand one way or another. Flaws in attitudes, in the way things are handled, in concepts and ideas – especially in motives – are all going to be revealed and corrected. With proper love attitudes, with a proper perspective on marriage, the future marriage will be more secure and long lasting.

Learning the art of forgiveness is going to be important this year. Friends will no doubt disappoint. Your lover will give you a hard time. Understand where they are coming from and forgive. Don't allow yourself to be a victim – protect yourself and forgive.

Month-by-month Forecasts

January

Best Days Overall: 2, 3, 12, 13, 20, 21, 29, 30, 31
Most Stressful Days Overall: 5, 6, 18, 19, 25, 26
Best Days for Love: 5, 6, 9, 14, 15, 18, 19, 23, 25, 26, 27, 28
Best Days for Money: 1, 7, 10, 14, 15, 16, 18, 19, 24, 25, 28

Your year begins with 70 (and sometimes 80 per cent) of the planets in the independent, Eastern sector of your chart. So you are in a cycle of independent action and personal initiative. Your actions will determine your happiness. You have the power now to create conditions as you desire them to be – and this power will only get stronger in coming months. So, if conditions are bothersome, change them. Others – the world – will adjust to you. You have less need for others during this period – you know what's right and all you need to do is act on it. The planetary momentum this month is overwhelmingly forward and thus you should see rapid progress towards your goals. There is only one thing to keep in mind now: With power comes responsibility. And thus you will be held accountable for your creations. You will have to live with their consequences – so build wisely.

Most of the planets are above the horizon of your chart – on the 'day' side of the chart. Also your 10th House of Career is strong (until the 24th). This shows that you are still in a strong career cycle – finishing up a career period – and this is where your focus still needs to be. Tie up all loose ends. Dot all the Is and cross the Ts. Career will become less important very soon, but not yet. You still need to focus here more than on home and family issues.

Career will benefit from a good detox – that is, the removal of all inessential things. Weed out the trivia and focus only on the essence.

Mars in your 4th House (and he will be there all month) is showing major activity at home, too – but still, more attention needs to be paid to the career than to the home. It looks like there is major construction, renovation or repair going on. You are spending more – investing – in the home and in family members. Perhaps there are more expenses there. But Mars is Retrograde all month, and you need to give more thought to – do more homework on – these expenditures. It is true that family unity and harmony will come from more financial support and from better material conditions – but it's the way that you go about it that's important. Family unity will also be enhanced by better communication, getting involved in group activities as a family unit, and through spiritual understanding (after the 8th).

The main headline of the month ahead is the incredible power in your 11th House of Friends. Some 50 to 60 per cent of the planets are either in this House or moving through there this month. A huge, huge percentage. A very social month. You are almost consumed with issues dealing with organizations and friends (and this area seems very important career-wise, too). You have the kind of aspects where you start your own organization or group. Many fondest hopes and wishes are coming to pass this month – especially in career and in love.

February

Best Days Overall: 8, 9, 17, 26, 27
Most Stressful Days Overall: 1, 2, 14, 15, 23, 24, 28, 29
Best Days for Love: 3, 4, 6, 7, 13, 14, 15, 21, 22, 23, 24
Best Days for Money: 3, 4, 7, 10, 11, 12, 13, 15, 16, 21, 22, 24

Spirituality is always an important interest for you, but this month even more so. It is the main headline of the month ahead. It's a kind of Pisces heaven. The cosmos impels you to do the things you most love to do – get involved in spiritual groups, organizations, charities, altruistic causes and the like – explore your personal spiritual powers and expand your abilities – go off on retreats or pilgrimages – spend more time in communion with the Higher Power within you. A month for taking those workshops and meditation seminars.

There are two eclipses this period. The 1st is a Solar Eclipse on the 7th (the 6th in the US) which occurs in your 12th House of Spirituality. If you haven't been careful, this eclipse will reveal health problems so you can correct them. Your health planet is the eclipsed planet. But it is even deeper than that – Neptune, your ruler, is also impacted here. So do take a reduced schedule – a few days before and after the eclipse. Physical detox could happen and there will be important changes in your health attitudes and regime. Job changes are also likely now. And those who employ others will have dramas with their employees or employee turnover. If you've been careful in health and dietary matters, you should go through this with no problem. You will just make changes to your regime.

The Lunar Eclipse of the 21st (the 20th in the US) is also strong on you, so take a reduced schedule for this one too. This occurs in your 7th House and will test a current marriage, love affair or relationship. Keep in mind that with Saturn in your 7th House all year, these things – especially marriages and partnerships – are getting tested anyway – the eclipse is only adding some more pressure. The cosmos wants you to have the highest-quality love, and nothing less will satisfy it – either the flaws of the present relationship are removed and purified or it must go and be replaced by something better.

Once the dust settles from the eclipses, health will be basically good. You can enhance it further by paying more attention to the heart, ankles (until the 19th) and feet (after the 19th). Ankle massage is powerful until the 19th and foot massage afterwards. (Foot massage is always good for you, but especially after the 19th.) The spiritual dimensions of healing are ultra-important this month, too. A month where you make great progress here.

On the 19th you enter a yearly personal pleasure peak. All the enjoyments of the senses are coming to you. With your health planet in the 1st House you will naturally be moderate. Excess is always the danger during these periods.

Jobs and work opportunities are seeking you out from the 19th onwards. A successful period for job-seekers or those who employ others. It also seems successful for those of you in the healing professions – personal healing power is unusually strong and clients and patients are seeking you out – you couldn't avoid them if you tried.

March

Best Days Overall: 6, 7, 15, 16, 24, 25
Most Stressful Days Overall: 13, 14, 19, 20, 27, 28
Best Days for Love: 4, 5, 14, 15, 19, 20, 24, 25
Best Days for Money: 2, 3, 6, 8, 9, 11, 15, 19, 20, 24, 29, 30

This month personal independence is at its maximum for the year. Some 70 to 80 per cent of the planets are in the independent East, your 1st House of Self is the most powerful in the Horoscope (40 and sometimes 50 per cent of the planets are either there or moving through there) and the Sun moves into independent Aries on the 20th. So if you haven't made those personal changes that you need to make – this is the month to do it. Not only that, but 90 per cent of the planets are moving forward this month – an overwhelming forward momentum. This is the time to have life on your terms, to take personal charge of your life and happiness, and to launch those new products or ventures into the world. The wind is at your back, all of nature is helping you – progress will be swifter than you can imagine.

You are still well into a yearly personal pleasure peak, so enjoy.

Job-seekers are still enjoying great success – you are in demand – jobs are seeking you and not vice versa. These jobs seem well paying, too. On the 4th your financial planet changes Signs – it moves from Gemini and into Cancer – this shows a shift in your financial interests. You are still spending on the home and family, but you seem more speculative this month. True, you are working for your money, but the lure of easy money is still there. Avoid speculations from the 4th to the 8th. There can be some short-term financial disagreement with a friend, too.

The two love planets of your chart move into your Sign this month. Venus, the general planet of love, moves in on the 13th and Mercury, your actual love planet, moves in on the 15th. So this is a good love month as well. Love seeks you out. Your lover or spouse goes way out of his or her way to please you. Your interests come first. You are having your way in love. Also you look especially good – both of these planets bring style and glamour to the appearance. You are magnetic and charismatic, and others take notice. But with Saturn still in your 7th House go slow in love and let it develop naturally. No need to rush into anything. Marriage is unlikely this month, in spite of your great charm and appeal.

Love is idealistic this period – lovers will tend to be very sensitive now – so watch your tone of voice and body language. Little things can trigger big reactions. (Be especially careful and more sensitive from the 4th to the 7th and from the 15th to the 17th.) These periods will be good for 'clearing the air' in your relationship.

Health is good this month and you can enhance it further by paying more attention to the feet (until the 20th) and to the head and face afterwards. Face and scalp massage will be very powerful after the 20th. Heat-oriented therapies are strong then, too. If you live in a cold climate, make sure you bundle up and stay warm.

April

Best Days Overall: 3, 4, 11, 12, 20, 21, 22, 30
Most Stressful Days Overall: 9, 10, 16, 17, 23, 24
Best Days for Love: 4, 5, 6, 13, 14, 15, 16, 17, 24, 25, 26
Best Days for Money: 3, 4, 5, 6, 7, 8, 11, 12, 16, 17, 20,
    21, 22, 26, 27

Last month on the 20th you entered a yearly financial peak – and the trend continues even more strongly this month. A prosperous period. However, it is not the Horoscope of the lottery winner – you are working for it – overcoming many challenges and difficulties. You are more speculative than usual, but this doesn't seem advisable. Money comes through work (job-seekers are successful), through family connections and support, through good communication, sales and marketing – but mostly from a will and determination to prosper – your financial drives are very strong and this is 90 per cent of success. Your drives are so strong that you are exploring all kinds of out-of-the-way places and things to increase earnings. You seem (and this has been true for a few months) 'out of bounds' – out of your usual haunts. Nothing daunts you. A business partnership or joint venture can happen after the 6th. Spousal support is strong then, too. Social contacts are very eager to cooperate in your prosperity. But it's not a smooth ride. Your financial planet is in the moody Sign of Cancer – so avoid making important financial decisions when you are in a bad mood – angry or depressed. Sleep on things and wait for a mood of peace before making important decisions.

Job-seekers should first check with their financial contacts (people who are involved in their finances) for job leads until the 19th. Afterwards, the normal kinds of ways seem best – putting adverts in the newspapers or reading the adverts. Letter writing – sending out those CVs – is important.

Most of the planets are below the horizon of your chart – this has been the case for the last three months. So the need now is to focus on home, family and psychological issues rather than the outer life. Your 10th House of Career is basically empty this month as well – only the Moon will visit there on the 23rd and 24th (a monthly career peak). So cultivate emotional harmony, the right mood and right state and, in due course, the outer life will straighten out. Work on the career by the methods of night – through dreaming and visualizing – rather than by overt action. In due course the necessary actions will happen – and very powerfully and naturally. You are in the night part of your year – let the night do her perfect work on you.

Communication and intellectual interests become important after the 19th – and this is the natural order of the cosmos. Wealth is for the purpose of buying free time to develop the mind. A good period for catching up on your reading, letter-writing and for taking courses in subjects that interest you.

Love seems happy for singles (and current relationships seem happier after the 19th). Your love planet, Mercury, moves very speedily this month – through three different Signs and Houses of your chart. You have confidence. You cover a lot of territory. You date a lot and date different kinds of people. These kinds of love aspects can be confusing (both to you and to those you are involved with) – for no sooner do you think that you know what you want (or that you've found what you want) when your needs in love change. Those involved romantically with Pisces should make note of this. The world might call you fickle, but the truth is that your love planet is just moving very fast.

May

Best Days Overall: 1, 8, 9, 18, 19, 28, 29
Most Stressful Days Overall: 6, 7, 13, 14, 20, 21
Best Days for Love: 4, 5, 6, 13, 14, 15, 16, 24, 25, 26
Best Days for Money: 1, 2, 3, 4, 5, 10, 13, 14, 20, 23, 24, 30, 31

Your financial planet changes Signs this month – it moves into Leo from Cancer on the 9th. But you still seem as speculative as ever – and this needs to be reined in. It is good to earn money in happy ways – in creative kinds of ways – which is what you've been trying to do for the past two months – but risk-taking doesn't seem advisable. This is a period, especially after the 9th, for earning the old-fashioned way – through work and productive service. Job-seekers are successful this period and there are various options for finding work. After the 9th people involved in your financial life can provide good leads. Until the 20th (like last month) send out those CVs and read all the adverts in the newspapers. After the 20th family connections seem helpful.

Your career planet goes Retrograde on the 9th. Most of the planets are still below the horizon. Your 4th House of Home and Family becomes very strong after the 20th, while your 10th House of Career is still empty (only the Moon makes a brief stopover on the 20th and 21st). So the message is clear: You need to give the family its due and let go of career issues for a while. You won't lose anything as there is not much happening there anyway – and many career issues will just need time to resolve. Your focus on family (and your personal emotional life) will set the stage for career success later on. You are still in the night period of your year (actually the midnight of the year) – and the function of night is to provide the pause that refreshes. Night is for sleeping, dreaming and feeling good. Night is for being at home, safe and secure. A good night's sleep will do more for your career than overt action right now. Enjoy the pleasures of hearth and home.

Family unity can be enhanced in various ways this month – through DIY projects at home (as a family unit), through common health interests such as going to the gym or yoga studio together as a family, through good communication and common intellectual interests, and through family gatherings and entertaining from home.

Love has been fast paced for the past month, and now it slows down a bit. On the 26th your love planet goes

Retrograde and it is time to take a breather – to step back and review your love life, love goals and relationships. Love opportunities will still happen for the unattached, but this (after the 26th) should not be rushed. Avoid making important love decisions after the 26th. Until the 3rd, love is in the neighbourhood and at educational settings. Intellectuals are very alluring. After the 3rd, intellectuals are still alluring but you want more – a good mind, stimulating conversation, intellectual compatibility AND emotional sensitivity and nurturing. A good mind and a good heart. People with strong family values are alluring now, too. In love you seem like a 'homebody' – a romantic evening at home, watching TV is as enjoyable (perhaps more enjoyable) than a night out on the town. Love is much more than about physical intimacy and some feverish physical gyrations – it is about intellectual and emotional intimacy as well.

June

Best Days Overall: 5, 6, 14, 15, 24, 25
Most Stressful Days Overall: 3, 4, 9, 10, 16, 17, 18, 30
Best Days for Love: 3, 4, 9, 10, 11, 12, 14, 15, 21, 22, 24, 25, 30
Best Days for Money: 1, 2, 7, 8, 9, 10, 17, 18, 19, 20, 26, 27, 28, 29

Retrograde activity will reach its maximum for the year this month – 40 per cent of the planets are Retrograde (the planets change, but the percentage is the same). The pace of events is slowing down in the world. And with your 5th House of Fun getting strong on the 21st, this is an excellent time for a holiday if you can swing it.

Last month the planetary power shifted from the independent East to the social Western sector of your Horoscope. Not only that but your ruler, Neptune, went Retrograde on the 26th of last month. So this is not a period for self-will or self-assertion. It is a period for personal review (not just in love, but your personal desires) and for cultivating the social skills and graces. People skills count now, rather than personal skills. Let others have their way so long as it isn't destructive. Your way is probably not the best way right now. Younger Pisces need to be sure to be around good types of people – positive and uplifting types of people – as they are more vulnerable than usual to peer pressure. Hanging with a bad crowd can lead to a lot of problems. A good crowd will lift them to the heights.

Friends have been having dramatic experiences in their lives. There has been tumult and upheaval in organizations you are involved with. This has been going on for a few months, but now it should start to ease up – later in the month. The worst seems about over.

Home and family are still the dominant interests until the 21st. Family unity can be enhanced in the ways discussed last month. With your family planet Retrograde until the 19th, avoid making important family decisions until then. Many of you are purchasing art objects or redecorating the home now – so do more homework on these things and be patient with delays.

On the 21st you enter a yearly personal pleasure peak. This is a time for leisure activities, sports, theatre, entertainment and for exploring the 'rapture' side of life. For singles this is a time for love affairs – not serious involvements. (Love can be looked at in various ways – as a partnership or just another form of entertainment, like going to the movies – you have this latter attitude now.)

The main challenge now (and this is tricky) is how to earn money and work in enjoyable and fun ways. In some cases there will be a need to make the present job more fun – this can be done through some creative approach. In other cases it is about finding a job that is fun. Job-seekers should check out resorts, theatres, and sports franchises for leads – especially after the 21st. The fun aspect will be the determining issue for you when having to choose between jobs – seems to me it will be more important than just the pay. You could easily choose the lower-paying but more fun job than the high-paying but dull one.

Health needs watching until the 21st. Enhance health through rest and relaxation and through more attention to the arms, shoulders and lungs (until the 21st) and to the stomach and breasts afterwards. Very important to listen to your body this period.

July

Best Days Overall: 2, 3, 11, 12, 21, 22, 30
Most Stressful Days Overall: 1, 6, 7, 14, 15, 28
Best Days for Love: 1, 2, 3, 6, 7, 10, 13, 22, 24
Best Days for Money: 6, 7, 16, 17, 23, 24, 25, 26

Health improved dramatically on the 21st of last month. With increased energy mysterious aches and pains simply vanish. A strong immune system is more than equal to any problem. This month, Mars' move into Virgo makes health more delicate. You can enhance your health with more attention to the stomach and breasts (until the 22nd) and to the heart afterwards. Emotional health seems important until the 22nd. Joy seems an important healer all month. Just having fun will solve many a seeming health problem. Rest and relax more and avoid risky high-stress activities. Though there are four long-term planets in stressful alignment with you (and these planets are not powers to take lightly) the good news is that you have a strong health focus this month. You are not ignoring things. You are on the case. You should come through with flying colours.

There are important financial changes happening this month – they can be disruptive – unpleasant in the short term – but good for the long haul. This happens from the 1st to the 8th. Avoid risky or reckless financial behaviour then. Your financial planet also changes Signs this month – he moves into Virgo (from Leo) on the 1st. This shows a possible business partnership or joint venture. Social connections are more important for the bottom line than mere 'hard work' (you've done that already). Spousal support should improve, too. (But it could be that you are spending more on your spouse or current love, too.)

With most of the planets in the social West and your 7th House of Others strong this month, your good – and especially your financial good – comes through the good graces of others. Your personal likeability is more a factor in earnings (and other things) than your actual talent or skills. Keep this in mind now. Avoid self-assertion and self-will (your ruler is still Retrograde) and get your way through compromise, consensus and negotiation. Adjust to difficult conditions as best you can. This is not a good time to make radical personal changes.

Once again you become your 'fickle' self in love – a mystery to yourself and to others. Until the 10th love is about emotional and intellectual compatibility – nurturing – the sharing of intellectual and emotional intimacy. After the 10th love is about fun and games – just another form of entertainment. While singles will be having fun – dating a lot, going to parties, etc. – nothing serious is likely to come from this. Still, it should be enjoyed for what it is. After the 26th love opportunities happen at the workplace, with co-workers or with people involved in your health.

You are still very much into a yearly personal pleasure peak. Retrograde activity is still at its maximum for the year. So, like last month, this is a great time for a holiday.

On the 22nd the party winds down a bit and you are into a more serious work-oriented mode. This will be a good period for job-seekers, too. Like last month, the challenge seems to be to find work that is enjoyable – or to make the existing job more enjoyable.

August

Best Days Overall: 7, 8, 9, 17, 18, 26, 27
Most Stressful Days Overall: 3, 4, 10, 11, 24, 25, 30, 31
Best Days for Love: 1, 2, 3, 4, 12, 21, 22, 23, 30, 31
Best Days for Money: 3, 4, 12, 13, 14, 19, 20, 22, 23, 24, 30, 31

With health more delicate this month, take a reduced schedule as much as possible – but especially around the periods of the two eclipses. Enhance health with more attention to the heart (all month) and to the small intestine after the 22nd. But the most important thing is to avoid risk-taking or high-stress kinds of activities – especially if they are elective. Things that really need to be done should be done, but only you can discern what is and is not 'elective'.

The Solar Eclipse of the 1st occurs in your 6th House of Health (and eclipses the health planet). This can bring health scares or dramas. But if you pace yourself and focus more on health, this should pass. Those of you who take good care of your health as a matter of course will probably change doctors, diets or health regimes. Flaws in your present regime will be revealed and you will know what needs changing. There are job changes in the works, too. Employers will have dramas with employees and probably turnover. There are dramas with aunts or uncles. Friends can have brushes with or encounters with death – most probably on a psychological level.

The Lunar Eclipse of the 16th is an almost exact repeat of the Solar Eclipse of February 7. More or less the same planets are affected and it occurs in the same Sign and House. (Whatever changes were not made after the last eclipse will get made now.) This eclipse occurs in your 12th House of Spirituality and impacts on Neptune, your ruler. Again there are important changes in your spiritual practice and regime (probably due to interior revelation). People will often change gurus or places of worship under these aspects. There is another shake-up in a spiritual organization or charity that you are involved with – and this is a likely cause for a change in your relationship with them. Like the last eclipse in February, you are forced to redefine your personality, your self-concept, how you think of yourself and how you want others to see you. (It seems to me that this too is coming from interior revelation – as a result of your spiritual practice.) Over the next few months you will have a new wardrobe, hairstyle and new 'look'. Often there is a detox of the physical body with these aspects – but this should not be confused with sickness – old, effete material needs to come out. Your spouse or partner can have job changes, employee turnover or a health drama. A love affair gets tested. There are dramatic changes in creative projects you are involved with and there can be dramatic events in the lives of your children or those who are like children to you.

On the 22nd you enter a yearly social peak. Your social life seems active and basically happy (the eclipses do create some bumps on the road). Singles have a huge menu to choose from – all kinds of different types are available – co-workers, health professionals, surgeons, athletes, entertainers, intellectuals and moneyed people. With 50 and sometimes 60 per cent of the planets either in your 7th House or moving through there, your problem is not lack of love but too much of a good thing – you have too many choices, not too few. It's a bit confusing. A business partnership or joint venture is still likely – but a romantic marriage? I'm not so sure. I hope you singles prove me wrong on this.

September

Best Days Overall: 4, 5, 14, 15, 22, 23
Most Stressful Days Overall: 6, 7, 8, 20, 21, 27, 28
Best Days for Love: 1, 2, 11, 12, 20, 21, 27, 28, 29, 30
Best Days for Money: 1, 2, 9, 10, 11, 12, 16, 17, 18, 19, 20, 21, 27, 29, 30

Last month the planetary power made a major shift from the lower, night side of the Horoscope to the upper, day side. Dawn is breaking in your year. The night is over. Time to stop dreaming and to start doing – to act on your dreams. Time to pursue the goals of your outer life. The timing of this is also very fortunate. For as this shift is taking place, Jupiter, your career planet, starts to move forward after many months of Retrograde motion. Beautiful. Hopefully you've spent the past few months reviewing your career and seeing where improvements could be made. Now you will have a clear mind, a clear plan, and the energy and enthusiasm to put the plan into action. Let go (or de-emphasize) family issues and focus on the career. Career is enhanced through social means – through networking or getting involved in organizations and group activities. Having the right friends in the right places is a key factor in success – and you seem to have this. Your friends are people of power and influence. Also good to keep up with the latest technology and be willing to travel.

You are still in your yearly social peak until the 22nd. Love opportunities happen in organizations, group activities, through the introduction of friends, at the workplace or as you pursue health goals. Healers and co-workers are highly alluring now. You seem very perfectionist about love (especially until the 22nd). Good health for you means a healthy love life and marriage as well as good physical health. But in your zeal for good social health, try not to focus overmuch on all the bad points. Look at the bad points and but also at the good. This will keep you in balance.

Love is very sexual this month. It's the physical chemistry – the passion – that allures you. And while this is an important part of it, try to remember that there is more to it than that.

The Retrograde of your love planet on the 24th signals another period for social review and analysis. This timing also seems good, as you have just come out of a major social peak. You've had so many opportunities you need time to sort things out.

Health is much improved over last month but still needs watching until the 22nd. The good news is that with the Sun in Virgo you will tend to be more focused on health and give it the attention it needs. Enhance health by resting and relaxing more (the simple advice is always the best) and by paying more attention to the small intestine (until the 22nd) and to the kidneys and hips afterwards. Detox regimes – herbal or mechanical – are powerful after the 22nd.

Finances look good. Spousal support is strong. A partnership or joint venture opportunity is still likely after the 22nd.

Your line of credit increases and you have the option to either incur or eliminate debt this period. Your spouse or partner is prospering and in a yearly financial peak – this is no doubt a factor in his or her generosity towards you.

October

Best Days Overall: 1, 2, 11, 12, 19, 20, 28, 29, 30
Most Stressful Days Overall: 4, 5, 17, 18, 24, 25, 31
Best Days for Love: 1, 9, 10, 11, 12, 17, 18, 21, 22, 23, 24, 25, 26, 27
Best Days for Money: 6, 7, 11, 13, 14, 15, 16, 19, 20, 24, 25, 28, 29

Your 8th House got powerful on the 22nd of last month and is still powerful until the 23rd. This is a period to pursue goals involving personal transformation and reinvention. It is wonderful now to clean house – both on the physical level and on the interior level – in your mind and emotions. A good detox of the love life is also in order. Get rid of attitudes, opinions and patterns that are no longer helpful or useful. Perhaps they are not 'evil' as we understand it. At one time they were good. Now, they no longer belong there and are just 'gumming up the works'. Keep your mind focused on the essentials of love and let the trivial things go. Work to get a right perspective on it.

Love is still very sexual. In fact this is a very sexually active month. Whatever your age or stage in life, libido should be stronger than usual. On the 15th your love planet starts to move forward and so does your love life. You have more clarity and more social confidence. Your social judgement is much improved. Your choices should be wiser. Love seems happy now. You and the beloved seem in synch. The unattached have wonderful opportunities – serious ones – on the 1st and 2nd and again from the 29th to the 31st. For those already in relationships, these periods bring a deepening of the existing relationship and happy social opportunities (invitations to parties and the like).

Even though health is improved over last month and looks good now, take it easy from the 1st to the 3rd and from the 12th to the 15th. Drive defensively. Avoid violent people or situations. There can be dramatic events in the lives of siblings and neighbours during these periods. Your spouse, partner or current love is forced to make some dramatic financial changes. (It seems to me that these changes come from prosperity and not because of problems.) Enhance health by paying more attention to the kidneys and hips (until the 23rd) and to the bladder, colon and sexual organs afterwards. Detox regimes are powerful all month. Safe sex is now more important for you. Prayer and metaphysical techniques are always good for you but especially from the 23rd onwards.

You can be making some important financial changes from the 17th to the 20th as well. Avoid risky financial behaviour then.

Your 9th House becomes very powerful from the 23rd onwards. Thus this is a period for religious and philosophical revelation – something you are always interested in. There will be more travel – both for business and pleasure. Financial opportunities are in foreign lands or with foreigners. Students have good fortune with scholarships and financial aid from the 4th onwards (and this would be a good time to make your application or interview). Students in general seem successful in their studies this month.

November

Best Days Overall: 7, 8, 16, 17, 25, 26
Most Stressful Days Overall: 1, 14, 15, 20, 21, 27, 28
Best Days for Love: 1, 7, 11, 12, 16, 17, 20, 21, 27, 28, 30
Best Days for Money: 2, 3, 4, 7, 8, 10, 11, 12, 13, 18, 20, 21, 27, 30

Most of the planets are above the horizon of your Horoscope. Your 10th House becomes very powerful on the 21st (and this is the beginning of a yearly career peak). Your

4th House of Home and Family, by contrast, is empty (only the Moon visits there on the 14th and 15th). Your career planet is firmly forward. Your career is moving forward. You have the drive and the interest to overcome any obstacle. With Mars crossing your Midheaven on the 16th you are willing to take on all comers, all competitors in either your company or industry. Also it shows you are working very hard. You are pursuing career goals aggressively (as you should). You are reaching the pinnacles now. Pay rises and promotions are likely. Your professional standing is elevated. But once you have tasted the pinnacles you are likely to ask, 'Is that all there is?' You are ready to move on to other experiences in life – to develop other areas and interests – most notably friendships and the pleasures of group activities – of associating with people of like mind and interests.

This is also going to be a very prosperous month on a bottom-line level. For as Mars crosses your Midheaven (the 16th) he becomes, for a time, the most elevated planet in the Horoscope. Your are reaching financial highs. Finance is important and high on your list of priorities. Elders, bosses, parents or parent figures, government officials are all cooperating in your prosperity. For those in your own business this is a good period to solicit government contracts or to seek favourable treatment from the government. Your good professional reputation now has bottom-line consequences – people refer work to you or other kinds of opportunities come your way.

But there are consequences to all this success – well deserved though it is. Energy is not up to its usual standards and you run the risk of pushing your body beyond its limits. Health needs much more watching all month – but especially after the 21st. Success is wonderful, but be aware of the messages of your body. If you are tired, make an excuse and take a nap. If you feel a pain somewhere, stop what you're doing and relax. Enhance health though better care of the colon, bladder and sexual organs (until the 21st) and to the liver and thighs afterwards. The heart needs more attention all month. The problem this month –

but especially until the 21st – is that you are likely to ignore health. You will have to force yourself to pay more attention here.

Love seems very happy, too. Your partner or current love also seems highly successful this month – especially after the 23rd. Family members too. In fact the family as a whole – the status of the family – is increased. Both your lover and family seem supportive of your career goals. Love is still very sexual until the 23rd. But afterwards you seem more interested in status and power. The unattached have opportunities with bosses or superiors after the 23rd. In general you mix with the 'power people' – the high and the mighty – after the 23rd.

December

> Best Days Overall: 5, 6, 13, 14, 22, 23
> Most Stressful Days Overall: 11, 12, 17, 18, 24, 25, 26
> Best Days for Love: 1, 7, 8, 11, 17, 18, 20, 21, 27, 28, 30, 31
> Best Days for Money: 1, 7, 8, 9, 10, 15, 16, 17, 18, 26, 27, 28

Last month the planetary power shifted from the social West to the independent East. Day by day you are becoming more independent and more able to create conditions as you desire them to be. No need now for compromise. Over the past six months you've had the opportunity to see how well your previous creations worked, and now you can fine-tune them or totally create something new. Always be polite and respectful to others, but chart your own course.

Your yearly career peak is still very much in progress until the 21st. But afterwards the interest shifts to friendships and the joys of collective activities with people of like mind. With your career planet also moving into the 11th House (permanently this time – on the 27th) this is a long, long-term interest. Pluto can stay in a Sign anywhere from 13 to 35 years.